14

WAYWARD SAILOR

Also by Anthony Dalton

Nonfiction
Explorations with My Father
Portraits of Bangladesh

Fiction
Nelson, The Arctic Adventures of Tristan's Old Sea Dog

WAYWARD
SAILOR

IN SEARCH OF THE REAL
TRISTAN JONES

ANTHONY
DALTON

INTERNATIONAL MARINE / McGRAW-HILL

Camden, Maine • New York • Chicago • San Francisco •
Lisbon • London • Madrid • Mexico City • Milan • New Delhi •
San Juan • Seoul • Singapore • Sydney • Toronto

The **McGraw·Hill** Companies

1234567890DOCDOC0987654

The Library of Congress has cataloged the cloth edition as follows:
Dalton, Anthony.
  Wayward sailor : in search of the real Tristan Jones / Anthony Dalton.
  p.   cm.
Includes bibliographical references and index.
  ISBN 0-07-140251-9
  1. Jones, Tristan, 1924–   2. Jones, Tristan, 1924–   —Journeys. 3.
Sailors—Scotland—Biography. 4. Voyages and travels. I. Title.
  G540 .D18 2003
  910.4′5′092—dc21   2002153773

Paperback ISBN 0-07-144028-3

Maps by International Mapping Associates

In memory of my grandmother,
Florence Mary Waterman,
who lost both her legs to diabetes late in life—
yet fought on with great courage

Where what is done in action, more, if might,
Shall be discover'd; please you, sit and hark.

William Shakespeare, *Pericles*

Contents

*Photographs appear following
page 206*

Acknowledgments

This book could not have been written without enormous help from others. Its preparation proved multifaceted, a task as labyrinthine as building a seaworthy wooden boat from the barest of materials. Tristan Jones provided the plans grudgingly, sparingly—one incomplete sheet at a time. His friends and acquaintances supplied the resources, drawn from the accumulated flotsam and jetsam of memory and memorabilia. Some worked side by side with me, sharing their knowledge as I, the builder, assembled a multitude of pieces into a coherent whole.

Arguably the greatest reward for taking on the task of writing Tristan Jones's story has been the friends I have made as a consequence. Their encouragement guided me every step of the way.

Jonathan Eaton, my editor at International Marine, gave me steady guidance and enormous encouragement as he showed me how to improve my manuscript. Thanks also to Molly Mulhern.

I am deeply indebted to Richard Curtis, Tristan's literary agent in New York. He gave approval to my project, loading my early research with a treasure trove of correspondence and associated papers, and allowed me to litter his office while I sifted through boxes of unexpected delights. My thanks, Richard, for more than two years of support.

Henry Wagner, Tristan's closest friend, has been unstinting in his efforts on behalf of this book. Henry lent me his archival collection of

Tristan's faded photographs, sent me video and audio tapes, books, and boxes of Tristan's correspondence, and shared his memories. After knowing you for a little over two years, Henry, I fully understand why Tristan thought so highly of you. I'm thrilled to have you on my side.

In the Highlands of Scotland I experienced the warm and considerate hospitality of two more of Tristan's special friends, Sir Wally and Lady Herbert. Wally and Marie gave me an overnight berth, wined and dined me, and talked passionately about the old sailor. Additionally, Sir Wally entrusted me with a file of correspondence and two of Tristan's logbooks. I am truly grateful to you both.

Few days passed during the research and writing of this book when I didn't receive a message from Mike Warburton in England. He was a staunch pen pal to Tristan who became my ally, friend, and confidant. Without his dedicated approach to research and his willingness to share, this book would not have met its publishing deadline. Mike and Carole Warburton graciously invited me into their home and their lives—I feel honored. So too in Switzerland, Willi and Irina Zeiss made me welcome and treated me as a member of their family. Willi, the German translator of Tristan's books, took his own time to drive me through much of southern Germany on two occasions to meet those Tristan touched in passing. Those journeys hold special meaning for me.

Kriemhild Ettenhuber is deserving of great accolades. She allowed a stranger to probe her saddest moments and did so with grace, composure, and courage. I'm proud to now call her my friend.

Rob Cohen, the late Arthur Cohen's son, hauled a small mountain of memorabilia out of his Pennsylvania attic for my benefit. We spent a nostalgic afternoon at his kitchen table studying relics from *Barbara*'s great adventure. Thanks, Rob, for your kindness—and for the Chinese food.

Among the many others who either added to my knowledge or lent me support, I appreciate the following:

In the United Kingdom: Anna Borzello, Jill Butcher, Euan Cameron, Mary Deacon, Clare Francis, Della Galton, Gillian Hughes, John

Hulme, Pete "the Manxman" Kelly (I'll see you in the Green Man), Jan Morris, Stephen Rabson at P&O History and Archives, Pete Ross, Terry Sipson, Miss S. Wallace of the Armed Forces Personnel Administration Agency, the staff at the Family Records Centre in London, the staff of the Public Records Office at Kew, and at the United Kingdom Passport Agency in Peterborough; plus Barry Cox, Derek King, Jeff Morris, and Stephen Nourse of the Royal National Lifeboat Institution, Abner Stein (Tristan's agent in the United Kingdom), and Emma Taaffe at Lloyd's Register.

In the United States: Mike Anderson, Robert J. Austin, Beverly Baroff, Deven Black, Chip Croft, Anton Elbers, Craig Grosby, Robert Grosby, Dave and Jaynie Horner, Rick Just, Brice Keller, John Kretschmer, Wilson McLean, Pat Miller, Carl Paler, Reese Palley, Tor Pinney, Alexander Pufahl, Jonathan Raban, Ron Reil, Jeff Ritchie, and Steve Rosse—thanks for all the help on Thailand, Steve—plus Hal Roth, Stuart Sarjeant, Chris and Carole Scott, David and Margaret "Magee" Shields, Shaun Simpson, Don Swartz, Laurel Wagers, Patience Wales, and Ron Wendt.

At home in Canada: Gael Arthur, Steve Crowhurst (who should take responsibility for persuading me to become a writer over two decades ago), Danny Evanishen, Jan de Groot, and Steve Sanderson; they all helped in different ways.

My travels in Germany introduced me to Manfred and Gabby Peter, Michael von Tülff, Werner Umwherle, Fredi and Rosemarie Vivell, in addition to Kriemhild Ettenhuber. With them I was fortunate to enjoy excellent meals, fine beers, and fascinating conversations. Thanks also to Dr. Michael Werder in Switzerland, Guus Schohaus in Holland, plus Hugo Vermeirsch and David Murray in Belgium.

Peter "Champy" Evans, in Grenada, allowed me to interrogate him by telephone. Per Holte gave me useful contacts in Norway. In Denmark Helge Schultz-Lorentzen assisted me with information on ships of the Greenland trade, and Keld Q. Hansen supplied photocopies of ice report charts of the Denmark Strait. Karen McCullough, editor of *Arctic* (Calgary, Canada), also directed me to useful sources of information on ice conditions in the Arctic. The Icelandic Maritime Administration guided me to harbor arrival and departure records in Reykjavík.

My gratitude goes to Paul Dark in Phuket, Thailand, for his assistance during a difficult time for him. Thanks also to Chris Forrester in Chiang Mai, Jos Souer in Phitsanulok, Scott Murray and Rafiq Tschannen in Bangkok, Derek Tonkin (former British ambassador to Thailand and Laos), David Morgan in the Philippines, and Euan Ferguson in Japan.

Leonard Surtees, designer and builder of *Outward Leg*, wrote from Australia, as did Dr. Ian Spooner. Lin Pardey phoned from New Zealand to chat about Tristan. Conrad and Lorna Jelinek interrupted their sailing lifestyle to answer my scores of questions, by e-mail and telephone, first from Antigua and later in the Mediterranean after a grueling Atlantic crossing. This book would not have been complete without your involvement. Thanks a million.

Tristan Jones's story dominated my life for two and a half years. I'm fortunate that Penny, my wife, understands my passion, and approves. Thanks for being there.

I must also extend my gratitude to Lothar Simon of Sheridan House, current publisher of Tristan Jones's books, for his help and for permission to quote briefly from *The Incredible Voyage, Ice!, A Steady Trade, Heart of Oak, Seagulls in My Soup*, and *Encounters of a Wayward Sailor*; to Imray, Laurie, Norie & Wilson Ltd., for permission to quote from Rod Heikell's *The Danube*, to Random House, which agreed to the use of a line from John Gardner's *The Art of Fiction*, and to International Marine/McGraw-Hill, which allowed me to quote two passages from Richard Henderson's *Singlehanded Sailing*, 2nd edition, and correspondence from Tristan Jones.

I am indebted to Tor Pinney and Ron Reil for allowing me to quote freely from their excellent websites. Finally, thanks to anyone I have inadvertently forgotten.

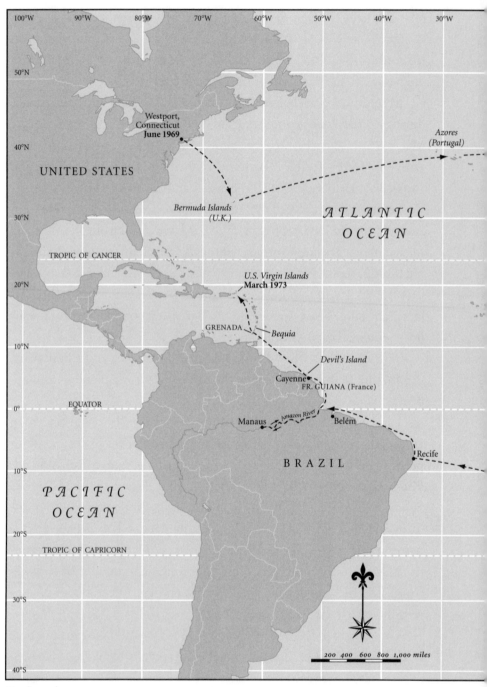

Barbara's route

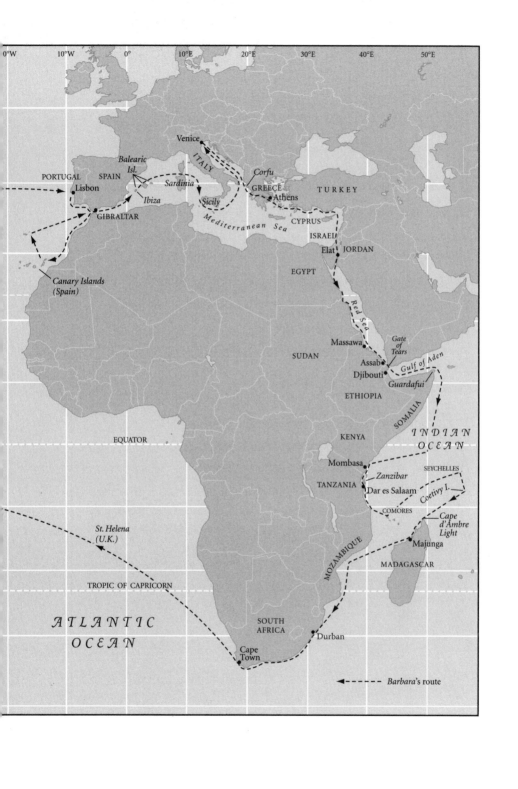

0°W 10°W 0° 10°E 20°E 30°E 40°E 50°E

Venice

Balearic
Isl.

PORTUGAL SPAIN

Corfu

ITALY

Lisbon Sardinia GREECE TURKEY

Ibiza Athens

GIBRALTAR Sicily CYPRUS

Mediterranean Sea ISRAEL

Elat JORDAN

Canary Islands
(Spain)

EGYPT

Red Sea

Massawa Gate
of
Tears

SUDAN Assab Gulf of Aden

Djibouti Guardafui

ETHIOPIA

SOMALIA

EQUATOR INDIAN
OCEAN

KENYA

Mombasa SEYCHELLES

Zanzibar

TANZANIA Dar es Salaam Coetivy I.

COMORES Cape
d'Ambre
Light

St. Helena
(U.K.) Majunga

MOZAMBIQUE MADAGASCAR

TROPIC OF CAPRICORN

ATLANTIC
OCEAN SOUTH
AFRICA Durban

Cape
Town

◄- - - - Barbara's route

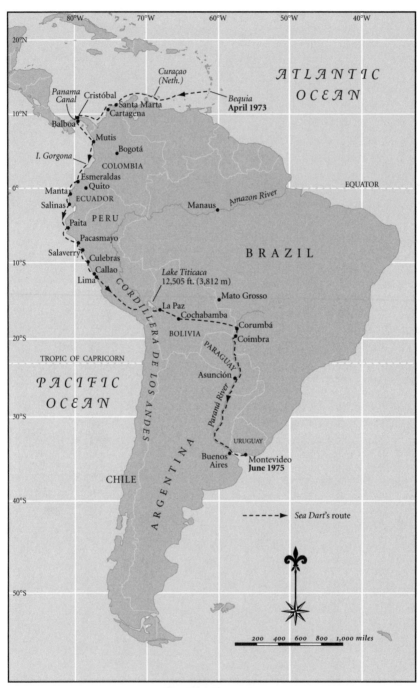

Sea Dart's route

The Kra expedition aboard Henry Wagner

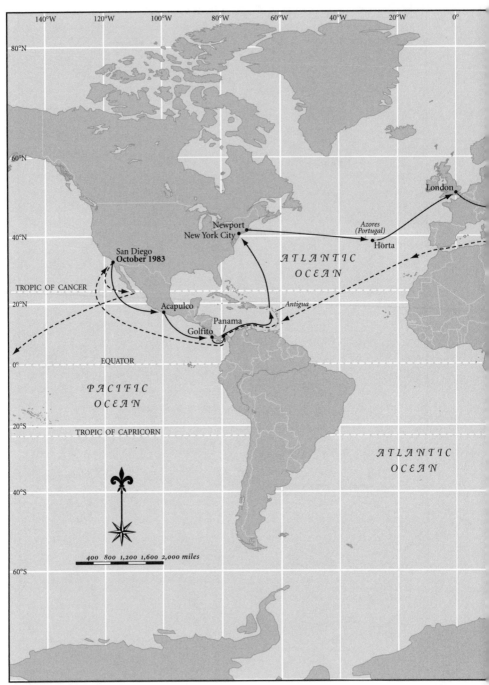

Outward Leg's Route

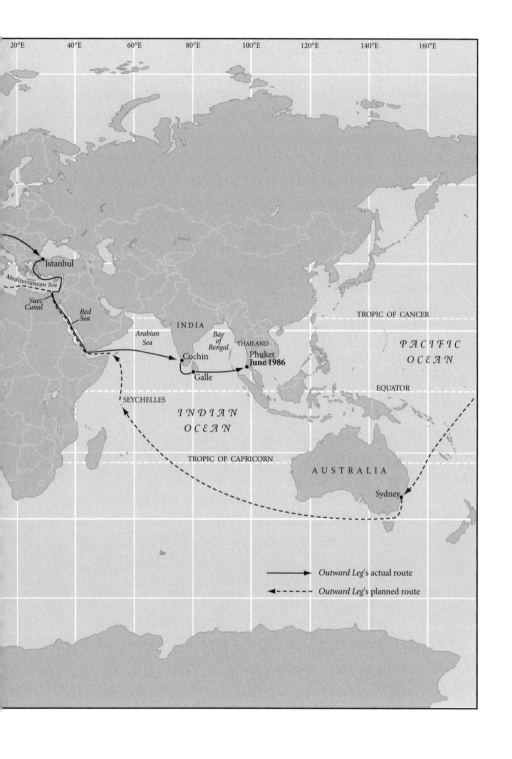

Istanbul

Mediterranean Sea

Suez
Canal

Red
Sea

Arabian
Sea

INDIA

Bay
of
Bengal

THAILAND

Cochin

Phuket
June 1986

Galle

TROPIC OF CANCER

PACIFIC
OCEAN

SEYCHELLES

INDIAN
OCEAN

EQUATOR

TROPIC OF CAPRICORN

AUSTRALIA

Sydney

Outward Leg's actual route

Outward Leg's planned route

Introduction

Wayward Sailor was originally intended to be a tribute to Tristan Jones, the Welsh sailor, adventurer, and author. It was to be an admiring look at his life: a mostly uncritical biography of a highly respected sailing author, based on the history he allowed his fans to experience in his books, magazine articles, and public appearances. Tristan Jones, however, did not want his biography written—not during his lifetime, and not soon after. His books were autobiographical, he insisted; there was no need for a biography. He felt so strongly about the subject that he included it in his will: no biography was to be written until at least thirty years after his death. Later he amended that to a financial condition: no biography without payment of $100,000 to the Tristan Jones Trust. His reasons for not wanting his true story told, I discovered, had little to do with modesty and far more to do with a lack of probity. Despite his wishes, I chose to continue. This book is in many ways a long and arduous detective story. It began, as any book about Tristan Jones should, on a sailboat.

All around me in the marina at San Pedro, California, tall masts rocked from port to starboard, starboard to port, as the breeze gusted from the northwest. A few loose halyards rattled against unyielding aluminum masts. Just beyond the dock a row of palm trees swayed under an almost clear blue sky. I stood silently alone, deep in thought, on the foredeck of *Retreat*, my thirty-three-foot auxiliary-motor sloop. On the end of an adjacent slip a great blue heron stood patiently, equally silent, waiting for an unsuspecting finny morsel to swim within range. A pelagic cormorant bobbed to the surface, shaking its head contentedly, savoring its own meal. The heron's stoic expression remained unchanged. Somewhere close by someone was using an electric sander. The rasping burr cut intrusively across the water; otherwise it was a quiet midweek morning.

Retreat trembled softly under my feet as her powerful diesel engine purred. Although it was a good day for sailing, with a promise of increasing wind in the early afternoon, I had no plans to go out. I was simply there doing odd jobs, charging the batteries and meaning to scrub dust, residual air pollution, and seabird droppings off her decks. The freshwater hose was running and I had a broom in my hand, but I felt distracted. Tristan Jones kept intruding on my thoughts, taking my mind off the work at hand.

Earlier that morning, before the sun woke enough to warm the sea air, I had been sitting in the cockpit with a mug of tea, reading Tristan's last published book, *Encounters of a Wayward Sailor*. Half a dozen of Tristan's entertaining tomes occupied the shelves in the main and fore cabins; ten more were at home. *Retreat's* small library held other adventure sailing volumes, at least one of them relevant to Tristan's life—as he had reported it.

A compendium of the eight mountaineering and sailing books by the late H. W. "Bill" Tilman stood there along with Tristan's *Ice!* and *The Incredible Voyage*, among others. I forgot about scrubbing. Instead I turned off the hose, went aft, and dropped down the companionway. On the starboard shelf I ran my hand along the spines of a dozen or more volumes until I reached Tilman's book, looking for an answer.

A chapter on Bill Tilman in *Encounters of a Wayward Sailor* preyed on my mind. Tristan wrote about the two occasions when he and Tilman supposedly met, both times in far northern waters. I knew neither story was true. I had read all of Tilman's books, and I had all of Jones's books. I knew they could never have met in Iceland or Greenland as Tristan claimed, because the dates he cited did not fit with known events. Having had doubts about the honesty of some of Tristan's stories, I began to wonder how many of his tales came more from his imagination than from experience.

Tristan Jones was reputed to be one of the great small-boat mariners of the twentieth century. Either that or he was one of the greatest frauds ever to put a sailing story on paper. Perhaps he was both. Though slightly built, he was tough, resilient, and determined—of that there was no doubt. His own books describe a man apparently cast in the iron mold of the finest British explorers, most of whom, like Tristan, were far from perfect. Many solo adventurers of the past five centuries who went off into the unknown to carve their names on distant lands and to raise the Union Jack for Britain might have recognized Tristan as one of their own. Sir Richard Burton, Alexander Gordon Laing, John Hanning Speke, and the Welshman Henry Morton Stanley, all of whom had their detractors, would have tipped their hats in homage to a man like Tristan Jones. But dynamic career sailors and navigators like Sir Francis Drake, Captain James Cook, and Sir John Franklin, to name but three, while they would have understood the motivation that drove him, they would not have admired Tristan's lack of professionalism in recording his exploits.

How much of what Tristan wrote in his books and articles was fact and how much was fiction, I wondered as I researched material for his biography. Many of his readers and critics had asked that simple question, but no one, to my knowledge, had taken the necessary lengthy steps to determine the answer. The only person who could solve the mystery quickly was dead. Yet I knew that everyone leaves a paper trail. If I wanted to be the one to discover the real Tristan Jones, I naively thought, all I had to do was follow the long line of vague clues he had left in his wake and pick up every scrap of information. I wanted my book to be an accurate portrayal of the man as well as a tribute: as faithful to his life as his writing, his friends, his enemies, and my research would allow. I knew I might have to probe unfathomable depths to accomplish my goal.

And so was set in motion a chain reaction. One accidentally discovered falsehood led inexorably to another and another. Gradually, over two and a half years, with a great deal of help from Tristan's friends and associates, I pieced together the elements of an extraordinary life. I became a fascinated bystander, an unofficial observer of one man's history, as Tristan clawed his way to success, reinventing himself on the way, first as a small-boat sailor, later as a writer.

I had no idea when I started this long voyage that my quest would take me more than halfway around the world. During my travels through a dozen countries, I interviewed scores of people and studied hundreds of letters—including Tristan's personal correspondence—plus faxes, e-mails, websites, and Tristan's logbooks and collection of faded photographs. As the weeks passed I found more and more evidence of embellishment and outright invention.

The man who claimed to have sailed more than 345,000 miles in boats under forty feet (12 m) long, who said he sailed 180,000 miles solo, and who told his readers he had crossed the Atlantic nineteen times under sail—nine times alone—in addition to alleging a page-long list of other adventurous nautical accomplishments, had far less experience at sea than he was prepared to admit. The man who claimed to have been torpedoed three times before his eighteenth birthday, who said he had taken a sailboat farther north into Arctic waters than anyone else, who told his readers of being trapped in polar ice for months at a time, was something of a fraud. The man who said he was born at sea on his father's ship in 1924 was actually born on land five years later.

That Tristan Jones had the soul of an adventurer was never in doubt. From whom he inherited the adventurous spirit that colored his life after he left the navy is not known: possibly from the father he never knew. His lionhearted approach to tackling enormous obstacles impressed friends and foes alike. That he became a highly skilled sailor through his own efforts is beyond question. He recovered from the amputation of his left leg in 1982 and then sailed more than halfway around the world. He endured the loss of his right leg in 1991 and still briefly returned to the sea. His courage was never in doubt—it was the outrageous claims of extreme achievements that bothered me.

Day after day, sifting through mounds of evidence, I uncovered the elements of a story woven from the exotic threads of deceit, ego, skill, courage, tenacity, sexual differences, and eventually murder. As the tally of deception rose, I had to ask myself how far I was prepared to go with Tristan's story. My quest had already uncovered unforeseen dangers, but the facts accumulating before me demanded to be heard. Just as Tristan had an obligation (which he ignored) to justify his extravagant claims, so I felt honor bound to present his story accurately— or not at all.

Based on what I already knew, and considering the controversial domains to which my quest would inevitably lead me, I was forced to make some difficult decisions. Did I have the courage to make a metaphorical voyage into perilous waters? Could I tell the truth about Tristan's life while offering his memory every courtesy? Was I prepared to risk shattering Tristan's integrity on the rocks of his own deceit?

The answer to all was a cautious *yes.*

Somehow I had to create an acceptable balance between Tristan Jones the superb sailor, the wonderful wordsmith, the hardy adventurer, the stoic amputee, the well-meaning mentor to disabled young men in Thailand and his alter ego—the teller of outrageous tales. I wanted to find a way to show that the real Tristan Jones was possibly something more than the mythical persona he created for himself. The task proved far more onerous than I could have imagined.

Tristan's inconsistencies and embellishments are a minefield for a biographer. There were so many false trails, so many dead ends. For a while I harbored a temptation to believe Tristan deliberately set and baited traps for any future biographer. An impossibility, I know. In 1976, when he wrote his first book, *The Incredible Voyage*, Tristan could not have known he would one day be famous among sailors.

After many false starts I chose to allow Tristan's life to unfold naturally—as much as possible—so that readers might understand the progression of events that led him to become first a skilled sailor and later an important writer of sea stories. Eventually, when I reached Tristan's midlife, when it became obvious that he had completely reinvented himself, when his career as a writer had firmly taken hold and his books spoke for themselves, I found I had little choice but to point out the anomalies in his stories. On one hand was the truth—on the other were Tristan's often grandiose exaggerations. The chapter on Bill Tilman in *Encounters of a Wayward Sailor* had kick-started my research. That fictional anecdote turned my quest into a much more difficult challenge than I had anticipated: far more complicated, yet infinitely more rewarding.

What follows is the saga of my probing voyage through the life of a man who—like many explorers and authors before him—had no wish to be subjected to close scrutiny.

CHAPTER 1

The Early Years

Brooding, craggy hills—the northern extent of the Cambrian Mountains, backbone of an ancient Celtic land—stand guard over Gwynedd, veiled in early morning mist. Only Snowdon, the highest, has a name accessible to the tongues of those not born in Cymru, or Wales. Aran Fawddwy, Aran Benllyn, Rhinog Fawr, Rhinog Fach, and Cader Idris protect their Celtic identities with the barely pronounceable syllables of a lyrical, evocative language. It is said of mighty Cader Idris, the "Chair of Arthur," that anyone who spends a night asleep on its heights wakes up either blind, mad, or a poet. In Wales, poets are many.

This was Arthur's land. According to myth Arthur, the legendary sixth-century king of the Britons who led Celtic resistance against Saxon domination, slew monsters among these hills, lakes, and forests of pine. Where terrifying fabled creatures once roamed, today small towns, villages, and hamlets, their houses built from hard-wearing local stone and slate, nestle snugly in lush valleys between the hills and an unpredictable sea. The forerunners of these gray settlements spawned Celtic saints who set off to sail to an emerald isle, as well as heroes like Llewellyn the Great and Owen Glendower. In more recent times poets Dylan Thomas and W. H. Davies, author Jan Morris, painter Augustus John, actors Richard Burton and Anthony Hopkins, composer Ralph Vaughan Williams, and young singer Charlotte Church with her haunting voice all came from Wales. So too did explorer Henry Morton Stanley, philosopher and Arabist T. E. Lawrence, and renowned statesman David Lloyd George. This is a land liberally sprinkled with poets and singers, actors, storytellers, and dreamers. Surnames like Davies, Williams, and the ubiquitous Jones predominate. One such Jones, who called himself Tristan, said he grew up where the west wind blows steadily over Merioneth—now South Gwynedd. He too was a poet, a writer, a storyteller, a dreamer, a sailor.

Tristan Jones claimed an impressive family tree of seafarers. He could, he said, trace his oceangoing ancestors on both sides of his family as far back as the seventeenth century. He hinted at a blood kinship with Christopher Jones, captain of the *Mayflower*. At times, inspired by the depths of his own imagination, he managed to dredge up a thousand years of nautical antecedents—weaving in salty grandmothers who roved the oceans as qualified mates on square-rigged cargo ships and adding seventeenth-century Welsh buccaneer Sir Henry Morgan to his family tree. It's an impressive and ambitious list by any standard.

He painted a particularly colorful picture of his father in *A Steady Trade*, the "autobiographical" story of his early life, published in 1982. Jones Senior, Tristan claimed, had been at sea since 1909, first serving as a cook and deck boy, then rising through the ranks until he became a master mariner. Captain Jones Senior's career on sailing ships lasted to 1916, with voyages to the far corners of the world. After World War I, we are told, he took command of an eight-thousand-ton tramp steamer, SS *Western Star*. His wife, Megan, accompanied him on his far-reaching voyages. And so Tristan cleverly set the scene for his own dramatic birth.

Jones's biographical details state that he was born at sea on his father's tramp steamer on May 8, 1924, in the South Atlantic. *Western Star*, we are told, was en route to Halifax, Nova Scotia, from a port in Western Australia, with a cargo of sheep bones and a roller-skating rink. Out in the South Atlantic, some 150 miles northeast of the lonely islands of Tristan da Cunha, Megan gave birth to a boy. Nothing was ever easy in Jones's early life. Memorable, certainly. Easy, never.

The baby, the story tells us, was in a breech position—difficult for mother and child in any circumstances. At sea, under the conditions Tristan described, the birth would have put both at enormous risk. On that day in May poor Megan suffered for ten excruciating hours, trying to deliver her baby in the master's cabin of a ship being callously tossed by a storm. The scene is as dramatic as it is far-fetched.

Western Star rolls at the whim of the tempest, buffeted by screaming winds and white-capped waves. One can almost feel the ship shuddering and moaning under the onslaught. Meanwhile, down below, a heavily pregnant woman struggles to give birth while standing upright and hanging on grimly to the ceiling of a cabin moving wildly in concert with the angry sea. One foot is on the captain's desk. The other finds a modicum of stability on a sofa that the mate has ripped from the wall with his bare hands. As if that weren't enough drama, Tristan then creates a near-perfect climax. He is born at sunrise and with a caul—a membrane—over his head. The first mate, Ebenezer Roberts, helping Megan's husband at the birth, recognizes the caul as a symbol of good luck. Avowing that the infant will always land on his feet, he adds that he might one day find himself the center of attention at a hanging. The baby boy, we are led to believe, was given the name Tristan in honor of the nearest land.

Having established that he was born at sea in 1924, Tristan then told of his boyhood in north Wales in the hamlet of Llangareth, near Barmouth, in the shadow of Cader Idris. Close examination of maps of Wales, however, fails to reveal the village of Llangareth, where Tristan supposedly spent his first fourteen years. There is, in fact, no Llangareth anywhere in Wales.

So the questions must be asked. Where and when was this Jones born? Where did he grow up? Where did he go to school? When did he first go to sea? The answers were buried so deep in the quagmire of Tristan's storytelling that at times it seemed they would never be found. Persistent digging in dusty archives, however, proved successful—to a point.

Tristan's seafaring Welsh mother, Megan Roberts, as described in *A Steady Trade*, was a fictional character. It is unlikely that his real mother had more than a passing acquaintance with the sea. She was a Lancashire girl from a landlocked region of England.

Margaret Jones probably lived with her parents in Brownhill, Lancashire, close to the east side of the British industrial city of Blackburn. In the late summer of 1928, possibly still a teenager and single, she discovered to her dismay that she was pregnant.

In late 1920s Britain, where sex education was virtually unheard of, illegitimacy carried an extreme social stigma. A girl who got pregnant out of wedlock brought disgrace on her entire family. She was considered a tramp and sometimes labeled mentally deficient. Working-class girls who got "in trouble" were often turned out of their parents' homes and left to the mercies of the church or, worse, the local workhouse. The more fortunate ones were sent into exile, often to distant relatives, for the duration of the pregnancy.

Margaret Jones, who may or may not have been of Welsh descent, appears to have been one of the luckier ones. She spent her pregnancy, perhaps with relatives, in the north Liverpool suburb of Crosby, where she worked as a waitress until her time drew near. Close to the end of her ninth month, Margaret entered Liverpool's Walton Hospital. On May 8, 1929, she gave birth to a dark-haired boy with equally dark eyes.

In 1929 Wyatt Earp, legendary marshal of Dodge City, died peacefully at the age of eighty, and the lovely actress Lillie Langtry passed away at seventy-five on the French Riviera. In the Soviet Union Joseph Stalin sent Leon Trotsky into exile. And in Chicago, on February 14 the notorious Saint Valentine's Day massacre took place. There was an aeronautical high in August when *Graf Zeppelin*, the German airship, flew round the world in twenty-one days from Lakehurst, New Jersey. The high was followed by a calamitous low: the financial world watched in horror as the stock market crashed on October 24, when close to thirteen million shares were traded on Black Thursday. It is unlikely that these historic events had any great impact on the Jones family.

Margaret named her son Arthur and registered his birth on May 14, 1929. The spaces on the birth certificate for the father's name and occupation had a line drawn through them: no name, no occupation. On leaving the hospital Margaret returned to her parents' home in Brownhill. Arthur Jones would carry his mother's maiden name as his surname for the rest of his life. He would never know his father, or even his father's name.

In an unpublished book completed only a few months before he died, Tristan wrote of growing up in a variety of children's homes until he was sixteen. That has the ring of truth. Although he would have been clothed and fed, life would have been harsh for the unwanted little boy, and discipline strict. Step out of line and suffer a beating from hard-hearted guardians. The boys in the dormitory started each day early by washing in cold water, making their own beds, and eating a communal breakfast of porridge with watered-down milk, followed by rudimentary lessons on weekdays—mainly reading, writing, and arithmetic, with a smattering of geography and history. They were served unappetizing meals of tepid tea, lukewarm gristly stew, and bread to sop it up. What little free time Arthur and the other boys had would have been on weekends when, if permission was granted, they could explore the intriguing world outside the orphanage's confining walls. Small and thin and inevitably labeled a bastard, Arthur would almost certainly have had to fight regularly to stand up to the bullying of bigger boys. It was a tough life for Arthur, one that molded the habits of a quarrelsome adult.

Four days after Arthur's eighth birthday, George VI was crowned in Westminster Abbey. A little over two years later, on September 3, 1939, the British government declared war on Nazi Germany. Allied shipping began to fall prey to German submarines. On October 16 the Royal Navy battleship HMS *Royal Oak* was sunk by an enemy torpedo at her base in Scapa Flow, in the Orkney Islands off Scotland's northern coast. Eight hundred men died.

The initial weeks of 1940 saw food rationing introduced in Britain as the country went on short supplies for the duration of the war. German forces stormed across Europe and by the end of May encircled British troops on the French and Belgian coasts. A vast fleet of naval vessels, fishing boats, ferries, and private boats crossed the Channel from English ports to evacuate over 300,000 allied troops. By mid-June much of Europe had fallen to the enemy, and Britain stood virtually alone against the combined forces of Germany and Italy.

That summer the Luftwaffe attacked British airfields, and the Battle of Britain began. Waves of German bombers dropped thousands of tons of explosives on London. Attacks on provincial cities soon followed, with emphasis on industrial regions. Liverpool suffered a heavy raid at the end of November. Wherever young Arthur Jones lived during those dark days of 1940, he, like the rest of the nation, would have been at constant risk and often in fear. Few in Britain who lived through the six years of World War II were left unscarred. Nightly, exploding bombs alternated with screaming air-raid sirens. As buildings crumpled into dust, the cries of terrified people mingled with the moans of the injured and dying. Death became a daily event, though none who survived really became accustomed to the violence.

On May 8, 1945, Arthur Jones's sixteenth birthday, the guns finally fell silent across a battle-weary Britain. The war was over. Arthur's youth had protected him from induction into the armed forces. By this time he was on his own, earning his keep as a truck driver's helper. On the day the war ended Arthur Jones was legally old enough to join the Royal Navy as a boy sailor. But he didn't. He continued to work on trucks. Peacetime, however, did not mean the end of Britain's military forces. All men, once they reached seventeen and a half or eighteen, were expected to spend two years of national service in one of the three armed forces. Arthur Jones was no exception. He had missed the war, but he still had to serve his time.

CHAPTER 2

Tristan's Navy

On November 26, 1946, when he was seventeen and a half years old, Arthur Jones of Liverpool signed on the Royal Navy's roster for his two years of National Service. He was assigned to HMS *St. George*, a shore-based barracks at Gosport, Hampshire, as a stoker 2nd class. (All Royal Navy shore establishments, known as "stone frigates," are prefixed HMS, for Her Majesty's Ship. Before the death of George VI in 1952, they were His Majesty's Ships.) Arthur Jones was given service number KX770680; his enlistment papers noted his date of birth as May 8, 1929, and his place of birth as Walton, Lancashire. They further recorded that he was five feet, eight inches tall with a thirty-eight-inch chest, and that he had brown hair and eyes and a dark complexion. There is no record of his weight at the time, but it would not have been much over 120 pounds, a weight he maintained for much of his life.

After eight weeks of basic training at Gosport he was assigned to HMS *Imperieuse* at Devonport—on the Tamar River at Plymouth—where he was trained to be a stoker. He remained there until June 5, 1947, when he was sent to HMS *Pembroke*, yet another shore posting, this time at Chatham Naval Barracks, Kent. There—as with future shore-based postings—he would have served in a boiler room.

Jones spent eleven months at HMS *Pembroke* before being transferred to HMS *Victory*—another shore base and depot at Portsmouth. Three months later he was sent back to HMS *Pembroke*. More exciting times were ahead. After two months at the Chatham base, close to the end of his two years of National Service, he appears to have signed on for a further twelve years. He soon received orders to proceed overseas— whether he crossed the Atlantic by military aircraft or by sea is not known.

On October 13, 1948, he arrived in the brilliant sunshine of Bermuda, at HMS *Malabar*. He was still based ashore, but at last he was seeing a different part of the world. Although we know little of his time at the Bermuda station, from later reports we can assume that he, or the ship he was on, may have helped position marker buoys in the approach channel to Hamilton Harbor.

After two and a half years in the navy, a few weeks past his twentieth birthday, Arthur Jones finally was posted to a real ship for four months. HMS *Snipe* was a 1,490-ton sloop of the Modified Black Swan Class, converted to a frigate. Launched in 1944, she was almost three hundred feet long.

HMS *Malabar* claimed him for eight more months before he once again went to sea, on a much smaller ship. He joined the 730-ton boom defense vessel HMS *Barbeque* on September 1, 1950, and stayed with her for a mere seven weeks before returning to England and HMS *Pembroke* at Chatham.

If Arthur Jones had expected to be at sea for much of his twelve years, plus his original two, he was sadly mistaken. Just over three months after returning to Britain's gray winter skies, he was issued a railway warrant and ordered north to HMS *Cochrane*, the navy's base at Rosyth, Scotland, across the Firth of Forth from Edinburgh. At times he must have wondered if the navy really had a reasonable system for rotating personnel or if it did so randomly. On July 12, 1951, he was returned to HMS *Pembroke* for another eight-month stint. Then back to Rosyth, where, during a posting lasting just over one year, he served for a time aboard the Onslow Class destroyer HMS *Orwell*, a veteran of the North Atlantic in World War II.

From Scotland he moved south again, this time to HMS *Osprey*, a base at Portland, on the Channel coast. Thirteen months later he was back at Rosyth to ship out for four months on the destroyer depot ship HMS *Woolwich*, presumably on North Sea or North Atlantic duty. Since he had served only on ships of considerably less than 2,000 tons, at 8,750 tons HMS *Woolwich* would have felt like an ocean liner. From Rosyth he returned to Chatham, where after a few weeks he was assigned to another destroyer, HMS *Aisne*, of the Battle Class. In her he sailed for Malta to spend ten months ashore at HMS *Phoenicia*, a supply base on Manoel Island for the Royal Navy's Mediterranean flotillas. HMS *Aisne* came back into his life on September 24, 1955, and he served on her in the Mediterranean and home waters until the end of May 1956, when he once again found himself at Chatham—briefly in the reserve fleet barracks at HMS *Neptune*. Toward the end of his time on HMS *Aisne* he obtained his first passport. Number 254986 was issued to Arthur Jones on March 16, 1956. This document, which would have echoed the details on his birth certificate and his Royal Navy identity card, would have given his date of birth as May 8, 1929, and his place of birth as Liverpool.

Posted back to HMS *Pembroke*, he again shipped out on destroyers—first HMS *Obdurate*, another of the Onslow Class, and later the C Class HMS *Chieftain* for the better part of a year. In January 1958 he received a posting to the Far East—to HMS *Sultan*, a shore base in Singapore, which employed him for nine months. Over the winter of 1958–59 he was once again at sea, experiencing life on a minelayer, the Manxman Class HMS *Apollo*. He returned to England in May 1959, spending a week at HMS *Drake* barracks at Devonport and a few weeks at the by then extremely familiar HMS *Pembroke* at Chatham. With less than two years of his service remaining, Jones was given one last posting to a destroyer, HMS *Cavendish*. Five months later, early in the new year, he was back in Singapore at HMS *Terror* shore base to begin his final year of service.

Official records show that Arthur Jones spent little more than four years aboard ships during his fourteen years in the navy. Almost all his postings were to shore bases. On September 9, 1960, Arthur Jones entered the Chatham Naval Barracks of HMS *Pembroke* for the last time. From there he was transferred to HMS *Drake*, where he was discharged on December 24, 1960, as "below naval physical standard."

Since navy records personnel were not forthcoming with additional information, we can only guess at the reasons behind his discharge. It is possible that Jones was either alcoholic or diabetic. (By the mid-1960s he was notorious for his heavy drinking; in later years diabetes *could* be blamed for two amputations.) An unsubstantiated report said he was invalided out of the service after injuring his back when he fell down a companionway aboard ship while drunk. Yet another such report said he only had one lung.

At this juncture one wonders if at thirty-one years old, after fourteen years of service, he had become so comfortable with navy life—perhaps the only real home he had ever known—that he tried to sign on for a further twelve years. Possibly his physical condition, whatever it may have been, became obvious only during a medical examination for reenlistment.

During his fourteen years of service Arthur Jones rose from stoker 2nd class to engineering mechanic 1st class. There is no known record of his taking any courses to further his education. Other than "naval history," there were few courses for lower ranks in those years; the old salts taught younger sailors everything they needed to know.

Arthur Jones's naval career may not have been distinguished, but he did his job efficiently. His character was assessed as "very good" throughout his first thirteen years and as "good" for his final year. For overall efficiency, his assessment began at "moderate," progressed to "satisfactory," and finished as "superior."

After fourteen years of Royal Navy regimentation, finding himself out on the street in winter—on Christmas Eve to be precise—must have come as a shock. Once again he was alone. Later, as an author, he would regularly time events in his life to coincide with festive occasions such as Christmas or New Year.

With Cresswell *and* Banjo

Although we don't know for sure what Jones did immediately after leaving the navy, we do have a clue to his next employment. In addition to a Royal Navy service number, his pension records show that he also had a merchant navy number. Although a search of the records (which contain scores of men named "A. Jones") failed to locate either this Arthur Jones or a Tristan Jones, it is highly possible that he went back to sea on commercial ships for the years 1961, 1962, and 1963. In the early 1970s he mentioned to a crew mate, Conrad Jelinek, that he had been in the merchant navy as well as the Royal Navy.

Chatham Naval Dockyard, where Arthur Jones was based many times during his naval service, is on the river Medway, which opens up into the Thames estuary. For hundreds of years the river Thames, gateway to London, has been used by private, commercial, and military marine traffic, including recreational sailboats and the last vestiges of Britain's coastal sailing barge fleets. Those latter images apparently had a profound effect on Arthur Jones, providing the aspiration to purchase his own sailboat.

In late spring or early summer 1964 Arthur invested his meager savings in a converted lifeboat that he found on the river Medway at Rochester, almost within sight of Chatham Naval Dockyard. *Cresswell* would be his floating home for the next two or three years.

Cresswell was built by the Thames Ironworks, of Canning Town, London, in 1909. She was a self-righting lifeboat originally given the name *Martha*. Designed by a Mr. Rubie, who was then the Surveyor of Lifeboats for the Royal National Lifeboat Institution (RNLI), she was thirty-four feet long with an eight-foot beam. *Martha* carried one water ballast tank and was powered by ten oars, double-banked. Her twin bilge keels were designed so she could be launched quickly from Britain's shingle beaches. The RNLI has always been supported entirely by voluntary donations. In 1909 the cost of the new lifeboat for the Cresswell, Northumberland, station (£723) was part of a bequest from the late Mrs. M. A. Vaughan of Highbury New Park, London. It was Mrs. Vaughan's wish that the new boat be named *Martha*.

There was to be no easy introduction to the lifeboat service. *Martha* was called out on September 23, 1909, her first night at Cresswell. (Although her crew searched until daybreak, no distressed vessel was found.) During her distinguished career in the lifeboat service, spanning thirty-five years, *Martha* was launched thirty times to assist endangered shipping and saved seventeen lives. The boat was withdrawn from service in the summer of 1944, when the Cresswell lifeboat station closed, and she was sold privately that same year.

The London office of Lloyd's Register of Shipping is on Fenchurch Street, a few minutes' walk from the Tower of London. In a large basement room, glass-fronted cabinets contain shelves of green cloth-bound volumes: the yacht registers, published in April of each year from the late 1800s to 1980. *Cresswell* is listed there. She makes her first appearance in the register for 1950, after she had been converted to an auxiliary ketch sometime between 1944 and 1949. She was owned at that time by a C. D. J. Benton, and her port of registry is listed as Rochester, Kent. *Cresswell,* the register states, was powered by a two-cylinder auxiliary engine of ten boiler horsepower, built by Cub Oil Engine Ltd.

Benton, a resident of nearby Chatham, owned *Cresswell* until 1960.

The registers for 1961 through 1964 show the ketch then owned by an E. Meredith, with Rochester still her home port. In the "Alterations and Editions to July 10, 1964," Tristan finally comes into the picture. A. (Arthur) Jones, using the General Post Office at Sandwich, Kent, as his address, is noted as the new owner. With Arthur in command, *Cresswell*'s port of registry changed from Rochester to Sandwich.

After carefully navigating the bad-tempered currents and swirling tidal waters of the busy Thames estuary, Arthur Jones piloted his charge east to pass Margate and round North Foreland. Turning south, with the notorious Goodwin Sands to port, he entered Pegwell Bay and motored up the river Stour to Sandwich, *Cresswell*'s new home port. He doesn't appear to have stayed long. He soon continued west, daring the busy shipping lanes between England and France to Guernsey, in the Channel Islands.

Twenty-one-year-old Ian Spooner met Arthur Jones in Guernsey and quickly moved out of his minuscule rented room and into *Cresswell*'s forepeak. Spooner came from a sailing family. His father was a lifelong sailor and had been captain of an East Coast sailing smack. The young Englishman would be a useful mate aboard *Cresswell*. Based alternately at St. Peter Port in Guernsey and alongside the wall by a pub in Alderney, Arthur and Ian enjoyed a riotous summer cruising from those harbors to the nearby island of Sark and to Dilette, in France. Spooner recounted a brace of anecdotes from those free and easy weeks.

"We did one whisky [smuggling] trip to France. Ended up scooting up the sand [and ran] aground in the harbour entrance as it wasn't obvious that there was no water inside the harbour wall at that stage of the tide . . . apart from the fact that there were about forty French holidaymakers up to their knees [in water] across the entrance! Ho hum. That's where I did the classic move; we were under full sail *and* engine, doing about 6 knots and when I saw what was happening I took the kedge off its coil of line and threw it overboard. [Unfortunately,] it wasn't made fast to the line for some reason. I don't think we found it."

On another occasion they tested the navy's nerve. "We took officers and their girlfriends from a navy ship to Sark, missed the tide and had a hairy trip back through the rocks north of the island at night. The navy men and girls were terrified, but Arthur's angel guided us through with good old *Cresswell* plunging between huge rocks with the swell. Rocks literally an arm's length away for quite some time. Great memory. Myself and my girlfriend were up in the shrouds singing, such was the spirit in those days."

On August 19, 1964, Arthur Jones obtained a new passport in London bearing the number 339558. As with his previous passport, that document would have listed his year of birth as 1929 and his place of birth as Liverpool. Within a year he would obtain a falsified passport, as well.

As summer turned to autumn, Arthur, after a long night's drinking, fell off the Alderney harbor wall onto *Cresswell*'s deck and broke his ribs. Unable to go a-roving for a while, he parted company with Spooner. We know Jones returned to the river Medway and Chatham sometime later that year or early the next, because he got into a brawl in a pub—one with significant repercussions for him.

As far as we know, Arthur Jones began introducing himself as Tristan sometime after his escapades with Ian Spooner. One wonders how much he knew about the new name he chose for himself. Possibly it was nothing more than a clever attempt to glamorize his identity by aligning himself with a few remote rocky volcanic islands in the South Atlantic. Perhaps, though, considering Tristan's love of literary sagas in midlife, his reasoning was closer to home. Steve Sanderson, who knew him in Ibiza from 1967 to 1968, recalled that Tristan occasionally quoted old Welsh sayings.

The name Tristan is said to be a corruption of Tristram—one of the knights of King Arthur's Round Table—whose love for Iseult, daughter of the king of Ireland and wife of King Mark of Cornwall, featured in a host of romantic medieval epics. As early as the twelfth century Tristan was in use as a surname in France. Derived from the French *triste*, "sad," Tristram was used in England in the twelfth century as a Christian name. The two similar names are also thought to be derivations of the Pictish Drostan or the Celtic Drystan. The latter, according to experts, bears echoes of *Drust* and *Drest*, both of which suggest tumult or din—fitting nomenclature indeed for rowdy Arthur Jones of Liverpool. By this time, though, Tristan had decided he was Welsh and therefore a Celt. And, with his dark, brooding looks, he could well have been.

Probably as a consequence of his lowly start in life, a difficult childhood, and perhaps his lightweight physique, Arthur Jones had developed a chip on his shoulder and a quarrelsome attitude. He was always ready to use his fists and his boots against anyone—regardless of size—who crossed him in any way. When he'd been drinking heavily, as he regularly did, he could become downright mean. He was quick, and he could be vicious. He was usually the instigator of trouble, and he never backed down from a fight. In Chatham he picked on the wrong person—a Celt much bigger than he was.

The Celts, a broad mix of Scots, Irish, Welsh, and Manx, are a close people—when it suits them. Once he became known as a writer Tristan trumpeted his Celtic background, whether real or assumed, whenever he got the chance and aligned himself with other Celts at every opportunity. One such Celtic figure, a fighter like himself, featured largely in Tristan's life for a while in the middle to late 1960s and appears in one of his books.

Pete Kelly, the Manxman from *Saga of a Wayward Sailor*, Tristan's third book, is a fraction shy of six feet tall, broad shouldered, and powerfully built. Pete has wavy gray hair and a neatly trimmed beard of the same shade. His eyes are blue flecked with gold, framed by steel-rimmed glasses. One eye appears to be lazy and wanders occasionally, as if restlessly looking for excitement. For a former fisherman his hands, though large, are surprisingly callus-free, with soft skin, although he has an iron grip. He wears a solid gold bishop's ring, adorned in the center by an amethyst bearing the Manx symbol and his personal seal in gold. His nails are long for a man's and perfectly manicured. They are the hands of an artist. Pete Kelly, the admitted former drug smuggler and ex-convict, is now an accomplished watercolor painter.

He was born, he said, on the Isle of Man in 1944, hence the appellation "Kelly," the traditional affectionate name for those born on Man. His mother was Manx, his father a member of the Polish Air Force serving with the RAF. Sadly for the infant, he never got to know his father, since the freedom-loving fighter pilot was shot down and killed during the war's final months. Pete Kelly's real surname, naturally, is Polish.

Kelly first encountered the man he knew only as Tristan Jones in a Chatham pub in 1964 or early 1965—he isn't sure exactly when. Tristan, in his habitual belligerent fashion after a few drinks, took it into his head to hurl abuse at Kelly—a man he had never met. Kelly, then twenty-one years old, some fifteen years younger than Tristan and a brawler by nature, had no qualms about the difference in their sizes; he picked Tristan up and threw him across the room. "Aggressive little men are dangerous. You never know what they will do. You have to kill them immediately," Kelly explained.

Tristan bounced off a wall and crumpled to the floor. Before he could get up and rejoin the battle, as he assuredly would have done, he was greeted by one of Kelly's large boots. It connected sharply with Tristan's head, and he stayed down. To avoid further unpleasantness when his adversary woke up, Kelly threw the recumbent wreck out the door and resumed drinking.

The two met again within a few days, on a street near the harbor. No mention was made of the fight, and they got along reasonably well from that day on.

~~~⌇~~~

Tristan claimed to have spent many long months trapped in Arctic ice in *Cresswell*. In his stories, he was there between 1959 and 1961, an impossibility considering that he didn't purchase *Cresswell* until 1964. He told convincing tales, though, with many variations in the telling. When asked what he knew about Tristan's Arctic adventures, Kelly replied, "I had fished off Iceland and told Tristan stories about the times up there," he said, "what the seas and winds were like. He knew nothing about Iceland in those days. I'm sure he'd never been there."

Continuing the Arctic theme Kelly said, "I think he was in the Arctic. I reckon he sailed up the North Sea toward Spitsbergen and got stuck in the ice for a while off Norway, until someone rescued him. It might have been the Russians. When I met him his boat was a mess, and he was very thin and still showing the effects of his earlier starvation. He hoarded food. He'd take a little tin, you know, like a tin for cough lozenges, and he'd put rice in it and stow it away behind a bulkhead for when he needed it."

Kelly admitted that his memories of events from thirty-five years before might be faulty, but he added, "I don't think he went to Greenland, but I believe he was in the Arctic. He was trying to beat Nansen's record." Despite Kelly's memories, which may have been clouded by reading Tristan's early books, it is most likely that Jones did not go to the Arctic. There are no records of Tristan or *Cresswell* in Icelandic ports, or in Spitsbergen, or in northern Norway. And there was hardly time for an Arctic voyage between his buying *Cresswell*, enjoying the islands with Ian Spooner, and meeting Pete Kelly in Chatham a few months later. *Cresswell* could have been a mess because her owner was habitually untidy. And Tristan's skinny frame and penny-pinching nature could well have reflected lack of income or been attributable in part to his recent rib injuries.

Kelly helped Tristan tidy up his boat and get her ready for sea, even rowing across the Medway in a fog to raid a naval supply depot for equipment. Once they were ready the duo sailed westward down the Channel, back to the Channel Islands, for a rendezvous with smugglers—a second chance at the game for Tristan. With navigation a hit-and-miss affair at first, the mismatched pair of rogues found their way from one port to another as much by luck as by intent. "I don't think he had a sextant on board in those days," Pete said. "I never saw him use one. In the Channel and the Med we navigated by dead reckoning." Discussing their combined knowledge of sailing, Pete added: "In those days, neither of us really knew what we were doing [technically], but Tristan was a natural. He became a superb sailor."

That matched Ian Spooner's comments. After learning more about his former skipper, he said, "I begin to understand why we had so many 'adventures' afloat due to less than perfect seamanship."

When Pete and Tristan took part in the smuggling they knew they were gambling with their freedom. But the opportunity for some fast money, with excitement thrown in, was too good to pass up. Without giving the names of any ports or regions, Pete made it clear that the goods smuggled—crates of fine Scotch whisky—traveled across the Channel from north to south, Britain to France.

Smuggling whisky across the Channel from river mouths, bays, and occasionally small ports was a time-honored profession among the Celts of Britain's western coastline. Cornishmen, Welshmen, Manx, and Scots all played a part in the lucrative illegal commerce. Tristan admitted to making two smuggling runs with Pete in *Cresswell*. In reality he probably did three or four, maybe more.

They spent a few months risking jail by undertaking irregular cross-Channel voyages, heavily laden with crates of Scotch. Tristan said he carried 150 crates on his first smuggling exercise. Assuming that each crate contained a dozen bottles, that night's work illegally landed 1,800 duty-free bottles of Scotch on the French coast. In separate interviews on British television two decades later, Tristan, with his flair for exaggeration, claimed to one host that he carried more than 90,000 bottles. The French, he said, understood it was 82,000. To another interviewer he lowered the total smuggled. The French thought the total was 65,000 bottles, "and they were absolutely wrong," he crowed. "It was 72,000."

The lowest figure, if true, suggests he made at least thirty-six smuggling voyages—a staggering number. But Pete Kelly scornfully disputed Tristan's figures. "It was hundreds of bottles, not thousands," he said.

The number of zeros is unimportant. The penalty for smuggling was incarceration, whether the boat had a hundred bottles on board or a thousand. Every run would have been dangerous. Officials on both sides of the Channel were well aware of the trade and would have been on constant watch for the smugglers. Each trip would have required the utmost vigilance, combining strong nerves and excellent sailing skills with a hefty slice of luck. The busy Channel is no place for anxious and unlucky amateurs.

Tristan's luck ran out one night. As he landed his cargo at the designated spot, he was apprehended by the French authorities. With little choice other than to surrender themselves and the boat, Tristan's crew (of either one or two) ghosted away to sea in the darkness. Tristan, stranded on land and caught red-handed, had nowhere to run. According to Pete he spent the next three months as a guest of the French government. Kelly, who was one who escaped to sea in the darkness, said, "There was nothing else we could do."

He went on to say that he thought the French police had knocked Tristan around a bit when they arrested him. Tristan, no stranger to using his fists, had probably put up a fight. When he gained his freedom once more, we can safely assume he was officially told to stay out of France. Happy to oblige, Tristan went to the nearby Channel Islands. In Guernsey, in July 1965, he had his legal passport renewed and almost certainly obtained a forged British passport as a backup. This late, illegal addition to his documentation bore the same identification number as his real passport—339558. It listed the bearer's name as Tristan Arthur Jones and gave him a new birthplace, Dolgelly (the correct name is Dolgellau) in Wales, and a new year of birth—1927. From Guernsey, he turned *Cresswell* toward the sun. Arthur Jones—aka Tristan Jones—had taken another step toward reinventing himself.

Pete Kelly did not go south with Tristan at that time. They met again some months later in Ibiza, in the Balearic Islands. Consequently Tristan's movements from the time he left Guernsey until he arrived in the Mediterranean can only be guessed. Kelly was sure Tristan followed the French canal system, as did delivery skipper David Morgan, who met Tristan in Ibiza.

With his typical "screw-you" attitude to authority, Tristan ignored earlier instructions to stay out of France. He likely entered the country using his false passport. It is improbable that he would have been allowed in using his real papers, since Arthur Jones would have been on a list of undesirables. A dedicated Francophobe, it's unlikely he lingered in France. He almost certainly unstepped *Cresswell*'s masts and motored directly to the south coast. On arriving in the Mediterranean, Tristan and *Cresswell* were at last safe in the sun, with a long annual cruising season to enjoy.

David Morgan remembered that Tristan knew little about sailing when he arrived in Ibiza: "Once I had to sail his boat from one side of the harbor to the other, because without his engine he did not know how to sail," Morgan said.

Novice or not, Tristan learned. And later, with Pete Kelly as mate, he occasionally found jobs delivering boats between a variety of Mediterranean ports. He also built up a small business taking day-trippers out from Ibiza on snorkeling trips.

Pete said Tristan had a talent for marketing and organization. Much as he disliked chartering, he understood its potential and was good at getting everything in place. Tristan made deals with assistant managers of Ibiza hotels. The hotels would advertise day excursions to nearby beaches and snorkeling sites for their guests and would supply food and drinks. Then, while Tristan and Pete reaped the benefits of the business, the assistant managers got introductions to a bevy of beautiful and not-so-beautiful girls.

Part of Spain, Ibiza, Majorca, Menorca, and Formentera comprise the four main Balearic Islands. Today Ibiza is known more for its hedonistic night life than for the sun, sand, sea, and cheap booze that attracted visitors, including hordes of hippies, in the mid-1960s. For Tristan Jones, Ibiza was an excellent base from which to earn a few dollars while continuing to sail, and a place to entertain with his own and other people's stories.

Many of Tristan's later tales, fiction and nonfiction, in books and magazines stem from this period. Although Kelly confirmed that he helped Tristan on a number of short deliveries within the Mediterranean, he denies the story of helping him deliver a luxury yacht to Dakar for the president of Mauritania, a tale Tristan claimed as true in his book *Yarns*: "We never delivered any expensive yachts, except one on a short run from Italy," Pete said.

In 1966 or 1967, while Pete and Tristan were negotiating yacht deliveries, they were rewarded with a contract to take the fifty-nine-foot (18-meter) *Antoinette* from Barcelona to Gibraltar. Tristan related a complicated story about Pete having a large Union Jack tattooed on a British traitor's forehead in Valencia after getting him blind drunk, then locking the unfortunate man in *Antoinette*'s forepeak and sailing him to Gibraltar. There he was set free to display his shame to the British populace. Confirming that, like other suspicious Tristan stories, this one was based loosely on a true event, Pete set the record straight: "The tattoo was only a small one. I got him drunk and had it tattooed on his arse, not his forehead. He wasn't a traitor. He just owed me money and wouldn't pay up."

Gibraltar—the name stems from the Arabic Jebel Tariq—is a tiny British crown colony on a narrow rocky peninsula jutting out from

Spain's southwest coast at the eastern end of the Strait of Gibraltar. Its most prominent feature is the "Rock" it is named for, a limestone massif rising 426 meters above sea level. Gibraltar, once a bastion of British naval might, has long been claimed by Spain. It is a busy seaport where both English and Spanish are spoken, and where bars are plentiful.

The Rock is home to Barbary apes, the only simians more or less native to Europe. There is a legend that when the twenty-two Barbary apes that inhabit the upper reaches of the Rock of Gibraltar leave, the tiny territory will cease to be British. Spain would, of course, benefit by annexing the colony immediately. Not surprisingly, in those days when the British Empire was shrinking all too rapidly, the apes were guarded day and night.

Tristan and Pete sailed *Antoinette* into Gibraltar at the end of a few rough days at sea. The harbor, as always, was crowded with small boats overshadowed by the gray hulls of naval ships. Mischief, which was never far from them anyway, could hardly ignore the strutting pair of cheerful mismatched mariners. Being sailors, they went looking for a bar as soon as they arrived. They would also have looked up at the Rock to study its canopy of cloud. Like the clouds over Cape Town's Table Mountain, those draped untidily around the summit of the Rock of Gibraltar are an excellent guide to current and approaching weather conditions. Steady and hardly moving means a calm day. Clouds in a hurry, tearing themselves to shreds on the rough limestone peak, warn of high winds and whitecaps at sea. That day, and the following few days, the clouds were sluggish. Ideal conditions for the mischief they had planned.

In company with new friends, Willy Clossart and Henry Willons, usually referred to as Closet and Deaf Henry, Tristan and Pete got involved in a wild scheme to sell Barbary apes to Spanish nationalists. Stealing a troop of apes from under the noses of vigilant British troops and smuggling them onto a boat in a busy harbor was out of the question. But the thought of getting 1,000 pesetas per ape was magnetic enough for the four to put their heads together.

Closet came up with a scheme to buy Barbary apes in Morocco for 100 pesetas each, give them a free cruise across the Strait of Gibraltar to Algeciras, and palm them off as Gibraltar apes at a huge profit. As Closet explained, the ancestors of the apes on Gibraltar originated in Morocco. No one in Spain would know the difference.

On board Deaf Henry's grubby motor launch *Fanny Adams*, the adventurers crossed the usually busy narrow straits to Ceuta, a Spanish enclave on Morocco's north coast. Tristan said they bought fifteen apes in the souk at Tetuan, about thirty miles to the south, inside Morocco. Pete disagreed. "We bought them in the market in Ceuta. We didn't even have to go into Morocco." Pete also disputed the number purchased. "I don't remember fifteen apes," he said. "We only got seven or eight."

Tristan's description of the apes and the return to Spain is, as one would expect, far more colorful than his former partner's. Pete remembered, "We housed the seven or eight apes in a cage lashed on deck. They were quiet most of the way, but they smelled awful."

Tristan makes no mention of using a cage for the overnight crossing. He had the "friendly little fellows" grinning happily and chattering loudly, tethered to the deck by ropes. In his tale he and his cohorts quieted the noisy apes by feeding them a fortune in bananas. The climax of Tristan's story, set on a Spanish shore, was played out under a brilliant moon with Disneyesque ceremony. Fifteen apes, with Deaf Henry in the vanguard, paraded down the gangway to a new country. Tristan said the scene reminded him of Noah's ark.

Promising to come back with the remaining apes in a few days, the four temporary primate dealers pocketed their money and cast off. The sooner they were far away from Algeciras, the better for them. With no intention of attempting the caper a second time, they turned *Fanny Adams* for the Balearic Islands.

Tristan rarely talked to Pete about his past, other than to say he was Welsh, but he did tell him a fictitious version of his birth. "My dad died at sea before I was born. I was born on a ship, but my mam died before we got to England. I was an orphan." "I don't think he had any family," Kelly said. "He never got letters from anyone."

Pete Ross, co-owner with his wife, Britt, of the George and Dragon pub in Ibiza at that time, disagreed. "I remember the night [Tristan] got news of his mother's death. It affected him badly, and he was roaring drunk for three days and had a vicious fight with an American photographer . . . who he left in a badly battered state, although Tristan was half his size and only had one lung."

No other habitués of the George and Dragon, or other local pubs, remembered Tristan's talking about his mother, and certainly not in association with her death while he was in Ibiza. In view of Tristan's known habit of dramatizing or fabricating incidents, the story of his mother's death in 1967 sounds like fiction. In those days Pete Kelly was the closest thing to family that Tristan had. Together they sailed for a living during the day and rampaged through bars at night. If Tristan's mother had died in 1967, Kelly would have known.

Tough though he undoubtedly was, Tristan did have a sympathetic side. He loved dogs and was happy to take them out on his boat. A Dutch girlfriend, Marlieka van Scheltema, owned a beagle cross named Wilson that Tristan often took sailing with him. Pete recalled another dog they met in Ibiza: "There was one mutt, we called him Rommel. He had long hair that reached to the ground and a long body like a dachshund. He had something wrong with his hips, so he walked a bit funny. From the back he looked like a furry tank. That's why we called him Rommel. He slept on board with us one night when we were pissed, but he got seasick with the motion and threw up."

In 1967 *Banjo*, a Folkboat, replaced *Cresswell* in Tristan's life for a little more than a year. "I think he sold *Cresswell* to German Willie in exchange for *Banjo* [in 1967]," Pete said, adding that he was sure there was no time lapse between selling the former boat and buying the latter. Tristan moved off *Cresswell* straight onto *Banjo*. Lloyd's Register of

Yachts, however, lists Arthur Jones as *Cresswell*'s owner until 1969, suggesting that he neglected to advise Lloyd's when he sold her. A study of subsequent years in the register produced no further mention of *Cresswell*, but she did survive for many years after Tristan sold her. An officer of the RNLI said she was seen off Maidstone, Kent, in 1990. She would then have been a remarkable eighty-one years old.

The only known photograph of *Cresswell* was probably taken on the French coast: a black-and-white shot of her having her masts stepped—or unstepped. Fortunately *Banjo* is the subject of many of Tristan's faded photographs from that era. Some of these have printed dates showing the month and year the photograph was processed. Thanks to those dated images, we can track Tristan reasonably effectively through 1967 and 1968. One of the last photographs taken on board *Banjo*, in September 1968, shows Tristan out at sea off Ibiza. With him are Marlieka and Wilson—the dog.

Of course, while all the photographs prove Tristan spent considerable time in the Mediterranean on *Banjo*, the captions on the backs—those in his own handwriting—have to be considered suspect. Many photographs in his collection bear deliberately misleading comments. A prime example is a color photograph of two naval ships taken during his later South American voyage in *Sea Dart*. On the image side is the printed date of December 1973. On the back Tristan wrote, "Peruvian Navy cruisers (Ex Royal Navy 'Sheffield' and 'Glasgow'). I served in 'Glasgow' 1947–8." Tristan did not serve in HMS *Glasgow* at any time. And neither of the two cruisers in question was sold to Peru. Both HMS *Glasgow* and HMS *Sheffield* were retired from the Royal Navy in 1958 and broken up.

Later in life Tristan regularly boasted of always having an extensive onboard library, listing many of the great works of literature. Pete Kelly disagreed: "He didn't have all those books he talked about. Not then anyway. He might have had a couple of cheap novels, but that's all."

Despite Tristan's lack of education, Pete firmly believes those few years based in Ibiza set his friend on course to be a writer. Pete recalled, "He was embarrassed by his lack of literary knowledge. In those days Ibiza was home to a lot of artists, writers, and actors. Tristan definitely felt insignificant. We used to drink in the same bar as them and [British actor] Richard Todd quite often."

Tristan, after a few drinks, usually tried to work his way into the often erudite conversations. Blithely unaware of the rudeness of his intrusions, he invariably pretended to know more than he really did, and trouble followed. "He could be an obnoxious little fucker. There was one occasion, in Wauna's bar, when we got into a fight," Pete recalled. Members of the local expatriate literati staged an impromptu Shakespearean drama—Pete didn't recall which—one evening. Tristan, pretentious as ever, and well into his cups, chose to join in, without knowing any of the lines. His loud and unnecessary interruptions finally provoked Wauna into shouting, "Shaddap, Tristan, for Chrissakes." Balked in his attempts at acting, Tristan snarled back, "Fuck you, Wauna."

Wauna, a large American former movie actress, not surprisingly took exception to his attitude and sprayed Tristan with the contents of a soda siphon to shut him up. Tristan threw a punch at Wauna, and she retaliated in kind. Shakespeare's prose ground to a bemused halt, and a good old-fashioned bar brawl ensued. Pete used his size and strength to force his way to Tristan, picked him up, and threw him over his shoulder. Wauna continued her barrage of blows on Tristan's body as Pete wrenched the soda siphon from her and hurled it over the bar, shattering a large mirror. The sound of breaking glass may have stopped the fight, but it did little to slow Wauna. She immediately turned her fury on Pete. Sensing a no-win situation, he looked around for a line of retreat. With Wauna in pursuit, Pete fled the bar, Tristan still over his shoulder. Forgetting a short flight of steps outside the door, he tripped and somersaulted to the street, conveniently landing on top of Tristan.

Others who knew Tristan in Ibiza confirmed his aggressive nature and his willingness to start a fistfight over inconsequential words or actions. A Dutchman, Guus Schohaus, who was a bartender at La Taberna, remembered him this way: "During the two years I spent in Ibiza I never saw the man sober. . . . He was very abusive, mostly verbally, sometimes even physically. He was not a nice person to have in the bar as a customer. He was loud, always drunk and, as I said, abusive, especially when unexpected tourists were around. He tried to impress them, as he knew that most locals were not very impressed with him anymore. I can still hear his loud voice thundering through the bar."

Many who encountered Tristan in Ibiza remember him similarly, as an obnoxious, loud-mouthed drunk who spent much of his time in bars—Wauna's, the George and Dragon, La Taberna, and El Isleno— all in the lower part of Ibiza town. David Murray, owner of La Taberna at the time, recalled hearing the story of Tristan's being born at sea off the islands of Tristan da Cunha. He also said one of his customers claimed you could tell Tristan was getting drunk when he started saying "pissed as a fish's tit." The adjective "obnoxious" occurs frequently when people talk of Tristan, in the 1960s and later.

In spite of his loutish ways and his lack of education, deep inside Tristan was a writer searching for an intelligent way to express his thoughts. He did begin to read serious books, Shakespeare in particular, and he quietly studied a new skill. A surprised Pete found a book on how to be a writer on Tristan's bunk one day. The rowdy sailor from Liverpool had secretly embarked on his voyage to an uncertain literary fame.

At close to forty years of age Tristan was frustrated. He could see no future for himself other than a few more years of playing with boats in the Mediterranean and eventually drinking himself to death. He wanted more than that—much more.

In the mid to late 1960s a veritable fleet of sailors were racing around the world, with the prevailing winds and currents working for some and against the more hardy. Long-distance sailing records were established and as quickly broken. Tristan saw other sailors becoming famous for their exploits while he wasted his sailing time taking snorkelers out on day trips from Ibiza. News reports of the much older Francis Chichester and Alec Rose separately circumnavigating the world, and gaining instant fame and financial rewards for their efforts, set Tristan thinking of a way to win recognition for himself as an adventurer and small-boat sailor. "I need credibility," he complained to Kelly. "I need to achieve something like these [guys]. Then I'll have something to write about."

Pete believes it was about this time that Tristan first mentioned going after a vertical record, a cynical gesture of contempt for the circumnavigators while establishing his own credentials. He talked of the Dead Sea and Lake Titicaca, the lowest and highest navigable bodies of water in the world. Pete soon forgot the conversation. Tristan obviously didn't. It lay waiting in the recesses of his mind for the appropriate time. Until then, there were yachts to be taken from one port to another, tourists to shepherd from town to little-known beaches, and drinks to be drunk.

Sometime during the second half of the 1960s, most likely in early 1967, when he and Kelly occasionally delivered boats from port to port in the Mediterranean, Tristan formed a small yacht-delivery company, Naviza (Navigators Association of Ibiza). Naviza's smart letterhead, in red and blue ink on a good-quality white bond paper, describes the director rather fancifully as Captain Tristan Jones, R.N. (Retd). One assumes that, being based in Spanish territory, Tristan felt he was far enough from the prying eyes of the Royal Navy to take considerable license with his former rank. The company's address is listed under Tristan's name as "Lista Correos, Ibiza, Baleares, Spain." In other words, the local post office took care of his mail. The bottom line of the letterhead lists all Naviza's services to boaters: Yacht Charters—Deliveries—Inspections—Repairs—Maintenance. It finishes with a grand flourish: "Correspondents in all West European countries, Scandinavia & USA."

Among Tristan's papers is a short letter dated June 26, 1967. Written by S. Morse Brown, from the yacht *Primorosa* in Almeria, Spain, it is an excellent reference for Tristan's abilities as a sailor and another reminder that he was involved in deliveries, no matter how short the voyages, and associated work on small craft in the Mediterranean. It reads in part: "Mr. Tristan Jones' skill and experience as a navigator was much appreciated."

Naviza did not make much money. The company did, however, keep Tristan busy and added immeasurably to his sailing skills and experience. And he must have studied celestial navigation. During Naviza's relatively short life Tristan roamed the western Mediterranean from Malta in the east to the Pillars of Hercules, gateway to the Atlantic Ocean. Kelly confirmed a visit to Malta: "That would have been for Nino Falzoun," he agreed. "We once delivered a forty footer, *Italia*, from Pescara [Italy] to Seville [Spain] for him."

Tristan made the mistake of chartering *Banjo* to a supposedly experienced American sailor in September 1968. That was the last time he saw her. The uninsured vessel was wrecked during a storm at Ensenada Hondo on Ibiza's northwest coast. Fortunately Tristan knew many other boaters and had arrangements to look after several yachts in their owners' absence. He still had a berth and a roof over his head when needed.

By 1968 Pete Kelly had tired of the Mediterranean scene and moved on to other endeavors. He never saw Tristan again. Although he remembers Tristan with affection, Pete Kelly lives with no illusions as to his former sailing partner's mendacity: "He was a great storyteller," Pete explained. "He could take someone else's story and make it his own. He was always convincing. He'd keep everyone entertained for hours."

Delivery skipper David Morgan confirmed Tristan's storytelling ability. Like others, he remembered Tristan's recounting the story of his birth at sea off the islands of Tristan da Cunha about this time.

After Pete left Ibiza, Tristan stayed on to keep Naviza operating.

Making use of his book on how to be a writer, in his spare time he also wrote his first "nonfiction" article, "Slow Boat to Barcelona," and sent it to *Motor Boat and Yachting* magazine in Britain. The article tells about Tristan's delivering a damaged *Cresswell*, after he sold her, from Ibiza to Barcelona in midwinter. Whether the article was truly nonfiction has never been established.

In February 1969 Tristan delivered *Alisca V* from Barcelona to Valencia, followed a few weeks later by taking a thirty-foot (9-meter) Dutch ketch from Ibiza to Santa Pola for bottom painting. It was well that he remained in the Mediterranean. Unknown to Naviza's principal, he was on the verge of the greatest opportunity of his life. Years later he would refer to such events as "fatalistic synchronism." A real long-distance delivery was in the offing. Soon there would come an American adventurer, a man with money who would help Tristan realize his dreams and turn him into an adventurer too.

CHAPTER 4

Barbara's Long Cruise

Arthur Cohen was a successful Connecticut businessman and a skilled engineer. He was also known as something of an adventurer, having ridden a motorcycle across the Australian Outback in his youth. In his middle fifties with, apparently, the prime years of his life ahead of him, Cohen seemed to have his personal world in excellent shape. He had a happy marriage, a son, and a daughter. But few people knew that he did not expect to live a long life. His father had died young. Although he looked healthy, he suffered from dangerously high blood pressure. His son, Rob Cohen, hypothesized that his father had opted to take early semiretirement and have some fun for a couple of years.

Barbara, named for Cohen's daughter, was an Alden Challenger, equipped with a thirty-six-horsepower Perkins Westerbeke auxiliary diesel engine. Arthur Cohen planned to take her on a three-to-four-year cruise around the world. Not having the time to spend himself, owing to his many business commitments, he chose to hire a professional captain and crew to move the boat from place to place. He would fly in with his family and his friends to join her whenever possible. The initial route would take *Barbara* across the Atlantic to the Mediterranean port of Alicante, on Spain's Costa del Sol. From that base she would cruise for up to a year, giving Cohen ample opportunity to visit the ports on his list.

Perhaps because he planned extensive cruising in the Mediterranean, where local knowledge is paramount, Cohen wrote to Naviza, Tristan's yacht delivery business in Ibiza, on February 21, 1969, in response to a small newspaper advertisement. It was a wise move. By that time Tristan had nearly four years' experience with the Mediterranean's capricious winds, sailing in all seasons. His own words tell of a potentially tragic incident off Majorca.

> *The passage between Dragonera and Majorca is subject to very strong gusts of wind which swoop down from the mountains with no warning. In 1967 I had been driving to windward up this passage in a breeze of 25 knots when suddenly I had a hurricane round my ears which very nearly knocked me down. The mainsail split right down the middle like a piece of tissue paper. Before I knew it I was running before this tremendous wind with the jib about to go at any minute. I headed for the lee of the lifeboat station, a desolate low headland, rounded up smartly and dropped the hook.* Banjo *came up all standing, quivering like a frightened pup.*

The Mediterranean is not for amateurs. Tristan Jones's knowledge of the middle sea would serve Cohen well.

Naviza quoted $12 a day for a skipper while at sea and $5 a day in port. Tristan wisely recommended hiring a mate and two deckhands in the States for the Atlantic crossing. Looking at a long-term possibility for himself, in a postscript to the quotation he said, "As an alternative, I can arrange a permanent Skipper for you (British) at 10 dollars per day on a yearly contract after a month trial period."

Arthur Cohen met Tristan in a Madrid hotel on the evening of April 23, 1969. Rob Cohen said his father was an excellent judge of character and could quickly calculate a person's worth. Tristan's charming and seamanlike manner, combined with references from his previous deliveries, must have been convincing enough to satisfy any concerns the astute American businessman might have. He hired Jones as *Barbara's skipper* for her circumnavigation. For Tristan, used to struggling from one short delivery job or day charter to the next, the extended contract was a dream come true. Fate, however, almost wrecked his prospect before it started. His flight home to Ibiza from Madrid came close to disaster when the plane skidded off a runway during a stop at Valencia and ended up in a potato patch. Unhurt, though unnerved, Tristan and the other passengers walked to the terminal. On May 23, 1969, eight months after he lost *Banjo*, Tristan flew from Ibiza to New York via Barcelona.

Barbara impressed Tristan the moment he saw her at her berth in the Cedar Point Yacht Club at Westport, Connecticut, on Long Island Sound. He wrote happily of his new charge:

> *A quick glance over her was enough to tell me that here was a boat which had been built with loving care, and that handled with the same care, she would stand up to anything. From the stainless-steel rigging to the varnished African mahogany cabin sides, here was a true sailor's craft. Down below she is as well appointed as any 38 footer could possibly be, with an all stainless-steel galley, huge refrigerator, hot and cold pressurized water system and even a shower in the head. Her engine is a 36 hp Perkins Westerbeke which gives her 6 knots under power. She is fitted with a Kenyon Log, wind speed indicator, Sperry R.D.F., Ray Jefferson 400 Depth meter and a Richardson MM Autopilot. Steering can be either wheel or tiller.*

Over the next four weeks Tristan provisioned *Barbara*, checked her gear, and occasionally took her out on short trips on Long Island Sound to get used to her rhythm. On many evenings Tristan drove to Greenwich Village to meet drinking companions. He also fell afoul of the law. Soon after his arrival in the States, Tristan—used to driving on the left in Britain—was stopped by the police for driving his borrowed car on the wrong side of the road. He was found to be intoxicated and spent the night in jail to sober up. He was released into Cohen's custody—for a fee—the following morning. Cohen's thoughts on the incident have not been recorded, but Rob Cohen thought his father would have been more amused than upset.

The night before *Barbara* sailed, Tristan was joined on board by Jim Brand, the owner's nephew, who was to serve as cook for the passage to Bermuda. Arthur Cohen and two friends, Howard Hanson and Ralph Glendenning, came on board early in the morning on Wednesday, June 25, 1969.

At departure the wind was light, out of the northwest. Few other sails were in sight. With no fuss, Tristan called for the mooring lines to be cast off, and *Barbara* pointed her bowsprit to the ocean. As the light on Montauk Point faded into the darkness late that night, Tristan was at the helm. His thoughts, however, were on the land he had so recently left. "I am sad to leave," he would write in *Track of the "Barbara,"* his first, unpublished, book-length work. "Sad to leave the land of getting things done properly, the land of open-hearted generosity, the land of my Friend, who sits in the canyons of Manhattan and only an ache goes with me." There is no hint who this mystery friend was, male or female. He or she is never mentioned again.

For the first two days the wind remained light. *Barbara* cruised lethargically toward her first foreign port of the voyage, taking her time to feel the ocean swells. Soon after they entered the warm waters of the Gulf Stream in the late afternoon of June 27, conditions were so calm that Tristan streamed a ten-fathom line over the stern and all hands except the skipper swam beside the boat for a while.

Next morning the wind arrived, slowly at first, rising from the southwest. By 4 P.M. the wind was force 4. Two hours later it was force 6. *Barbara* frolicked contentedly over the swells throughout that night, eating up the miles. As dawn broke the wind dropped to a whisper. With a strict deadline to meet—Cohen and his friends had a plane to catch in Bermuda—there was no choice but to run the engine for long hours until the wind returned. The skipper had *Barbara* under sail, a light genoa pulling her along at better than six knots, for the rest of June 29 and throughout June 30.

Surprisingly, for someone who would later claim to have crossed the Atlantic under sail so many times, Tristan wrote in the log when 140 miles from Bermuda, "When we heave to in the calm ocean we are astonished by the prolific life in the Gulf Stream, all kinds of fish and jelly fish."

Tristan picked up Bermuda's Gibbs Hill Light at 5 A.M. on July 1. An hour later, with no appreciable wind, the rains came. Visibility dropped as the captain picked his way under power along the twenty-mile buoyed passage between the dangerous coral reefs. He wrote in the log, "08:00 Off St. Catherine's Point. We are now passing buoys I helped to lay in 1950."

Barbara tied up in Hamilton Harbor about 11:30 on the morning of July 1, 1969. For some reason a .22-caliber rifle was on board. The Bermudan customs officer promptly relieved the vessel of that small burden before granting it port clearance. Later events suggest that the rifle was returned in time for departure.

Arthur Cohen, Howard, and Ralph left immediately to fly back to the States. Tristan and Jim stayed on in Bermuda to touch up the varnish, move the boat to St. George's Island, and prepare *Barbara* for the next leg of her voyage. While they waited in the heat, Tristan received a letter from Arthur Cohen telling him the next crew would consist of Hank Kelly, Dan Burt, and Anton Elbers. Young Jim Brand would not be among the crew when the boat sailed. His culinary skills would be sorely missed. Brand flew to Europe as the replacement crew arrived to fill the empty berths. Over three decades later Anton Elbers, a captain himself, remembered Tristan as an exceptionally competent skipper.

After Bermuda Tristan began sending long and articulate reports on the voyage to Arthur Cohen. Those reports, added to his letters and *Barbara*'s logbooks, were incorporated into *Track of the "Barbara."* That work eventually would be trimmed to a mere six pages in *The Incredible Voyage.* At first he was content to tell the story exactly as it happened. Later he fabricated scenes for effect. Crossing the Atlantic that summer of 1969, Tristan kept his writing honest.

Tristan's log read, "At 9:15 A.M. on Sunday, July 13th, we at last cast off from St. Georges and were soon off Five Fathom Hole in a S.W. breeze, Force 3, moderate swell, sunny and bright and headed for the wide open immensity of the Western Ocean, and what lay beyond it, over the rim of the world." With the hurricane season only two or three weeks away, he was keen to get far to the east—six hundred nautical miles was his figure—as quickly as possible. Speed may have been essential, but *Barbara* was in a contrary mood. Tristan's words tell the story:

> *The first two days and nights were rough. The sea was high, the wind increased by the hour and* Barbara, *heavily laden with stores, was not easy to steer. She insisted on broaching to and only by hard work could we keep her to her course. She yawed like a mad thing. We were under reefed jib and mizzen only during the first and second nights and still the motion was violent and sickening. Every effort was multiplied ten times. By 1 a.m. on the 14th it was blowing Force 7 Southwest. I try to ease her by shifting some of the weight from the forepeak into the saloon and this helped to a small degree, but still she yawed. By 9 a.m. the sea was as bad but the wind had moderated to Force 3, so we unreefed the jib and were still steaming along at 6 knots. She charged down the leeward side of the seas then surged into the next one. Slowly she developed a rhythm, until at last we began to anticipate her and could move about the boat more easily.*

"At 2 A.M. on the 15th," Tristan told his boss, "just as we were changing watches, with Dan on the wheel he shouted 'she won't steer!' I grabbed the wheel and turned it hard over to stop her from broaching, but there was no tension. The steering cable had snapped. All hell broke loose. I ordered the mainsail down and Anton dropped it within a second, so fast that the boom caught Dan a glancing blow on the bottom of his neck, knocking him to the side deck."

The tiller was stowed at the bottom of a sail locker. Tristan and Hank frantically pulled out sails and spare equipment to reach it. Less than a minute after she broached, *Barbara* was under control again. For the rest of that night Tristan and the crew took turns at the tiller, working hard to keep the boat on course in the long rolling seas. A shaken Tristan wrote to Cohen, "It was a bad moment when *Barbara* broached to, but it certainly 'settled in' the crew!"

When they finally had time to check why they lost the steering, Tristan found that one of the wooden blocks securing the steering cable pulleys, a thick plank of hardwood, had splintered. Mechanical and electrical problems continued to plague them. They had trouble with the alternator pulley. Then the refrigerator compressor quit. The wind, however, stayed in their favor. All day on July 15 *Barbara* ran at six knots under winged-out roller jib and mizzen. Once again the wind dropped a day later, and the sea settled into a flat calm. The motor propelled them forward for four hours until Tristan decided to heave-to and make repairs to the steering.

On July 18 a small whale, about twenty feet long, the second they had seen since Bermuda, surfaced about ten yards from the boat. One quick look at the wooden intruder was enough for the future leviathan. Before Hank could record the scene with the Polaroid camera, the whale dived.

Barbara's position at noon on July 21 was 36°47′ N, 47°00′ W. Nearly a quarter of a million miles away, two American astronauts, Neil Armstrong and Buzz Aldrin, were walking on the moon—mankind's first foray onto truly alien soil.

Back on *Barbara*, for much of the next week the sailing was comfortable. Then the glass began to drop. Stormy weather was on the way. The crew soon found themselves thrashing along in a near gale under reefed roller jib only. With lengthening seas—Tristan estimated the distance between crests as about 400 yards—*Barbara* yawed up to sixty degrees with the autopilot correcting each swing. Mistrustful of all things mechanical and electrical, Tristan made sure one of the hands stood by the wheel at all times while the autopilot steered. Just shy of sixteen days after leaving Bermuda, *Barbara* entered the port of Horta and tied up at the mole. The time was half past midnight on July 29.

Dan Burt continued to suffer constant pain from the blow to the base of his skull. At daylight he left for a medical checkup at the U.S. military base at Tercera and was advised to return to the States for treatment. Tristan was not pleased and complained, rather unfairly, in a letter to Arthur Cohen that he thought Dan was faking.

At Horta the crew first heard the chilling news about Donald Crowhurst, the British solo sailor from the trimaran *Teignmouth Electron*. Crowhurst had been lost overboard somewhere near the Azores a few weeks earlier during the Golden Globe round-the-world race. Tristan referred to the information he received that day as a "sketchy account." The natural opportunist in him filed the information away. He found his chance to use it to his own credit seven and a half years later.

With a spare berth after Dan Burt's departure, Tristan took on a new hand in Horta. David Tomblin was an Englishman, about twenty-eight years old, a cameraman who had recently been filming scenes for a documentary on whale hunting. Tomblin agreed to sign on as far as Lisbon.

After a brief stop at Ponta del Garda, on San Miguel Island, *Barbara* continued east on a mostly uneventful eight-hundred-mile leg to Lisbon. On August 9, Tristan noted in his log, they encountered the highest seas of the whole Atlantic crossing. Rolling out of the northwest, they attacked sharp and steep, agitated by a force 5 wind that excited itself to gale force 8 by dawn. *Barbara* arrived off Cape Espichel, twenty miles south of Lisbon, driving along at six knots, reefed down and under sunny skies.

A few hours later *Barbara* motored up the Tagus River past the sixteenth-century Belém Tower, followed by the monument to Prince Henry the Navigator. Ahead the Salazar Bridge, longest in Europe, welcomed the ocean travelers. *Barbara* slowed to a stop in Doca de Belém on the north bank of the Tagus, close to two sloops, *Minx of*

Malham and *Sea Laughter*. Her transatlantic voyage was officially over. The crew headed home, and Tristan was alone for the first time in many weeks.

Arthur Cohen and Harold James flew to Lisbon to join *Barbara* on August 23, 1969, and found the boat immaculate. Arthur's plan was to cruise through the Strait of Gibraltar to Málaga, visiting selected ports en route. At 10:00 A.M. the following day Tristan hauled anchor, after digging it out from under half a dozen others, and sailed out of the Tagus. The Atlantic greeted them with a steady breeze from the north, force 2, and steep seas. With her headsails wing and wing, *Barbara* cruised sedately south under clear skies. Off Cape Espichel, in the middle of the afternoon, the wind rose to force 5. Anticipating stronger winds, Tristan ordered the genoa lowered and continued under mizzen and roller jib. Before long they were being whipped by a gale and forced to seek sanctuary in the lee of the cape. Tristan's embryonic book described what came next: "We were racing along with the wind increasing by the minute and the sea rising as quickly. When we tried to reef the roller jib more we found that it had wrapped itself around the forestay and would neither wind out nor in. We were now doing seven knots and bouncing about like a yo-yo. Arthur went forward and managed to wrap a halyard around and around the sail to dowse it. A tricky job in the circumstances. We just got the sail killed as we came into the anchorage [at the fishing port of Sezimbra]."

Moored to the stern of the famous gaff-rigged cutter *Jolie Brise*, *Barbara* was stable enough for Arthur and Tristan to change the roller jib. Outside the harbor, increasing wind kicked the sea into turmoil. For six days, with brief calls at three ports en route, the trio fought lumpy seas and occasional gale force winds as they made for Gibraltar. At 3:15 P.M. on August 30 a jubilant Tristan wrote and underlined twice, *"Passed into Mediterranean."* He'd been away for a little over three months, but he seemed happy to be back in familiar waters.

With *Barbara* safely across the Atlantic, Arthur Cohen was content to have his boat explore the western Mediterranean for a year and to visit Morocco and the Canary Islands. The eastern Mediterranean could wait for the following summer. On *Barbara*'s first cruise, along the Spanish coast from Gibraltar to Málaga, Tristan and Arthur sighted three people clinging to an overturned dinghy off Torremolinos. Quickly streaming a stern line, Tristan expertly rounded on the capsized vessel and rescued one woman, who was showing signs of exposure, and two men. After wrapping the trio in blankets and pouring a tot of whiskey for each, Tristan and Arthur took them to Málaga. Tristan wrote afterward, "They had no idea at all of the jeopardy which they had been in, for when we picked them up the wind was increasing to Force 5 or 6 and veering to the North. They could have been adrift for hours or even days, but they treated it as a huge joke, even though they had been having difficulty hanging on in the sea which was running."

In the log for September 3 Tristan noted that it was one year since he lost *Banjo* because of another's carelessness. After Arthur flew home *Barbara* spent a month in Málaga. Apart from a weeklong battle with influenza, Tristan spent his days cosseting his charge. Cohen came back alone, it appears, and he and Tristan sailed via Alicante to Palma, Majorca, and then Ibiza—base for Tristan's former escapades—and back to Palma.

These short voyages became an irregular pattern that *Barbara* followed for the next year. With Tristan in command and a constant change of guests aboard, plus Arthur Cohen and his family at times, *Barbara* visited many ports on Spain's Costa del Sol, in addition to Morocco and the Canary Islands.

In Ibiza, on a subsequent visit, he was delighted to learn that "Slow Boat to Barcelona," the article he had submitted months before, had been accepted for publication by Britain's *Motor Boat and Yachting* magazine. With the acceptance was a check for thirty-five pounds and an invitation to submit more work. That first published article was a huge boost to Tristan's morale, and it showed him he could combine sailing with writing to sustain himself financially. Much later he explained, "Now I had found the key to the solution of my problem."

A young Portuguese fisherman, Albin de Jesus Alves, signed on as crew in Gibraltar on December 16, 1969. He was joined by an English student, Neil Ogilvy, who lasted long enough to put seawater into *Barbara*'s freshwater tank before being summarily fired by an irate skipper. Albin was a competent sailor. He and Tristan, with newcomer John Westerguarde for part of the way, proved to be a solid professional team as they worked *Barbara* south along the Moroccan coast to Agadir for a rendezvous with Arthur Cohen. The winter voyage, battling high winds and heavy seas, proved an enormous strain on crew and boat.

Westerguarde was paid off in Mogador (now Essaouira) on December 23. Tristan and Albin continued to suffer abominable weather on Morocco's coast until ordered to the Canary Islands in mid-January 1970. Uncomfortable though it may have been, the Moroccan voyage was not a complete waste of time for Tristan. He described his experiences in "Coasting the Sherifian Empire" and sent the article to *Motor Boat and Yachting*, where it was published in March 1973.

American lawyer Bob Grosby, his wife Ellie, and their son Craig joined the boat for a two-week cruise in the Canary Islands. Albin, in his late teens, and eleven-year-old Craig quickly formed a friendship. Bob Grosby, who had not met Tristan before arriving in the Canaries, showed his appreciation for the family's island cruise a few years later by giving immense help to a destitute Tristan. He also showed up under another name in one of Tristan's books.

From the Canary Islands Tristan sent Arthur Cohen his manuscript of *Track of the "Barbara"* with a covering letter: "Dear Arthur, Here is a rough draft of the account of the cruise of *Barbara*. It is about 60,000 words I think. It has many shortcomings. . . . I think what is needed is for the whole thing to be tidied up and perhaps re-arranged into shorter chapters. If Mr. Knopf is interested I can do this on board."

Cohen read the manuscript "with interest" and sent it to his friend Alfred Knopf Jr. at Atheneum Publishers. Knopf rejected the submission.

Albin was discharged at Port Mahon, Minorca, in the Balearic Islands, on May 31, 1970, and returned home to Lisbon to join the Portuguese army. A few months later he was killed in Portugal's Angolan war. Many years later Craig Grosby spoke of Albin with affection and said he was sorry his Portuguese friend did not live to fulfill his potential.

From Port Mahon to Malta, via Sardinia and Sicily, Tristan had the company of Arthur Cohen plus Harold James, Cliff James, and George Llewellyn. As usual Cohen and his friends flew directly back to the States when they arrived in port. Sometime during the first week in July, in Malta, Tristan got really lucky. A young English wanderer named Conrad Jelinek joined *Barbara* as a deckhand. He would prove to be one of the stalwarts of the sea. Conrad would spend the next two years sailing with Tristan—on the Red Sea, the Indian Ocean, the South Atlantic, up the Amazon, and in the Caribbean. His memories of those many months on *Barbara* add immeasurably to Tristan's published versions. As a direct result of those two years with Tristan, Conrad went on to spend most of the next thirty years in small boats. As 2001 drew to a close, he and his second wife, Lorna, were in Barcelona aboard their Hallberg-Rassy 382, *Arcturus*, after a rough Atlantic crossing from Antigua.

From Malta *Barbara* cruised the Adriatic, wandering north among the idyllic islands off the coast of Yugoslavia to Venice with members of the Cohen family and their friends. On the way south, at the beautiful walled city of Dubrovnik, Tristan gave Conrad a few additional sailing lessons. For a few hours they practiced mooring stern-to under sail alone and leaving the mooring under sail instead of using the engine. As each day went by Tristan and Conrad learned to trust each other more and more.

Crossing the Adriatic on a choppy sea, *Barbara* called at the southeast Italian port of Brindisi, where, to his delight, Tristan found he could buy English newspapers. The southern Adriatic continued choppy as *Barbara* followed her course to the Greek island of Corfu. From there, often fighting heavy seas and high winds, Tristan made for Patras and the entrance to the historic Corinth Canal.

Separating the Peloponnese, the southernmost section of the Balkan peninsula, from mainland Greece, the Corinth Canal was started by the Roman emperor Nero. He struck the first blow with, it is said, a golden pickax. Despite Nero's gesture, Rome's wars against the Gauls caused the project to be abandoned before it really got going. A French concern finally completed the canal in 1893, cutting through solid rock. When it was finished the canal created an important shortcut for shipping from the southern Adriatic to Piraeus, the seaport of Athens.

Barbara began the 3.4-mile journey, under power, at 12:15 P.M. on October 6, 1970. Transiting the canal, which is only 23 meters wide, with vertical walls up to 90 meters high, takes not much more than an hour for a yacht, but is an awe-inspiring experience.

Although he was justifiably proud of his ability as a sailor, Tristan rarely performed stunts to prove his skill. He was by all accounts an extremely safety-conscious skipper. Occasionally, however, he allowed himself to show off a little. After leaving the Corinth Canal, Conrad saw a first-class performance from Tristan when they arrived at a Greek marina.

"*Barbara* was approaching Turkolimano in Athens with thirty knots of breeze. Instead of fenders TJ got me to tape two eggs to lengths of line and hang them over each side of the boat. He then sailed into the tiny harbor with only the headsail rolled to handkerchief size, turned the boat and backed her into the jetty between two other boats. Eggs intact and no engine."

Conrad had every confidence in his captain by this time, and Tristan was comfortable with his mate. They needed to be a strong team. They had the latest orders from Arthur Cohen. After cruising the Aegean and visiting Turkey and Cyprus, they were to leave the Mediterranean and proceed, via Israel, through the Red Sea to Massawa, Ethiopia. From there, after cruising the East African coast, they would set course to cross the Indian Ocean to Singapore.

CHAPTER 5

Israel and Hostile Shores

Barbara dropped anchor in the ancient harbor of Haifa, in northern Israel, on Thursday, November 12, 1970. That same day in Paris a requiem mass was held for Charles de Gaulle, the architect of modern France, who had died on November 9. Three weeks earlier, from Rhodes, Tristan had asked Arthur Cohen to send charts of the coast of Israel and the Red Sea. With the Suez Canal closed to international maritime traffic since the Six Day War in June 1967, the only reasonable access to the Red Sea and the Indian Ocean—for the continuation of *Barbara*'s circumnavigation—was overland across Israel to the Gulf of Aqaba.

Soon after arriving in Israel, Tristan solicited shipping quotes from a few haulage companies in the Haifa area for transporting *Barbara* overland one-way from Haifa to Eilat by the most direct route. While he and Conrad waited for replies, there were numerous odd jobs to do on *Barbara* and a few personal details to look after. Among the mechanical and cosmetic chores, the freshwater pump needed replacing. A compression test had to be performed on the engine. Injectors required testing and maintenance. The inside of the hull needed repainting. Tristan, too long a stranger to the medical profession, also needed attention. He visited a local dentist and had six teeth filled.

He wrote to Arthur Cohen on November 24, "If the price and conditions are o.k. with Israeli Shipyards we should be going out of the water about 8th December and I guess we will be in Eilat on or about the 10th o.k. The move through north Israel will have to be by night because of the length of the trailer, but we can go through the Negev [desert] by daylight I believe. I don't know how we could have managed here without the [rental] car as everything is very far flung."

With the boat's transport arranged and the way ahead looking smooth, Conrad Jelinek dropped a bombshell. He announced he would be leaving the crew the first week in December. He had decided he wanted to spend the winter on a kibbutz. Tristan, who never liked being crossed, wrote to Cohen, "I thought there was something in the wind. He's not the kind of guy who could stick at anything for very long, I believe. Pity, he's a nice bloke most of the time."

Privately Tristan was disturbed about losing a valuable crew member. He wrote a long letter to Conrad's parents in England, asking them to persuade their son to stay on and help him with *Barbara*. Leo Jelinek, Conrad's father, was happy to oblige. He wanted Conrad to continue the voyage anyway—to its conclusion if possible. Unfortunately, Leo Jelinek's letter failed to reach Israel before *Barbara* sailed from Eilat. But it didn't matter: Conrad made his own decision to stay a while longer. Tristan, predictably, did a complete volte-face. In a relieved letter to his employer he explained, "Conrad is very loyal and can see what the situation is. . . . I personally think that once Conrad gets clear of Israel he will want to go on further with the boat. . . . there is a girl involved and he's a bit soft, but once we get some salt water between him and her then he'll come to his senses about it."

In the meantime a Frenchman, Jacques de St. Henry, was hired to join the crew at the beginning of December. For Tristan the paperwork and negotiations continued. Getting quotations for the overland shipment and haggling with haulage contractors caused him daily anguish. A letter to Arthur Cohen on December 2 tells of his growing frustration.

Dear Arthur,

Since speaking to you on the telephone there has had to be another shift in plans, for I went round to the shipyard this morning and when I told them that in principle we accepted their quotation for the transit the foreman in charge said that they were sorry but it would be another week before they could start on the job. As the complexities of the move demand that the work start now, that police permission be sought, that insurance be arranged, that customs clearance be obtained, etc, etc, it looked to me like we were going to get sidetracked once the contract was signed, so I have pulled away from them and got the same terms from HERCULES and SNAPIR. . . . They are experts at this work, but quoted very high until I told them of the Shipyards price when they agreed to come down to 1840 dollars for the work plus 200 dollars for the insurance.

They are to commence building the cradle tomorrow and already a diver has been down about the placing of the wires for lifting. Tomorrow one of Hercules' men is going round to the customs with me to get that side sorted out.

The cradle will be completed by the sixth.

The lifting will be between the 8th and the 10th.

The Harbour Master here said that Hercules were the best people for the job when he was on board here this afternoon. I am relieved about the shipyard as I have been going over there several times a day and it is always a case of waiting around to see people for two or three hours. With Hercules we are already moving. They have moved many boats and everyone says they know their stuff.

After details of the work done to prepare *Barbara* for her return to the sea, Tristan raised a concern about time. "I had your cable re sailing from Eilat on the 24th [of December] which will be pushing it a bit but we'll do our best of course."

Cohen's plan was to fly in to Tel Aviv on December 21 and be in Eilat on the twenty-third ready for a few days' sailing on the Gulf of Aqaba until the twenty-seventh. On December 3, in a one-page letter mostly concerning general repair work to *Barbara*, Tristan added, "Hercules is going to let me know on Monday about Police terms such as time of moving etc. They will probably move us thru the night as far as Beersheba."

Tristan worked hard to accommodate his employer's plans for re-joining the boat. *Barbara* was hauled out on December 8. On the tenth, loaded on the low flatbed trailer of a powerful truck, she set off for the Red Sea. Traveling through the first night as planned to avoid disrupting traffic, then crossing the Negev by daylight, the convoy shuddered to a halt on the dock at the head of the Gulf of Aqaba two days later, on December 12. Tristan wrote from Eilat that night. "Dear Arthur, what a trip we had from Haifa to Eilat . . . first of all we couldn't get the wedges to stay put and were continually stopping on the highway to re-shore up the boat. Then of course when she lost sight of the sea she settled down and we roared away across the plain to Beersheba, then through the desert, down 2000 feet to the Jordan Valley, round hair pin bends with a gradient of 1 in 20 and heeling over as much as 20 degrees. I was in the tail car, watching the boat the whole way, and I lost a couple of pounds, believe me."

Although he wrote an honest magazine article called "Across the Desert," accurately describing the haulout and *Barbara*'s subsequent overland journey across Israel, Tristan later used the occasion to claim the first half of a vertical record in his first book, *The Incredible Voyage*. To do so, he had to transport *Barbara* to the Dead Sea. On paper it was simple.

Ignoring commercial enterprise, Tristan has the Israeli navy supply a tank transporter to haul the boat. He describes driving on a superhighway to Tel Aviv with the local people watching in awe, some even raising a friendly cheer as the convoy trundled past. That evening, he wrote, they arrived at Bethlehem, a holy site for three major religions, where they stopped for the night. With the boat outside on its giant trailer, Tristan and Conrad settled down at an inn. Conveniently, it was Christmas Eve. There is no mention of passing Jerusalem, although, considering the size of the truck and trailer, the road they would have had to travel, and the holy city's proximity to Bethlehem, they could hardly have avoided it.

On Christmas Day, according to Tristan, they continued south through Hebron, then east to the shores of the Dead Sea. Though Tristan was delighted to have reached the first of his two "impossible destinations," the Israeli authorities refused to give him the Christmas present he craved. Despite intervention by Tristan's friends in the Israeli navy, the officials refused to let him launch *Barbara*. Tristan found an alternative. He says he borrowed a small boat for a day or two, cruising as far south as Masada. But in an article for *Rudder* magazine, published in early 1977 just before *The Incredible Voyage* (and two years after Arthur Cohen's death), he claimed he had sailed *Barbara* on the Dead Sea.

Having announced his triumph of sailing on the lowest body of water in the world, he raised his sights. Half a world away in South America, Lake Titicaca awaited.

To complete his Dead Sea story and bring it in line with reality, he has the huge truck, with its valuable cargo, crawl back over the Hills of Judea to the main road. From there the convoy rumbles south, through Beersheba and across the Negev to Eilat, on the Gulf of Aqaba.

Many years later Conrad Jelinek confirmed that the Dead Sea story was false. He wrote, "I usually backed Tristan with his poetic license when people ask[ed] me about *The Incredible Voyage*. It was an amazing trip in those days in its own right, despite not actually sailing on the Dead Sea. . . . Apart from the Dead Sea embellishments TJ recounts it well."

By December 15, 1970, *Barbara* was back in the water, at Eilat, with both masts standing and fully rigged. Lowering the heavy boat from the dock into the sea had entailed extreme tension for Tristan. That day he wrote to Arthur, "I had a bit of heart-burn here, I can tell you as machinery and labour are the devils own job to get hold of . . . and when the boat was dangling twenty feet over the water the crane ceased to function and the boat was jerking up and down like a yo-yo about a foot or so, all 14 tons of her on a fifteen ton mobile crane. I said to the foreman (joking) 'is the driver a learner then?' 'Oh no,' said he, 'the driver is ill at home. This is the mechanic and he's never driven a crane before!' I nearly died."

Amateur or not, the crane operator settled *Barbara* as gently as he could into the Gulf of Aqaba to the great relief of Tristan and crew. After stepping the masts they took her out for the sailing trials on December 18. Her skipper pronounced himself satisfied with the rigging tension and pleased with her performance in a force 5 to 6 wind on a flat sea. "We got her up to 7 knots with a reefed main and jib," he reported.

The Christmas season passed in short sailing trips on the Gulf of Aqaba, with Arthur aboard. To the west lay the Israeli-occupied Sinai Peninsula. To the east were Jordan and Saudi Arabia's desert shimmering under a scorching sun. As soon as Arthur returned to Tel Aviv, planning to meet the crew again in Massawa, Ethiopia, Tristan made ready for sea. Conrad's girlfriend, Maureen, a twenty-one-year-old American nurse working her way round the world, joined the crew in Eilat.

The original plan, devised months before in Westport, was to sail *Barbara* around the world via the Mediterranean, across the Indian Ocean to Southeast Asia, thence to Japan, and on to the west coast of the United States by way of Alaska. Reports of piracy in the eastern Indian Ocean and the South China Sea made Arthur worry about the safety of boat and crew. Tristan arguably may have been the ideal man to captain a small boat through such dangerous waters. Brave yet not foolhardy, he would have done all in his power to avoid pirates. But if challenged, he would never have given up the boat or his crew without a major fight. Arthur Cohen decided to have *Barbara* explore the coast of East Africa while he assessed the situation.

A small boat flying the Stars and Stripes, sailing between hostile

Islamic shores, was sure to encounter trouble somewhere. Since she had visited Israel, feared enemy of many Islamic nations, and her presence in the Red Sea had been reported in the press, she was an inviting target for troublemakers. Her skipper recognized this and determined to keep her out of sight of potential enemies as much as he could.

The wind blew steadily from the north as *Barbara* sailed nonstop the 110 nautical miles of the Gulf of Aqaba, the safest part of the long run to the Indian Ocean, running under all working sail. Slipping through the four-mile-wide strait between Sinai and Tiran Island, she entered the Red Sea.

Tristan's report to Arthur Cohen, dated January 14, 1971, and mailed from Massawa, detailed their progress. On December 29 *Barbara* sailed out of Marsa el-At, close to the most southerly point of the Sinai Peninsula. As on the previous day, the wind blew from the north, force 5. Tristan radioed the Israeli military base in Sharm el-Sheikh to report that they were clearing their area. The base radio operator in turn wished *Barbara* good luck. Good wishes were not enough. The autopilot failed during the night, leaving the crew to take turns at the helm.

By daybreak the wind had increased to force 6. *Barbara* heeled over and raced before the wind. A little over a hundred miles from Sinai they sighted the Brothers, a series of low-lying islets thirty-five miles from the Egyptian shore. Unable to repair the autopilot because of the boat's motion or to fix the freshwater pump, which had also failed, Tristan chose to stop long enough to get the work done. Cautiously he approached the lee of the islands, with the U.S. flag clearly visible. When the boat was about a cable's length from a jetty, a group of Egyptian soldiers dressed in khaki uniforms appeared. Tristan was at the helm, Conrad on the foredeck. Before the two realized their danger, the soldiers opened fire with rifles.

"Some shots passed very close to the boat and the armed men made many threatening gestures," Tristan wrote to Arthur. A few years later, in *The Incredible Voyage*, he created considerably more drama, with *Bar-*

bara subjected to a hail of machine gun and rifle fire and taking two hits on deck and two more shots through the mainsail.

Conrad recalled the event clearly: "There were not the amount of bullets flying like he says. I was on the foredeck whilst they were firing and then crawled back to the cockpit. It was then that Tristan was standing up in the cockpit . . . he was also shouting at the Egyptians, 'You can't shoot me, I'm British!' "

Presumably Maureen and Jacques were off watch and belowdecks at the time. Their reactions to the attack have not been recorded. No matter how many bullets were fired, the situation could have been deadly. Though no one received a scratch, the effect on their nerves would have been considerable. Tristan immediately put into action one of his favorite expressions: "When in doubt, fuck off out." He turned *Barbara*'s bow away from the shore, hoisted all sail, and fled.

Steady northerlies continued throughout that day and night. Having recovered from their fright, the crew celebrated New Year's Eve with a dinner of English sausages and Israeli wine. The year 1971 dawned with a change in the wind, gusting out of the northeast at force 4 to 5. Tristan noticed the island of Zebirget off the Egyptian coast, but mindful of the events at the Brothers, he bore off in spite of a vicious swell from the southeast and variable winds. Within a few hours they crossed the Tropic of Cancer.

The next few days kept all on board busy as the Red Sea lived up to its reputation for harsh conditions. Tristan's log entries are brief and to the point.

> January 2nd. Gale force wind from the east split the roller jib. Very bad sea from the SE forced us to beat out thirty miles to the east.
>
> January 3rd. Wind abating and veering to the south. Beating hard all day to get ourselves away from outlying reefs.
>
> January 4th. Wind east, force 6 rising at times to 7. Sailing hard all day and night. Sight [with a sextant] increasingly crazy, owing to the heavy haze all around. Visibility at times down to two miles.

On January 5 at dusk Tristan said he managed to get a snap sight on the moon and another on Polaris. The sights placed *Barbara* right in the middle of the Suakin reefs. "So I sailed a safe triangle all night, hoping my estimate of the current is correct. Wind storm force. Jib split again."

Conrad remembered the worrying occasion thus: "It is night and Tristan realizes we are lost. For six hours we sail a reciprocal course, not really knowing that in fact we are. As the sun comes up we see that we have been sailing into a horseshoe reef and then out of it."

The anxiety continued. Morning showed they were sailing over shoals off the poorly charted Sudanese coast. Exercising great caution, Tristan maneuvered into the lee of Talla Talla Saghir, a desert island, where they spent the rest of the day waiting for the wind to abate. The crew was tense as reefs and shoals stretched around the boat. The perils, while not lost on Tristan, prompted a rare note of humor in the log: "January 8th. Tip-toed our way out of the reefs and shoals in a force 6 wind from the SE. Electric bilge pump packed up and the engine cooling system has developed bubble trouble. I spent most of the day and night wishing I was in a good pub!"

Barbara's trials continued for a few more days. Her crew grew more and more tired from the constant strain.

> January 9th. Beating and bashing wetly we at last sighted the coast of Eritrea. Looked for port of Taclai but, when within a cable of the coast, find it to be washed away. We fought our way off the coast in a terrific wind which split the mainsail at the head. I kept it up as better to have a sail carried away than to be on that vicious coast of coral. It took us fourteen hours to make six miles into the offing! The current was, I estimate, three knots running NW. The wind was SE at least Force 7.

> January 10th. After fighting all night we found ourselves ten miles north of where we were yesterday. I sent radio messages to any receiver to inform you of the delay, but no reply. During the day it

got so bad I heaved to under storm sail. By midnight the seas were
PRECIPITOUS.

January 11th. The wind abated during the night though the seas were
still bad. Then the wind backed around to east and we hightailed it
down here in good conditions, picking up the lee of Difnein Isle at
3 A.M. on Jan 12.

January 12th. In Paradise, with an even keel, and a warm sun to dry
things out, and to rest up before making for Massawa in halcyon
conditions.

January 13th. Arrived in Massawa after racing an Arab dhow into port.

Tristan's cable to Arthur on arrival in Massawa, Ethiopia, tersely
states, "Arrived Massawa bloody but unbowed thirteenth [after] three
gales. Some damage fixing now ready sail twentieth stop informing Uncle Sam was fired upon by Egyptians Brothers Islets December thirti-
eth stop send five hundred dollars."

A day later, explaining the usual list of necessary repairs to the boat,
Tristan's cynical mind added, "Well, as I write it is evening . . . we have
been here twenty four hours and life is gradually resuming normality in
little ways, like blades of grass peeping up after an atomic holocaust."

Arthur had originally planned to meet the boat in Massawa, but
on leaving Israel he and Ruth had gone to East Africa. That, plus a quick
trip back to Connecticut on business, had removed the possibility of
coming to Massawa. At this point Tristan knew little about his immediate destinations. His impatience began to show as he wrote his regular letter to Arthur with questions and suggestions: "I am awaiting
firmer indications of future programme from you. Personally I think
you should join the boat here. There is a fabulous cruising ground right
here [the Dahlak Archipelago]. But if you wish I'll make for Djibouti
and meet you there. Or even the Seychelles." He then promised to have
the boat ready to sail from Massawa by January 20.

Tristan had grown tired of Jacques by the time he reached Massawa and fired him, complaining that he was completely unteachable

and "about as useful as a clockwork orange. If he stays on board I will go nuts." Conrad, whom Tristan now relied on more than ever, agreed to remain, as did Maureen.

Before Jacques was sent home, Tristan invited half a dozen Ethiopian naval cadets on a two-day cruise to explore the Dahlak Islands. The navy personnel had been extremely helpful in solving technical problems on board, so Tristan repaid their kindness. The grateful cadets wrote Tristan and his crew a thank-you note that he had reproduced in *The Incredible Voyage*. For some reason, in the book's reproduction of the letter Maureen's name has been crossed out. In fact, Maureen was never mentioned, not in the log or in reports to Arthur during her extended stay on *Barbara*. Her name also fails to appear in *The Incredible Voyage*. Although Jacques did rate a note or two in letters to Arthur, he too failed to appear in the book. Tristan apparently preferred the fiction that only he and Conrad were aboard during the fight against the Red Sea.

Letters from Arthur are full of notations about which of his friends and business associates would be availing themselves of *Barbara* next. Two were supposed to board in Mogadishu, Somalia, if *Barbara* received permission to visit. Two more planned to join in Mombasa, Kenya, for a leisurely coastal cruise to Dar es Salaam, Tanzania. Arthur expected to next meet his boat in the Seychelles at the end of May.

Captain Bob Jones of the USS *Glennon* visited *Barbara* in Massawa. He advised against calling at Mogadishu because the people were rabidly anti-American. Having heard the same from others, Tristan chose to leave his decision until he had made further inquiries in Djibouti.

A fifteen-year-old Ethiopian boy joined the crew in Massawa, although Tristan neglected to mention that to Arthur until he reached Djibouti. Employed to perform unskilled tasks such as cleaning, Alem Desta was supposed to have left the boat in Djibouti, but Tristan chose to keep him on, citing his value as a local. Conrad approved of Alem and commented, "In hiring Alem as crew in Ethiopia . . . Tristan went to incredible trouble to get Alem the first Ethiopian seaman's passbook ever issued, No. 0001."

Barbara sailed from Massawa on February 3 after a stay of three weeks in high humidity, constant dust, and a plague of flies. Back on the Red Sea the voyage became a test of skill—Tristan's seamanship against harsh winds and a powerful current. When they anchored at Shumma Island on the fourth to ride out a southeast gale, the Danforth anchor dragged, almost putting *Barbara* on a reef to leeward. Tristan ordered the crew to weigh anchor to move to a safer location. But the anchor rode parted, and the valuable Danforth was lost. All efforts to retrieve it with a grapnel failed. Then, fighting to clear the reefs, *Barbara*'s keel touched bottom twice, fortunately without damage. They spent the night desperately trying to hold ground with two anchors out. To add to the misery, a rat gnawed through the freshwater hose and flooded the cabin, wasting precious drinking water. The strain of the hard-won passage shows in Tristan's description of the daily battles: "The difficulty is that at noon the wind rises to gale force and more, and I just don't make any southing, even though I beat to the point of exhaustion. So we go to anchor in as open a place as we can, but out of the current, then we have to wait for the weather to ease about midnight, then take off. This is dangerous too, as the currents are not plotted and the coast is a nightmare of uncharted reefs, and low islands which are impossible to see if there is any cloud about—which there usually is. It is risky in the extreme."

Constantly pushing himself, Conrad, Alem, Maureen (one assumes), and the boat against natural forces determined to keep him in the Red Sea, Tristan was getting worried about his timing. He noted from Assab, Ethiopia, "It is vital to get away from Djibouti as soon as possible to catch the NE monsoon, which ends at the middle of next month." Frustrated, he continued, "There are continuous strong S.E. winds which raise very bad seas (much worse than the Strait of Gibraltar) and the current runs at times up to 4 knots, setting NW. It has taken me 8 days to get from Massawa even pointing her up with the engine and at times carrying more sail than is safe."

Assab, though within reach of Djibouti, was far from a safe haven. Tristan secured *Barbara* to a jetty, wide open to the wind and sea, with six mooring lines. There was no alternative. "Assab is the last place God made," he moaned. He and Conrad did make good use of some of the wasted hours, however. They smoked out the verminous stowaway and, after Conrad had beaten it to death on deck, hung it from the rigging as an example to other illegal boarders.

With Yemeni gunboats threatening to fire on small vessels entering their sea space without permission, Tristan was forced to plan his escape from the purgatory of Assab and his passage through Bab al-Mandab, the Gate of Tears, by keeping close to the African coast. His exhaustion shows in a letter written from Assab: "Well Arthur, this is the longest continuous beat to windward I have ever made, reefs to one side and fanatics the other, and we are hardened, frustrated, weary and worried, but definitely not beaten by any means. Another 80 miles direct (probably 200 miles sailing) and we will be out of this hostile Red Sea."

On February 12, although two deep-sea tugs and a dozen or so dhows were unable to make any appreciable way for Djibouti, *Barbara* slipped her moorings and attempted to escape from Assab during the early morning, a time Tristan optimistically referred to as "the easy period." At the outer point of the reef, he noted, "the sea ran in at a tremendous rate." A force 6 wind blew out of the southeast, punching *Barbara* right on the nose. She could not make any headway, although she logged twenty-eight miles tacking back and forth. With strong currents setting on shore, others pushing farther up into the Red Sea, and the wind right in her face, *Barbara* fought in vain. Once again a depressed Tristan started the engine and ran back to the doubtful shelter of Assab to wait.

Finally the weather relented, and *Barbara* made the most of her freedom. She raced through the Bab al-Mandab, out of the Red Sea and into the Gulf of Aden. With great relief the crew motored her into Djibouti on February 15. Her trials, and Tristan's, were far from over. Two days later someone broke into the boat and stole $420. All Tristan and his crew wanted was to get out of the area as soon as possible. But first they had to check on the political situation in Somalia, in case they were forced to land for any reason. The Somali consul in Djibouti, despite the reported anti-American sentiments in Mogadishu, gave Tristan a *laissez-passer* (literally, "let pass"—a permit, in this case, to make a stop in Somalia) in case he needed it.

The short stop in Djibouti dragged on for over two weeks. With himself, Conrad, Maureen, and young Alem to feed and take care of, Tristan took on yet another hand. Gerard was a twenty-four-year-old French army officer, on leave from his regiment. As with hiring Jacques, signing Gerard was not one of Tristan's wisest decisions.

Barbara's crew had beaten the Red Sea and was ready to tackle the Indian Ocean. The wildlife reserves of East Africa lay ahead. Conrad Jelinek remembered their March 2 departure from Djibouti with amusement. "The yacht club escorted us out of the harbor in small boats, passing bottles of whisky around. TJ got very drunk and set a wrong course. I argued with him, but he would not listen to reason, so I had to lock him in the forward cabin. Fortunately my course was right, and after he had slept he was fine again with no recriminations on either side." Conrad had further comment about that departure. "I would like to add TJ did *not* [normally] drink at sea. Needless to say, he made up for it in port."

Pushing hard for the Indian Ocean, they encountered strong easterly winds, force 6 to 7, in the Gulf of Aden. Although the log shows an average speed of five to six knots, it took *Barbara* ten rough days—constantly beating to windward over short steep seas—to cover the 580 miles to Cape Guardafui. Off the cape the mainsail tore at the head and was quickly replaced with a new sail. After rounding Guardafui, the Horn of Africa, and with the northeast monsoon wind breathing steadily on the port quarter, *Barbara*'s rhythm changed. As if aware that the worst of her trials were over for a while, she settled down. At last the crew members, with the exception of the skipper, could lower their guard a little.

CHAPTER 6

Indian Ocean Saga

After two months of struggling in the Red Sea, the first weeks on the Indian Ocean proved a pleasure cruise. Once past the Horn of Africa, *Barbara* bowled happily along at five knots in sight of a flat, desolate Somalian coastline with few distinguishing marks. Occasionally the crew started the engine to charge the batteries. Otherwise they let the wind and sails carry them resolutely south.

Minor mechanical problems intruded on the otherwise enjoyable sailing. Air began to seep into the fuel lines, so the system had to be bled regularly. Then Tristan was burned. In a letter to Arthur he said, "Whilst messing about around the fuel heater, I got a blow-back of flame which scorched both arms and face." Although the injury was not serious, there was cause for concern because of the hot climate. Tristan applied burn ointment to prevent blistering and wore bandages for protection from the sun.

Gerard, like his countryman Jacques before him, was not a great success as a small-boat sailor. His disgusted skipper referred to him as a "dud squib." "He knows absolutely nothing at all," Tristan bitched in a letter to Arthur, "but at least he can steer the boat which is a God-send. His eye-sight is very, very bad which doesn't help. His English is (or was) pretty near zero. He is leaving at Mombasa. He is supposed to be an Army officer, well God help the French Army is all I can say. It's incredible. Absolutely no initiative whatsoever."

Alem Desta was more useful. Adapting to a nautical environment with boyish resilience, he soon learned to stitch and repair sails and to take a confident turn at the helm. Conrad, as always, was strong and reliable, never failing to accept any necessary chore, no matter how messy or unpleasant. Of Maureen's competency as a sailor we are told nothing. On the Indian Ocean leg Conrad began to study celestial navigation. After a year together under a variety of extreme conditions, he and Tristan had developed into an efficient sailing team. Before Mombasa Tristan gave Conrad a raise in pay, hoping to keep him on board indefinitely.

Crossing the latitude of Mogadishu, which they chose not to visit, *Barbara* ran free all night under mainsail, roller jib, and mizzen. There was some concern about a fifty-mile-an-hour (80 kph) cyclone sitting off the north coast of Madagascar, but at the time they were not affected. Nearing the equator Tristan, though by now a skilled navigator, had trouble finding his latitude with the sun. "If you don't catch it on the moment of noon, [it's] impossible," he explained. "It takes about five minutes to go from bearing due east to bearing due west."

Moon sights helped considerably, and he enjoyed learning the southern stars, making use of Canopus, Regulus, and Aldebaran, which gave him northeast, south, and northwest at dusk (that would suggest, though not confirm, that he had never before sailed or navigated south of the equator). He wrote in his log, "Equatorial lesson: To cross the equator and know position during the day, be there when the moon is out during the day. Then you can get a two-sight fix."

A large shark kept pace with the boat for a while on March 18. Estimated at twenty feet long, it was just one of many big fish they encountered. Losing lines and hooks to sturdy sea dwellers became a regular occurrence.

On March 22, 1971, they reached the latitude of Mombasa. At 8:00 A.M. *Barbara* changed course for the west. Anticipating a landfall at

3:00 A.M. the following day, Tristan was prepared to stand off until dawn and go in by daylight, about 5:30. His report to Arthur said they entered port at 4:00. The logbook says 2:00. By this time his burns were healing well and his eyelashes were growing back.

A strong element of frustration with Arthur Cohen shows in one letter Tristan sent from Mombasa. In an earlier communication Arthur had inadvertently written Massawa as a rendezvous for two of his guests (the Jackson family) instead of Mogadishu. Tristan was confused and said so. After explaining why he needed clarification, he grumbled: "I wish I knew what you and they had in mind for them. I suggest that we cruise locally on the Kenya coast and then return to Mombasa to complete further work after such a long haul in such weather as we have had, before taking off for the Seychelles at the end of April, in the SW monsoon season."

He obviously did not really want to tackle the long trip out to the Seychelles and back. His letter continued, "It will be a job to get back from the Seychelles in May as we will be beating into the ocean swell, sometimes with weak winds, sometimes with near gales. In other words p . . . ing against the wind as we say and to make a good trip from the Seychelles to Madagascar you would have to wait for the NE monsoon again in October. It can be done, but it won't be a pleasure ride I can assure you on that. And it will be slow, slow."

Having tried to eliminate one destination, he had little choice but to recommend alternatives. "My suggestion is to cruise south down the African coast, Dar Es Salaam, Mozambique, etc, then take off east for the Comoro Islands and Madagascar or to continue south later (September) into the southern summer and forget the islands, for by heading for the islands you are placing yourself to leeward until October, but by remaining on the African shore you will be a lot on a weather shore and there are many ports and harbours of refuge."

Then came a stern warning: "The SW monsoon is not to be played around with. It is much harder than the NE monsoon. But if you decide in any case to head for the islands then we can head south very well in October and be in South Africa in November as previously envisaged."

From Mombasa Tristan mailed a series of articles to boating magazines in the United States and Britain. Among them was "Across the Desert," his factual account of hauling *Barbara* overland across Israel. While in Mombasa he began work on an article called "Tropical Cruising." Filled with useful advice on topics as varied as keeping cool, clothing, swimming, religion, eyewear, and how to deal with local residents, it was not finished and mailed until months later, but it did get published. He was writing; his initial success with "Slow Boat to Barcelona" had inspired him to write articles about his voyage for magazines whenever he found time.

The ineffectual Gerard left in Mombasa, as did Maureen. Conrad and Alem remained as crew. With able assistance from an engineering company, they repaired the refrigerator, which had been hiccuping for weeks. In addition Conrad replaced a faulty saltwater intake valve, essential for the engine's cooling system. They also had the engine tuned. With those chores accomplished, the crew went on safari. Of that expedition Conrad said, "It's as well something helps fools, drunkards and sailors."

Back in the early 1970s, before the world became so safety conscious, tourists could rent small, open-topped British cars called minimokes. Tristan, Conrad, and Alem set off from Mombasa in a minimoke to see big game in the wild. Their first fright occurred while wandering in the bush, about two hundred yards from the car. They came upon fresh tracks of a big cat, almost certainly a lion. The naive trio retreated to the car and made a quick getaway, but they failed to learn much from the lesson. Later that same day they stopped to stretch their legs in a clearing surrounded by scrub. They soon heard noises from beyond the bushes, followed by the pounding feet of a large animal. Once again the three ran for the safety of the car. Before they could drive more than a short distance a rhino burst out of the scrub and thundered toward them. Conrad said, "The rhino had not reached full speed but, for a heart-stopping moment, neither had the moke. We were both gaining speed with the rhino about fifteen feet astern. The moke proved faster."

Their adventures for the day continued. That evening, in the dining room of a safari lodge in Tsavo Game Reserve, a snake interrupted their meal. In his book Tristan has the reptile, a spitting cobra, drop from the rafters directly above his head. Conrad described the encounter differently.

> For ventilation there was a two feet gap between the walls and the ceiling. In one corner of the restaurant there was a chest of drawers and our table. We saw the snake come over the wall and then stop with only its tail showing behind the chest. I got up to tweak its tail, thinking I could jump back before it turned around. I was wrong, but it only looked at me then carried on under the chest and came towards us. We all put our legs on the table and, beginning to feel foolish, called a waiter over. Within seconds the restaurant was empty, except for us—who couldn't move. Our waiter killed the snake with two broom handles lashed together. A hunter told us that spitting cobras are known to spit with very little provocation.

Conrad could easily have been blinded or killed when he foolishly touched the snake. Spitting cobras have evolved the unique ability to rear up and propel a fine spray of venom. Their aim is accurate enough to splash a person's face from up to six feet away. The venom inflicts intense pain and can cause permanent blindness. A bite would probably have been fatal.

There seems to have been an exchange of letters between Tristan and Arthur Cohen from Mombasa regarding the future direction for *Barbara*, although they have not survived. In a letter dated April 5, while at Shimoni, Kenya, with the Jacksons on board, Tristan wrote, "As we shall not be calling at Durban, as originally planned, this means that Mombasa is our last hope of good work and resources until we arrive at either Colombo [Sri Lanka] or Singapore, so there are a few more items to be done there when we return."

This comment suggests that circumnavigation was still a possibility. A week later Tristan estimated he would need another $750 to pay bills and buy provisions for the Indian Ocean. Cohen was due to rejoin *Barbara* in the Comoro Islands in May, once Tristan had cabled to report his arrival from Moroni.

After they added a few coats of fresh varnish where necessary and repaired a couple of sails, *Barbara* sailed south again for Tanzania. They anchored off the yacht club at Tanga but did not go ashore. For a few days Tristan was in regular morning radio contact with another yacht, *Foxtrot,* somewhere north of Tanga. On April 26 *Barbara* headed for exotic islands, following the coast within sight of land, with her first major stop expected to be Dar es Salaam, Tanzania. South of Pangani the wind picked up, blowing from the south. Unable to make much headway, Tristan radioed to *Foxtrot* that he was going in to Zanzibar.

In squally conditions *Barbara* crossed the Zanzibar channel to Mwana Mwana lighthouse on Tumbatu Island. Keeping well clear of the long coastal reef, Tristan motored south to the port; he claimed *Barbara* was the first yacht to call at Zanzibar for many years. Customs, health, and immigration officials boarded the vessel outside the harbor. All were courteous, Tristan noted. He stayed in Zanzibar one day before returning to the mainland of Africa. On May 1 *Barbara* safely reached Dar es Salaam, and they stayed until evening of the next day.

Until this time Tristan had faithfully recorded all details of the voyage for Arthur Cohen. After Mombasa, as far as can be ascertained, he changed his style. The letters, other than a few, either stopped or have been lost. Instead of regular reports Tristan typed thirteen double-spaced legal-size pages under the heading "Islands of the Moon," a story of cruising to the Comoro Islands. Obviously the rejection of *Track of the Barbara* had not dulled his enthusiasm for writing long stories. "Islands of the Moon" is not an accurate account of the voyage, being rather banal and an odd mix of fact and fiction. In it Tristan, Conrad, and Alem have hearty conversations, each in his own dialect of English, with Tristan always the teacher. "Islands of the Moon" was almost certainly intended to be a part of *Indian Ocean Saga*, another book-length manuscript that never got published but was incorporated into *The Incredible Voyage*. Parts of "Islands of the Moon" were later published in a U.S. magazine under the title "Hot Passage." Fortunately a couple of letters to Arthur relate a few facts about the voyage, and Conrad was able to add his memories to the logbook's basic itinerary.

Barbara arrived off Moroni in the Comoros at midnight on May 13. The crossing from Tanzania had not been easy. After clearing at Kilwa Masoko, one day out the log line somehow got wrapped around the propeller. They lost both line and spinner, leaving them with only a rough idea of their speed.

"What a struggle to get here from Dar es Salaam!" Tristan said. "The current was running anything up to four and a half knots, direction between NE and NW. On the Africa shore the winds were strong . . . always SE or S of course and the coast and reefs are unlit. This with the rain and clouds at night kept the party going as you may imagine. We are looking forward very much to Trade Wind sailing after the last lot."

The harbor, which Tristan reported as drying up completely at low tide, was in darkness, so they dropped anchor just outside to wait until daylight. Arthur Cohen had not visited his boat since Israel, at the end of December, nearly five months before. Tristan acknowledged the gap with a pleasant close to his letter: "I am sure looking forward to seeing you again after so long in time and distance. Please let me know as soon as you can when you will arrive so we can have all ship-shape."

When he arrived at Moroni Tristan had received a letter from Arthur about the Seychelles. "The Seychelles sound so good that after looking them over I may decide to give the *Barbara* a rest there and to return there myself." He then added a sentence that took Tristan by surprise. "I have all but abandoned the idea of going further east and now believe South Africa and South America will be the fall and winter program."

Tristan shot back a concerned reply: "The change of voyage plan has come as a bombshell because I have ordered charts for the Singapore run from the Seychelles in London and they are probably waiting in the Seychelles right now." But ever accommodating to his boss, he shrugged and continued, "Well, I guess we can always return them and order others in place." The cautious skipper then added notes about the new plans. "Weatherwise the run from Seychelles to South Africa is o.k. but the later the better. Up to the end of August there is a frequent southerly content in the wind. From then it backs slowly to the east. The current is westerly running at about 70 miles a day, from Lat 5S down to Madagascar. So we would be close-hauled coming south in July and August, unless we head for Mozambique."

Moroni was an uncomfortable berth for *Barbara*. In the same letter Tristan talked of the difficulties in staying there:

> *There is a continual swell at all times. In fact this is a very, very bad anchorage. During the last four days, over the spring tides, we have had to leave the port and hang on to a refueling buoy way out in the offing. But a tanker came in for two days [causing us to move again]. The holding ground is soft sand and we continually dragged. There is no respite from the swell and surge here. It is far worse than Malaga. Also it has rained continuously for the last ten days, very heavy downpours. . . . Whenever a coaster comes in we have to shift berth, the room is so constricted. So most of our effort in the past two weeks has gone into preventing disaster.*

The long letter, much of it about the impending Seychelles visit and the problems to be overcome in obtaining landing permission, bears a crew list with passport details. Along with Conrad and Alem's particulars are those of the skipper. It reads: "Tristan Jones: date of birth—May 8, 1927. Place of birth—Dolgelly." Then there is the passport number, 339558, plus place and date of issue—London, August 19, 1964. Tristan was using his forged passport. As we have seen, the real U.K. passport number 339558 was issued on August 19, 1964, to Arthur Jones, born May 8, *1929*, in Liverpool.

Permission to land in the Seychelles was granted. Arthur flew in to Moroni alone on June 9 to sail the long haul, via Aldabra Island, to Victoria, the Seychelles capital on Mahé. The eleven-day voyage was uncomfortable, as Tristan had predicted. The logbook describes the seas alternately as mountainous or long and steep. Tristan wrote, "Motion of boat v. tiring and discomforting."

Tristan's anecdote in *The Incredible Voyage* about Conrad's dropping the only sextant and damaging it annoyed Conrad. He said, "I never dropped a sextant. I don't know why he would write that." The sextant did get broken, though not by Conrad. Tristan surmised that heat and humidity melted the fixing compound, allowing the bottom mirror to fall out.

Despite being a forgery, Tristan's passport passed scrutiny on arrival in the Seychelles. After cruising the islands for a week, Arthur flew back to the States from Victoria. *Barbara* stayed in the islands for five more weeks, with the crew readying her for the southbound leg to Majunga, Madagascar, while waiting for opportune departure conditions.

Tristan's last surviving letter for some time was sent from Victoria, Seychelles, on July 22, 1971 (he incorrectly dated it 1972). He finished with, "All on board are well and well-rested, but the stay here has palled somewhat and all are anxious to get away and around the Cape of Good Hope. Some of the flash [expensive] boats here now, awaiting the same trip, provide an incentive to us to show them our heels, and get around before they do."

While waiting for a thirty-knot southeasterly to subside, the crew had a chance to relax for a change and enjoy La Digue Island, their final port in the Seychelles. On Tuesday, August 10, *Barbara* weighed anchor at 1:00 P.M. and set course for Coetivy Island under working rig. The wind was southerly, force 3 to 4. For two days they ran close-hauled under overcast skies, with intermittent rain. At 11:30 A.M. on August 12 they sighted Coetivy Island, bearing 170 degrees, and worked their way in against the weather.

They rested at Coetivy for two nights before making an exceptionally fast run for Cap d'Ambre, Madagascar's northern tip. Tristan wrote of August 14, "Going like a train all day at 6.25 knots." The morning of the fifteenth was a repeat of the previous day, a fast run. From noon to noon *Barbara* covered 144 miles, her best run to date. The sea, however, became increasingly disturbed in the early afternoon. Tristan handed (furled) the mainsail and continued under mizzen and jib until 6:00 P.M., when he felt conditions were safe enough to set the main once more. Through the night they raced south. After another morning of exhilarating sailing, high winds once again forced Tristan to reduce sail. At 2:00 P.M. he again handed the main. Two hours later they found themselves being battered by a full gale out of the southeast. Tristan set the storm jib in preparation for a rough night. In the morning the force 7 to 8 gale continued to blow, punctuated by rain squalls. *Barbara* began to take seas over her decks. Taking sights became exceptionally difficult. By nightfall huge seas dominated the boat, and black squalls constantly threatened. Tristan noted somewhat laconically, "Situation getting rough."

At 1:00 P.M. on August 18 they sighted Cap d'Ambre light through a squall. Running free at seven knots, aided by a three-knot current, *Barbara* raced before storm-force winds through heavy rain for the shelter of the cape. Conditions became so rough Tristan considered heaving-to and letting the boat drift into the lee of Cap d'Ambre. He resisted the temptation and maintained his course. By 7:00 A.M. sea conditions had improved as Madagascar's bulk gradually deflected the storm. At 4:00 P.M., on a glassy sea, the exhausted crew dropped anchor in a mix of sand and mud two miles northeast of Cape Saint Sébastien, on the extreme northwest coast of Madagascar.

There must have been regular letters between Tristan and Arthur over the next few months, from Madagascar and from South African ports. Tristan was a conscientious skipper and usually kept excellent contact with his boss by mail. Although Cohen's son, Rob, was able to supply many letters from Tristan to Arthur and a number of Tristan's written reports on the voyage, sadly, he found no communications sent between the Seychelles (in July 1971) and arrival in Brazil (February 1972). We are left with Tristan's unreliable later version of events as written in *The Incredible Voyage*, the much more reliable logbooks from *Barbara*, and Conrad's memories.

Tristan spent a week wandering from one small port to the next along Madagascar's northwest coast. At Hell-Ville he careened the boat, cleaned and painted her bottom, and replaced worn zincs for the propeller. Although the crew only stayed six days in Majunga, they managed to get into trouble.

Ian Orde, an Englishman, joined *Barbara* as additional crew, probably in Madagascar. Tristan and his merry men quickly initiated him into their shore-going lifestyle. In Madame Chapeau's bar in Majunga, described by Tristan as the biggest whorehouse he'd ever seen, Tristan and crew got into a brawl.

"Tristan took a dislike to the fact that a British Union Jack hung behind the bar alongside an equally large swastika," Conrad explained. "The plan was TJ starts a disturbance, Ian is at the bar buying drinks while I go to the toilets to short the lights. I got a large flash and darkness [and then] went back to the bar to find *light*. Ian [was] trying to look nonchalant before leaping over the bar to snatch the swastika and poor Tristan [was] by now trying to extricate himself from a fight."

With bruised knuckles and broad smiles *Barbara*'s piratical crew sailed out of Madagascan waters for the Mozambique coast in the afternoon of September 1. Ahead of them stretched close to a thousand nautical miles of the Mozambique Channel. On this passage Tristan employed a self-sailing technique that he named the "Eureka system." Throughout one night *Barbara* sailed herself at 4.5 knots, maintaining a course of 210 degrees, with the wind on her port quarter. Tristan was thrilled enough with his idea to sketch it on a blank page in the log. Basically the system employed a mizzen flattened to leeward and a backed genoa. Tristan noted that the system worked best with the wind broad on either quarter.

There is some confusion as to the events of the next few days. Although there is a stamp and clearance from Mozambique's Inhambane Port Authority, signed by a lieutenant commander in the Portuguese navy and dated September 14, Conrad disputed the Mozambique visit. He could not recall having entered Mozambique. The Port Authority stamp suggests that Conrad's memory let him down on that point.

In his writing Tristan regularly made use of the names of people he met at sea and on shore. The Portuguese officer who signed *Barbara*'s log at Inhambane, Ruy Vital Pinto Molarinho Cahno, also appears, with a slightly different name, on the dedication page of *Saga of a Wayward Sailor*. That book recognizes, among others, Ruy Vidal Molinharo, commander, Portuguese navy. One assumes Tristan included the name to add credence to his claim in that book of being rescued by the Portuguese navy after being sunk by a whale in *Two Brothers*. The story is fiction.

From Inhambane or its vicinity to Durban, South Africa, took five days of torture as high winds from the southwest pushing against the Agulhas Current created violent seas. Tristan noted the sea was "unsailable" at the hundred-fathom line. Conrad remembered the seas as being close together, steep, and high. The rough passage did have a compensation. Conrad told the story this way:

> Barbara *found herself in 50+ knots [of wind] against probably a couple of knots of current. We threw a bottle in the water and it marched to windward as if being towed. At one point we were running before the wind under bare poles, maybe towing warps. The seas were so steep, it was like going up and down in a fast elevator, and we would leave our stomachs behind. When in the troughs looking astern, the crests must have been 45 degrees above us. Then, out of the heights of the next following sea, appeared the heads of two killer whales, riding the top of the wave and looking right down on us. They dove out of sight as the wave lifted us up and passed under us. As we settled into the next trough they appeared again.*

As we craned our necks to see them, they appeared to be grinning at us
and were certainly only being inquisitive.

A battered *Barbara* entered Durban harbor at 10:30 P.M. on September 22 to learn that the winds had been gusting to eighty knots. She remained in Durban until November 14, waiting for the right season to round the Cape of Good Hope and cross the South Atlantic. Conrad took a holiday, taking advantage of the hiatus to travel the coast—on land for a change—with John Costello, who like Ian Orde had joined the crew somewhere in the Indian Ocean. Conrad thought it might have been in the Comoros. His name fails to appear in the log or in letters to Arthur. Costello left the boat in Durban, as did Alem Desta. Conrad agreed with Tristan about Alem: it was hard to have a black on board as crew in South Africa.

"Tristan," Conrad said, "was wonderful with Alem from beginning to end. In South Africa Tristan tried to buck the system to make a place for Alem, but of course it was not possible. He flew Alem back to Ethiopia." Conrad added a sad finale to Alem's story. "I was back in [what is now] Eritrea and inquired after Alem. He was well known but had died in that shitty war."

Alem's departure probably spared him one of Tristan's wild days ashore. Fighting in bars was nothing new to Tristan—he'd been at it for much of his adult life. In Durban Tristan and his crew sat in a bar where the skipper held a dozen people enthralled with his tales of adventure. "And then," said Conrad, "a big Afrikaaner joins our table. He is twice TJ's size and Tristan picks a fight with him over apartheid. After fifteen minutes the Afrikaaner gets fed up and sensibly gets up and goes to the toilets. Tristan stupidly follows him. After three to four minutes the Afrikaaner comes out looking sheepish. Then a bit later TJ emerges covered in his own blood. Unbowed but a little quieter."

Back at sea in November the violent winds and conflicting currents continued to create heavy seas and difficult sailing conditions.

Barbara called briefly at Port Elizabeth and Mossel Bay before the tired crew finally arrived at Cape Town late at night, twelve days out from Durban.

Although he couldn't recall the precise location, Conrad had the last words on the Indian Ocean saga, words that—once again—demonstrate Tristan's superb seamanship: "In the Indian Ocean, sailing toward a low sandy atoll. I am navigating and plot the final course. Tristan says to tack for another fifteen minutes and then resume my course. After half an hour or so, there [the atoll] appears, right on the nose. There is no cloud to reflect [it] or any other sign that I can see. I know now that he felt it, and that is having experience and a real affinity with the sea. I might also add that whilst GPS is a lot safer in many respects, it also kills that affinity."

CHAPTER 7

The Amazon and a New Banjo

A young American, Phil Teuscher, joined *Barbara* in Cape Town. Tristan did not like the new addition to the crew and often complained about him in the log. Thirty years later Conrad commented, "I only vaguely remember him. I seem to recall he was an American family friend of Arthur Cohen's and that he was a bit arrogant and so did not fit in with *Barbara*'s crew."

After three weeks in Cape Town, one of which Tristan spent in a hotel, *Barbara* slipped her mooring at the Royal Cape Town Yacht Club at 1:00 P.M. on December 19, 1971. She motored out until due south of Robbin Island, where the skipper ordered three sails to be set: main, jib, and mizzen. The long haul to the northwest had begun, across the South Atlantic from the tip of Africa to the mouth of the Amazon. It would be Tristan's second confirmed transatlantic crossing.

Tristan made a habit of noting details of his personal history in the log and in his letters to Arthur. Surprisingly, therefore, although he sailed *Barbara* through the same South Atlantic waters where he claimed he was born, there is no mention of Tristan da Cunha or that momentous dawn in either logbook or letters.

At one o'clock Christmas morning, under nine-tenths cloud, *Barbara* was breasting the seas at six knots. The wind dropped three hours later, and light rain fell. The skies cleared at daybreak, and the crew celebrated Christmas by cleaning the boat and enjoying a Christmas pudding and a glass of wine each. By 10:30 A.M. *Barbara* was ghosting slowly north-northwest at three knots under spinnaker, main, staysail, and mizzen. Toward nightfall the wind freshened. Tristan doused the spinnaker, handed the staysail, and continued all night under main, genoa, and mizzen.

On New Year's Eve they crossed the prime meridian. The log notes they had covered 1,227 miles from Cape Town. Throughout the voyage from South Africa to St. Helena, which they sighted on the morning of January 4, 1972, Tristan kept the crew busy with constant sail changes to take advantage of all wind conditions. Day after day they did whatever was necessary to make northing. The night before they arrived off St. Helena, Tristan expressed some concern in the log: "18:00 Rain Showers. Down Spinnaker—running under main and mizzen at 5kts. 20:00 wind freshening. Don't want to go too fast—might miss St. Helena."

As St. Helena came in sight at 7:25 A.M., Tristan ordered Teuscher below, since he was on deck naked. At 3:00 P.M., with Teuscher modestly dressed, one assumes, *Barbara* dropped anchor in St. James Bay. During the two days and three nights on St. Helena the Standard Pub received the crew's undivided attention for many hours, and Dot's Café and Mrs. Baines Grocery Store each earned a few dollars from the short visit.

Barbara showed St. Helena her stern at 7:30 A.M. on January 7. The next stage of the voyage was a repeat of the slow approach to St. Helena. Constant sail changes kept the crew too busy to think about dwindling supplies of fresh food. The tomatoes ran out after five days. The carrots lasted a few days longer. The bread began to get moldy. Only the meat receives a positive mention in the log. "Meat lasting well," Tristan wrote.

Apart from the routine of changing sails to complement the wind, there was little else to liven the voyage until the sixteenth. The log records the sea as being "regular" and *Barbara* being under mainsail and mizzen only. The speed is not recorded but would probably not have been more than five knots. While Tristan and crew watched, a Chinese fishing boat, *No. 22 Chin Ying Chang*, approached to within about two hundred yards to leeward of *Barbara*, dropped her nets, then proceeded across the yawl's bows and hove-to. Tristan, swearing loudly at the Chinese crew, worked his boat skillfully to avoid the submerged obstacle.

Barbara entered Brazil's Recife port at 6:30 A.M. on January 23. The South Atlantic crossing of 3,280 nautical miles from Cape Town had taken thirty days at an average speed of 109 miles per twenty-four-hour day, or 4.5 knots. Phil Teuscher left the boat at Recife, to the skipper's relief.

Tristan, Conrad, and Ian enjoyed Recife so much that they stayed two weeks. By day they worked on *Barbara*, preparing her for the Amazon. At night they explored the multitude of bars near the port. *The Incredible Voyage* gives the sense that Tristan found himself perfectly at home in Recife. "It was a sailor's shore-going paradise. . . . If ever there was a place where you could fuck yourself to death, free, gratis, and for nothing, Recife was it. There must have been, and I'm not exaggerating, at least ten thousand available women and boys within half an hour's stroll from the boat."

But a big river called, and the boss was due to arrive in Belém in a few weeks. At daybreak on February 6 *Barbara* slipped her yacht club mooring and motored past the breakwater. Off the harbor's outer buoy the skipper called for all sail. The well-traveled yawl bowed to the waves as the equatorial wind played around her, urging her north.

Three days of steady running before a pleasant east-southeast breeze saw them off Mucuripe, the port for Fortaleza. Early-morning squalls lined the horizon as the crew dropped anchor at the yacht club for a day's rest. The squally weather continued as *Barbara* made her way along Brazil's north coast to the mouth of the Amazon. Tristan obviously expected to encounter the Amazon's notorious power some distance from Belém. On February 12, north of Parnaíba, the log notes with some surprise, "No sign of current." The following day's entry reads, "There is no sign of any current still."

Off Salinópolis, for the first time, *Barbara* took on a pilot. He advised that high water at the Amazon was four hours later than at Salinópolis. Tristan now found his current. At 7:00 A.M. on the fifteenth the log states, "Course 280 Current 2½ knots gives us 9 knots." Two hours later off Espardate Tristan recorded, "The current sets up upwelling (green)." By midafternoon, well into the Rio do Pará, the current pushed against them, slowing their progress. The water became muddy brown. Many fishing boats shared the river with them; all *Barbara*'s crew could do was be patient and wait for the incoming tide. At 7:30 P.M. the tide turned, and Tristan wrote with glee, "Now whizzing along in a cocoa sea." They dropped the pilot at 11:30 P.M. and went to anchor until daybreak. During the next three weeks in Belém they careened the boat at Ver-O-Peso Harbor and scraped and painted her bottom. Later they moved her to a pier within sight of the eighteenth-century cathedral and waited for the boss.

The Amazon, second longest river in the world, stretches over 4,000 statute miles from source to sea. Almost on the equator, it is invariably hot and humid. Fed by some 1,100 tributaries, it has a total volume of water twelve times that of the Mississippi and a current varying from three to eleven knots. The Amazon is not a river to be tackled lightly. Arthur Cohen, however, had an adventurer's heart and an inquiring mind. He wanted to experience the great river for himself.

Arthur and an unidentified friend flew into Belém to join *Barbara* and her crew of three in early March. Shortly after midnight on the eleventh, under a cloudy sky, they slipped away from land—with a certified river pilot in the cockpit—and powered down the Rio Guajara to the Rio do Pará. The Amazon adventure, which Tristan would later turn into an epic fictional struggle against enormous odds, began quietly.

Although ocean freighters regularly traveled as far upriver as Iquitos, 1,730 nautical miles beyond Belém, Arthur Cohen's plan was to take *Barbara* only 930 miles—to Manaus, the great city in a jungle. From there he and his friend would fly home. Tristan and crew would return on the fast-flowing current to the Atlantic and position themselves in the Windward Islands, or Lesser Antilles, to await further orders.

Up to this time few if any foreign pleasure craft had attempted the Amazon. To most small-boat sailors, the experience of traveling the enormous river was not worth battling the Amazon's powerful current. Arthur Cohen was made of sterner stuff.

Without a knowledgeable pilot, the maze of islands and rivers that make up the Amazon River estuary would have baffled even Tristan's navigational instincts. Evangelino, the pilot, would remain with the boat for the next thirteen days—until one day shy of Manaus. After a morning stop at Abaetetuba to purchase wood for a boomkin, Evangelino unerringly led *Barbara* between two islands to once again find the Rio do Pará. Circling the dangerously shallow waters over Banco Otelo, they spent the rest of that day working through the chain of islands off the river's north shore. After a cool morning, rain and humidity prevailed throughout the afternoon. This was to prove a regular pattern for the next few days. They tied up that night at Boa Vista, with the Amazon proper still over two days away.

Each day, except for one late start owing to a leak and another for a sightseeing excursion, *Barbara* slipped her mooring between 4:45 and 6:00 A.M.

Following the western fringe of Ilha Marajó, a swampy island the size of Belgium, they reached the Amazon at 2:00 P.M. on March 14. As usual in the early afternoon, it was raining lightly. Keeping about fifty yards off the south bank, they reached Gurupá at 10:00 P.M. The log offers no zoological surprises on the Amazon. The "thousands of alligators," "millions of fearsome piranhas," and "swarms of dangerous snakes" Tristan reported in his book stayed hidden. The upriver voyage, as many other travelers on Brazilian riverboats have found, is less exciting than one might expect of the famous Amazon.

The jungle itself is represented by a seemingly unbroken wall of green beyond which nothing can be seen. Of far more interest are the changing colors of the river as tributary after tributary empties contrasting hues to mingle with the main flow. The yellow waters of the Amazon become decorated with patches of green from the Tapajós, and the near black of the Rio Negro and the Solimões. Multicolored butterflies and birds dressed in exotic plumage perform ballets over the river by day. At night, when the lamps are lit, huge moths preen like actors in a spotlight.

Occasional views of crowded riverboats break the monotony of a benign-looking jungle slipping by. The city of Santarém, exactly halfway between Belém and Manaus, is a welcome break from the tedium of the river. Dating back to 1661, and with a population of over 300,000, Santarém is the fourth-largest city in Brazil's Amazonia. On at least one occasion the crew dined at Restaurante Mascote, which Tristan referred to as "the only decent one twixt Belém and Manaus." It stands on the waterfront opposite the old Royalty House, close to their mooring. *Barbara* stayed two nights and one day in Santarém.

Four hours after casting off his mooring Tristan notes that they passed red cliffs and for the first time mentions "flights of pretty gray, white, & red birds." An air of urgency is reflected in the logbook as *Barbara* forces her way upstream. The engine is in constant use, aided by sails when possible. Other than at Santarém, stops are rarely for more than overnight. Time, one assumes, was running out for Arthur and his guest.

On March 26, with the boat preparing to depart from Itacoatiara, the pilot went missing. Tristan set off anyway, at 6:00 A.M. Apart from a fuel pipe failure, the rest of that day was uneventful. Evangelino met them at Eva that evening, and Tristan fired him. His services were no longer important anyway; their destination was close at hand. In midafternoon the following day they moored alongside another boat at Manaus. *Barbara* had reached the zenith of her upriver Amazon voyage.

The journey had taken sixteen days from Belém. Arthur and his friend flew home to the States from Manaus. Tristan, Conrad, and Ian had standard boat maintenance to take care of.

In *The Incredible Voyage*, Tristan led his readers to believe he was on the Amazon solely to reach the great river's headwaters, where he could arrange transport for the boat to Lake Titicaca. This not only added drama to the story but stressed his indefatigable pursuit of a single-minded goal—to get his boat to the remote mountain lake. In the book it is high adventure indeed as dramas unfold in quick succession. The intrepid pair, Tristan and Conrad (no mention of Ian), drag the boat from tree to tree, some with a girth of eighty feet, gaining on the Amazon yard by tenacious yard until finally, too exhausted to continue, they tie up to a rubber collector's grave on May 20 and admit defeat. Actually, by that time they were already safe in Grenada.

In the book we hear that the two were fading fast from starvation, their bodies debilitated by malaria. Forced to admit defeat, they retreat to Manaus. Too late in the season for another attempt, they lash *Barbara* to floating tree trunks and drift the hundreds of miles to safety where the Amazon meets the sea. Tristan tells a ludicrous story about the starving pair catching a capybara, and later a manatee, and stuffing them into a pressure cooker.

Conrad remembered the Amazon excursion rather differently from his former skipper. "Old Tristan did rather let his imagination go overboard on the Amazon. None of us had malaria. The only thing we suffered from was the humidity."

Conrad also confirmed that *Barbara* did not go west of Manaus. The boat stayed put in Manaus from March 27 to April 6 at 10:00 A.M., when she commenced her downstream run to the open sea. The run east, downriver from Manaus to Macapá, took fourteen days under sails and engine. With time to spare, the crew took it easy most of the way, occasionally stopping at midmorning to spend the rest of the day moored to another boat or riding at anchor. On May 1, having moved from Macapá to Curuá Island some days earlier to wait for the tides to lessen, they made for the open Atlantic.

On the evening of May 3 they tied up against the mole in Cayenne, French Guiana, after suffering an unpleasant beam sea for much of the way. In Cayenne they met Peter Tangvald, a flamboyant Norwegian sailor who was there with his beautiful young French wife, Lydia, building a sixty-foot (18-meter) ketch to circumnavigate the world.

Barbara stayed five days in Cayenne, long enough for her crew to see some of the sights and have a few hearty meals and for Tristan to prepare his charge for the next stage of her voyage. At the same time he and Ian began to make plans to return to the Amazon and start a boatbuilding business. Tristan came up with the idea of fabricating a series of catamarans from marine plywood. Based on a James Wharram design, the fifty-one-foot (15.5-meter) cats would be built in Macapá, where there was a marine-plywood factory and a small boatyard equipped to do the job inexpensively. Tristan planned to use the prototype (to be named *Banjo Too*) on a six-month cruise up the Amazon with paying guests. As he explained to Arthur Cohen in a letter from Cayenne, "This kind of craft is ideal for the Amazon, where you need plenty of deck space and shelter."

Tristan and Ian estimated building costs at not more than $2,500 per vessel. The pair aimed for a September 1972 start, with the first boat ready in December. According to Tristan, the project included Conrad. He was scheduled to captain the first cruise up the Tapajós River. Thirty years later Conrad had no recollection of any such plan. Tristan hoped to sign a party of wildlife watchers from the United States and England for the maiden expedition. He confided to Arthur, "I am fascinated with the Amazon. It's so vast, and it's growing. I can't see that we'll get much competition either as it's such a way-out area. If we can knock out one craft every three months or so it might even be possible to do bare boat charters on the Tapajós."

Tristan's idea was basically sound, although too ambitious, as

Arthur pointed out. Building one catamaran as an Amazon expedition boat made sense. A series of identical craft would be financially unsupportable. In the meantime, while his mind massaged the idea, Tristan had to steer *Barbara* to the islands.

Anxious to escape the unrelenting humidity of the South American coast for a while, the crew prepared for the Caribbean. Following advice from Yves Massel, owner and skipper of a large schooner, who recommended the marina facilities at Grenada, Tristan notified Arthur that he would be sailing for Grenada instead of Trinidad. On May 9, in squally weather, he weighed anchor and set course for Isle Royale, one of the Îles du Salut, French Guiana. Once a French penal colony, the islands include Devil's Island, made famous by the escapades of "Papillon"— Henri Charrière.

Studying the tides and currents with his professional eye, Tristan concluded that Charrière could not possibly have been telling the truth when he said he drifted the twelve miles from Devil's Island to the mainland on a bag of coconuts. The current, Tristan observed, flows offshore at three knots or more—even against the incoming tide. The nearest islands to the northwest are Trinidad and Tobago, well over five hundred nautical miles away. Tristan, with a certain amount of unintentional irony, went on to write, "But the old rogue told a good story, so let him lie in peace." Based on the fictional aspects of many of his sixteen books and his magazine articles, that could be Tristan's epitaph as well.

Barbara's log records the departure from Isle Royale on May 13 at 1:00 P.M.: "Anchors aweigh. Course due W. to clear reef off Devil's Island. 14:00 Up main, Genoa and mizzen."

As readers of *The Incredible Voyage* know, Tristan wrote that *Barbara* was the first yacht to anchor off Devil's Island and said he went ashore for a while. He repeated the claim in a magazine article called "In the Wake of Dreyfus." His logbook disagrees with him.

After six days of variable winds, occasionally uncomfortable seas, often overcast skies, and some equipment breakage, *Barbara* reached St. George's harbor in Grenada. They tied up at the fuel dock on the east side of the finger at 11:00 A.M. on May 18, 1972. Tristan had not been up to par for a few days. He complained in the log of feeling weak, but a letter to Arthur written on the day of arrival in Grenada makes no mention of any sickness. The first half of the letter revolves around Ian and a change of heart. "After all the fuss and palaver about building a vessel in Brazil, Ian has got cold feet and wants to go home."

At this point Tristan had no clear idea how much longer he would be needed as *Barbara*'s skipper. After a few months cruising the Caribbean she would be returning to Westport, Connecticut, and he would be out of a job. Meanwhile his sojourn in Grenada was not always happy. He did not get along well with other yachties and complained of their malicious gossip. His own truculent attitude may have been partly to blame.

An eyewitness account of one aspect of Tristan's stay in Grenada tells of the problems: "They were right near my boat," recalls Grenadan sail racing champion Peter "Champy" Evans. "They were there for quite a while. A few weeks I think." Champy's recollections of Tristan mirror those of other Caribbean sailors. Most remember his temper, and his capacity for drink, more than anything else. "Tristan was a very strange person. One minute he would be fine. Then he'd have a few drinks and become a raving crazy man." Champy told me. "He was very sometime-ish. That's a saying in the Caribbean. Sometimes he was fine. Other times he was a complete arsehole."

Conrad, being much younger than Tristan, was a contemporary of the then twenty-year-old Champy and his friends who were—according to Champy—"all hippy types." Conrad, however, did not remember Evans.

Conrad met a woman in Grenada and fell in love, sparking Tristan's unpredictable temper—not an unusual event. "After I had found my confidence on boats, Tristan and I had terrific rows on occasion. He fired me half a dozen times, and I left the same amount. It was the only way we could keep our own individuality and keep sailing together. Once they were over they were forgotten."

Champy Evans recalled, "They were always fighting. Shouting at each other. I think they [Tristan and Conrad] had split up after one big fight. Oh, it was a real spectacle: the talk of the marina for a long time. Tristan was raving and throwing things. Conrad was shouting back. It was a big scandal in the marina. I think there was a girl involved, someone with Conrad. Tristan was mad."

The woman was Wendy, who later became Conrad's first wife. Conrad vividly recalled the fight. With *Barbara*'s voyage effectively over, Tristan had offered to take Conrad with him to Lake Titicaca (apparently the first time this subject had come up between them). Conrad refused because he was in love with Wendy and wanted to stay with her. He felt Tristan was jealous of Wendy. While the three were having drinks on board, Tristan became extremely insulting to Wendy, provoking a violent response from Conrad. "Then I lost the plot and remember having my hands around his [Tristan's] throat and somebody pulling me off. I'm glad he did."

Tristan's mercurial character obviously bemused, perhaps offended, the laid-back Caribbean sailors. "Sometimes he would shout at us," Champy laughed, as he mimicked Tristan's rage: "'You blasted hippies!' Another time he just walks on board [my boat] into the cockpit and expects to have a long social chat. He was a crazy man."

The fight made Conrad decide to leave Tristan, which he did at the end of June. He was fortunate in immediately finding work as mate on *Dana*, an old but shipshape charter boat. With no partner for his boatbuilding enterprise, Tristan dropped the idea for a while and concentrated on writing articles for boating magazines and trying to finish *Indian Ocean Saga*. He still had accommodation and a job for a while. All he needed was to stay in one place for a few weeks and write. The last paragraph of a letter to Cohen on May 30, 1972, explained, "I am looking for a place to do some writing for a month or two, so if you

want me to stay around [and] look after the boat until say October . . .
I can do that okay and it would help out. I still haven't quite figured out
what I'm going to do . . . building in Brazil, now, looks bloody complicated, getting stuff in like fittings, etc. So I may either build in Britain
or the Med, but I'd like to do some writing too."

Barbara's regular logbook entries cease on June 1, but Tristan's letters to Arthur continued for a few more months. At the end of June,
after announcing Conrad's departure, he expressed his personal lack
of direction.

> My own position is that it looks as if nothing will settle until September
> at the earliest. Until then I won't know if there's:
>
>   a) a demand for an Amazon voyage.
>
>   b) a publisher interested in Indian Ocean Saga (now completed).
>
>   c) If the book is published, if there is a suitable smallish boat around
>   to do another trip in, either to West Africa or Turkey. In this respect
>   I have written away all over the place to see if there's a suitable boat
>   going reasonably.

These comments suggest that Tristan might have temporarily
dropped the idea of attempting to reach Lake Titicaca, possibly because
Conrad refused to join the adventure.

Tristan's position as skipper and caretaker on Barbara for the summer remained unchanged. Whenever possible he took time out to
write. With his tenure as Barbara's skipper gradually coming to an end,
he also kept his eyes open for a boat of his own. Before July was half
over he had found her. A letter to Arthur explains, "I fell into a stroke
of luck [I think]; a thirty-five foot yawl, Alaska Pine on Oak, with a
brand new Volvo 16h.p. diesel engine, all stainless rigging and enough
gear to cruise for the next five years."

Tristan bought her for $5,000 and said the only snag was that she
had been constructed in Japan with two substandard marine-plywood
bulkheads. He doesn't say what the boat was originally called, only that

he changed her name to *Banjo II*. He planned to have her renovated over the summer. By good fortune, Conrad had quit his job on *Dana* and was looking for employment and somewhere he and Wendy could live. The argument forgotten, Tristan lost no time installing them on *Banjo II*.

Now that he had a boat of his own again, new plans began to surface. Tristan talked of sending *Banjo II* to the Mediterranean under Conrad's command once the Atlantic hurricane season was over. There she would be a crewed charter boat among the Greek islands. He also considered a similar project in the Caribbean, where he still had responsibility for *Barbara*. Neither idea reached fruition. Conrad and Wendy left by air for England in late July. Tristan was less than pleased to lose his longtime mate again and refused to pay his airfare, reneging on an earlier agreement to fly Conrad home eventually.

In August he sent the manuscript for *Indian Ocean Saga* to United Kingdom publisher Michael Joseph, who, Tristan said, forwarded it to Nautical Publishing. Then he waited for a reply. Good news arrived when he learned he had sold three illustrated articles to a British magazine.

In mid-September he wrote to Arthur from Grenada, complaining of the cost of keeping his boat there and worrying about his book. "I don't think I can keep *Banjo* here much after December; so I'm hoping something comes up. I'm daily looking for news of the book. If that comes off then I can see my way forward."

In the same letter he moaned about finding more rot in *Banjo*'s coach roof coaming, but he expected to have all work finished within a week. At the end of the month he proudly announced that her sea trials had been a success. He had another mental boost when he received word that a French boating magazine had purchased his story of the rat from the Red Sea.

At some unknown date, bad news followed: *Indian Ocean Saga* was rejected. Undeterred, Tristan promptly sent the manuscript to Donald Copeman, another publisher in England, even though he had changed his mind about the scope of the book. He decided to amalgamate his writing into a trilogy about *Barbara*'s voyage, with the overall title *A Sailor's Odyssey*. Book 1 would be on the Atlantic and the Mediterranean (almost certainly taken from the rejected *Track of the Barbara*), book 2, the cruise from Israel to St. Helena (this one appears to have been *Indian Ocean Saga*), and book 3, the story of the Amazon voyage. He sent the manuscript to Arthur Cohen for review, commenting on book 1, "I wrote a load of trash on this two years ago. I will have to tear it apart and do it all again."

In the same letter he wrote, "I remember that you showed that last terrible MS to Alfred Knopf, and of course he wouldn't touch it with a barge pole. This one is very different. I've never seen a cruising book like it, except Slocum's, and there you had to read between the lines to see what a rascal he really was."

In October Tristan suffered a bout of dysentery, which he said left him feeling shaky. He still managed to continue his maintenance work on *Barbara* but, perhaps as a result of the dysentery, his spirits dropped to an unusual low. He sent Arthur an update on *Barbara*, then surprisingly added, "I found a buyer for *Banjo* who will complete the purchase at end of November. Quite frankly, Arthur, I do not feel that I can undertake any serious voyages for some time as I feel worn out and the heat is getting me down. So I will be going to London for a month or two before looking around for something else."

For unknown reasons the rifle carried on *Barbara* had at some time been transferred to *Banjo*. When the two yachts were slipped to have their bottoms cleaned in October, the undeclared rifle was discovered, and Tristan found himself in trouble. He discussed the situation with Arthur by phone, then followed up in a letter on October 19: "I'm up the creek for the rifle and expecting a big fine—this is the word I got from the grapevine. No one asked if there were arms aboard when we arrived."

Although he was worried, his mood had changed drastically from the lethargy of a few days before. He continued with, "On selling *Banjo*—I was very, very down before the doc started injecting me with massive doses of vitamins. Now I could do a transatlantic right away. The sale offer is open at both ends until the end of November, so chances are—if I can get my bastardy back in running order—I'll keep her. I really want to."

Fortunately for Tristan, the local magistrate chose to turn a blind eye to the rifle incident, and Tristan got away with nothing more than a fright. He decided to leave Grenada as soon as possible and find somewhere less expensive to moor the boats. With Arthur's approval, and assisted by two Australians, Tristan moved both boats from Grenada to Bequia, where they dropped anchor in mid-November. In late November Arthur asked Tristan to have *Barbara* available in Grenada by Christmas. A group of his friends would then take her on a short cruise to Antigua. For the first time in nearly four years Tristan would not be in command, or even on board. He confirmed his agreement in writing, adding once again that he planned to sell *Banjo*. He then announced he would buy a forty-five-footer named *Singora*. The latter, he explained, was going cheap, and although she needed a lot of work, he would be able to sell her for a good profit, then look around for a fiberglass boat.

He had more to tell Cohen, "Good news! Donald Copeman, a big London publisher has told me that he is determined to get *Indian Ocean Saga* launched. He is trying to get hold of a professional to polish up the literary style."

A few days later, while detailing a few mechanical problems for Arthur, he wrote, "The deal with *Singora* fell through as she is too rotten, so *Banjo* will stay here until I can join her again and maybe something else will turn up."

He delivered *Barbara*, then flew back to Bequia. Arthur's friends spent a couple of weeks enjoying the islands by sea and incurred Tristan's professional disdain when he subsequently saw her anchored on a lee shore. He admitted to finding life without *Barbara* "a bit strange."

This was the beginning of the end of Tristan's relationship with Arthur and *Barbara*. First, though, he had to skipper her one more time. Arthur asked him to fly up to Antigua in mid-February to meet the Cohens and another couple. From there they would sail her on to the U.S. Virgin Islands together. Tristan agreed.

There is no record of that 350-mile voyage other than a note that they called at St. Martin and Tortola before arriving in St. Thomas. Thanks to another's anecdote, however, we can surmise that Tristan took on a deckhand for the voyage.

Jan de Groot, owner and skipper of the fifty-five-foot yawl *Ring Anderson*, remembered Tristan well from that cruise. De Groot's West Indian crew had an altercation with Tristan and a Dominican deckhand at Village Cay Marina on Tortola, in the British Virgin Islands. A few days before, the Dominican had made insulting remarks about "Uncle Toms" and accused *Ring Anderson* of being a slave ship. De Groot believed Tristan had instigated the taunts. In Tortola *Ring Anderson*'s muscle-bound crew, without their captain's knowledge, decided to confront their tormentors. *Barbara*'s crew, Tristan and the Dominican, came off second-best. One can assume that the Cohens and guests were ashore at the time.

In St. Thomas Arthur gave Tristan the rest of his pay before they parted—with regrets on both sides. After nearly four years the disparate pair of adventurers had developed a healthy respect for each other. That was the last time the two met. Arthur and his friends took *Barbara* home to Westport, while Tristan flew back to Bequia and *Banjo II*. Although a ship's logbook is part of the vessel's standard property, Arthur Cohen must have agreed that his former skipper could keep *Barbara*'s logbooks for a time after he left the boat, probably to help him complete *A Sailor's Odyssey*. Neither Cohen nor his family would see the two logbooks again. Arthur Cohen died while Tristan was next in South America, and Tristan kept the logs.

CHAPTER 8

Tristan Meets Sea Dart

A communication with Arthur Cohen after the Amazon trip suggests that between planning charters in the Mediterranean on *Banjo*, talking of boatbuilding on the Amazon, and maintaining two boats in the Caribbean, Tristan had discussed with Cohen the old idea of attempting a vertical sailing record. Originally proposed back in the Mediterranean with Pete Kelly and more recently revived in the Caribbean with Conrad, the venture continued to intrigue him.

Sometime after Tristan returned from St. Thomas to Bequia, he first set eyes on *Sea Dart*. He knew immediately that she was the boat for him, and he turned his attention away from other ideas and, once and for all, toward Lake Titicaca. The crusty mariner and the tiny cutter were made for each other.

Tristan wrote in *The Incredible Voyage* that he found *Sea Dart* at anchor in a beautiful bay on Bequia on his first day sailing in *Banjo II*. At the back of the same book, however, he has a list of ports *Barbara* visited on her voyage from Westport, Connecticut, via the North Atlantic, Mediterranean, Red Sea, Indian Ocean, South Atlantic, and Amazon to the West Indies. Photocopied directly from Tristan's own papers and printed with incredibly uneven type, it includes the number of days spent in each port. An addendum in pen states that he traveled 1,420 miles in *Banjo II* looking for *Sea Dart*. Then follows a list of his ports

visited during that supposed search. It is extensive, listing twenty island stops from Barbados to Puerto Rico and back to Bequia. Until he
arrived in Bequia after leaving *Barbara* for the last time, he had not even
heard of *Sea Dart*.

Sea Dart's owner, Ron Reil, a young American—who was on board
when Tristan arrived—was happy to show a fellow sailor his boat. After some discussion, according to his own version of the story, Tristan
put down a deposit and took possession two days later. Reil had been
based in Bequia with *Sea Dart* since the end of the first week in January 1973. He remembers the occasion quite differently. Although neither
story has been substantiated by a third party, Reil's version is longer and
livelier. It has the ring of fiction, yet it sounds enough like Tristan to be
true: "In early March of 1973 Tristan Jones came into my life with a rush.
My first glimpse of Tristan occurred one early morning when I was
brought to Dart's deck by a big ruckus ashore. High up on the hill, in
town, I could see Tristan running down the road toward the bay, as
fast as he could go, with the local sail maker right behind him waving
a big machete and screaming profanities at him. Apparently Tristan had
pulled a fast one on the sail maker and was about to pay for it with
his life."

Reil continues the story on his website with obvious enthusiasm:

> *Tristan was fleet of foot, however, and reached the town dock about three
> steps ahead of the sail maker's machete. Tristan launched off the dock
> gracefully, clearing twenty feet of water before entering the sea in a head-
> long dive. He swam out to* Banjo *and climbed aboard in a fierce temper.
> He could be heard all over the bay cussing at his two young black crew-
> men. It has been said that Tristan couldn't swim, but, if that's true, his ac-
> tions are a testament to quick learning in a pressing situation.
> If Tristan couldn't swim, I think he must have forgotten that fact for a
> moment.*
>
> *I got to see Tristan quite often after that. Tristan loved the rum bot-
> tle, especially someone else's rum bottle. He would often come back to*

Banjo *in a fierce roaring mood that would get the whole bay up on deck to watch. One such event occurred one afternoon when Tristan returned to the beach after some heavy socializing. He yelled to* Banjo *for his crew to come in to the beach and pick him up in the dinghy, but received no response. He continued to bellow from the shore while his thermostat moved steadily up into the danger zone. Finally he couldn't take it any longer. He waded in and swam out to* Banjo, *once again forgetting he couldn't swim. When he climbed aboard he was in an extreme temper and stormed below decks. A few moments later he showed up on deck again with one of the little black boys held high above his head and threw him into the sea. He immediately went below again and brought up the second one to repeat the gesture.*

Reil said it didn't stop there. The two boys climbed back aboard *Banjo II* only to have Tristan throw them overboard again. He was still yelling profanities. According to Reil, all the yachties in the bay were on deck to watch the amazing scene.

Although he's not explicit as to how long Tristan was in Bequia before he purchased *Sea Dart*, Ron Reil said, "After some time passed, Tristan became aware that I had put Dart up for sale. He hailed me from shore one afternoon, and I went to get him in Dart's dinghy. We spent the afternoon on board discussing Dart and working on the gallon and a half of rum I kept on board. That night, Wednesday 13 March, Tristan and I reached an agreement on the sale of Dart. That night the bottle of rum also became history."

April 1 was the date agreed on for the transfer of ownership. In the meantime Reil's leg became badly infected from a spider bite. Although he tried to treat it himself, it got worse. About that time Hillary and Neil, two of his friends, sailed in. Fortunately for Reil, Hillary was able to operate on the wound and clean it properly. A few days later Reil told his friends that he had sold *Sea Dart* to Tristan Jones. They were upset by the news and said they had sold their boat to Tristan too.

Before the leg infection confined him to Bequia, Reil was planning one final short cruise to the Grenadines, in *Sea Dart*. Without knowing Reil's intentions, Hillary and Neil had decided to go there too. At this point the local bank held Tristan's deposit on Hillary and Neil's boat in trust, and Tristan needed that money back. Hillary and Neil quickly learned that, after arranging to buy *Sea Dart*, Tristan had told the bank that the first deal was off. The boat's owners had sailed away in her, he claimed, and he demanded that his money be refunded. It was returned and passed over to Reil as a deposit.

Hillary and Neil, confident their boat had been sold, had purchased nonrefundable airline tickets and made other arrangements back in England. Tristan's canceling the sale caused them considerable financial distress.

Ron takes over again: "I immediately decided that I would cancel my deal with Tristan in order to force him to go back to the original arrangement, but Hillary and Neil would have no part of it and insisted that I complete my deal. I felt horrible over the situation, and all the joy I felt in having everything come to a smooth close was gone. I was filled with anger towards Tristan."

Although one man was angry and the other probably complacent, the two sailors somehow agreed to get along. "An uneasy truce" is how Reil describes the situation. Tristan and Ron shared *Banjo II* and *Sea Dart* for close to two weeks. They ate dinner together on *Banjo* because it was roomier than *Sea Dart*, though Reil at this time was still living aboard *Sea Dart* and Tristan aboard *Banjo*.

Having restored *Banjo II* to cruising condition, Tristan was able to sell her for a reasonable profit. Ron Reil, who was soon to be without a boat, agreed to act as captain for *Banjo*'s new owners, a retired pharmacist and his wife, due to arrive from New York within two weeks. One day while Reil was away on the other side of the island, Tristan went aboard *Sea Dart*, although Reil was still the legal owner.

"[He] went through all of my stuff looking for my ship's log. He was very concerned about what I had recorded in it about the incident with Hillary and Neil. After searching through everything (I always had the log well hidden), he found it and read it. He then wrote a note, and left it in the log, stating that if I ever published anything that was in my log about the boat deal he would sue me for everything I was worth! He was very concerned about his image to his readers since his income came from his books."

Reil is incorrect there, of course. The events he recounted took place in March 1973. Tristan hadn't seen many of his articles in print up to that time, and his first book, *The Incredible Voyage*, wasn't published until May 1977.

During the changeover, while the two were transferring possessions from one boat to the other, a pile of assorted rubbish built up in *Banjo*'s cockpit. On top was an old atlas. Reil said, "I picked it up and looked through it."

He was stunned to see that on every ocean there were lines drawn in red and blue pencil. Reil guessed that they were Tristan's private record of his ocean voyages, and he was suitably impressed. It is far more likely that the lines represented Tristan's imagination sketching out voyages he would like to sail in the future—even, perhaps, voyages he convinced himself he had already sailed. At that time, in 1973, Tristan's only major sailing voyage was the one he had just completed—*Barbara*'s odyssey from Westport to Grenada via East and South Africa. He would make only two more extensive voyages in the next twenty years—one in *Sea Dart* and the other, many years later, in a trimaran.

On April 1, 1973, Tristan took ownership of *Sea Dart* and moved his gear aboard. Reil moved onto *Banjo II*. Tristan said he paid Reil a total of $5,000 for *Sea Dart*. Reil disagreed. He said the price was $3,500, plus a couple hundred dollars for ancillary gear. As a bonus she was well equipped with charts of the Caribbean and Pacific. Though much smaller than either *Barbara* or *Banjo II*, she was perfect for Tristan's needs.

One of the debutante class from marine architect Robert Tucker, *Sea Dart* was built in England in 1960. Originally she was intended for an attempt at the Northwest Passage, the ice-choked waterway across the top of North America; consequently she was sturdily constructed from mahogany marine plywood. An additional advantage for tropical waters was that her hull had been sheathed with twenty layers of a silk and rubber compound that Tristan identified as Cascomite, which protects against the teredo worm.

Crammed into her hull, which was twenty-one by seven feet, she had three full-length berths, a table, stowage lockers sufficient for three months' supplies for a solo sailor, and a small kerosene stove. Tristan recorded that with no inboard engine—meaning no batteries for power—there was no radio, no refrigerator, no electricity. He wasn't concerned, he said; to him these were luxuries. Although she didn't have an inboard, *Sea Dart* was equipped with an old outboard motor.

On April 10, 1973, with the trade wind filling the sails, Tristan and *Sea Dart* embarked on the initial stage of their great adventure, which would eventually make *Sea Dart* known around the world and turn her abrasive owner into a highly regarded sailing author.

CHAPTER 9

Cruising to Peru

Although it is over a thousand nautical miles on a great-circle route (the shortest distance) from Bequia to the Panama Canal, Tristan was in no hurry. He spent three months exploring the southwest Caribbean before dropping anchor in the Flatts, off Colón, at the Caribbean end of the Canal. And those months were not without incident.

Tristan left *Sea Dart* in Cartagena, Colombia, where he arrived on May 1, 1973, and a few days later he traveled inland to Bogotá, the nation's capital. *The Incredible Voyage* tells us he went there to buy an outboard motor because, he said, he didn't have any form of engine on board and would need one for the Panama Canal transit. *Sea Dart* was in fact equipped with an old outboard, but Tristan wanted a newer one. But Cartagena, being a coastal city, might have been a better place to find a motor than Bogotá. It is more than likely that Tristan visited Bogotá just to see the city. Whatever the reason, he did not get an engine, but he did get far more than he bargained for.

A Bogotá newspaper reported that Tristan Jones was mugged and robbed of all valuables, including his passport, not long after he arrived. When he complained to the police about the assault—Tristan spoke passable Spanish—he was promptly arrested for failing to carry identification and tossed into a cell for three days. Fortunately the British embassy staff took pity on Tristan and issued him a new passport on

May 7. Passport number 281164, valid for one year, was the first legitimate piece of identification to refer to him as Tristan Jones, born in Liverpool on May 8, 1929. All previous papers—except his forged passport—had been in the name of Arthur Jones.

Sea Dart was little more than half the size of *Barbara*, yet Tristan took on crew to help him—probably in Cartagena. A Canadian, Eric Eugene Freeborne, and Carlos Arturo Ramirez Parra, possibly a Colombian, are recorded in the log with their passport numbers. With three men on a twenty-one-foot boat, *Sea Dart's* compact cabin would have been crowded. That Tristan felt a need for the company of two others emphasizes his dislike of sailing alone.

As far as can be ascertained, the only occasions when Tristan might have sailed alone were first in *Cresswell*, early in his sailing career, meandering through the French canals and across part of the Mediterranean to Ibiza, and possibly in *Sea Dart* from Bequia to Willemstad on Curaçao in the Netherlands Antilles and onward to Cartagena. On the other side of South America he also may have sailed alone for a few days on the Platte River between Buenos Aires and Montevideo. Despite his extravagant claims of having sailed hundreds of thousands of miles alone, there are no other confirmed solo voyages, either earlier or later in his life.

Between the Colombian island of Fuerte and Cape Tiburón on the border between Colombia and Panama, a three-day run, the old outboard motor's piston rings failed. Tristan sailed on to Punta Escoces, Panama, where the crew went ashore to explore the vague remains of the seventeenth-century Scottish Fort St. Andrew. It is unfortunate that, rather than telling the truth, he chose to write nine pages of fiction in *The Incredible Voyage* about the zigzag cruise along Panama's Caribbean coast. It is a fascinating region peopled by colorful Cuna Indians. A series of well-written articles about the Cunas and their lifestyle would have made far more sense and been infinitely more interesting than the silly tale he chose to tell.

The book has Tristan—alone, of course—arriving at Punta Escoces and persuading the headman of the village to tell him about a lost
tribe deep in the jungle. The "legendary" tribe—descendents of Scottish immigrants, we are told—were known locally as Cabellos Rojas, or
Red Hairs. After spending a week at Punta Escoces, Tristan and two
villagers, Willie and Charlie-Boy, sailed up the coast a few miles to
Caledonia Bay. From there, leaving Charlie-Boy to guard *Sea Dart*,
Tristan and Willie trekked inland for many days through thick brush
until they met the Red Hairs. After surviving a nervous night in the
jungle village, they made their way back to the coast. The journey of
discovery, more appropriate to a boy's adventure magazine than an
adult's book on sailing exploits, had taken more than two difficult
weeks. There is no mention of that excursion in *Sea Dart*'s logbook.
Tristan said he then continued his voyage to the Panama Canal on
June 14, 1973.

In reality the crew stayed one day at Punta Escoces, which included
a visit to the local village. On June 9 they moved on, beating hard to
windward between the mainland and offshore islands, to Sasardi. The
log says they spent a hot and humid week at Sasardi. An entry for June
11 says, "E. F. [Eric Freeborne] is trying to get to Panama today to get
an engine and stores." It doesn't say how he planned to accomplish such
a feat, since there is no road from the village to the outside world.

While Eric Freeborne made his way to civilization, probably by
coastal freighter, Tristan and Carlos spent the week doing odd jobs on
the boat. Somehow Freeborne made the round trip to Colón in six days.
He returned on the afternoon of June 16 with a new four-horsepower
Johnson outboard motor. After cruising sedately along the Mulatas archipelago, exploring the world of the Cuna Indians, *Sea Dart* passed
through the breakwater to enter Panama's Canal Zone on the afternoon
of Sunday, July 8. Moored to a buoy in the Flatts anchorage, she was
measured for her canal transit, and Tristan received a vaccination. He
doesn't say which one.

The canal transit, which Tristan would one day falsely use to claim a record for the first boat to sail through without engine power, is recorded in the log as follows:

> Saturday, July 14, 1973: The move through Panama is postponed until tomorrow.

> July 15: 06:00 Slipped with 4 line-handlers and Pilot.
>   08:00 Cleared Gatun Locks. Under all sail and engine.
>   16:00 At Pedro Miguel Locks.
>   18:45 Tied up at Balboa Y.C. to mooring buoy.

At the bottom of the page a handwritten note records the new engine's hours at twenty. The log does not tell us who the line handlers were or whether Eric and Carlos were among them. Neither man is mentioned after arriving at Panama.

Sea Dart remained at Balboa for thirteen days. During that time Tristan purchased and loaded stores and ordered new sails. On July 29 he sailed the eight miles to Taboga Island to careen *Sea Dart* in order to prepare her for the long haul down the Pacific Ocean. After cleaning *Sea Dart*'s hull and applying antifouling paint, he sailed back to Balboa on August 10 to collect his new sails.

Although the log is not explicit about when they joined, Tristan had young male companions on the hard slog south against the Humboldt Current, all the way from Panama to Callao, Peru. One of the early crew was an Englishman, Derek Kerley. The other was Peter Dieterle. Their job was to help Tristan get his boat from Panama down the Pacific coast of Colombia to Esmeraldas in Ecuador.

At 11:00 A.M. on Saturday, September 8, *Sea Dart* slipped her mooring and left the Panama Canal Zone. For six and a half hours Tristan was forced to beat to windward, passing and being passed by numerous general cargo and container ships inbound for Panama and outbound for the Pacific. A relieved crew dropped anchor by Taboga pier at 5:30 P.M.

Constantly beating into southerly winds, with visibility often limited by rain, Tristan found time to catch an eighty-pound hammer-head shark. One week out of Taboga *Sea Dart* passed Point San Francisco Solano, a peninsula with rocks extending well out to sea. It's probable that *Sea Dart* hit one or more of the half-submerged rocks. Two hours later Tristan dropped anchor in four fathoms of water, half a mile from shore in Solano Bay, off Mutis. He cleared into Colombia, noting that the port captain was courteous and reasonable.

With a seabed of hard-packed sand beneath the keel, Tristan moved *Sea Dart* closer in, to anchor within eighty yards of the high-water mark. As the tide ebbed the cutter gradually settled until she sat level on her keels for inspection, her hull drying in the sun. Tristan was furious to find two blades missing from the propeller and patches of antifouling paint rubbed off from hitting the rocks. He repainted the bottom where necessary and ordered two more propellers from a local distributor, which arrived eight days later.

While he waited for the propellers, Tristan kept himself and his crew busy cleaning the boat inside and out. They also rubbed down and painted scuffed areas in the cockpit. When the chores ran out he wrote a couple of articles for boating magazines—one, title unknown, for *Sail* was rejected, as was an idea for *National Geographic.* "On the Spanish Main" went to *Motor Boat and Yachting,* where it was accepted. He also submitted a story on dairy farming along the Amazon to *Yachting World.* In addition he wrote letters to acquaintances, including one to Arthur Cohen referring to *Barbara*'s logbooks.

I'm a bit worried about Barbara*'s logs which I had sent to you from St. Vincent [Bequia] way back at the end of April, for I had a letter from Blackheath, London, when passing through the Panama Canal and they said they hadn't received them from you yet. Donald Copeman is yelling for them as he wants to include some extracts in* Indian Ocean Saga. *Could you please let me know the situation? I left them with Nolly Simmons to post, but he's in Canada now and I won't be able to contact him until Christmas. It is possible that, being West Indian, he didn't post them . . . in which case they must still be at his house.*

This letter smacks of a lie. At the end of April Tristan was approaching Cartagena, Colombia. He was not in St. Vincent. Also, on one line he tells Arthur he sent the logs to him. On another he says he left them with a man named Nolly Simmons to post. One wonders why Tristan would consider sending the logbooks on such a circuitous route, from the southeastern Caribbean to a London publisher via Arthur Cohen in Connecticut. Certainly Arthur Cohen never received the logs. In fact, they remained in Tristan's possession until the summer of 1983, when he sent them to his friend Wally Herbert in England for safekeeping. The letter continues to speak of Tristan's plans for the future.

> *With luck I expect to arrive in Mollendo, Peru, about the end of October and from thence haul* Sea Dart *over the Andes to Lake Titicaca. . . . There I hope to find a nice hut or something ashore and write* South American Saga. *What I'll do after that I'm not quite sure. A Jap rounded the Horn last year in a 25 footer, yawl rigged and, if the boat is in decent shape, I may try to top the rising sun. On the other hand, if my stuff [writing] sells, and I can raise the wherewithal, I may try to cross over Bolivia with* Sea Dart *and emerge from the River Platte. Failing that, if things get tight, I'll cross to New Zealand and Australia to earn some living.*

He noted that several of his articles on the West Indies and Colombia had been accepted for publication and that *Sail* magazine in Boston was considering his Amazon features. After discussing the local people of Colombia's Pacific coast he wrote, "Donald Copeman was at a dinner given by the Royal Cruising Club and he wrote me that everyone was tickled pink at the idea of getting a *vertical* record, whilst everyone else is whizzing round and round the oceans. I guess by the time I get to the Dead Sea I shall just about be ready to pack it all up and go into farming or driving a steam roller!"

Obviously, if he had truly embarked on a mission to achieve a vertical sailing record, via Lake Titicaca and the Dead Sea, he was not in any hurry—as the vagueness regarding his future course testifies.

That was almost the last time Tristan mentioned *Indian Ocean Saga*. It apparently was rejected by the publisher. Undeterred, and hopeful of finding a publisher one day, Tristan continued writing a long book of his adventures, adding the Amazon and *Sea Dart*'s South American odyssey to the earlier tales. We know he fictionalized parts of *Indian Ocean Saga*; consequently we can assume he did the same with the rest of the story. *A Sailor's Odyssey*, the planned trilogy, appears to have died a natural death, although parts of it eventually appeared in *The Incredible Voyage*.

Patience Wales, then managing editor of *Sail*, recalled his first submissions to her as dreadful. But, she added, his cover letters were wonderful. She advised him not to write what he regarded as articles; rather, she said, "write me a long letter and tell me what you are doing." The advice worked. Tristan's next attempt for *Sail* would make the grade.

In Solano Bay Tristan performed a fifty-hour engine check and fitted a stainless steel forestay on the bowsprit before weighing anchor on September 25, 1973.

Sea Dart continued beating relentlessly to the southwest. Staying mostly within sight of the landmass, rarely much farther out, she plowed on—through heavy rain on some days, as well as under light winds. Crossing a tidal rip under motor to gain an additional five miles of sea room, the boat hit a floating tree trunk. At 2:30 P.M. on Monday, October 1, *Sea Dart* anchored in a bay off the Colombian convict colony of Gorgona Island. Not allowed to land, Tristan made use of a rainy day on the hook by repairing seams on the genoa and staysails. The collision with the tree trunk had loosened the bowsprit stem, so he made temporary repairs with large screws.

The published version of this part of the voyage does not mention a stop in Solano Bay. It also, once again, fails to mention the crew on board. And its account of the damage to the bowsprit is much more exciting than hitting something as mundane as a drifting tree trunk. Tristan the author had collisions at sea with whales, not trees. On this fictional occasion, in the early morning hours during a storm, the collision capsized *Sea Dart*. Tristan then managed to spin the routine stop off Gorgona Island into five pages of adventure in *The Incredible Voyage*. First he had to clear up the mess created by the capsize. Then, to captivate his readers, he conjured up an army of uniforms with rifles and handguns, as well as hundreds of prisoners who pointlessly carried rocks from one end of the beach to the other and back again—all day long.

On October 3, 1973, *Sea Dart* weighed anchor at 7:00 A.M. She spent all morning beating hard to windward against steep seas and had to fight a strong north-flowing current off Viudo Rock. The struggle continued throughout that day and night. At noon on October 4 she was five miles north-northwest of Pasa Caballos lighthouse. By daybreak on the fifth, in choppy seas, she was in sight of Gallo Island. There was no letup. The seas remained choppy all day and night as *Sea Dart* pounded the waves. At midnight she passed Cape Manglares, the final promontory in Colombia and entered Ancón de Sardinas Bay. For the rest of that night she stood off in heavy seas under staysail and main, waiting for daylight. *Sea Dart* entered the harbor at Esmeraldas, Ecuador, and at 9:30 A.M. on October 7 she anchored close to the port captain's office. She had been at sea four days and two and a half hours since leaving Gorgona.

Tristan did not like one of his crew and said it bluntly in the log for October 8, 1973. "Many problems with Derek Kerley of Poole, who shows his true colours. A lazy coward. The son of a bitch screwed me for $20.00." We can assume Kerley left soon after arriving in Esmeraldas. Ernst Kraft, a young Dutchman who had been working in Peru and Bolivia for two years, took his place.

The blond Kraft, who, *Sea Dart*'s log notes, joined the boat on October 19, can be seen in later photographs showing *Sea Dart* being lowered into Lake Titicaca at Puno. *Sea Dart* stayed in Esmeraldas until October 26. During the prolonged stay of almost three weeks, Tristan moved her to the foreshore where she could safely take the ground at low tide. "Mud, mud, mud!" he scribbled happily in the log. After repairing the bowsprit, Tristan went inland to Quito to pay a call on the British ambassador while Peter Dieterle cleaned out the galley. On October 18 Peter left the crew. "A fairly good lad, but very slow," Tristan noted.

Busy though he may have been at sea, in port the crew certainly gave Tristan time to pursue his writing. From Esmeraldas he sent articles and photographs to three publications in the United States and United Kingdom. Tristan's life at sea, with no stable home base, meant he always had to wait months, sometimes a year or two, before learning whether his articles had been published. The same was true for receiving payment. British magazines deposited his checks directly into his London bank account. Once he became published in magazines in the United States and Australia, they sent payment to whichever poste restante or British consulate he had recommended.

Tristan's hardy adventurous embellishments aside, the truncated book version of the brutal haul south against wind and current fails to do justice to *Sea Dart*'s stellar performance or to his own seamanship. Instead of beating nonstop from Panama to Salinas by detouring far out on the Pacific, the courageous little cutter fought her way south from one port to another. That pattern would be repeated all the way to Callao.

Clearing Esmeraldas in the early afternoon of October 26, with the wind out of the southwest at four to five knots, Tristan set his course to pass north of Galera Point. Under main and genoa, with *Sea Dart* performing well, they continued the punishing voyage, beating hard all the way. The pounding went on throughout that night, with one change to starboard tack, recorded at 3:00 A.M. Galera Point came in sight at 9:00 A.M. The day was overcast with no hint of sunshine, and the wind blew cold from dawn to dusk. At 9:00 P.M. Tristan tacked to port. No silvery moonlight brightened the crew's passage. The cold wind created steep gray seas that made life miserable for all on board, whether on watch or resting below. *Sea Dart* creaked and groaned, complaining every step of the way yet never faltering. In the early hours of Sunday,

October 28, Tristan tacked once more to starboard. Nine hours later, on another rough, cold day, *Sea Dart* crossed the equator. Her logbook records that she had sailed a thousand miles from Balboa.

With both crew and boat desperately in need of a rest, Tristan went to anchor at 5:30 P.M., due east of Ballena Point, 10′ south of the equator, and settled in for a long sleep. At 7:00 A.M. they weighed anchor again and set course for Cape Pasado. The Pacific Ocean refused to live up to its placid name. Heavy seas seemed determined to block *Sea Dart's* southerly progress. Midday saw them a little to the southwest of Borracho. Another afternoon of hard sailing in unpleasant waves took them abeam of Cape Pasado, with Caráquez Bay due east of their position. Tristan altered course for Manta.

Conditions must have been difficult to say the least. That night, fighting rolling waves, a northbound current, and winds out of the southwest at five to six knots, *Sea Dart* gained some ground, but only just. For the past twenty-four hours she had covered a pitiful sixty-eight miles. A disappointed Tristan noted in the log: "Must have been set back all night. At 07:00 only ten miles on!"

"Beating! Beating! Beating!" Tristan wrote at the top of one page. The rest of the log for Tuesday, October 30, 1973, tells the cryptic story of another wearying day off the coast of Ecuador: "Noon—abreast Churapato. 13:30 sighted Manta. Wind rising to 25 knots. By 14:00 up to gale force. Beat hard on full main and staysail. 15:30 entered [Manta] to anchor by church."

The following day Tristan moved *Sea Dart* to the yacht club inside the fishing harbor, and there he stayed for a week. There is no mention of his or the crew's activities in the log for those seven days. We can only assume they took a well-earned rest. The next entry is for November 8: "Wind southerly at three knots. 05:30, slipped. Under working sail and engine to Punta San Mateo. Sea fairly choppy. Full and by."

Progress against the Humboldt Current continued to be slow. At noon they were due west of Cape San Lorenzo, having covered no more than fifteen miles. By late afternoon they had only reached a point just south-southwest of Canoa Point. After another night of hard beating they were a little west of Salango Island, where they took time to clean the boat. At dusk Puerto La Liberdad came in sight, but not quite within reach. They spent all night beating up to Santa Elena Peninsula, sighting the light at 3:30 A.M.—due south of their position. Tristan dropped anchor off Salinas beach at 7:00 A.M. Four hours later he moved four miles southeast to Liberdad, but the heavy swell made his anchorage uncomfortable. He returned to Salinas at 3:00 P.M. Thirty-five days had passed since they left Gorgona, of which nineteen days and nights had been spent in port, plus one night at anchor. A rather different story from his reported "twenty-eight days of continuous hammering into the wind, day and night."

Sea Dart spent ten days in Salinas, although—once again—we know little about what the crew did during that time. The log tells that they straightened *Sea Dart*'s mast again; that they met the U.S.-registered catamaran *Illusion*; and that Jack Leeper of the Anchor Restaurant made roast beef. Also, "Tony Lichfield's wife gave us a fruit cake. So we will eat well."

On November 20, 1973, *Sea Dart* weighed anchor at 6:30 A.M. This was the beginning of a hard beat across the Gulf of Guayaquil. As usual the wind was out of the south-southwest, seas sharp. All day and all night the boat plowed south, her bowsprit alternately pointing at the sky and the sea. The crew was exhausted by the constant fore-and-aft motion, accentuated by rolling from port to starboard. At daybreak on November 21 the wind dropped. Tristan fired up the motor and went looking for a breeze. He found it ten miles to the southwest. His seaman's instinct once again proved accurate.

By 9:30 A.M. they were on a "broad run" with the wind out of the northwest for a change, blowing at force 2. A happier Tristan wrote in the log, "Well. Well. Sea easing." His joy proved premature. By early afternoon *Sea Dart* sailed close-hauled again, battling that same old south-southwesterly wind, which gradually increased in strength from force 3 to 5, then up to 6. The sea hammered them all night long. By dawn they had covered only fifty-three miles, an increase of a little more than two miles over the previous twenty-four hours.

With Cape Blanco in sight to the south-southwest, the wind dropped briefly. At 9:00 A.M. they were close-hauled again on course to round Cape Blanco. Tristan was ecstatic. At last he had reached the Peruvian coast. Mollendo, however, was still many hundreds of miles to the south. Out in the offing, a fleet of Peruvian fishing boats kept *Sea Dart* distant company.

He may have reached Peru, but the elements had more torment for Tristan. With Cape Blanco due south at noon, the wind remained strong and dead against him. *Sea Dart* stood out to sea eleven miles and found a welcome change. The seas lessened; the Pacific blessed them with a good breeze, and the boat responded with enthusiasm. That night was cold, the air temperature dropping to about forty degrees Fahrenheit. The log recorded the sea temperature at a much warmer sixty-one degrees. In the morning Tristan discovered they had been set out a further ten miles to the west. Altering course to due east they again closed the coast, eventually sighting lights on land at dusk. At 10:30 P.M. they dropped anchor off Telegraph Point. There was little time to rest. For some reason, probably a heavy swell, they moved to the fishing port at 3:30 A.M. A few hours later, at 7:05 A.M., they moved again—this time to the main mole at Paita.

Entering *Sea Dart* and crew into Peru, obtaining a permit to travel to Lima, and clearing out of Paita proved frustrating. Tristan drew a diagram in his log to show the number of journeys he made between the police, the harbormaster's office, immigration, and the shipping agent. On his twentieth walk he finally made contact with the harbormaster himself. While Tristan paced from office to office, the crew performed a fifty-hour overhaul on the engine. Once he had the all-important permits in hand, Tristan chose not to linger in Paita. At 3:30 A.M.

on November 29 he weighed anchor and motored out, past Telegraph Point again. For two days they alternately sailed and motored as the wind dictated. Off Negra Point they sighted a pod of whales.

December 1 found *Sea Dart* beating along the coast in light winds under a warm sun. As dusk reduced visibility, Tristan prudently put more sea between his boat and the shoreline. His caution proved well founded. At 8:00 P.M., as they were on course for Lobos de Tierra Island, the wind failed altogether. Once again Tristan had to start the motor. Two hours later they sighted the island's light. At dawn, *Sea Dart*'s position was six miles southeast of Saena Point. Tristan decided to go in to top up his gasoline tanks. An added comment in the log says, "Sighted many big seals, albatross and pelicans."

At 10:00 A.M. *Sea Dart* passed northeast of Lobos de Tierra Island and entered Juanchuquita Bay, where she tied up alongside a fishing boat. Close by lay the wreck of a two-masted sailing ship, probably one that had played a part in the lucrative guano trade. The opportunity of stretching cramped legs on shore may have appealed to the crew, but the brief island call proved fruitless. There was no gasoline available. Back on board the captain wasted no more time. He immediately stood out to sea and set course for Pimentel. With little wind, no more than a southerly whisper, Tristan rigged his number two genoa as a large staysail.

The wind dropped again at 9:00 P.M. Even so, with two genoas pulling their weight, the going was better than it had been. *Sea Dart* stood off to the southwest. When the wind returned at 4:00 A.M. on December 2 her captain pointed his bowsprit due east, once again looking for the land. They spent that day and another night beating steadily toward the coast. The log complains of "light winds making slow sailing." The nights became colder. Daybreak must have come as a great relief each day, an opportunity for the crew members to warm themselves in the sunshine. On December 3 they shivered all morning under a thick overcast, waiting impatiently for the sun, which finally appeared in the early afternoon. That day they caught a six-pound dorado on a horsehair lure. Optimism begins to creep into the log on December 4. "Going fair all night. Stopped pounding at 22:00. Came about 23:00 to close shore. At 08:00 sighted shore and headed in. At noon ½ mile SW of Cherrepe Point. Trying the desert coast routine. It works."

Tristan's rules for sailing a continental desert shoreline on sunny days were simple: try to be about four miles off by 8:00 A.M. Head in as the sun rises and stick close to shore—say half a mile out. He warns to watch out for mountain deflection and to be ready at any time to come about and go hard to windward.

As *Sea Dart* worked south the sea temperature began to drop. On December 4 it was down to fifty-eight degrees Fahrenheit: not icy cold, but cooling down. Pacasmayo light came in sight at 4:00 P.M. *Sea Dart* continued beating all night under a bright, clear moon. Tristan noted the cockpit temperature had risen to a balmy sixty-two degrees Fahrenheit at 11:00 P.M.

A surprised entry began December 5. "At dawn find we are set out to west 15 miles! Estimate current NW 1½ knots. Standing in for convection winds." He continued, "Then we motor during quiet calms, usually from midnight to 06:00."

With only $10 left in the kitty, Tristan planned to go into Chimbote because it was within easy reach of Lima. In the capital city he would have been able to draw funds from his account at Lloyd's Bank in London. Weather conditions called for a different approach. Obviously using the outboard motor far more than anticipated, Tristan changed his mind about heading directly for Chimbote. The logbook's final entries for December 5 tell the story: "At noon ½ mile off huge breakers. Arcana Point coming up. 19:00 Wind failing. Bugger it! On motor—going in to Chicama. A slow haul against wind, currents and wash from fishing boats gets us in at 19:00. An uncomfortable anchorage, with a big swell rolling in."

Ashore the crew refueled and purchased fresh food. Before departure a tug somehow managed to bend *Sea Dart*'s long-suffering bowsprit. Then getting out at 6:00 A.M. on December 7 proved difficult. The anchor had fouled a sunken wreck. Once free they stood out to sea and into a dense fog. The day proved just how changeable conditions could be in the Humboldt Current, as witnessed by the log entry: "At 10:00 fog lifted and showed Macabi Island on port bow! Current is shoving me off 30 west! On engine at 11:00 in a flat calm. Steering 140 dead against current. Just before dusk sighted Mt. Campana bearing 048—which surely gives a south-going current. Anyway, I am going hell for leather on 125 to pick up Salaverry Lighthouse—if it's lit! At 01:00 [December 8] picked up Salaverry. Heading in fast before fog descends! Course 075! Entered harbour at 02:00. On main anchor with trip line. A thick fog came down 20 mins after we anchored!"

Salaverry roads did not suit Tristan. He found the anchorage uncomfortable. As with much of the coast, the incoming swells were almost certainly the problem. At 2:00 P.M. he weighed anchor and set a course of 185 degrees to take him clear of the Guañape Islands. Between Guañape and the shore *Sea Dart* encountered a strong northwest current and ran into more fog. A note written across the top of the logbook page, describing the voyage from Salaverry to Chimbote and beyond, complains, "Still beating hard against fickle headwinds and contrary currents with thick fogs." The log continues: "December 9th, winds light S.E. (of course). At 07:00 sighted Chao Island. Heading in. Current is definitely offshore. Clearing. Noon—Santa Island in sight, on range 145 M [magnetic]. 16:00 Cleared Santa Passage. 16:30 entered Chimbote Harbour."

Having reached Chimbote, Tristan was ready for another stretch ashore. Leaving Ernst in charge of *Sea Dart*, he traveled overland to Lima, presumably by bus, to collect funds—payments for articles submitted weeks or months before, and to visit the British embassy. He was gone five days.

Weighing anchor at 6:00 A.M. on December 15, and probably happy to be back at sea, Tristan set course to pass North Ferrol Island. Two hours later the fog closed in again. By 9:20 A.M. he was motoring once more. At 12:00 noon, the fog apparently gone, *Sea Dart* sailed a starboard tack—three miles east of Seal Island, where the crew saw many big seals and pelicans.

Sea Dart may not have been a greyhound of the seas, but she was determined. Slowly, mile by exhausting mile, she made her way south. At 10:00 A.M. she passed due west of Culebras. Another eighteen miles of beating against a coastal breeze and northbound current saw her enter Huarmey harbor, where she anchored at 3:00 P.M. The log notes that there was "lots of wind but [the] swell [was] not too bad." Tristan went ashore for gasoline.

Early next morning the crew rose early, preparing to depart before daybreak. At 6:00 A.M. they weighed anchor and set course to round Lagarto Head. Within fifteen minutes they were enveloped in thick fog, which lasted over an hour. As the gray veil slowly dispersed with the sun's return, *Sea Dart* headed south-southeast against a rough sea. Most of that day she spent beating hard to cross Gramadol Bay. By 4:00 P.M. Callejones Point stood due east. The wind dropped at midnight, only to be replaced by more thick fog at 3:00 A.M. Tristan crept on, hoping for a breeze. With the dawn *Sea Dart* headed to shore once more. He was pleased to find his dead-reckoning position was correct. He was three miles south-southeast of Supe and working against a northwesterly current running one to two knots. They dropped anchor in calm conditions in Supe Bay soon after 9:00 A.M. There, sheltered to a great extent from winds and currents, the crew cleaned a field of grass off *Sea Dart's* hull and gave the engine its latest fifty-hour check.

At 2:00 A.M. on Wednesday, December 19, 1973, *Sea Dart* crept cautiously out of the dark bay in a medium fog. As she rounded Tomás Point and headed south the fog became thicker. At 8:00 A.M., with daylight well advanced, visibility was no more than a hundred yards. Two hours later, two miles northwest of Baja Point, the fog began to clear. Salinas Point came and went over midday. Then the wind picked up a little, blowing from the south-southeast at force 2 to 3. They spent the afternoon beating hard while overhauling the outboard motor.

The wind began to die at 7:00 P.M. An hour later, when they needed it least, the just-serviced engine seized up. "Disaster strikes!" Tristan wrote, underlining the words. The log further notes that conditions were calm all night, though—not surprising without wind or engine—it was a struggle to keep moving. They must have been quite close to shore earlier because the log records that at 10:00 P.M. they lost the sound of the surf. They found a wind, too, for a brief note states, "Up 2nd jib." The log reports: "Thursday December 20th. Winds SE 1–2. 09:00 wind out of SE. Close hauled. 15:00 Into Playa Grande Bay. Dropped lunch hook, on 25 fathoms line as wind failed, but it rose again after a few minutes so carried on close hauled. I will try to make Ancon, but if not can fall back on Chancay if urgent. Beating along coast all night. Saw many huge (10 ft–16 ft) jelly fish, red, blue, green."

Tristan wrote about those monsters in *The Incredible Voyage.* Typically, he changed the location, to the Guañape Islands—which he actually passed on December 9, and he doubled the size of the jellyfish to twenty-five feet. The color too became a "scarlet red." Many years later, in *Encounters of a Wayward Sailor,* his final book, Tristan's overactive imagination returned to those jellyfish. On that occasion he remembered seeing a blood-red undulating mass with tentacles ten feet long waving threateningly around the creature's perimeter.

The final two days on the Pacific were a great improvement over the previous weeks of hard sailing. "Friday 21st. Wind calm at 04:00. Creeping south. Not quite as foggy. At 11:00 wind picked up (SSE-1) Fog and mist clearing over coast. Very light zephyrs all day. Rigged jury mizzen using storm jib. [This is the first indication of damage to the mizzen sail.] 17:00 Identified Isla Grande de Pescadores ahead. 21:00 South of Isla Grande. Sighted Aero Beacon at Lima Airport. Wind steady force 2. Making good [time]. Midnight, approximately one mile SW of Punta Pancha. Heading SW."

The cold facts of the log belie the excitement *Sea Dart*'s crew must have felt. Callao and Lima were almost in sight. The Pacific ordeal was nearly over. Originally Tristan had planned to continue as far as Mollendo, nearly five hundred nautical miles to the south of Callao. From there he would have had a relatively short overland journey over the Andes to Lake Titicaca. But the exhausting weeks against the Humboldt Current appear to have changed his mind: "December 22nd. 06:00 Heading SSE. 06:30 Calculated position 12 S 77 20′ W. Course 105. 12:00 approximately 6 miles NNW of Isla San Lorenzo. Very weak zephyrs. Working hard. 14:00 breeze improving. 15:00 Yacht *Calypso* met us and welcomed. Working into Callao Port and at 18:15 [went] to anchor at Yacht Club."

In *The Incredible Voyage* a tired and lonely sailor was met not only by *Calypso*, but also by the flagship of the Peruvian yacht club, which towed *Sea Dart* into port. The Johnson outboard motor, Tristan said, was still in its original wrapping, having never been used. One assumes that Tristan's false declaration, that he did not have an engine on *Sea Dart*, was made to lend authenticity to his claim of making the first transit of the Panama Canal under sail alone, and to enhance the difficulties of his voyage off the west coast of South America. When he wrote the book he could hardly have forgotten the two outboard motors that gave him so much trouble. Either way, Tristan and *Sea Dart*, with considerable help from others, had completed stage two of their incredible voyage.

After the many flagrant distortions in *The Incredible Voyage*, Tristan went on to tell his readers he arrived in Callao at 6:15 P.M. on the twenty-fourth of December. He loved to make use of internationally recognized festive occasions: Christmas Eve and New Year's Eve were his favorites. Three years before, he had already claimed in his book, *Barbara* sat on a large truck outside an inn in Bethlehem on Christmas Eve. At the end of his voyage to Callao, he reminded his readers of that fictional occasion when he told of sleeping contentedly aboard *Sea Dart* by the wharf at Callao and remembering a previous Christmas Eve.

CHAPTER 10

Reaching for the Stars

On December 23 Tristan landed the damaged engine in Callao for repairs. While ashore he met with the port agent to arrange for haulout. Although there are few references to crew in *Sea Dart*'s log, we know Ernst Kraft sailed with him on the long passage from Esmeraldas to Callao. There obviously was one other person on board, at least for some of the voyage. A note in the log for December 23 reads, "Paid E & S $1,000 advance on amount due." On the twenty-seventh another note, in pencil, comments, "Paid E $650 off amount due. I owe E now $12 US."

The crew unstepped *Sea Dart*'s mast on December 26 and hauled her out with the help of the yacht club crane. A long voyage was over; a rough ride lay ahead. Tristan always claimed he took *Sea Dart* across Peru without a permit. In other words, he smuggled her in: "And all the time *Sea Dart* sat on the truck, contraband, smuggled, paperless, probably being searched for high and low right now by the Peruvian customs service!" That tale was told for effect and to explain why he did not return to the Pacific through Peru after sailing on Lake Titicaca.

The version of events between Christmas Eve and New Year's Day as told in *The Incredible Voyage* is exciting. The players are Tristan and a truck driver, Salomon, plus Salomon's argumentive bowler-hatted girlfriend. One can't help urging Tristan and Salomon on, spurring them to achieve the impossible as they smuggle a rickety old truck loaded with its illicit cargo of an oceangoing cutter, past customs and up into the Andes to the highest navigable lake in the world. It's a grand story. It might even be believable but for a few inconsistencies.

Tristan described *Sea Dart* loaded on the bed of the truck facing forward, with the bowsprit hanging over the cab, but black-and-white photographs in the same book clearly show the transom facing the cab and the bow pointing astern. Another photograph, published in *El Pueblo*, a newspaper from Arequipa, shows *Sea Dart* with her bow over the rear of the truck. In that picture are four Peruvians and, the accompanying article advises, "Ernesto Kraft—a Dutch sailor aged 21 years."

Considering Tristan's claim of having smuggled *Sea Dart* into Peru, the photo and article in *El Pueblo*, and a subsequent television appearance in Arequipa, would surely have alerted the authorities to his presence.

The claim to have smuggled *Sea Dart* into Peru also falls apart with a glance at a Spanish document reproduced in *The Incredible Voyage*. Tristan's caption in English emphatically states: "Permission to enter Peru, not a customs document, just permission, and to navigate on Lake Titicaca." Apparently Tristan thought none of his English-speaking readers could read Spanish. Halfway down the page that same permit advises, "Temporary importation certificate number 150 issued 28 December 1973 for sailboat *Sea Dart.*" *Sea Dart*, no matter what Tristan wrote, was in Peru legally. Future tales of a price on her skipper's head ($1,000, he claimed) for smuggling her into the country are untrue. *Sea Dart*'s log for December 27 confirms the permit: "Spent a lot of time in various offices getting permission to cross Peru. Eventually Mr. Goodwin, of Voll & Co., arranged temporary import license. Also much chasing about re-transport."

With all official paperwork in hand and transport arranged, everything was ready for the overland drive to the Andean heights. The journey was not a comfortable one. The log continues with the true story:

Truck No: 5-13 (44-2) owner Salomon Aragon, with co-driver Hector
Bedregal, loaded on Wednesday 2nd January [1974] and left YCP at
12 midday. Height of load was 13′ 4″. The coast road to Arequipa was
fairly smooth, but many hair-pins. Much curiosity. At Arequipa we
were received by Alcade [the mayor] on January 4th and appeared
on TV Channel 6. On Saturday 5th at 03:00 we left Arequipa and
started the long haul up the un-made mountain track 300 kilometers to Juliaca, where a good road goes 40 k to Puno. We passed
many crosses and wrecks [of vehicles] on the precipitous passes. Lla-
mas and Indians on the Altiplano. Snow covered crests. Mountain
sickness. Jolting truck. Many stops. At long last at 7 pm by the light
of a nearly full moon—saw the lake. Parked in Plaza de Armas.
Again much curiosity. Sunday—no place open.

Thus *Sea Dart* did not arrive at the shores of the lake on New Year's
Eve as reported in *The Incredible Voyage.* She was still on the jetty in
Callao at that time. And she was not launched on Titicaca on January 1, 1974. As the log tells us, the boat arrived in Puno on January 5. It
was another two days before Tristan received permission to off-load
her—and then only onto a railway siding. *Sea Dart* finally wet her bottom in Lake Titicaca on January 12. Tristan made use of an old steamer
close by to step the mast. With that accomplished, *Sea Dart* was ready to
sail on the highest navigable body of water in the world—and achieve
one half of a world record.

With *Sea Dart* afloat on the lake at last, Tristan told his readers
about his desperate need to hide himself and his boat from the eyes of
Peruvian customs authorities. That $1,000 "price" on his head haunted
him. He said he slipped out of Puno in the dark, sculling his boat
silently so as not to be seen or heard. It's an exciting lead-in to his adventures on Lake Titicaca, but it is pure fiction.

For the next seven and a half months Tristan half-heartedly explored parts of Lake Titicaca. He said that there were no charts of the
lake, so he set out to survey it and draw his own: an ill-considered statement, since the Peruvian and Bolivian navies both had ships on the lake

and there were ferries and steamers, all of which would surely require navigational charts. Perhaps to support his claim, *Sea Dart*'s logbook contains thirty sketch maps of various aspects of the lake.

On crossing into Bolivia he wrote an insulting account of meeting members of the Bolivian Yacht Club. He described the Bolivian yachtsmen: "All looking very German, with close-cropped heads, rimless glasses . . . and the blue-peaked caps so beloved by Teutons." The yacht club, he wrote, was surrounded by a chain-link fence topped by half a dozen strands of barbed wire. Adding to the formidable security precautions, he produced two armed and uniformed patrolmen with "huge German police dogs." It didn't take long for Tristan to massage the scene into a coarse verbal contest, based on World War II, between himself and the local sailors. His words would come back at him a few years later.

Robert J. Austin was appointed to the American embassy in La Paz as a political officer in 1979, only six years after Tristan was there. During his two-year stay he purchased a twenty-seven-foot German-built sailboat to cruise Lake Titicaca. He found Tristan's book *The Incredible Voyage* so imbued with fiction as to be useless as a guidebook to the lake. In 1982 Austin would challenge Tristan's report of his Lake Titicaca travels in a strong letter to Jones.

That fictional theme, so loosely based on the facts, runs right through *Sea Dart*'s travels, not just on the Pacific coast of South America or on Lake Titicaca. It continues to haunt the gallant little cutter's overland journey to the Brazilian frontier and down the Paraguay and Paraná Rivers to Buenos Aires. Little of what Tristan wrote in *The Incredible Voyage* resembles the original entries in *Sea Dart*'s logbook.

Ernst Kraft left *Sea Dart*, probably soon after she was launched on Titicaca. For a while Tristan may have sailed alone, although he occasionally took new acquaintances out for a day. At some point he took on a new crew member who was apparently not suitable. On March 17, in

Bolivian waters, the log reports, "Having problems with D. He will go at Guaqui."

For five of his seven and a half months at Titicaca Tristan lived ashore, in two rented rooms in Suriqui, Bolivia. Using the accommodations as a base for writing, he sailed regularly, though only on short excursions, rarely more than a dozen miles a day. Continuing to work on his book manuscript and stories for magazines, he sold a series of "nonfiction" articles—later proved to be almost as much fiction as fact—to *Motor Boat and Yachting*. One, "Bringing the Ocean to Bolivia," mentions that he had drawn what he believed to be the first sailing chart of the lake. He also sent two articles to *Sail* magazine, presumably in the form of long letters, as Patience Wales had suggested. Both were accepted. "The Longest Haul," about the recently completed voyage against the Humboldt Current, would be published in September 1974. The following issue contained "A Sea to Myself," tales of sailing on Lake Titicaca.

Sometime during Tristan's sojourn on and near Titicaca, Edwin Mejia joined him. Edwin, an eighteen-year-old Bolivian, makes his first appearance in the log on Thursday, August 29, when *Sea Dart* was loaded on a truck in La Paz waiting to be driven through the mountains to Cochabamba, the last major city in the Bolivian Andes before the Gran Chaco desert. "Edwin off at 8:00 am. I to Embassy and collected motor. No sign Edwin so took off mid-day. After very hairy haul across Oriental Andes arrived Cochabamba about midnight."

Huanapaco, the Quechua Indian who features so heavily in *The Incredible Voyage* from Lake Titicaca to Buenos Aires, did not exist. The photograph of "Huanapaco" wearing a *Sea Dart* T-shirt in *The Incredible Voyage* is actually a picture of Edwin, on whom his character was based. Edwin traveled with Tristan as far as Asunción, Paraguay. The tardy Edwin caught up with *Sea Dart* in Cochabamba's city center. Tristan noted with wry humor, no doubt referring to his leaving his crew unannounced in La Paz, "He will have to be shook up."

The truck left Cochabamba at 8:00 A.M. and followed a rough road, up and over the Siberia Pass through thick fog to Santa Cruz, where they arrived at 9:30 P.M. There Tristan had to wait for funds from London and for clearance to enter Brazil from that country's consul. He and Edwin lived on the boat, perched on its keels in the station yard, and did not enjoy the weeklong stay in the desert city. "[It's] hot, dusty, dirty, poor, crowded, what a place. . . . More than a week here will be a nightmare!" He later moaned, "The Station Master at Santa Cruz is one of the most unpleasant men I have ever met."

With *Sea Dart* safely aboard, the train for the Bolivia–Brazil frontier departed Santa Cruz at 8:00 P.M. on Saturday, September 7. Throughout the night, the next day, and another night, the train rumbled across the hot and dusty Gran Chaco. Sitting on a flatbed railcar beside the carefully chocked and secured *Sea Dart*, Tristan and Edwin had a miserable journey. After such a ride, arriving in Puerto Suárez must have been a great relief, in spite of the return to humidity. Crew and boat cleared outward Bolivian customs on September 9.

Tristan wrote a bizarre account of the trials of the next few weeks in *The Incredible Voyage*, much of it reading like another story out of a boy's adventure magazine from the 1950s. For a description of leaving Puerto Suárez for the Paraguay River he delved deep into his youthful memories. With no alternative, he said, he and his helper commenced hauling the boat through thick jungle to the river. Then came a tale of great heroism as he and Huanapaco braved poisonous snakes while hacking their way with machete and ax through sixteen miles of almost impenetrable jungle. At night, shut up in *Sea Dart*'s stifling little cabin, they avoided the danger of vampire bats. There was more to come. Diurnal and nocturnal torments did not end with the ultimate arrival at the riverbank after twenty-one terrible days. The hard-pressed pair then had to get their charge down to the river, nearly forty feet below them. It took another eight days for the intrepid adventurers to slash through foliage and carve a ramp to the water.

Tristan wasn't finished. With the bit firmly between his teeth, he then inflicted additional suffering on himself and poor Huanapaco as they constantly got lost in the maze of narrow dead-end channels of the Paraguay River's tributaries in the green hell of the Mato Grosso. The trials and tribulations of those weeks seem as exhausting to read as to experience.

Actually, Tristan did not have to manhandle his boat through a jungle. A sketch map he drew on a blank page in the logbook shows the Brazilian border town of Corumbá. The Paraguay River flows past its front door, and a side stream flows east into Lake Caceres, which shares part of its shoreline with Puerto Suárez. Published maps of the region show identical features. Tristan's sketch even has an arrow pointing along the waterway to Puerto Suárez. We can safely assume that *Sea Dart* could have sailed from Puerto Suárez to Corumbá in a few hours. Tristan, however, had paid to take his boat by train all the way to Corumbá, and take the train he would. On September 12 he did just that. *Sea Dart*'s train pulled into Corumbá station in the middle of the evening. She had reached Brazil, and she was only a short distance from the naval base beside the river. The log makes interesting reading: "Mon. 16th Sept. To Naval Base and Port Captain early. Feet very sore— hot day. No help. Finally got Alcaldia to send crane and found a truck, which first took SD [Sea Dart] to a rough shore, finally to Porto Principal for $50!" The crane must have lowered *Sea Dart* into the river, because under the same date Tristan wrote, "Afloat again! We don't seem to take water."

Considering her size, the valiant *Sea Dart* had withstood the battering of her overland experiences on trucks and trains extremely well. On September 17 the crew stepped the mast and bent on her sails. While waiting for more money to arrive they painted the toe rails and deck surfaces and gave the galley and cabin a thorough cleaning. In the evenings they fished for piranha, catching ten for supper one night. Tristan complained of the mosquitoes after dark. Besides cleaning with

Edwin, Tristan took care of the paperwork and passport stamps necessary to get them on their way again. Still, he was bored and frustrated. Even occasional lunches with a new friend, Fernando Carneiro, failed to cheer him up. "V. Depressed. Hot," he wrote in the log.

With time on his hands, Tristan wrote "Grueling Haul to the Green Hell," one of a handful of articles based on *Sea Dart*'s fictional trials en route to Brazil. When the long-awaited payment for a previous article arrived, $130 Australian, a disgruntled Tristan complained, "Aussie dollar just devalued." Nothing less than being back under sail would improve his mood. At noon on October 1 they set sail to pass the naval base, running with the current at about six knots. Four hours later, with a headwind bucking the current, Tristan started the motor. A few hours later it overheated. They went to anchor and cleaned the sparkplugs. A laconic note in the log, "[I] think it works. If not—long, slow trip."

For the next couple of days *Sea Dart* sailed downstream on the wide river, when necessary tacking back and forth across the current against the unfavorable wind. The book description of constantly getting lost in the many small channels and creeks of the Mato Grosso can be discounted. Equally, the rapids of Paso de Moros, which featured in an exciting anecdote in *The Incredible Voyage*, effectively blocking the Paraguay River with a wall of white water just upstream from Coimbra, do not seem to have been charted on any maps, and they also failed to rate a mention in *Sea Dart*'s logbook.

On October 2 *Sea Dart* weighed anchor at 6:30 A.M. to spend the day under sail, tacking back and forth across the river against a strong headwind and under a scorching sun. Tristan had his shirt off too long and suffered severe sunburn to his back. By 5:30 P.M., tired and hot, they went to anchor for a few hours in sight of Manga. The motor sounded rough again, worrying Tristan. Guessing he would need it later, he chose to sail until he could get it fixed properly. Under way again at 2:00 A.M., to make use of the cooler temperatures of the night, they drifted downstream with the current. Dawn brought a favorable wind, out of the northeast. For a change they had a good day of running free, which even the heat could not ruin. As the light faded they anchored for the night, tired but content. The log reads: "Friday 4th Oct. 07:00 Anchor aweigh. Strong SW wind raising a sea way. Beat under reefed main and stays'l. At 11:00 heavy rain. Cold! At 13:30 anchored under 200 yr old fort at Coimbra, a military town. Officers very hospitable. Doctor gave me insect repellent and mechanic fixed engine where cooling pump had been blocked."

The officers did indeed offer their hospitality. Before *Sea Dart* left early next morning, the crew received an invitation to breakfast in the officers' mess. For six and a half days *Sea Dart* then sailed and motored downstream through southern Brazil. Crossing the frontier at noon on October 11, they had another two days of traveling through Paraguay before reaching Concepción, the first opportunity of clearing into that country. The logbook tells us Tristan and Edwin were not getting along well by this time. On Monday, October 14, after clearing customs, Tristan wrote: "Am having problems with Edwin. He is very reluctant to get into a swing in cleaning. Dirty, slow & . . ."—here a few words are carefully crossed out under multiple lines of ink, making them illegible. Tristan continued with, "I had a showdown and told him he must leave in Asunción. I will pay his fare back [to La Paz]. That leaves me a lot freer financially. We are both weary with the heat & strain of voyaging rapidly, so I must be careful to keep my cool."

Evidently he was able to keep his temper, although whether Edwin left *Sea Dart* in Asunción is not made clear: his name never occurs again in the log. There are, however, occasions when "we" is used, most noticeably on arrival in San Nicolás, Argentina.

Five days out of Concepción *Sea Dart* tied up at Club Náutico in Asunción. Tristan stayed there for one month. All we know of his true activities is recorded in the log, two notations only: "Made several sail trips in Asunción Bay. Including one to Fray Bentos factory, where Mr.

Lynn gave me a box of corned beef." Then, "Painted sides and galley and inside coach roof."

For the rest, we can only assume that Tristan spent his time writing articles for magazines and exploring the city and the waterfront bars. Among his written works was "Downhill All the Way," a pseudofactual account of the recent river voyage from Corumbá. Like many of his other adventure articles, it was published in Britain by *Motor Boat and Yachting*. And he sent "Where the Prairie and Ocean Meet—Cruising down the Paraguay River" to *Sail*, which accepted it for a 1975 issue.

We can certainly discount his story in *The Incredible Voyage* of being visited on *Sea Dart* by President Alfredo Stroessner and his booted bullyboys. Equally, we can ignore the many tedious references to arrests by security police and other authorities that pepper that book and a later one. For some reason, perhaps because he saw the newspaper report of his being jailed in Bogotá, Tristan seemed to think his readers would be fascinated by tales of incarceration at gunpoint in each country en route. The only time Tristan went to jail during his two years in South America was in Bogotá, and that occasion is unlikely to have been quite as hellish as he so enthusiastically described it.

Leaving Asunción on November 20, 1974, *Sea Dart* sailed south all morning. At midday the wind swung to the south and heavy rain began to fall. After covering fifty-one miles for the day, Tristan dropped anchor at 7:00 P.M. opposite Paragi Island and settled down for the night. A thick, cold fog delayed departure for one hour at daybreak. Another long day, the last in Paraguay, ended with Tristan attending a fiesta of sorts. He wasn't overly impressed with the occasion. "Everyone just sat and looked at each other," he reported.

Approaching Formosa on the west bank of the Paraguay River, the northern port of entry into Argentina, *Sea Dart* ran aground about eight miles upstream. Fortunately the riverbed was mud, so a little effort with a pole pushed the boat off safely. About Formosa Tristan complained, "a terribly noisy place at night & mosquitoes & heat make life a misery."

Tropical rain fell hard to mark the final seventy miles before reaching the vast Paraná River. At the confluence Tristan followed the buoyed channel to Corrientes, where he tied up to the landing stage and took a well-earned rest of two nights and one day. There too he found help from the military. The Argentine navy donated charts of the river as far as Esquina, some two hundred statute miles to the south.

Life on the big river proved far more complicated for the crew of a small sailboat than had life on the relatively peaceful Paraguay River. The wind gusted hard from the south, creating an unpleasant chop in the narrow shipping channel as *Sea Dart* beat against wind and incoming tide. "Sunday December 1st, 07:00. Slipped but fierce southerly at 07:10 raised such bad sea forced a return. 08:00 slipped. Under power (sail when able) again threading against nasty chop. At 15:30 reached Lavalle where anchored alongside cliff, very fed up and tired."

On the two-day run to Esquina via Goya, *Sea Dart* briefly ran aground twice without damage. The navy was less inclined to be helpful in Esquina than farther north. No charts changed hands. Tristan continued without benefit of professional assistance or local knowledge. As a consequence *Sea Dart* ran aground again on leaving. Once more she was able to wriggle off.

On December 8, after a few more days of sailing, drifting, and motoring, boat and crew were welcomed at the yacht club in Santa Fe. Invited to present an illustrated talk at the club on the tenth, Tristan was happy to relax for a couple of days—and get some laundry done. His first day back on the river, under sail, Tristan progressed as far as Diamante, which he referred to as "a miserable place." One more day took him to Rosario and his first sight of an oceangoing ship since Callao one year before. *Sea Dart's* next port of call was San Nicolás. And there, as so often happened, Tristan's log and *The Incredible Voyage*, rarely compatible, tell vastly different stories. The log has a few simple entries: "20/12/74 In San Nicolás—life a misery. Small boys begging cigs and money. But invited [to] supper—So! [invited by local yacht club member]. Then Commodore said we weren't dressed well enough. 21/12/74 Left in a huff."

The Incredible Voyage, being a combination of fact and fiction, has a novel version of his reasons for visiting San Nicolás. While in Turkey on *Barbara*, he says, he visited the ruins of another Church of Saint Nicholas. There he took a color photograph of the remaining structure and carried away a piece of stone from the walls. He did this, he explained, so he could deposit the items in the town of the same name in Argentina, as thanks for surviving the long voyage between the two distant locations. Actually, when Tristan was in Turkey he had no inkling that he would one day be in San Nicolás, Argentina. At that time he had no plans to visit Argentina at all.

In the book the approach to the Argentinian San Nicolás is conducted with urgent fantasy. Tristan and *Sea Dart* race down the Paraguay River, stopping rarely and then only for an hour or so. All the while, international news agencies spy on their progress, ready to report the news of Tristan's arrival at the church to eager readers. The international news agencies, if they even knew Tristan Jones was in Argentina, had no interest in his progress toward San Nicolás. Just over a year before, sailing down the Peruvian coast, he had made similar self-promoting claims.

The simple invitation to supper at the yacht club in San Nicolás, as reported in the log, became in the book an invitation for Tristan and crew to attend a grand Christmas occasion. And that gave Tristan another golden opportunity for letting off literary steam. Tristan's passion for expressing his anger at imagined injustice was given full rein in *The Incredible Voyage*. With "Huanapaco" denied access to the party, Tristan shows us again just how rude he could be when angry—even when the story is untrue. The last two and a half pages of that chapter, pure fiction though they may be, are a deliberate insult to the yacht club members of San Nicolás—just as he had insulted yacht club members in Bolivia.

On Christmas Eve 1974, the log reports that *Sea Dart* dropped anchor at the Yacht Club Argentino in Buenos Aires. Hal Roth, noted American blue-water sailor and author, was in Buenos Aires—at the Yacht Club Argentino—prior to and during *Sea Dart's* arrival. Hal Roth remembered, "I was on my hands and knees doing some grubby job on my boat when I looked up to see a British naval officer in a dazzling white dress uniform (with ribbons and gold braid) standing in front of me on the dock. The officer was handsome, perfectly groomed, and looked about nine feet tall. 'Have you seen Jones? Where is he? Where can I find him?' he asked. The story going the rounds was that Jones was coming down the Rio Parana and into the Rio de la Plata and was due to arrive shortly.

"The officer, who was the naval attaché at the embassy, had apparently been sent on an official mission to greet Jones. He arrived a few hours later in his tiny boat that was filthy, as was Jones and a scruffy crewman. I vaguely recall an argument or some unpleasantness between Jones and his crewman. The contrast between Jones and Co. and the British naval officer in his immaculate white uniform and impeccable stature was incredible."

Roth continued, "The officers of the Yacht Club Argentino arranged to haul out Jones's boat at no charge as was often done for foreign yachtsmen, particularly those who were short of money. His little boat was grubby and desperately needed various repairs along with scrubbing, paint, and varnish. Shortly after he arrived, Jones went out drinking in Buenos Aires and caused a big disturbance in one of the bars. When the police were called, Jones boasted that he knew the commodore of the yacht club and had all sorts of influence with him. The police had better look out. Unfortunately for Jones, one of the people who came with the squad cars was the police reporter for the *Buenos Aires Herald*, the English language newspaper read every morning by the intellectuals for local gossip, news, and the latest foreign exchange rates. When the commodore read about Jones's boasts, he grew incensed and had Jones and his boat thrown out of the yacht club."

Once again Tristan's mouth had created unnecessary unpleasantness.

Despite her skipper's transgressions, *Sea Dart* had become the first oceangoing sailboat to travel the width of South America, from the Pacific to the Atlantic. She almost certainly had the right to be known as the first such vessel to sail on Lake Titicaca, and to sail the rivers of the Mato Grosso. Tristan's falsifications aside, the twenty-one-month voyage from Bequia to Buenos Aires, calling at nine countries, was a magnificent achievement—not only for the diminutive *Sea Dart*, but also for her stubborn, determined captain.

At last, with a few hard years and thousands of voyaging miles behind him, plus a handful of published magazine articles to his credit, Tristan had a solid adventure story to tell. It was almost time to announce himself to the world. First he had to survive a few more adventures before finding a place on shore where he could settle down to complete his book.

What Tristan did during a half-year sojourn in and near Buenos Aires, plus a few weeks in Montevideo, is unknown. In three books, spaced over nearly two decades, he wrote of exotic adventures featuring secret police and political prisoners. On many points the three versions conflict, however. His logbook, not surprisingly, tells yet another story.

On the factual side we know that about three months after he arrived Tristan moved *Sea Dart* back upstream a short distance, from Buenos Aires harbor to the suburb of Olivos. It was cheaper to live in Olivos, and he could keep his small boat safer from the hazardous traffic wash from commercial shipping. What he really did, other than write and drink in sailors' bars, is anyone's guess. There is nothing revealing in his logbook about the three months he spent in Buenos Aires between Christmas 1974 and March 22, 1975, when he moved to Olivos. Similarly, the log tells us nothing from March until mid-June, when he sailed the forty-seven miles across the river Plate to Uruguay.

In *The Incredible Voyage* Tristan told of sneaking away from Argentina at 2:00 A.M. in mid-July, without clearing customs. He describes being enveloped in thick fog and caught by a pampero wind off Montevideo and forced onto jagged rocks, where *Sea Dart* was badly damaged. After a herculean effort Tristan guided his craft into Montevideo harbor, where he cleared customs and immigration without any questions regarding the lack of exit papers from Argentina.

A later book, *Adrift*, has more drama. On the secret police list of undesirables and needing to avoid Perón's trigger-happy soldiers, the gallant captain slipped out of Olivos under the shelter of a foggy night in mid-July, without the obligatory clearance papers. Once again he got caught by the pampero wind (though this time the fog failed to arrive) and was driven onto rocks. In this version Uruguayan customs doesn't get a mention. *Sea Dart's* log, the most believable document, reads:

June 12 [Departed Olivos] To Colonia, Uruguay. Very light wind and haze. Cold.

June 14 To Puerto Sauce—under sail on close reach. Wind NE. 11:00–17:30.

June 15 Anchor aweigh 09:45. Under sail on a broad reach until 15:00 when wind changed to SE so sought lee of Punta Pavon until morning. Anchored in 1 fathom 1 mile out.

June 16 No wind. Under power from 07:00 to 21:15 when reached Santiago Vazquez, also known as "La Barra."

Tristan stayed in or near La Barra for a week. On June 25 he powered for an hour to a rotting jetty to examine a cave in a cliff. Anchoring off the jetty for the night, he returned to La Barra the following day. On the morning of June 27 he made way for Montevideo. He wrote in the log, "Wind variable, all around 360 degrees, Force 1–6. Passed bridge at 08:00—made two abortive exits from river, but weather unstable. 15:00 Sallied and, halfway down the 12 mile stretch fog came down. Anchored in swell. Cleared at 21:00, but came down again at 22:30. Anchored again. Sea very lively. Eventually entered [Montevideo] harbor at 24:00. Very tired. 16 miles or so in 9 hours. Made way to SE corner of Port, where is located Club Nacional de Regattas. This is very close to city center, so may stay here if all goes well."

And there, safely in Montevideo, without damage to *Sea Dart*, her log comes to an end. A local newspaper article mentions a Roberto Zaldivia, from Chile, who sailed from Buenos Aires with Tristan.

We know Tristan shipped the hardy cutter home to England on the SS *Hardwicke Grange* in late July 1975. With her he sent all standard sailing equipment, including sails, outboard motor, sextant, tools, and anchors, as the manifest shows. The total listed value—boat and equipment—was $4,920. (He wrote in *Adrift* that he sold most of that equipment to pay his airfare.) We don't, however, know why he sent the boat home by commercial transport. *Sea Dart*, with a skipper as experienced as Tristan Jones, was certainly capable of handling the long ocean voyage. It's possible that Tristan had planned to live aboard *Sea Dart*, in England, while he wrote the book of his adventures. A long sea voyage would have delayed that project by some months.

CHAPTER 11

A New Life

With his boat on her way to England by sea, Tristan flew to London early in August 1975. It would be his first visit to his native land in a decade. For three or four weeks he worked in the boiler room at Harrods in Knightsbridge while he waited for his boat to arrive. When the ship carrying *Sea Dart* docked at Newhaven he was appalled to learn that he had to pay a tax of hundreds of pounds—which he did not have—before she could be legally imported into Britain. Writing the book had to be put on hold. Homeless and desperate, knowing his job at Harrods offered little chance of saving the money, Tristan wrote to friends and acquaintances about his plight. At least one replied, far more positively than Tristan could have hoped.

Robert Grosby, who had sailed with his wife and son on *Barbara* in the Canary Islands early in 1970, received Tristan's letter and reacted quickly. Grosby arranged a job for him as skipper of a charter yacht and sent him traveling money and an airline ticket to New York. Bob and his wife, Ellie, met Tristan at Kennedy Airport at the end of August and took him home with them for a few days. They also bought him new clothes because, explained Grosby, "Tristan was a mess." Craig Grosby, by then in his middle teens, was pleased to see Tristan and talked to him for hours about his friend Albin, the Portuguese deckhand employed on *Barbara* during the Grosbys' sailing vacation.

Bob and Ellie took Tristan to *Sunshine* a few days after his arrival in New York and opened a bottle of champagne to celebrate his new command. *Sunshine*, a Columbia 45, was on limited charter to the Chalet Club—owned by Greg Swofford and Buddy Bombard. Bob Grosby described the Chalet Club: "a sophisticated singles club in its own townhouse in a tony Manhattan neighborhood. The Chalet Club did more than the usual mixers. It sponsored an ongoing series of lectures and discussions by well-known and not so well-known adventurers, explorers and writers."

Hearing Grosby's stories of *Barbara*'s voyage, Swofford had helped persuade Bob Grosby to find Tristan and bring him to the United States, presumably to deliver a series of lectures on his adventures. Tristan's letter to Grosby therefore had arrived with perfect timing. It's not known whether Tristan did speak at the club. His habitual untidiness and truculent attitude might have precluded his appearing there.

Bob Grosby had told Tristan right from the start that the skipper's position was only a temporary measure to get him into the States. For Tristan, down at the heels and with the debt of *Sea Dart*'s impoundment hanging over his head, even a temporary position on a boat in New York should have been better than slaving in the boiler room at a London department store. It should have been a golden opportunity, but it wasn't. For well over a decade, ever since he purchased *Cresswell* in 1964, Tristan had been his own master. At the beck and call of a boss for the first time in years, he missed his freedom and was desperately unhappy with his job on *Sunshine*. Bob Grosby said, "Tristan hated being a charter boat captain. I visited him several times on *Sunshine*, and he was very sad."

After his rough-and-tumble existence, most recently in South America, playing skipper for day sailors and acting as a hired curiosity at the club's disco by night did not sit well with Tristan. Once reasonably good at mixing in bars when sober, he would have been conspicuously out of place in an upscale nightclub. Much as he enjoyed the vibrancy of New

York, Tristan was still broke, and his beloved *Sea Dart* remained locked up in a British port. He passed a few weeks taking passengers with whom he had nothing in common on pointless excursions. Tristan became despondent. Having no permit to work in the United States, and allowed to visit for only a limited time, he found his prospects slim—though he did hold one potential ace: his writing. He called *Motor Boating and Sailing* magazine and spoke to Joe Gribbins. That contact earned him an agreement to supply a few published articles, six he said, and gained him a valuable friend for the future. When not writing he continued to search newspapers and marinas for an offshore yacht delivery. Tired of his employer and the club and with the local sailing season coming to an end, he needed a new direction. He soon found what he was looking for, a forty-four-foot yawl named *Sundowner.*

Strongly built of wood in Nova Scotia, *Sundowner* was destined for delivery to St. Thomas, in the U.S. Virgin Islands. The job was perfect for a skipper of Tristan's ability, with only one drawback: on arrival in St. Thomas, he would have to be a charter captain again. Much as he hated that part of the bargain, Tristan knew he couldn't refuse the offer. He also saw an opening for adventure on the way, and a possible magazine article. The notorious Bermuda Triangle lay across his planned course. What better for an experienced sailor with a curious mind than to sail through the triangle and see for himself what mysteries were hidden there?

Tristan and his crew of four left East Rockaway Inlet, on the south shore of New York's Long Island, on the evening of October 25, 1975, and headed south. Their final landfall on the mainland was at Morehead City, North Carolina. After an uneventful ten-day passage they passed under the forbidding gray walls of Morro Castle and tied up in the harbor at San Juan, Puerto Rico. The Bermuda Triangle had offered none of its secrets en route, though that didn't stop Tristan from writing intelligently about the weather phenomena he believed responsible for much of the triangle's reputation.

From Puerto Rico *Sundowner* continued to St. Thomas to work in the Virgin Islands. For most of the next few weeks Tristan had little to do other than daily maintenance on the boat. She was chartered only once. He stuck with the job for three months, until he and the owner argued about Tristan's drinking. Tristan either quit or was fired. Alone once more, with little money and no income, he more or less became a waterfront bum.

When David Shields, his wife, and a couple of friends arrived in St. Thomas from New York to sail among the British Virgin Islands for a week, their captain, Mike McMineman, pointed Tristan out as a down-on-his-luck Welsh skipper. Shields chatted with the scruffy sailor and found him an entertaining raconteur. He and his group invited Tristan to join them aboard their boat for the duration of their charter, some six or seven days. When Tristan returned to New York close on the heels of his new friends, he lost no time in calling them. Knowing that he had nowhere to live and little money, they invited him to stay in their guest room for a while. The visit lengthened to two months or so while he worked on the manuscript of *The Incredible Voyage*.

The tedious job on *Sundowner* had not been a total waste. Tristan had earned a few dollars with little or no personal expenses, had made influential friends, and while in St. Thomas had met Martin Luray, editor of *Rudder* magazine.

Determined to succeed as an author, with a host of ideas for magazine articles and with a book to finish, Tristan recognized that New York probably held the key. After his uptown sojourn, he rented an apartment in Greenwich Village, at 246 West 10th Street, and settled down to write. About once a week he joined the Shields family for dinner at their apartment, and he shared Christmas with them. On one occasion, despite knowing Margaret was terrified of snakes, he brought a garter snake in a large fishbowl as a present for her son. Margaret said she felt he did it deliberately to see her reaction.

Some writers attend classes to learn their craft. Others struggle on their own to find their literary voice. Many never see their works pub-lished. Tristan, by contrast, may have been born with the talent to write. His literary voice welled up from deep within him. Once pointed in the right direction by a series of rejections and by Patience Wales's careful prompting, he adapted his storytelling skills to writing. What others labored for years to learn, he grasped quickly. As with his sail-ing ability, he proved to be a natural. In New York he put that embry-onic faculty to a monumental test. He set himself a new goal: to write six books in three years. To achieve this end he applied himself dili-gently, regularly typing for twelve hours at a stretch. His dedication paid off. The years in Greenwich Village became his most productive time as a writer.

Soon after returning to New York he met with Martin Luray again. Over lunch Luray purchased three stories, as much fiction as fact, taken loosely from the unfinished manuscript of *The Incredible Voyage*, for a to-tal payment of $900. Three important American sailing magazines were now publishing Tristan's stories, in addition to British and Australian monthlies. He was reasonably solvent at last, and life began to improve.

While writing *The Incredible Voyage*, Tristan revised his past for a new set of readers. The true story of his first four decades of life, he seems to have decided, would not have the impact required to make him a public figure. He made a conscious decision to go public with a new and rather exotic past, a life story to fit the image he wanted to por-tray. His background had always been obscure. It wasn't difficult to change it in a foreign country, where he knew few people. As far as is known, no one who spent time with him in the 1960s and 1970s was privy to his real history. He had told a few fictions about his early life in conversations, but not in print. Expanding that personal reinven-tion for a large audience was easy. The three articles for *Rudder*, and his book, would set the stage for the future.

There is no doubt that Tristan firmly believed that for him the way to success as an author was in writing tales of adventure *based on* his experiences. Truth had little bearing on his resolution. He realized intuitively that the average reader wanted escapism. A fan of Jack London, he took a leaf from the master's book and turned the long, messy manuscript for *The Incredible Voyage* into a successful combination of fact and fiction, while leaving the impression that the book was nonfiction. His genius did not stop there. He had already changed his given name from Arthur to Tristan, his place of birth from Liverpool to Dolgellau in Wales, and—in his forged passport—his year of birth from 1929 to 1927. Now, as he prepared new biographical details to help promote his book, he made a few more alterations. Instead of being born in Liverpool or Dolgellau, he added the tale of being born at sea aboard his father's ship, and he changed his year of birth again, this time to 1924. He approached the complex task of his personal reinvention with astute planning—even cunning.

In his first book, as we have seen, he skillfully interwove fact with fiction and passed it off as true-life adventure. One wonders if Tristan had read Laurence Sterne's epic, *Tristram Shandy*. Sterne, an eighteenth-century British humorist and Anglican clergyman, wrote, "Oh Tristram! Tristram! Can this but be once brought about, the credit, which will attend thee as an author, shall counterbalance the many evils which have befallen thee as a man."

Those lines, written more than two centuries before Tristan's birth, contain an unwitting prophecy for him. He was successful in getting his stories published, and he did rise above his past. Much of the credit for that should go to the late Arthur Cohen. Without Cohen's appearance in February 1969, Tristan might have waited much, much longer to achieve his goals. Arthur Cohen handed him the wherewithal, but the rest was up to Tristan's natural talents, his imagination, and his skill as a sailor. He employed all three to his advantage.

In New York, he finished *The Incredible Voyage*. He found an agent, Peter Matson, and a publisher—Sheed, Andrews & McMeel of Kansas City—who paid him a $3,000 advance. Tristan was well on the way to sustaining himself by writing. He delivered the revised manuscript in October 1976. Soon after, based on the accepted manuscript, Sheed, Andrews & McMeel contracted for two more books, for which they paid an additional advance against royalties.

Tristan had looked into his future and seen the potential for more books based on the adventures of the persona he was inventing, and the three-book contract was proof that his inspired metamorphosis was going to succeed.

Many other authors have supplied enigmatic versions of their pasts that the public initially accepted without question. Four spring to mind.

Grey Owl, the great champion of Canadian wilderness conservation, claimed to be half Indian, the son of a Scots Indian scout and an Apache mother, born in Hermosillo, Mexico, in 1888. He was in fact born Archibald Belaney, of English parents, in Hastings, England. He first arrived on North American soil, in Canada, in April 1906.

South African explorer and literary figure Sir Laurens van der Post rose from obscurity to international fame on the strength of his apparent knowledge of the bushmen of the Kalahari Desert. As a result of his success he became friends with former British prime minister Margaret Thatcher and Prince Charles, among other luminaries. Yet much of van der Post's life as he described it had little to do with reality. And he, like Tristan Jones, found it opportune at one time to increase his age, by six years.

Patrick O'Brian, author of the popular series of Napoleonic-era naval novels featuring Aubrey and Maturin, changed his name and made a valiant attempt to bury his past. He said he was Irish, but his biographer proved he was born Richard Patrick Russ in England. His parents were Charles Russ, a German, and his English wife, Jessie. Richard Patrick Russ married Elizabeth Jones in 1936 and had two children by her. He then effectively abandoned the family in 1940. He later remarried, and when World War II ended, he changed his name to Patrick O'Brian.

And then there's the enormously successful British novelist and disgraced politician Jeffrey Archer. Archer changed the salient details of his past so frequently and erred so often that his biographer, Michael Crick, was faced with a monumental task in assembling the facts.

As was true for those four, Tristan's talent was in his ability to weave convincing stories from fragments of vaguely related incidents. And he, like Jeffrey Archer, was an expert at handing his public and the media a jigsaw puzzle of false information.

It is unlikely that Tristan's personal transformation was based on impulse. Considering the extent of his deception and its gradual progression, the decision to create a new life for himself was almost certainly premeditated, and the paths to be trod were carefully examined and prepared. Although it may not have been connected with later events, obtaining a false passport with spurious personal details was an early step on the road to a new life. But there are other questions begging for answers. Was the reinvention a self-delusion on Tristan's part, or simply a response to necessity? By 1977 he had already filled one book with most if not all of his true sailing exploits. To write more books to satisfy his newly acquired audience, either he could go back to sea and find new adventures—a slow process at best—or he could save time and energy by making them up.

Pete Kelly said that Tristan craved credibility as a small-boat sailor in order to attract a publisher for a book he had yet to write. As a published author he knew he would acquire a certain amount of fame as well as credibility. With fame, he hoped, would come financial stability. In that respect his metamorphosis was based on a perceived need.

Though his transition from a poorly educated, fun-loving charter boat captain taking day-trippers snorkeling in secluded coves in the Balearic Islands to a literate author was still in the embryonic stage, he was confident of success. Whereas for most the formidable journey from obscurity to fame requires much time and a monumental leap of faith, Tristan was too impatient to spend years compiling a valid list of achievements. He chose the short-track approach. At some point, while preparing his manuscript, he took a giant step: he decided to claim records he was not entitled to.

In New York Tristan continued to promote himself as Welsh. Having Jones as a surname certainly helped, and his dark Celtic looks added weight. But to anyone with an ear for British accents, his speech denied the Welsh connection—although that does not mean he could not have been of Welsh descent. The "lilting Welsh accent" that many American journalists referred to did not exist. His speech patterns were those of the Midlands, somewhere between Liverpool and London. Conrad Jelinek remembered Tristan as having "a sort of South Midland accent: certainly not Welsh."

In January 1977 *Rudder* magazine published the first of the three-part series based on *The Incredible Voyage*, which Sheed, Andrews & McMeel was to publish in May. Each of those articles, like the book, was riddled with fiction—including the author's claim that he had completed two circumnavigations, had crossed the Atlantic thirteen times under sail, and had sailed *Barbara* on the Dead Sea. In the book Tristan contradicted his own story of sailing *Barbara* on the Dead Sea, and on the dust jacket his Atlantic crossings were elevated to eighteen.

Cataloging-in-Publication data in *The Incredible Voyage* gave Tristan's year of birth as 1924, a date the Library of Congress retained for his author record for all of Tristan's later books. Biographical details on the dust jacket announced that he had been born at sea on his father's tramp steamer and told of his long line of sailing antecedents. We learned there that he left school at thirteen to go to sea and that he served in the Royal Navy during the dark days of World War II. There too we read brief teasers telling us he was torpedoed three times before his eighteenth birthday. For the first time we marveled at his outstanding record of sailing in small boats in the 1950s and 1960s. And then a forthcoming second book received a mention: the story of a historic voyage to the Arctic ice. None of these things was true. Tristan had deceived his publisher and was about to mislead his public.

So why did Tristan tell his readers—and publisher—he was born in 1924 rather than the truth of 1929, or even 1927, as stated in his forged passport? There can be only one answer. Among the list of books Tristan planned to write was one about the Royal Navy. That book, eventually published in 1984 as *Heart of Oak,* could not logically have been written as autobiographical nonfiction by a man born in 1929 or 1927. He would not have been old enough to star as the main character.

We have seen Tristan change his year of birth, his first name, his place of birth, and the circumstances surrounding that initial momentous event in his life. Reality and fantasy appear to have engaged in a bizarre dance in his mind, a ritual more suited to the adventurous dreaming of an impressionable young boy than to a hard-bitten sailor. What prompts someone to publicly offer such falsehoods?

The nineteenth-century German philosopher Friedrich Nietzsche said, "The most common lie is the lie one tells to oneself." Few of us are able to avoid telling the occasional lie, whether we admit the misdemeanor or not. Often, to avoid the denigration of being labeled a liar, we arbitrarily grade the severity of the offense. Parents are particularly good at doing this. We all experienced it as children, we all do it as adults. Parents caution their offspring never to tell lies, then confuse them by telling what they refer to as "white lies." To spare another's sensitive feelings, we all use white lies at times. The intent is rarely to truly deceive. Politicians, a notoriously mendacious breed, are renowned for using lies to gather votes. Others use falsehoods to attract attention or to impress. Sales and marketing people know the potential of stretching the truth in advertising campaigns and use that tactic to great advantage.

Tristan Jones appears to have been a compulsive, or pathological liar—also known as an habitual liar—one who tells lies out of sheer habit. One lie inevitably leads to another in a never-ending cycle. Habitual liars, according to psychologists, are often a product of low self-esteem—possibly for Tristan a by-product of a childhood without parents or other family. A further clue can be found in the knowledge that habitual liars have been known to have antisocial personalities, particularly rebelling against authority. Throughout his life Tristan showed little but contempt for those in positions of command, such as police, customs officials, and immigration officers.

Habitual liars often relate complicated stories about their lives, telling them with enough conviction to persuade listeners or readers of their veracity. They tend to employ great skill in blending fact with fantasy. Just a few examples in Tristan's case would be his stories of serving in the Royal Navy during World War II and his claim of having sailed on the Dead Sea. Believable though the tales may be, they eventually become confused as Tristan inadvertently—and inevitably—introduced contradictory statements in later retellings.

Lying convincingly is a complicated art that takes constant practice. At that Tristan was a master—to a point. Lying convincingly with consistency, however, is almost impossible. The truth about one's life, unpalatable though it may be at times, is much easier to keep straight than fabricated stories. For a writer, remembering and recording each untruth is elemental if one is to keep one jump ahead of one's readers. In books, inconsistencies created by half-forgotten lies signal their presence like beacons. If an author makes a statement of fact in one supposedly autobiographical book, it makes no sense to change that fact in another book or in a magazine article. Using one's own work as reference material for later writing should come naturally to an author. There Tristan failed. He regularly contradicted himself from book to book and article to article.

The Incredible Voyage is a masterpiece of adventure, with echoes of H. Rider Haggard, Edgar Rice Burroughs, and even Richard Halliburton. In view of its content and scope it is possible the book would have garnered reasonable sales from the sailing and boating communities, in addition to armchair travelers, had Tristan been satisfied with telling the story straight. In his defense, however, it is likely that he cared more about entertaining his readers than about telling the truth. Maybe he was looking for a far wider audience when he elected to magnificently fictionalize his tale—and to pass it off as true-life adventure. Having successfully done so, even to the extent of employing John Hemming, then director and secretary of the prestigious Royal Geographical Society and an acknowledged expert on South America, to write a foreword to the book (Dr. Hemming later admitted he had not read the manuscript), Tristan had to produce a follow-up, then a third adventure. Unknown to him, his lies almost caught up with him before he'd had a chance to savor his initial success.

After reading *The Incredible Voyage*, the late Ruth Cohen (Arthur's widow) tried to interest the media in exposing Tristan's false claim of sailing on the Dead Sea. She wrote at least one indignant letter, probably more. The one we know of, to *Motor Boating and Sailing* magazine in New York, was answered by editor Jeff Hammond, who politely asked her to verify the allegation. It is not known whether Ruth Cohen responded to Hammond's request. In any case nothing much happened, and Tristan was left with his reputation more or less intact. If the Cohen family had been in possession of *Barbara*'s logbooks, Tristan would probably have had some explaining to do.

Having committed himself to a fabricated course with his first book, Tristan chose to continue the deception with later volumes. One drawback to that irreversible decision was his logbooks. Those of *Cresswell* and *Banjo* have long since disappeared, leaving researchers no option but to explore other avenues to determine the truth. The logbooks of *Barbara* and *Sea Dart*, the two main players in *The Incredible Voyage*, fortunately were in safekeeping. In their original state, they would have told a story quite different from the published version. Tristan, however, chose to doctor the logs after the fact by adding comments and narrative lines to match the action in his book. He went further and carefully cut out of the logbook the crucial page describing *Barbara*'s real journey across Israel.

The afterthoughts scattered throughout *Barbara*'s and *Sea Dart*'s logs are classic examples of Tristan's stretching truth to the breaking point. They are most apparent in those short narratives that reflect the fictional elements of *The Incredible Voyage*. Tristan used a particular ballpoint pen with black ink to add comments on events that took place sometimes as much as three years apart. In each case the writing style is consistent, with none of the sudden errors or slips of the pen that might be expected from hurried log entries on a constantly moving vessel. There is a uniformity of pressure and formation of letters about the additions—an overall tidiness that arouses suspicion.

There are far too many such entries in both logs to record here. A few examples from the Amazon will suffice. On the same page as the arrival at Manaus, terminal point on the upriver voyage, a few lines in Tristan's handwriting have been added to suggest they went much farther: "30/3 to 7/4/72. To Codajas and Barrenca. Hot—Hot! This was one of the worst most arduous and difficult passages ever made in a sailing craft. Starvation and illness forced us to turn back 200 miles or so above Codajas. Crazy with hunger, sick, and me very bloody furious with this fuckin' continent!" And later a theatrical note: "I am ill, sick and faint-hearted. I do not think I can take any more now. BLOODY AMAZON!"

On the following page we see *Barbara* departing Manaus on April 6 for the Atlantic. This part of the log is correct. But on the same page, under April 7, immediately after the true entry regarding the second day of their downstream passage, there is another entry in black—once again in Tristan's hand: "Our state is very bad. No one has ever done this before!" A note on May 2 adds, "Thank God we are out of the Amazon!"

Even clumsily altered, the original information in those logs contradicts enough of *The Incredible Voyage* to prove that there is much fiction in that book. Tristan obviously viewed the embroidery in a different light. He was not prepared to run the risk of failure when, with a nod to the late Jack London, he could combine fact and fiction to create a livelier and potentially more salable book.

To help promote *The Incredible Voyage* he needed *Sea Dart*, still in England. With money in the bank from publisher's advances, he could finally afford to have her released. *Sea Dart* crossed the Atlantic on a ship for a second time. Off-loaded in Bayonne, New Jersey, she arrived in New York in time to be feted at the annual dinner of the Explorers Club at the Waldorf Astoria in April 1977, where Tristan was a guest speaker. *Sea Dart* stood behind Tristan on the stage. During that speech Tristan told his audience the fiction that he had been searching for the late Donald Crowhurst while crossing the Atlantic in *Barbara* in 1969.

After the Explorers Club event, *Quest* magazine used *Sea Dart* for a colorful promotional stunt. In return for permission to publish excerpts from the about-to-be-released book in the current issue, it collected her from the Waldorf and had her hauled through Manhattan for three days on a horse-drawn wagon before depositing her at South Street Seaport. Bob Shnayerson, then editor of *Quest* (circulation then roughly 450,000), commissioned the selections. Twenty-five years later he commented, "I don't recall doing any heavy editing on his writing. I had no intention of altering his singular voice. I hope the pieces we ran were faithful to him—a defiant rogue telling a tall tale of one man's picaresque bumming around the planet's high seas and low dives and unforgettable backwaters."

Sea Dart's overland travels continued. When *The Incredible Voyage* was released in May, Tristan set off on a coast-to-coast book-signing tour. With *Sea Dart* on the back of a truck, he talked to fans and sold books in twelve cities. In Boston he had his driver park the truck and boat outside *Sail's* offices, disrupting traffic on Atlantic Avenue. Two mounted policemen asked the truck driver to move. Tristan immediately turned on the charm. *Sail's* staff, watching from the window, saw him chat with the officers, autograph a copy of his book for each of them, and see them on their way. The truck stayed put.

Tristan and *Sea Dart* finished on the West Coast in Washington, where, according to one report, the young truck driver had become so tired of Tristan that he smacked him in the face.

By any standards Tristan's first book had been given an impressive launch. Few first-time authors receive such attention. It was to be his best-selling book.

Sea Dart remained in Washington State when Tristan flew back to New York City. He did talk of returning and sailing north, through the Bering Strait and beyond, to attempt the Northwest Passage. It would have been a fitting expedition for Tristan, another shot at the Arctic— for real this time. The idea faded as he sat down to write about more fictional adventures.

CHAPTER 12

Cold Facts, Arctic Fiction

No one knows where Tristan found the idea for his second book, the Arctic epic *Ice!* Perhaps Pete Kelly's tales of Icelandic waters inspired him, or maybe it came from reading Dod Orsborne, another rough and ready adventurer of the sea, whose books were similar to Tristan's.

Between 1949 and 1956 Dod Orsborne wrote three books about his own wild adventures in the Arctic, the West Indies, and South America, in the Royal Navy during World War II, and along the dangerous West Coast of Africa. Possibly they were the catalyst for Tristan's outrageous tales; there are many similarities.

Orsborne's three supposedly "nonfiction" books are liberally sprinkled with wonderful characters with unforgettable names, including Rummy Nose McBain, Stucco Willie, Australian Jack, Screamin' Jimmy, and Silent George. Tristan, in his turn, gave us Rattler Morgan, Rory O'Boggarty, Mr. Jeffries-Geography, Sissie St. John, Tony the Specs, and Shiner Wright.

Dod Orsborne served on a whaler off Greenland and in the Arctic. Tristan says he went to Greenland and the Arctic. Orsborne wrote his theory of the loss of the crew of the *Mary Celeste*. Tristan wrote a short story on the same theme. Orsborne suffered serious injuries during his days in the Royal Navy during World War II. Tristan claimed his own war injuries. Orsborne took a decrepit yet sturdy hull and restored it to sailing condition. He did this three times, once at Whitstable in 1953. Tristan said he restored *Cresswell* at Sheerness, not far from Whitstable, in 1958–59. One of Dod Orsborne's sailboats was the *Lonely Lady*, later renamed *Lovely Lady*. She was wrecked at sea, and Orsborne was rescued by a Liberty ship. Tristan claimed to have been wrecked at sea in *Two Brothers* and rescued by the Portuguese navy. Orsborne was injured when he fell from the mast and had to attend to his own serious wounds, including broken ribs and a bad gash on his leg. Tristan injured his eye on *Cresswell*. One of Orsborne's crew proved to be a German spy. In one story Tristan too had a spy on board in the Mediterranean. Orsborne encountered a lifeboat drifting in the Sargasso Sea. It contained what looked like a human body floating in water. He also tells of a fisherman in the Thames estuary who finds a body, gets a line on it, and tows it to shore. Tristan in turn wrote of discovering a body in the Mediterranean, getting a line on it, and towing it to shore. Orsborne survived wild adventures in the South American jungles, as did Tristan in his first book.

The parallels between Dod Orsborne's three books, which may or may not be true, and Tristan's tales are so many as to provoke serious speculation. In *Saga of a Wayward Sailor* Tristan even told of meeting Dod Orsborne in Toulouse, early in 1964. While it is unlikely that Orsborne and Jones really met (Tristan described Dod as a frail man of about eighty, at a time when he would have been, in fact, just over sixty), Tristan had almost certainly read Orsborne's books. If Tristan did recruit some of his plots from Orsborne's books, then perhaps we all owe the late skipper of *Girl Pat* a vote of thanks. The major difference between Orsborne's books and Tristan's is in the writing. Tristan's literary talents were far superior to Dod Orsborne's.

Ice! was the story of the two years Tristan Jones said he spent in the Arctic from 1959 to 1961. It was presented and published as a nonfiction book. It offers us three potential heroes. We can choose from *Cresswell*, the sturdy converted lifeboat; a black Labrador named Nelson; and Tristan Jones, sailor and teller of tall tales.

Tristan told us little about *Cresswell*'s history other than a few vague lines. He suggested she was once named *Mary Eleanor* and was one of the hundreds of "little ships" that crossed the Channel in 1940 to rescue British troops from the beaches at Dunkirk. He said he salvaged her decaying hull from a boatyard beside the River Medway, where he converted her to an auxiliary sailing ketch over the winter of 1958–59. None of this is true. He was vague about her dimensions too, creating confusion by his lack of attention to detail. In *Ice!* *Cresswell*'s hull length is variously said to have been thirty-four, thirty-two, and thirty-six feet. Similarly, her beam was either six or seven feet. In *Ice!* her masts were beautiful hollow British Columbian pine; in his final book she had a hollow Norwegian pine mainmast and a solid mizzen.

Nelson, the lusty, crusty canine bachelor with a singularly roving eye and a lifelong knowledge of the sea, was one of Tristan's most endearing characters. Supposedly inherited by Tristan in the dog's twelfth year, Nelson managed perfectly well at sea on three legs and saw enough out of his one good eye to keep his skipper out of trouble. In later years Tristan enjoyed amusing his audiences on television, at lectures, and at book signings with tales of Nelson's intelligence. With his dark eyes twinkling and a knowing smile on his lips, he'd say, "You know, the only time I disliked that dog was when he beat me at chess in the Arctic."

Pete Kelly expressed doubts about the existence of the dauntless Labrador. "I never saw Nelson," he said with a shake of his head and a bemused expression. "We were together in Kent, in the Channel Islands—where we were smuggling booze, and in the Med, on *Cresswell* and later on *Banjo*. Nelson is bullshit. I don't think he existed."

Tristan Jones, *Cresswell*'s enigmatic skipper, is well known to us. His single-minded determination to be famous, to earn credibility through his sailing exploits and his writing, drove him as few are driven. *Ice!*—his second published book—although beautifully written and exciting in content, tried its readers' credulity even more than its predecessor, *The Incredible Voyage.*

Ice! chronicles Tristan and Nelson's two-year voyage to push a small sailboat farther north into the Arctic ice than any similar vessel had gone. Unabashed by his obvious inventions and apparently unconcerned that some members of his reading public might know more about geography than he did and be more proficient navigators than he gave them credit for, Tristan insisted his Arctic tales were all true. His goal, he said, was to better the record set by the experienced Norwegian explorer Fridtjof Nansen, whose farthest north, at 85°55.5′, was reached in 1905, in the specially designed expedition ship *Fram*.

More than half the book is dedicated to finding a boat in 1958, preparing *Cresswell* for the sea, and smuggling crates of Scotch whisky into France before roaming leisurely from a variety of Channel ports, via Ireland and the Hebrides, to Iceland in the summer of 1959.

So let's look at the voyage, and the story, from its earliest days and, with a critical eye, ascertain what could have happened and what certainly did not. With *Cresswell*'s history so well documented, there is no doubt that Tristan was not involved in her renovation or conversion from an abandoned hulk into a seagoing vessel. Further, the records show that he did not purchase her in 1958 and could not possibly have sailed her to the Arctic in 1959. In 1958 and 1959 Tristan was in the Royal Navy, alternately based in Singapore, aboard ship, and in southern England.

Cresswell's Arctic voyage, as told by Tristan, poses innumerable questions, any one of which raises serious doubt in the minds of competent researchers as to the honesty of the reports. For example, the description Tristan gives of the island of Barra, in the Outer Hebrides, shows either sloppy note taking or poor research and includes a contradiction in names.

He said he spent the night before arrival hove-to in the Barra passage, waiting for daybreak to enter Castletown. With the dawn came the final few miles and a resting place for his anchor in "a lovely bay with a wide, white, sandy beach."

Tristan said he and Nelson spent a week merrymaking in the community. If so, he failed to notice much about the harbor. He did, however, comment on the island's airfield, which he gave the impression of having viewed from overlooking hills. Barra's airstrip, which in fact was the main beach, could be used only at low tide. He also mentioned the fishing boats in the harbor, suggesting that the working fleet on the sea was in sight of aircraft on the sand.

From Tristan's scattered account we revert to facts. The town on the south side of Barra is Castlebay, not Castletown (in *Ice!* he uses both names on different pages). It is the main harbor, and as such is busy with fishing boats and occasional ferries. Castlebay's harbor is distinguished by the prominent fifteenth-century Kisimul castle, a feature no visitor from the sea could possibly miss. It stands on a huge rock 150 yards offshore. If Tristan was in Castlebay, or overlooking Castlebay, he could not have seen the island's airfield without a substantial cross-island hike or some form of wheeled transport.

Traigh Mohr (Great Beach), more commonly known in those days as Cockle Strand for the crushed cockleshells that litter its length, was the airstrip and the main beach on the north side of the island. Its use for aircraft was dictated by the tides and weather. In the late 1950s BEA (British European Airways, now part of British Airways) used to fly De Havilland Herons, small four-engine propeller passenger aircraft, onto the beach airstrip as part of a scheduled service to the Hebrides.

Tristan's knowledge of St. Kilda, his next landfall, was no more accurate than his account of Barra. St. Kilda, comprising four islands (Tristan counted only three)—Hirta and Boreray, plus Soay and Dun—and a few pinnacles of rock known as *stacs* is, with the exception of Rockall, the most remote and difficult to reach part of the British Isles. It stands almost at the crossroads of 8°30′ W, 57°50′ N. A direct course from Barra, Outer Hebrides, would have a mariner first come abeam of the prominent 203-foot Stac Levenish, followed soon after by Dun Island to port. Hirta, the largest island, would form a backdrop of green and gray to Dun Island's green slopes. In the distance to the north, over four miles from Hirta, is Boreray. That island's impressively steep southwesterly coast, facing Hirta, is covered in lush green grass.

Hirta is blessed with two bays, which can be used safely by ships and boats in acceptable weather conditions. Glen Bay is in the northwest. Village Bay, where the settlement once housed the last thirty-six inhabitants, is on the southeast coast in a bowl almost surrounded by steep hills. Boreray cannot be seen from Village Bay. Tristan seemed to think that Village Bay was on Borerary.

Somehow, Tristan would have us believe, he made enough noise by accidentally dropping his gaff spar on deck that he disturbed a million birds, which took screaming to the air from the white cliffs of Dun and Boreray. Those birds on Boreray must have been blessed with acute hearing, separated as they were from *Cresswell* by miles of open sea. And the "white cliffs" of Dun and Boreray are actually green.

On land, wandering about the abandoned village, Tristan tells of the derelict stone cottages, their thatched roofs long scattered by the constant Atlantic winds, and says he found the ruins of three churches, one dedicated to Christ, one to Brendan the Voyager, and the last to Columcille (Saint Columba).

Tristan's description in *Ice!* of the dilapidated manse is another colorful work of fiction. "I looked into the manse, the old preacher's house, the biggest in the village, with its tin roof clattering away in the wind, and found old *Encyclopedia Brittanicas* [sic] from 1840. The dining table had collapsed, and the glassless windows swung in the breeze. There was an air of complete and utter hopelessness about the place."

Obviously Tristan's research was not sufficiently detailed for him to learn that, although abandoned in August 1930, St. Kilda had become a National Nature Reserve in March 1957. It is also obvious that he didn't know that a small but significant portion of Britain's military might had invaded the island in 1957, two years before he says he arrived.

In five months, from June to November, over three hundred officers and men—engineers and laborers—built a road from Village Bay to the summit of 1,200-foot Mullach Mor. By the end of 1958 a military camp and radar installation had been firmly established on Hirta. All the deserted, weather-beaten stone cottages were left as found. The lone church (not the three churches Tristan named), however, was commandeered by Royal Air Force personnel, as was the manse. The glebe—arable land adjacent to the church, once used for grazing the clergy's sheep and for cultivating crops—was overlaid with concrete foundations to support a permanent camp of wooden huts. Other concrete huts were built on the heights of Mullach Mor and Ruiaval to house the radar installation.

In early summer 1959, during *Cresswell*'s reported brief visit, there were more than just a million birds on St. Kilda. Hirta was also home to men of the Royal Artillery Guided Weapons Range (Hebrides), and the former manse was where some of them lived.

At the end of the chapter on his "visit" to St. Kilda in *Ice!* Tristan adds a final short paragraph to explain that in 1977 St. Kilda was a British government wildlife reserve. He acknowledged that by then there was a rocket-tracking station on the main island of Hirta. That information was already old news—twenty years out of date when he wrote it.

To liven the story, en route to Iceland from St. Kilda Tristan gets himself clobbered by a hefty wooden pulley block—an accident disturbingly similar in detail to that suffered by English single-hander Edward Allcard on *Temptress* in 1949, although Allcard played down the seriousness of his incident. Not content with suffering an appalling gash over his right eye, which he had to stitch himself (as other solo sailors have been forced to do), our hero tests his readers' gullibility by gruesomely recounting how his eye popped out of his head and lay unseeing on his cheek until he popped it back in and repaired the considerable damage to his brow with a needle and thread. Battered and cut, his head draped in blood-soaked bandages, Tristan struggled on to his next land-fall, Iceland. His knowledge of that country is also suspect.

The shortest sea route between St. Kilda and Iceland would have had *Cresswell* fetch the land off Dyrholaey (Door-hill-island), also known as Cape Portland. Dyrholaey, an enormous rocky peak, rises 370 feet above the foreland. Geologists believe it may be the last visible remnant of an ancient volcano. Changing course to the west, *Cresswell* would then pass within sight of the Vestmann Islands. Another day would have seen her abeam of Reykjanesta, where she would have passed through the ten-mile-wide channel between the peninsula and the great 226-foot rock named Eldey, home to an enormous colony of gannets.

Tristan says he arrived off Reykjanesta ten days out from St. Kilda. As a safety measure he stayed well off shore, giving himself plenty of sea room to clear the peninsula that he described as long, rocky, and dangerous. For some reason he failed to mention the extremely visible Eldey, which he could hardly miss if he could see the peninsula of green-carpeted lava.

After a visit to the hospital in Reykjavík, Tristan, with Nelson, set off to claim the first solo circumnavigation of Iceland in a small sailboat. On the twenty-day voyage, with eight nights at anchor, he was always within sight of the coast and said he went ashore at one point. For his circumnavigation claim to be valid, he would have needed to be considerably more accurate in his descriptions of the Icelandic terrain.

Iceland has some 3,300 miles of heavily indented coastline, though an oval shape around the island would cover only approximately 1,000 miles. On *Cresswell*'s alleged circumnavigation of Iceland, unless Tristan was exceptionally fortunate with weather and sea conditions, glaring errors are manifold. He managed to cruise the north coast in June, virtually on the Arctic Circle, even crossing it briefly, without encountering or even seeing drifting ice: a possibility, but unlikely.

The *Arctic Pilot*, a handbook for mariners, has a multitude of entries to cause considerable concern to any sailor in Icelandic seas, whether in a small boat or on a ship. One such item refers to the waters off Cape Langanes at the northeast tip of Iceland. It spells out the region's perfidious reputation for frequent fog, along with strong tidal streams and currents, and it warns that magnetic compasses are unreliable near Cape Langanes. All these dangers, it notes, have contributed to the loss of numerous vessels. The entry concludes with a reminder about drifting polar ice and the warning, "Finally, Langanesrost, a heavy race, may extend far out to sea even in calm weather."

Bill Tilman and his crew in *Mischief*, in late June 1968, passed Cape Langanes twenty-five miles out to sea. Tilman remarked on a strong westerly current that seemed determined to push him onto the dangerous shore he was equally intent on avoiding. Tristan, it seems, had an easier time, although he chose to ignore the peninsula's true name and referred to it as the Fontur peninsula. Fontur is the name of the lighthouse on the northeast extremity of Cape Langanes. With uncharacteristic restraint, he chose not to tell his readers about the dangers to be experienced on the seas off Cape Langanes. He says he had "splendid sailing."

Cruising comfortably through the night, he rounded the cape and hurried in to the shelter of the south side of the peninsula to gain protection from the north and the southwest. The next day *Cresswell* spent the afternoon and part of the evening beating to windward until Tristan was finally in a position to drop anchor. His friend Pete Kelly would have wondered at that. Kelly knew *Cresswell*'s sailing ability well. Expressing his doubts about the Iceland voyage, he said, "*Cresswell* sailed like a pig to windward. She went better sideways than forward. He'd have had to motor all the way to Iceland in that thing."

His chosen anchorage, Tristan explained, was sheltered in the lee of high land at the head of the fjord. If *Cresswell* was indeed beating to windward that long day and evening, the wind would have been out of the southwest. There would have been little protection from that same wind anywhere in the fjord. The high land to the southwest is miles from the low-lying coast.

Farther round the circuit, sighting one of Iceland's most readily distinguishable geographical features, Tristan either misread the map or allowed his imagination to obscure reality. He wrote of a great rocky plateau called Vatnajökull, and announced it as an ancient refuge of his beloved Celtic Christians, a safe haven from the bloodthirsty Viking marauders. Not content with the romantic projection of a tormented race hiding among rocks and boulders to elude vicious adversaries, he made the mistake of taking his spellbound readers to a historic anchorage under Öræfajökull, where, he avowed, the Celts had settled a millennium and a half before.

His gravest error was in not knowing, perhaps not caring, that Vatnajökull is not a rocky plateau. It is one of the great permanent ice caps of the Northern Hemisphere, and its eternal white quilt is clearly visible from the sea in good weather. Furthermore, Öræfajökull is the southernmost part of Vatnajökull, with a handful of rugged glacial fingers reaching for the sea. The area where Tristan says he went ashore, far from being grassy slopes and rocky ground, is a low-lying delta of glacial meltwater streams flowing over black volcanic sands. The nearest rocky land is a few miles away, and two small villages, Hof and Fagurhólsmýri, stand three miles apart at the foot of Öræfajökull.

The facts prove that Tristan's claim of making the first recorded circumnavigation of Iceland under sail can be considered specious nonsense. Apart from the glaring discrepancy in dates, itself a problem of some magnitude, Tristan should have known that if he truly wanted to claim a "first," he had an obligation as an explorer, however unrecognized, to accurately record data concerning his voyage. Daily chart positions noted in his log or personal journal as expressions of latitude and longitude should have been faithfully recorded, along with the times of day when he passed geographical features on shore. Photographs of recognizable geographical features would have helped immeasurably. His word alone, nearly two decades after the event, with no acceptable material evidence, could hardly be considered authority enough for others to endorse his achievement, particularly since his knowledge of the land was so faulty.

Tristan's voyage to Greenland, and his later declaration of reaching farthest north in a sailing vessel, also lacks reliable substance. Of his crossing of the Denmark Strait from Reykjavík, he wrote that he left on July 2, passed through a fishing fleet, and entered the Denmark Strait. For five days he ran before the wind with a northeaster blowing over his starboard quarter. Winds are ever fickle, and Tristan's northeaster was no exception. As suddenly as it started it died, and *Cresswell* lay motionless for two days, apart from a slow roll in concert with the North Atlantic swells.

Tristan explained that as he drifted, waiting for a wind, he passed his time by fishing. The floes, he said, were drifting south at about half a knot. Common sense dictates that if the floes drifted south with the surface current, *Cresswell* would have drifted in the same direction at an equivalent speed without a wind to hold her back. Tristan said he tied up to a floe for a while and walked on it. He recalled being at sixty-nine degrees latitude because he caught a large halibut that evening.

For three days he drifted, carefully avoiding the increasing number of floes. When the wind returned it came out of the southwest; the sea remained calm. Hoisting all working sail, he resumed his voyage. Inexplicably, immediately after collecting the breeze, he wrote that July 9 saw him sailing due west along a big lead between two sheets of pack ice. The ice packs, he said, were heading south, as they would with a southwesterly current. With luck a favorable lead opened up on July 11, and Tristan altered course to follow it north. Three days later, after following a shore lead—against the current, he said—he arrived off Cape Brewster.

The course Tristan described for *Cresswell* would have placed seemingly insurmountable obstacles in the courageous old vessel's path. A well-defined current flows south along the east coast of Greenland. *Cresswell* would have been forced to fight against it every step of the way, from Tristan's crossing of the usually ice-choked Denmark Strait before his landfall off Scoresbysund to his stated farthest north of 76°10´. Moreover, the annual limit of the permanent ice pack extends a long frozen finger as far south as the latitude of Cape Bismarck and less than fifty miles from Greenland's east coast. Permanent ice encroaches on Greenland's northeast coast at latitude 82°30´—roughly three degrees south of Tristan's goal of farthest north—making further northerly progress by sea impossible.

Any other sailor bound from Reykjavík for Scoresbysund would have set a course to cross Flaxafloi and Breidafjord to a point west of Bjargtangar light. From there the shortest track is almost due north to Scoresbysund. That, in fact, is the route plotted on the endpaper maps in *Ice!*

If *Cresswell* had a northeaster blowing over her starboard quarter for the first five days, she had to be sailing west, not north. For the three days of drifting with ice floes, waiting for a wind, she would have been carried south and west. On that grossly incorrect course, after sailing five hundred nautical miles across the southwesterly current, *Cresswell* would have fetched up on an exceedingly dangerous stretch of Greenland's east coast, south of the settlement of Angmagssalik and hundreds of miles south of Scoresbysund. We are expected to accept that by sailing due west from Reykjavík—which is at latitude 64°10´ N—and drifting to the southwest with the current, *Cresswell* somehow reached latitude 69° N.

Simple analysis shows that, using Tristan's description of his passage, by the time the wind came up to propel him north, he would have been some six hundred miles south of Scoresbysund. To fetch Cape Brewster in three days *Cresswell* would have had to average well over seven knots, an impossibility under any conditions. And she was bucking a current and dodging drifting ice floes.

A U.S. Hydrographic Office publication warns of the dangers from ice along the eastern Greenland coast: "East Greenland has much more pack-ice than West Greenland and no ship should attempt to navigate in the waters of the former unless it is specially designed."

The British *Admiralty Pilot* paints a slightly less gloomy picture yet cautions that "in an average year, the ice in this region is mainly navigable by ordinary vessels in August to October inclusive." For "ordinary vessels" read "ships," not fragile wooden sailboats. Also written for reasonably large vessels, the *Arctic Pilot* says of Scoresbysund, "The approaches to Scoresby Sound are more likely to be free from ice in late September than at any other time but in severe ice years they may not uncover at all."

Bill Tilman, in *Mischief,* took seven days to come in sight of Greenland's mountains from Reykjavík in July 1965. Halfway across the Denmark Strait he ran into heavy drift ice. Tristan, in *Cresswell,* says he left Reykjavík on July 2, 1959, and arrived at the mouth of Scoresbysund twelve days later. Considering the distance and the stated fortunate conditions, the passage time is about right for a vessel aiming directly for Scoresbysund from Iceland's west coast. Unfortunately for Tristan he had already told us he was headed in the wrong direction, which would have made for a considerably longer passage. Adding to that, ice reports prepared by meteorologists for the Denmark Strait during the summer of 1959 show it would have been virtually impossible for *Cresswell* to reach Scoresbysund.

Once he finally gets to Greenland, despite gross navigational errors, Tristan's vivid imagination, combined with a modicum of factual knowledge, has *Cresswell* surge into the narrow leads between enormous tables of virgin ice. All sails are pulling hard—aided by an icy Arctic wind. At the helm, his sailor's cap at a jaunty angle, dirty scarf wrapped around his neck, and layers of old clothes protecting his scrawny body from the cold, the skipper stands with eyes screwed up against icy particles on the breeze, constantly alert for danger. In the bow, one shoulder braced against the forestay, black nose sniffing the air, single eye casting from left to right, Nelson stands his ice watch.

The intrepid pair beat northward against the freezing current, dodging drifting ice pans and warding off a vicious attack by a giant polar bear, until they are eventually blocked by impenetrable ice just south of Cape Bismarck. Their northern progress into history stymied, they swing *Cresswell*'s bows through 180 degrees and retreat south, hunting seals for food as they go. Eventually they meet a ship.

Tristan's anecdote about his excitement at boarding the Greenland trading vessel *Gustav Holm* is interesting; it is also fiction. Had he really seen *Gustav Holm*, it is unlikely that a writer with Tristan's talent, especially considering his love of ships, would have been able to ignore the potential for a full explanation of that grand old vessel.

Gustav Holm enjoyed a long career in Arctic and sub-Arctic waters. She was built of wood and launched as *Fox II* in Copenhagen in 1893, for the Cryolite Company. The ship, of 409 gross registered tons, and 145 feet in overall length, was powered by a 230-horsepower steam engine. She also carried three masts for sail and was rigged as a barquentine. Her maritime role was to carry passengers and cryolite, also known as "Greenland spar" (sodium aluminum fluoride, used in aluminum production), between Copenhagen and the Greenland port of Ivigtut.

In 1924 *Fox II* was sold to the Scoresbysund Committee, who changed her name to *Grønland*. In her new role she transported Eskimo families from Angmagssalik to remote settlements in Scoresbysund. She was later sold to the Greenland Trading Company, which renamed her *Gustav Holm*. From 1925 to 1951, apart from the war years when she was laid up in Copenhagen, she sailed regularly between Denmark and Greenland. At times during her far North Atlantic years she was also chartered for use on Arctic expeditions. In 1951, however, *Gustav Holm* went to new owners in Finland. For the rest of her working life she sailed only in the Baltic. She did not return to Greenland waters during Tristan's Arctic voyage; therefore he could not have seen her. It's possible that Tristan chose the name for his imaginary ship from a map without knowing there was a real *Gustav Holm*. Cape Gustav Holm, on Greenland's east coast, sits right on the Arctic Circle.

Tristan is still determined to achieve farthest north in *Ice!* But with winter fast approaching, a safe haven is the only thing between him and a chilling death. Far up a fjord in Scoresbysund, he finds what he's looking for—a beach where he can haul his 4.5 tons of boat out by brute strength, aided by a little mechanical knowledge, to sit out the darkness of the long polar night. He could, of course, have sailed to Iceland and found a comfortable berth instead.

Undeterred by an eight-month ordeal throughout the winter, with the obligatory life-threatening adventures thrown in, Tristan sets off once more for the north in the summer of 1960. This time, using a smattering of navigational reasoning, he lets the dwindling Gulf Stream help *Cresswell* along to a point near the west coast of Spitsbergen. Once again he gets the long-suffering *Cresswell* stuck in the ice. For one full year, plus a day for good measure, Tristan and Nelson survive magnificent adventures as they wait for the surrounding ice to crack and free them to tell the world their incredible story.

Although we know Tristan did not go to the Arctic in the late 1950s, and it is highly unlikely he was there anytime in the 1960s, he told a good story. Assuming he really had planned to attempt to beat Nansen's farthest north—as he wrote in *Ice!*—it would have made sense to follow a course up the North Sea to the latitude of the Shetland Islands. From there a course north-northeast, past the dramatic Norwegian fjord lands to Spitsbergen, would have served him well, rather than going up the coast of eastern Greenland as he so eloquently described in his book.

Spitsbergen, which would have been a far superior jumping-off point for the polar ice pack, enjoys a unique position in Arctic waters; the mountainous archipelago stands at the farthest outflow of the warm Gulf Stream. It therefore has a considerably milder climate than

any other land on the same latitude. In summer this beneficial temperature translates into a boon for sailors bent on reaching the ice.
The complete west coast of Spitsbergen is almost always free of ice all
summer. More important to an expedition planning an assault on the
"farthest north" record by sea, the north coast—with fingers of land extending to eighty-one degrees north latitude—is less than five degrees
shy of Nansen's mark.

Farthest North, Fridtjof Nansen's detailed and fascinating two-vol-
ume account of his three-year Arctic expedition of 1893–96, gives explicit scientific analysis—in layman's terms—of the currents affecting
the drift of polar ice in the Northern Hemisphere. Nansen's expedition
ship, the Colin Archer–designed *Fram*, followed the fjord-indented
Norwegian coastline as far as Vardö, just about as far north and east as
it is possible to go and still be in Norway. From there she sailed almost
due east to the Russian island of Novaya Zemlya and continued
through the Northeast Passage to the New Siberian Islands—where
she entered the ice of the polar pack before attempting any significant
northing. Deliberately trapped, *Fram* drifted westward with the ice, far
to the north of Franz Josef Land and Spitsbergen, until she reached
her farthest north on November 15, 1895. Her position was latitude
85°55.5′ N, longitude 66°31′ E of Greenwich. From that point the Arctic
current carried her gradually west and south until the weakening ice allowed her to shake off her frozen chains a short distance north of Spitsbergen. *Fram*'s farthest north had taken her within 240 nautical miles of
the North Pole.

In selecting the eastern Greenland route as a means of beating
Nansen's farthest north in his book, Tristan made a monumental error.
Farthest North, which should have been required reading for him before embarking on the project, would have told him so, had he read it
properly.

A review of *Ice!* in the Royal Geographical Society's prestigious *Geographical Journal* of July 1980 contains the line, "Can best be described

as rollicking in style and should be taken with plenty of salt." Sir Wally Herbert, the renowned British polar explorer, agreed to a certain extent. "Of course some of his tales are 'tongue in cheek'—and most of these are pretty obvious to anyone who knows anything about the Arctic."

As the evidence weighs firmly against Tristan's having made the first solo circumnavigation of Iceland, so it is equally unlikely that much of what he wrote about his long Arctic sojourn can be taken seriously. Yet that hardly detracts from the value of his book. Writing *Ice!* was a clever idea, which would have been so much more effective had Tristan taken greater care with his research. In addition to the main theme, his introduction of one-eyed, three-legged Nelson brought the book alive and gave Tristan a new set of fans. Dog lovers were drawn to the image of a crippled canine exploring Arctic ice and fighting off marauding polar bears. Whether Nelson was fact or fiction, his future as an important character in two later books was assured.

The remaining tales of Tristan and Nelson's high adventure trapped in the winter ice, being threatened by collapsing bergs, and almost sinking before arriving at Spitsbergen are thrilling reading in the extreme. And that is the great joy of *Ice!* It is a gripping and entertaining read, but it has no place on a bookshelf for nonfiction. *Ice!* is adventure fiction—excellent adventure fiction.

CHAPTER 13

Blending Fiction with Fact

Once *Ice!* was out of the way, there was to be no letup in Tristan's quest to complete six books in three years. He immediately began writing *Saga of a Wayward Sailor*, the third book in his contract with Andrews & McMeel. This too would be more fiction than fact.

In *Ice!* Tristan stretched his credibility to the limit when he suggested that between late 1952 and the summer of 1958, in the course of his yacht deliveries, he crossed the Atlantic Ocean eight times under sail and managed a two-year circumnavigation of the world. In a magazine article he modestly claimed two solo circumnavigations of the globe, and he told his readers he had lived with New Guinea savages, the Indians of Tierra del Fuego, and other peoples on remote Indian Ocean Islands. *Saga* would describe traumatic transatlantic voyages. In a much later book he would tell of shorter deliveries in addition to the major ocean passages during the same years. To have accomplished all those voyages and lived with those exotic groups in less than six years would have made Tristan the busiest delivery skipper afloat, and one of the most experienced. His Royal Navy career alone proves he did not spend the six years between 1952 and 1958 delivering yachts.

Claims of his expertise and experience in delivering sailing boats under forty feet long are grandiose in the extreme. On the dust jacket of *The Incredible Voyage* he claimed to have sailed more than 345,000 miles in small boats, 180,000 of them solo. Then he added eighteen Atlantic crossings under sail, half of those as a single-hander. It is a remarkable list.

Was Tristan the highly experienced long-distance sailor or delivery skipper he claimed to be? It is unlikely. There are too many contradictions in his own stories, published and unpublished, for us to place any great faith in his claims. Plus, his fourteen years in the Royal Navy left little time for delivering yachts.

Apart from the fact that he couldn't possibly have been a delivery skipper in the 1950s, obvious questions arise from Tristan's excessive claims. Why would anyone deliver a yacht on a complete circumnavigation of South America? Or the world? Common sense dictates that in each case the boats would have ended up being delivered to their starting points. Tristan chose to ignore such questions. He expanded on the theme of being a long-distance delivery skipper in *Saga of a Wayward Sailor,* but unfortunately for him, his passport records let him down badly.

In 1964, we are told, he delivered *Rose of Arcachon* from St.-Nazaire, France, across the Atlantic to Martinique. He and a crew of two—Jean Pierre from Brest and Jacques, a Parisian—left France in early April. It's hard to imagine Tristan Jones, a committed Francophobe, being cooped up in a small boat for weeks with two Frenchmen. After the safe delivery, Jacques flew home via New York and, in the story, was conveniently killed when the Paris-bound airplane crashed outside Nantes. Strangely, there is no record of such an obviously newsworthy aviation accident.

For the return journey, Tristan said he and Jean Pierre took charge of *Quiberon* in Cayenne, French Guiana, on July 2. *Quiberon* fetched Antigua on July 17 and departed two days later. After a difficult Atlantic crossing, filled with adventures, *Quiberon* picked up a mooring in Fayal, in the Azores, on September 18. They continued to Cherbourg, arriving on October 17, 1964.

Neither of those deliveries can possibly be fact, since the dates conflict with public and government records. We know Arthur Jones was in England between April and July 1964 because that's when he purchased *Cresswell*. And while he claimed to have been far out on the Atlantic battling the waves in an unseaworthy boat, he was in England obtaining a new passport.

Fictional deliveries aside, *Saga of a Wayward Sailor* is a wonderful collection of sailing stories. Once again Nelson played a starring role, and Pete Kelly was featured. *Saga* also introduced us to another delightful fictional wanderer—Sissie St. John, the bishop of Southchester's sister. Sissie, Tristan's flamboyant sailing partner, was the bane of his and Nelson's life aboard *Cresswell*.

A photograph from the Ibiza years features a Rubenesque woman in a pale green one-piece bathing suit sitting on *Banjo*'s deck. On the back of the print, in Tristan's hand, is a single word: Sissie. But Sissie was not a real person, despite what the photograph suggests. Pete Kelly identified the woman as a Norwegian secretary. He believed Sissie's character was taken from a combination of at least two women they met in Ibiza. "One was Wauna. She was a big lady who ran a bar. Another was a little plum-in-mouth woman. A former head of British Intelligence in Paris, I think she was Dame something or other. We knew her as Fifi, I think."

Kelly's memory let him down there, and Tristan erred again. Among Tristan's personal collection of photographs is one of Tristan, an elderly lady, and another man holding a flyswatter. The caption, in Tristan's handwriting, reads, "Miss Lulu was Chief of British Intelligence in Paris, 1940–42." The photo is dated "Ibiza, 1968." Pete Ross, owner of the George and Dragon in Ibiza, identified the woman as Mimi Ashburnham Sutton, heroine of the French Resistance in World War II, usually referred to as "Old Mimi."

Toward the end of *Saga*, after Nelson died of old age and Sissie left for new adventures, Tristan wrote of selling *Cresswell* and buying a

Folkboat, *Two Brothers*, in Vigo, northern Spain. He managed to turn that fictional episode into a near disaster when, en route across the Atlantic to the Caribbean, he said he was sunk by a whale and rescued by a Portuguese naval vessel—conveniently commanded by the officer who admitted *Barbara* to Mozambique in 1971.

Although he often took little care in checking his own magazine articles and previous books to be sure of his "facts," Tristan did go to the Mediterranean in the spring of 1979 to research material for two future books. One he planned to call *The Sound of a Different Drum*; the other, almost certainly, was *Seagulls in My Soup*, a follow-up to his most recent offering, *Saga of a Wayward Sailor*. *Drum* was never published. *Seagulls* was not finished and published until 1991. Its release told all of Tristan's readers what many had long suspected. The last paragraph of his foreword reads: "This book, originally written in 1979, is in the recently 'discovered' and much acclaimed literary mode of *fictionalized fact*. But all human memory is that. Embroidering memories is what makes us human. God forbid the day when none of us can do that! Over the past twenty years, unrecognized by most shore-bound critics, I have done much to pioneer this mode of storytelling."

The year 1979 proved a milestone for Tristan. In March he was among ten writers to be recognized by the Welsh Arts Council. He won the top prize of £500 for *The Incredible Voyage*. In New York that year Tristan also met Welsh literary giant Jan Morris. Learning she was in town on a book-signing tour, he phoned her Upper East Side hotel and asked to see her. "What a grand sight he was when he breezed in," Jan remembered, "all sunburn, high spirits and Welshness, straight from the sea. I was immensely proud of this exotic visitor, and introduced him to everyone in the hotel, from the general manager down, and they were vastly impressed, and fawningly called him Cap'n Jones, and treated me with extra respect for the rest of my stay."

Although the two met only twice, both times in New York in the late 1970s, they corresponded for many years. A decade later Tristan would tell Jan Morris, referring to something she had written, "You make me remember my pride on being Welsh myself."

Busy though he was with his new career, Tristan still made time for others. Shortly after *Ice!* was released in 1978, he began corresponding with Wally and Marie Herbert, British explorers who knew the Arctic intimately. The friendship engendered by that initial letter was to last the rest of his life. Tristan's sympathetic side, expressed in his occasional consideration for others, came to the fore as letters flowed back and forth between them. Perhaps patriotism lay at the root. Whatever the reason, Tristan offered to publicize Wally Herbert's Arctic achievements in the United States gratis while on tour to promote *Ice!* He went further and donated $500 to Herbert's campaign to complete a circumnavigation of Greenland. And he offered useful advice on marketing the project to American companies at a time when the polar veteran needed it most.

In November Tristan accepted an invitation to sail on two Antarctic voyages from southern Chile as a guest lecturer on the *Lindblad Explorer*, a luxury adventure cruise ship.

Saga of a Wayward Sailor hit the bookstores in 1979, one year after *Ice!* Tristan's transition from a rowdy drunken sailor to an author of captivating adventure fiction was well under way, although he insisted his first three books were nonfiction, just as he claimed all his personal stories were true. *Ice!* and *Saga* sold well in their first editions, though neither was as successful as *The Incredible Voyage*. All three continue to sell to this day in trade paperback editions.

By this time, whether he understood it or not, Tristan was trapped in the mold he had created for himself. Most of what he wrote as nonfiction had been believed by his fans. His fabricated background had been accepted unconditionally. He now had to lie constantly to perpetuate the legend in which he supposedly starred.

Like other popular authors and recognizable public figures, Tristan lived to some extent in a fishbowl. No matter how deeply he sought to bury the truth about his life or how well he thought he had covered his past, there would always be a few people who knew the truth. Pete Kelly knew some of the facts. Conrad Jelinek's memory contained many more. Other crew members from many boats and voyages, whether or not they were aware that Tristan had found fame as a writer, held other clues.

Captain Tom Drake had made the same mistake many years before. One of the early solo sailors, Drake developed a reputation for inconsistencies and a tendency for personal aggrandizement in lectures about his voyages. He was well known for telling each interviewer a different story, the only consistent features being his own skill and bravery. By contrast, the doyen of circumnavigators, Joshua Slocum, avoided publicity when he could. He wanted reporters to stick to the facts. It has been said that Slocum let his adventures speak for themselves rather than embellishing them for public consumption. In such honesty he may have been unique.

In assessing the reasons behind Tristan Jones's fraudulence and the extent of his duplicity, we need to explore not only elements of the psychology of deception but the history of bogus claims in exploration. Most explorers or adventurers are individualists. While some shun publicity of all kinds, others revel in the often fleeting limelight. Those who practice deception invariably fit into the latter category. They rarely don a mantle of humility. Without exception they exhibit an urgent need for public acclaim. To wear the victor's laurels, they are prepared to risk almost any censure. It is a sad reflection on the characters of men like these (few if any women have made false claims in exploration), because with minor exceptions, adventurers who fraudulently claim records tend to be extremely capable in the field.

Dr. Frederick Cook was an accomplished mountaineer and a skilled Arctic traveler. His rival, Commander Robert Peary, was a highly experienced polar explorer. Both claimed they were first to reach the North Pole. Without question, both were capable of getting there. Neither in fact reached his goal—as proved by Wally Herbert in his excellent book *The Noose of Laurels.* English sailor Donald Crowhurst, who almost certainly committed suicide in the Atlantic Ocean after faking his positions for months in a round-the-world yacht race, possessed the knowledge and seamanship skills necessary to win the race. Yet he chose a calamitous alternative.

Tristan Jones was endowed with courage, tenacity, intelligence, and extraordinary talent as a sailor. Given time, he could have accomplished all that he claimed. He could have sailed over 345,000 nautical miles in small boats. He could have crossed the Atlantic nine times solo. He could have forced his boat farther north than any other man. He could have, but he didn't.

At nearly forty when he decided to write adventure sailing books, Tristan had little to show for his years. More than half his allotted life span had passed. He hadn't time to rack up the necessary nautical miles under sail—a slow process for one in a hurry. So he faked much of his experience. To his credit, however, he pursued his new calling with enormous zeal in order to catch up. Arthur Jones's development into a respected author of adventure sailing books was rapid; it needed to be. If that meant lying about his past, so be it.

In later life Tristan regularly lied even in letters to his closest friends, and sometimes about insignificant issues. Often—as we have seen and will see again—he went to great pains to distort the truth of major events or to rewrite history as it applied to him. He seemed to have inordinate faith that no one would ever notice his lies. The question is, was he more interested in deluding himself than in deceiving others? Quite possibly. There is a pattern of such behavior in Tristan's life.

That he was able to maintain most of his deceptions for over two decades, until the end of his life, suggests that he often deluded himself. That could be considered mythomania or a strong case of selective memory, an ability we all possess. In recounting an event—especially from the distant past—few of us can avoid coloring our memories.

Many narratives, inadvertently or not, bear little resemblance to historical facts. Author and sailor John Kretschmer quoted Tristan as saying, no doubt with tongue firmly in cheek, "All my stories are true. I just remember them differently each time."

Was Tristan's constant exaggeration, or lying, a legacy of his childhood without a real family, a product of his low self-esteem? Did his pugnacious attitude stem from his low social status? There are no positive answers, only conjecture. And that is based on limited psychological analysis, an inexact science at best. The answer to both questions is probably yes. Tristan definitely had a chip on his shoulder. Pete Kelly remembered it from the mid-1960s. Conrad Jelinek saw it in the 1970s. Henry Wagner and many others experienced it in the 1980s and 1990s.

While some may have doubted the veracity of his wilder tales, no one who met him believed that the cocky little yachtsman was anything other than what he claimed to be—a courageous sailor prepared to endure almost anything for adventure. His strength, perhaps, and his advantage, was that he apparently had mesmerized himself into believing his own fiction. Eventually that belief would develop into reality. Arthur Jones would become the Tristan Jones of his books.

David Roberts, author of *Great Exploration Hoaxes*, identified an interesting common feature among exploration frauds. Each perpetrator had a perceived enemy, often a rival. Tristan too had real and imagined enemies, usually rivals, but they appeared much later, once the knowledge of his books began to circulate around the marinas and yacht clubs of the world. He was intensely jealous of the success of circumnavigators Sir Francis Chichester and Chay Blyth, and he attacked both in letters to friends. He also fell afoul of a handful of boating journalists, most of whom considered him a beguiling writer while placing little credence in his tales of adventure and his transoceanic claims.

As a nonfiction writer it is important to be scrupulous about facts. Only then can one be sure of telling a story accurately. Tristan had no such concerns. Perhaps he would have felt more in tune with a line from John Gardner's *The Art of Fiction*: "Whatever the genre may be, fiction does its work by creating a dream in the reader's mind." Tristan certainly did that.

Admitted fiction came soon enough. *Dutch Treat*, a novel of wartime, followed *Saga*. Then Tristan reverted to type. He produced *Adrift* in 1980 and passed it off as another in his autobiographical series. *Adrift* tells of fictional adventures in South America at the end of his voyage in *Sea Dart* and his early days in New York. *Aka* came next, a lovely novel about a solo round-the-world sailor and a dolphin tribe.

The inconsistencies and inaccuracies in Tristan's "nonfiction" books somehow escaped his editors. It's hard to believe stories about stuffing a manatee into a pressure cooker, as reported in *The Incredible Voyage*, or about a monkey with an extra hand on its tail, in the same book. Yet editors allowed those fantasies to pass. His fans, too, either didn't notice them or didn't care. Most of them were in awe of the wayward sailor by this time. They would believe almost anything he told them, because they wanted to.

Samuel Taylor Coleridge's brilliant line, "That willing suspension of disbelief for the moment, which constitutes poetic faith," fits a high proportion of Tristan's readers perfectly. They don't care whether he told the truth about his experiences or made them up. Fact or fiction, his works are damned good stories written by a superior craftsman— and that is why he was so popular with real and armchair sailors alike.

Photographer Carl Paler met Tristan in 1980, in New York. Paler's first contact with him, in a bar named Patrick's, reflected the experiences of many others, especially from the Ibiza years. Tristan was drunk and noisy. Annoyed, Paler had words with him. Instead of throwing a punch as he so often did, Tristan gave him his business card. Paler read "Author, Explorer" and commented that it was a "bull-shit card." Far from being angry, Tristan urged him to go to the nearest B. Dalton bookstore, where all his books were on display. Paler did so, saw the shelf of books, and was suitably impressed. The two became friends and regularly drank together, often to excess, in a variety of Greenwich Village bars: Patrick's, Julius's, and the Lion's Head. Tristan told Paler the same old stories of being born at sea on his father's ship and of his wartime experiences. Paler supplied the black-and-white portrait photograph of Tristan for the cover of *Adrift*.

While in California on a book-signing tour that year, Tristan met the famous sailing couple Larry and Lin Pardey and the noted French single-hander Bernard Moitessier.

Early in 1981 Tristan received a fan letter from respected New York literary agent Richard Curtis. The two met soon after and got along well enough for Tristan to terminate his agreement with Peter Matson. In March a fifteen-year association began. It was to be a rocky ride for both, though it was launched spectacularly when Curtis discovered his latest client was owed more than $18,000 by his publisher, a considerable coup. But Tristan never quite understood that he was only one of many authors represented by the Richard Curtis Agency. He expected his agent to be available at any hour of day or night and to be all things, from friend to super salesman. When he submitted a manuscript he expected an immediate response from Curtis, accompanied by a publishing contract and an advance against royalties. He would tolerate no delays, no excuses.

Tristan gave acquaintances the impression that he hated Richard Curtis, and many of his letters reflect that sentiment. Twice he sent Richard short, sharp letters warning him that their agreement had to end. On at least one occasion he actually signed with another agency. Within a couple of weeks he was back with Curtis, who bore his client's tantrums with phlegmatic calm. Curtis wasn't alone. Tristan was equally difficult with Abner Stein, his agent in Britain.

Living in Greenwich Village, perhaps because of its proximity to Broadway, prompted Tristan to think in terms of the stage. With a J. Doyle, he wrote a stage play called *Purity*, now lost, and he drafted a stage monologue based on a major scene from *Ice!* The one-act play about the Arctic, never published or performed, suffers from an over-abundance of references to characters from Celtic mythology. More than half the manuscript is taken almost word for word from a 1949 translation of *The Mabinogion* by Gwyn Jones and Thomas Jones.

Tristan knew the eleven tales from the *Mabinogion* well and often quoted from them. Closely associated with the old legends of King Arthur, they are magical stories from Celtic history. Tristan made an English translation of *The Mabinogion* while living in New York, called *Echoes of Distant Thunder*. He said he wrote the tales down from memory as they were told to him in Welsh when he was a boy. That he could read, write, or speak Welsh has never been confirmed. In any event the manuscript was rejected by publishers. It is quite possible that his version was taken from an earlier translation of the work, probably the 1949 edition, and rewritten in a modern style.

Claiming to be Welsh, as his surname suggests and as his mother may well have been, Tristan felt he needed a Welsh background. In 1981 he planned a visit to England and Wales. On August 10 of that year he wrote to his friend Wally Herbert, "I may be in Wales for a couple of weeks in late September, to research a book to be called 'A Steady Trade,' which is the tale of my childhood among the Victorians."

His visit to Wales was delayed by a few weeks. He actually went there in November, after visiting Wally and Marie Herbert at their home in Devon. Although we don't know exactly where in Wales Tristan went, we can safely assume he roamed the area between Barmouth, on the coast, and Dolgellau, a few miles inland, observing life in Welsh villages and towns. Knowing his admiration for the late mountaineer and sailor Bill Tilman, who lived in the Barmouth area for many years, it is probable that Tristan chose that region of northwest Wales as a setting for the fictional story of his own childhood. One assumes he also studied the history of British coastal sailing barges during his stay in the United Kingdom, in order to more accurately portray the lifestyles of hardworking barge sailors. A few months later he would tell Wally Herbert in a letter, "It *[A Steady Trade]* was written at white heat in 3 weeks last Dec."

After his trip to Wales Tristan went to London, where, as so often happened, he managed to find trouble. In Earls Court, he wrote to Wally Herbert, he stopped a man from assaulting a woman and suffered a severe knife wound requiring twenty-six stitches for his pains. If the story is true, the injury must have been hidden by his clothes. Photographs taken seven months after the fact show no new scars on his face or on his hands and arms. It's possible he was cut on the leg.

After a few years in New York, with a modicum of success as a writer, one wonders whether the stability of marriage, a more settled way of life, might occasionally have been on Tristan's mind. He once told Conrad Jelinek that he had been married in the States and had a son, but that both wife and son had died in a car crash. Conrad, conversant with his skipper's penchant for fallacious tales, took the comment with a grain of salt, and nothing more was ever said of the mysterious family ties. Not surprisingly, none of Tristan's other friends recall hearing the story.

Early in their friendship he told Wally Herbert he planned to marry an American woman named Demetra. Wally sent his congratulations, and that was the last anyone heard of a potential spouse. She has earned a certain limited fame, however. In the acknowledgments in *Ice!* Tristan recognized Dimitra Nicolai, who typed the manuscript for him. Allowing for the slight difference in spelling, the name is unusual enough for us to suspect that the two are the same person. The woman, unfortunately, has vanished into the dark corridors of time.

Perhaps marriage and a family would have been good for Tristan, if any woman could have put up with him for long. He loved children and regularly invited them aboard his boats. Nature, however, had something else in store for Tristan Jones.

Carl Paler recalled that Tristan often had an attractive "boy" in tow, though he expressed doubts about any physical involvement. Patience Wales thought he had "eclectic sexual tastes," implying that he was bisexual. Lin Pardey recognized him as gay. Another friend, video producer Chip Croft, believed Tristan's years in Greenwich Village contributed to the development of his homosexuality. Many years would pass, however, before Tristan would allow any hint of his sexual preferences to surface publicly.

CHAPTER 14

Down but Not Out

Invited to appear on a BBC Television show hosted by well-known ocean sailor and author Clare Francis, Tristan flew to London again in January 1982. Clare and Tristan, who had not previously met, declared themselves mutual fans. Tristan had included Clare's name in a long list of sailors and friends in the dedication to *The Incredible Voyage*. The platonic friendship that blossomed that evening was to last, although the two met rarely. Sadly, that live broadcast, on January 29, 1982, was the last time Tristan would be seen on television standing on his own two feet.

From London he went to Amsterdam, perhaps to visit friends or to research locations for a new novel, possibly for baser reasons. In a later book, *Outward Leg* (*A Star to Steer Her By* in the United Kingdom edition), he wrote of wallowing in the fleshpots of the seamy side of the city.

Amsterdam's red-light district is notorious for its lewd window displays and live sex shows performed behind closed, but not locked, doors. Any form of sex known to those who deal in the oldest profession is for sale in three-, four-, and five-story red-brick buildings beside a series of narrow canals. Brazen hustlers, straight and gay, tout their wares from doorways and windows framed with red and blue neon lights. This colorful hard-core advertisement for depravity covers many blocks close to the Centraal Station.

After his night of debauchery in the bars and clubs of Amsterdam's low-life community, Tristan wrote in *Outward Leg*, he was still thirsty. He said he was happy when he crossed the Leidseplein on that February morning in search of more beer. The Leidseplein is a long walk from the red-light district. What, one wonders, took Tristan to the outer limits of the inner city when everything he required was so much closer to the central area? Whatever he was doing in Amsterdam, the visit wreaked havoc with his life. As an indirect result, he lost his left leg.

As usual Tristan told a variety of stories about the events leading up to his amputation, most of which revolved around fictional wounds from World War II: "Some tiny bits of magnesium shrapnel in my left heel bone shifted somehow into my bloodstream, and were forming a clot." Or in *Outward Leg*, "An occlusion, he [the surgeon] called it." Journalists added to the confusion. "In 1982 he was knocked down by a tram in Amsterdam and subsequently lost his left leg to gangrene," one wrote. Another chose "He lost his leg to cancer." An obituary noted, "Complications from old shrapnel wounds led to amputation of his left leg." Tristan confided to Lin Pardey that he suffered from phlebitis.

In *Outward Leg* he wrote that the first indication of trouble with his leg came when a searing pain in his hip caused him to fall in front of a tram at Leidseplein. Many years later, when reprising that scene for an article, Tristan placed the accident at the cobblestone square in front of the Centraal Station, where trams scurry in all directions.

Tristan usually preferred the war wound theme when discussing his operation, often expanding it to shrapnel from a phosphorus bomb, or star shell, entering his right shoulder and left foot and lying dormant for forty years.

David and Margaret Shields received a phone call from Tristan later that February. He was in St. Vincent's Hospital in Greenwich Village, and he was in trouble. When they visited him, that same day, they found him in bed in a ward full of down-and-outers—one leg so rotted with gangrene that, the doctor told them, his life depended on immediate amputation. Tristan would not, could not, give his approval for the surgery, even though he had been told he would die without it. He needed someone close to him, in this case David Shields, to hold his hand and lead him to the inevitable. After consulting with the surgeon, David gave his permission for an operation to sever the leg below the knee. In doing so he saved Tristan's life. That operation was not entirely successful, for the gangrene was too far advanced. Further surgery was required to remove the knee, leaving just the stump of a thigh.

Why Tristan developed gangrene is not known. That information was long ago discarded by the hospital records staff as an out-of-date file, but all the evidence points to his being a diabetic. (An obituary published in Thailand mentions his diabetes.)

Perhaps the altercation in London's Earls Court the previous November had something to do with the amputation. An injury serious enough to require twenty-six stitches, assuming it was to his left leg or foot, could turn gangrenous in a diabetic if not properly looked after. But it's most likely that Tristan, drunk, fell in front of an Amsterdam tram in front of Centraal Station. Many a tourist has come close to grief by thoughtlessly stepping in front of a fast-moving tram at that busy railway and tram junction. Tristan received some injuries to his leg or foot and failed to obtain adequate treatment. As a result, gangrene set in as the leg began to die. Amputation became necessary to save his life. That analysis of the situation is nothing more than a theory, but it is a theory based on the most likely circumstances.

A letter Tristan wrote to Wally Herbert told a different version. And, it must be accepted, Tristan was not always honest in letters to his friends, as much later events would prove. On March 12, 1982, while in St. Vincent's Hospital in New York, he wrote: "I had a foot complaint in Holland which was mis-diagnosed as gout. Ten day's exquisite pain later in the USA it was diagnosed as three blood clots in my left leg. I have just had the leg amputated just below the knee as septicemia had set into my lower foot. 36 days of bloody hell."

The contents of that letter glaringly contradict his story of the shrapnel wound. Perhaps he was still groggy from the effects of his operation and not thinking clearly, for he was also wrong about the extent of the surgery. Wally, ever the friend, replied with a terse telegram: "Don't fret Tristan. An arse can be kicked with either foot and you have lots more kick in you yet. So get well and get moving old sailor friend and take care of the parts you have left for they don't make men in your mould any more and the spare parts department have got no replacement for the spirit of Tristan Jones."

Following the amputation Tristan sank into depression. He became increasingly bad-tempered and aggressive. He blamed his plight on the world, on incompetent gods, on the injustice of life. Ever an enthusiastic drinker, he began to imbibe more heavily still. Fortunately friends and acquaintances rallied round him in spite of his failings. David Shields bought him a reclining chair with a high back to make him more comfortable while writing and reading. Author and underwater archaeologist Dave Horner and his wife Jaynie invited Tristan to recuperate at their Florida home. The visit had its inevitable ups and downs, and its humorous moments.

Jaynie Horner did not always enjoy Tristan's presence in her home. He was dirty and smelly, and so were his clothes. Jaynie threw his underwear out in disgust and bought new for him. His attitude was the biggest problem—but even that had its lighter side. "He could be really obnoxious," Jaynie said. "As you can imagine, he was not the easiest houseguest. I was getting a little tired of having him there. Then, one morning he was outside by the swimming pool and I heard him call, 'Jaynie! Jaynie?' I thought, Oh my God, he's fallen in the pool. I was afraid to go out and see what had happened, but I did. He was so excited and thrilled because he had just learned to use his artificial leg and he wanted me to see him. He was like a little child just learning how to walk. That warmed my heart and I began to feel more kindly towards him. But, nevertheless, he was with us for a while and difficult at times.

I did not regret his leaving, but I do have a special place in my heart for him."

Dave Horner arranged a speaking engagement for Tristan at a local yacht club. After the event the commodore invited Tristan to spend the night at her home. As so often happened, Tristan drank too much and became boisterous. When the woman and her husband went to bed Tristan positioned himself outside their bedroom door and sang ribald sea chanteys to them for half the night. He finally passed out where he was and snored loudly the rest of the night. Horner was politely ordered to retrieve his guest that morning.

Larry Pardey offered a piece of teak so that Tristan could carve himself a peg leg. Tristan responded that he would be delighted to have Larry carve it for him and sent the dimensions. He was rewarded with a beautifully fashioned appendage, which he wore only occasionally.

While recuperating from the operation Tristan finished writing *One Hand for Yourself, One for the Ship*, a project he had started several years before. Subtitled *The Essentials of Single-Handed Sailing*, it is a useful volume for small-boat sailors considering venturing offshore. Unfortunately, he plagiarized significant parts of the book from Lin and Larry Pardey's writings. When gently confronted by the Pardeys, Tristan apologized and sent a check for $200. All subsequent editions of the book acknowledge the Pardeys' contribution.

Desperately in debt after his amputation, Tristan built sailboat mobiles from teak and brass for sale to his fans to supplement the unreliable income from his books. While he adjusted to life on one leg in New York, he learned that his old sailing partner, Pete Kelly, was close by. After the two parted in 1968, Kelly had moved on from the Mediterranean to the Caribbean. By 1982 he was a guest of the Manhattan Correctional Center, awaiting trial on a drug-smuggling charge. Eager to see an old friend and offer support, Tristan attempted to visit Kelly in prison. He took copies of his books with him as gifts, and that created a problem.

Hardcover books can be used for hiding contraband, which Tristan probably did not know. He arrived at the center on one good leg and one wooden peg, carrying a walking stick for support. A gigantic security guard at the center took Tristan's books and ripped the covers off to make sure nothing was hidden inside. Horrified, Tristan lost his temper and attacked the guard with his stick. Needless to say, he did not get to see Pete Kelly. Without further ado the guards forcibly evicted Tristan, who should have considered himself fortunate not to join his friend for a while.

Tristan discovered a teenage boy eating from a garbage can on Washington Square one day and took a shine to him. He installed the vagrant in his apartment as a helper and companion. Carl Paler thought the boy was crazy and told Tristan so. Tristan ignored the suggestion and kept the boy for a while, partly because he played chess well. The association ended when the boy attacked Tristan in his bath. Paler's assessment of the boy's mental health seemed confirmed when he later saw him wearing a ski jacket and carrying skis on a Manhattan street one hot summer's day.

As his health and his locomotion improved, Tristan attended East Coast boat shows to sell his books and meet his public. As much as possible, he hid his curmudgeonly attitude. Lady Luck smiled on Tristan at the Stamford (Connecticut) Boat Show in 1982. Joan Wagner, from Sailor's Bookshelf, a leading retailer of boating books, recognized him hobbling through the show and called him over. Telling her assistant, "Go and get Captain Jones a beer," she invited Tristan to sit at the booth and autograph his books. Joan's husband, Henry Wagner, was working the Houston Boat Show at the time. He and Tristan met soon after and became firm friends—another friendship that would last until Tristan's death. More than a friend, Henry became a stabilizing influence and did more to help promote Tristan than anyone else. In many ways Wagner acted as an unofficial manager for Tristan and his whims.

Tor Pinney met Tristan at Annapolis that year. Pinney was captain of the prototype Morgan 60, a modern-rigged schooner named *Paradigm*, on her debut tour of five East Coast boat shows. He remembered Tristan clearly: "Among the patrons on the bar's raft was a crusty old mariner, off by himself, leaning against the rail, drinking and smoking a cigarette. He didn't look like much of an exhibitor to me. Slim, shaggy-haired and bearded, he sported a worn pea jacket, rumpled trousers, black rubber sea boots and a squashed Royal Navy cap that had seen better days. Compared to the slick, blue-blazer clad yacht brokers all around us, this guy looked like he'd been washed ashore by an errant squall and hadn't quite dried out yet."

The two captains started a conversation and talked about Tristan's one-legged status. "Have you ever tried sailing a multihull?" Pinney asked. "Maybe a broader, more level deck would be easier to move around on for you." Neither man knew it then, but a multihull would figure largely in Tristan's future. That evening they met again aboard *Paradigm* for another chat. "What are you drinking?" asked Pinney. "I'll have a rum and coke, if you please," answered Tristan, who chain-smoked throughout the evening and managed to finish most of a bottle of rum.

Pinney fell afoul of the irascible sailor's unpredictable wrath in Fort Lauderdale at a later boat show. Tristan hobbled up to *Paradigm* soon after she docked. He and Pinney greeted each other in sailorly fashion. Then, Pinney wrote: "His eyes flickered to my boat laying alongside the dock, then to the nearby sea wall. He looked hard at me and snapped, 'But after getting your vessel safely down here, what the hell are you doing docking her like that? You fancy yourself a bloody captain? What in bloody hell are you going to do if the shit hits the fan and you suddenly have to move that boat out of here? You going to back her out in a blow in this claustrophobic little space, are you? Don't you know any better than to put your bow to a sea wall? Don't you think the weather matters in port?' "

Pinney was stunned at the unexpected tirade and embarrassed that others couldn't help overhearing. He started to babble some excuse about the sales manager's telling him to put the boat there. Tristan interrupted. "Sales manager? What in bloody hell does he know about your ship? You're the bloody captain, aren't you?" "Tristan then relented somewhat," Pinney continued, "his attitude softening a little." "Listen, mate," the old salt cautioned, "you don't ever, ever want to put your bow in towards the shore. Always dock so you're facing outward. You have to be ready to escape from any harbor if things turn nasty, be it bad weather, unfriendly government officials, or some wench's angry husband. Now, I've said enough. What say we sit down and have us a drink? Give the old stump a bit of a rest."

"Later, when Tristan [and another bottle of rum] were gone, I switched on the VHF radio to catch a weather update," Pinney said. The report was not good. What Pinney heard worried him, especially after Tristan's harsh warning. A cold front with strong winds was due in the area before dawn. Pinney sensibly moved his boat to safety, against company orders. It was a wise decision. The storm wrenched the temporary dock from its moorings and slammed it into the sea wall. Had he left *Paradigm* where she was, she would have suffered considerable damage. Pinney was hailed as a savior by his employers and paid a bonus. "But for myself," he said, "I know who the real hero was. That crusty old salt who had probably forgotten more about seamanship than I'll ever know. Thanks, Tristan! You were bloody well right!"

Bob Grosby and his friend (later second wife) Esther sailed in to Newport during one of Tristan's lecture tours. Not having seen Tristan since 1975, Bob was intrigued when he saw a poster announcing a lecture by Tristan Jones at a local junior high school auditorium. Naturally, he and Esther bought tickets and took a seat among the mostly young people in the sold-out room. Bob briefly described the evening: "The major part of the lecture concerned long solo passages and the need for self-reliance, not only on the sea, but in life in general. When the lecture ended the discussion was spirited. I was amazed [at the way he handled the audience]. Essie and I worked our way to the lectern and caught Tristan's attention. We embraced. We all then left for a local restaurant, lifted a few, ate some food and talked [of] old times."

Solo sailing was an interesting choice of topic for Tristan, considering his dislike of sailing alone. It is to his credit that he was able to handle the subject intelligently and successfully.

Tristan, like many of his countrymen at the time, particularly former servicemen, had a xenophobic attitude toward Germans that surfaced in *The Incredible Voyage* with an unpleasant anecdote about his experiences at the Bolivian Yacht Club. That unnecessary inclusion brought him trouble in the summer of 1982. Robert J. Austin became so angry at Tristan's published accounts of his adventures on Lake Titicaca that he wrote a scathing letter to him on July 22, 1982.

> *Dear Mr. Jones, I used to take everything you wrote with a grain of salt, but that was only until I myself lived in Bolivia (1979–81), had my own 27-foot sailboat for a year on Lake Titicaca, and got to know Bruno Boehme, the respected Bolivian Doctor and pleasure boater you did a hatchet job on in* The Incredible Voyage. *Only then did I realize what incredible rubbish you are capable of writing about your single-handed (with good reason: nobody to hold you to the truth) experiences. While a lot of* The Incredible Voyage *should be questionable even to the uninitiated, for those who know Bolivia and Lake Titicaca it is a compendium of inaccuracies, hyperbole, and outright invention. Examples: If you look at your map again, Captain, you'll find Illampu and Illimani not "far to the west," but quite to the east and southeast; try to anchor in "Kona Bay" and you'll not find bottom in 20 feet of water (maybe one of your famous "submarine earthquakes" lowered the bottom 120 feet since 1974): and, especially, have another look at the Bolivian Yacht Club from a viewpoint of "overwhelming egoism."*
>
> *Do you really expect people to believe that the YCB [Bolivian Yacht Club] is a stalag? Why? Peaked caps, Sam Browne belts and jackboots, Alsatian dogs, chain link and barbed wire? Give me a break, Tristan. Dr. Boehme's "heavy German accent?" Dr. Boehme was born and raised in Bolivia and speaks not a word of German. If the YCB has a distinctly Eu-*

ropean flavor, it's because boating for pleasure is not a Third-World con-
cept. A middle-class Welshman has a certain social freedom stemming
from attitudes alien to the average Bolivian or Indonesian, or Turk. Your
smug attitude seems to have alienated about everyone I talked to on the
lake, including the boatbuilder Limachi on Suriqui, who was polite
enough to say only that he vaguely recalled you and that "there had been
some problem" with you. Nor are you any darling of poor Bolivia's tiny or-
ganized yachting community which, by the way, includes "true" Bolivians,
as well as Americans, Canadians, and Brits among its members.

If, in your recollections which led to the writing of . . . Voyage (I say
recollections because you obviously didn't keep notes), you recall having
seen a lot of German-looking Bolivians, it's because the incident where
you made yourself persona non grata *with them did not take place at*
the yacht club at all, but at the German Club in La Paz, where Dr.
Boehme had the kindness to invite you.

I have a gentlemanly proposition for you: you'll find enclosed a pre-
written apology to the Bolivian Yacht Club. Sign it and return it to me be-
fore 14 August 1982 and I promise to ignore you forever. What Dr. Boehme
decides to do with it is up to him, but I suspect it will never leave Bolivia.
If you choose to ignore this chance to set things right, I will forward a copy
of this letter to both Sail *and* Cruising World *and will appear at your 21*
August program in Newport, near where I will be vacationing, and at-
tempt to present Dr. Boehme's and my statement on the nature of the YCB
and the incident on which you based your . . . Incredible . . . account.

The apology, typed in English and Spanish and addressed to Dr.
Bruno Boehme and the membership of the Bolivian Yacht Club, is
worth reprinting because Tristan so rarely backed down when confronted with his inaccuracies. His usual reaction was to fight. On this
occasion he subdued his natural tendencies. The apology reads:

In 1977, after sailing my boat Sea Dart *on Lake Titicaca in 1974, I wrote*
a book called The Incredible Voyage, *in which I made certain allega-*
tions about the Bolivian Yacht Club and its membership which might
have caused mistaken impressions among readers of my book. I realize
and recognize that some of my impressions might have been mistaken or

*that my memory might not have served me entirely well between the time
I sailed on Lake Titicaca and the publication of* The Incredible Voyage,
*and hereby apologize for any inconvenience or embarrassment I might
have caused the Bolivian Yacht Club and its members and Bolivian pleasure boaters in general through some of the statements I made in my book.*

*I also thank Dr. Bruno Boehme for any kindness or help he offered me
on behalf of the Bolivian Yacht Club and/or the German Club in La Paz
during 1974.*

Sincerely,
Tristan Jones
August 5th, 1982

Tristan signed both copies and returned them with no further comment. His Newport appearance went off without interruption.

Henry Wagner's memories of Tristan's stage presentations, and his
storytelling style, remain vivid. His admiration for Tristan's ability to
handle an audience under any conditions is exemplified in one of his favorite stories. Tristan was booked to deliver a talk to a holistic medicine society, although he wasn't aware of his audience's interests.

"He was drunk when we arrived, and wearing his usual twenty-
five dollars worth of clothes, with cigarette burns on his lapels," Henry
explained. "Tristan walked up to the microphone, obviously the worse
for wear, and started to talk. He was leaning at about forty-five degrees
and obviously drunk. Some people got up and left. Those that stayed
were treated to Tristan at his best. Drunk or not, he gave a marvelous
performance."

Henry also said: "Tristan was always adamant when he told a tale
that it had happened just the way he told it. Maybe, in his mind, he believed all his own stories: really believed they actually happened just
the way he told them. And he could make other people believe them too.
Often when strapped for cash, and with nothing new to write about,
Tristan would simply rewrite a previous article to suit his current needs."

At one boat show, Henry Wagner recalled (he didn't remember the year), Tristan went to the bar with a couple of editors of *Cruising World* magazine. Tristan had recently read comments that sailing author Webb Chiles had made about Bernard Moitessier. He decided the comment was derogatory toward Moitessier and prepared to avenge the Frenchman. While the boating journalists were trying to hold a sensible conversation, Tristan, well into his cups, kept calling loudly, "Bring me the head of Webb Chiles." He was more or less ignored as his companions attempted to continue their talk. Tristan was not to be put off. "Bring me the head of Webb Chiles," he bellowed again and again. "He'd take a drink," Henry said, "then he'd shout for Chiles's head. Finally, after too many drinks, he yelled, 'Bring me . . .' and that's as far as he got. His chair went over backwards, Tristan hit the floor hard, and passed out."

A Steady Trade appeared in bookstores that same year. This book, the story of his birth at sea and his childhood in a Welsh hamlet—the version of his life he wanted the public to believe—was written as only Tristan could do it, with style and a unique literary flair—if not with the most honest of intentions. To most readers, as Tristan intended, *A Steady Trade* is an autobiographical look at his early life. Unfortunately, wonderful though the book certainly is, there is far more fiction than fact on its pages. Having said that, it is a fascinating tale and, if one ignores the overdramatization, well told. Tristan's research, however, shows many inaccuracies.

Tristan uses a roller-skating rink as a literary prop in both *Ice!* and *A Steady Trade*, as part of *Western Star*'s cargo. Originally destined for Nova Scotia, Tristan told us, the roller-skating rink was sold at an earlier port, and his father therefore diverted *Western Star* from Halifax to Liverpool. Megan, Tristan's fictional mother, then took her newborn son home to the tiny hamlet of Llangareth, in north Wales (where three years later she gave birth to a daughter), while her husband went back to sea.

In *Ice!*—written two years before *A Steady Trade*—Tristan suggests that Jones Senior led a rather different life after his son's birth. He tells his friend Kiwi that his father imported the first roller-skating rink ever landed in Britain, back in 1924. He then suggests that instead of returning to sea after his wife and son settled in Llangareth, his father operated the rink himself for a year or more. Eventually there was an economic slump, and the good captain went broke.

The truth is, the roller-skating rink stands at the Palace complex in New Brighton, across the river Mersey from Liverpool. It was installed as far back as 1871, with other amusements, when the Palace was built. Owned by the Wilkie family, now the Boswell Wilkie Circus group, much of the site was destroyed in a fire in 1916, during World War I. The roller-skating rink and the theater were saved. Tristan's father obviously could not have imported the rink in 1924.

He spread similarly confusing versions about his schooling. There's the lovely fictional story in *A Steady Trade* about how he and his younger sister, Angharad (who is almost certainly fiction), attended a one-room school presided over by Mr. Jeffreys-Geography. Or there's one he told to a journalist that has the young, orphaned Jones receiving little more than a rudimentary education before being shuffled off to sea as a barge hand. Another told of his juvenile march though nineteen elementary schools around the world as the family followed Jones Senior, a Trinity House pilot, to his many places of employment. He told one interviewer his education had been next to none because his nomadic father's itinerary had dragged him to fourteen church and municipal elementary schools all over Britain. He went on to tell of one school in a dreary Manchester suburb—he thought the year was 1937 and the teacher was a Miss Gore.

The second half of *A Steady Trade* relates the story of a young boy—Tristan Jones—working himself to exhaustion on a traditional sailing barge trading on both sides of the Channel. The book is arguably Tristan's best work. Among pages of superior writing, his considerable literary talent weaves ethereal images of an unreal world surrounding a ship at sea. There are echoes of Welsh poet Dylan Thomas's "Poem on His Birthday" in the following passage: "Our ship a poor intruder in the halls of the Mighty and the words of mere men nibbling at the moon's face under the Aurora Australis and the frosted Cross over the edge of a frozen universe, and shadows of priestlike clouds traipsing over rimed beaches like mammoths tramping over stones, and a scavenger's wind, cold and vengeful over the world. In those seas' dark coming it is all a man can do to remember the presence of Jehovah . . . and the penguins (Welsh word that is, bach) debating over bleached bones of deep-diving right whales, like landlords arguing a rent raise on the day before the crack of doom."

His description of a boy left to steer a ship without supervision is haunting: "I was awakened from my half-reverie suddenly, as a seabird cried over the starboard quarter. I turned my head to see it. Tansy was no longer on his bucket; he must have crept away down the companionway and left me to steer the ship alone. There was no one else on deck. I was in command of the ship. Silently, without a word, the accolade of trust had been bestowed on me, and I knew then that I was considered to be more of a man than I thought myself to be. Almost mechanically, I peered down into the compass binnacle. The ship was a point off the course. Joyously, proudly, I shoved the helm over and lifted my head and checked the wind and the sails."

It is beautiful, expressive writing, though it had nothing to do with Tristan's life. Those tales of a boyhood at sea appear to have been taken from stories Ian Spooner had told Arthur Jones in 1964 about his father's life on coastal sailing vessels. Once again he had delivered personal fiction packaged as fact.

Unable to resist any opportunity for exposure, and adapting more and more to his self-made piratical image, one-legged Tristan could often be seen in Greenwich Village during his New York years with a parrot on his shoulder, a pipe in his mouth, and a drink in his hand.

Another invitation to be a guest on BBC Television took Tristan to London once more, in November 1982. Irish interviewer Frank Delaney had three guests: Patrick Leigh Fermour, Sir Laurens van der Post—

godfather to Prince William and himself to be the subject of a revealing biography a few years after his death—and Tristan.

Van der Post and Fermour wore dark business suits, shirts, and ties. Tristan wore what appeared to be the jacket of a navy blue suit and the trousers from a light brown suit. Underneath could be seen a pale blue open-neck shirt covering a yellowish T-shirt. His lack of sartorial style compared with the others did not bother Tristan. He was there to entertain, not to impress with his fashion sense.

On two occasions during the program, discerning viewers may have had the impression that Tristan was trying to flirt with his handsome, married host. Asked about the eye he injured in the North Atlantic, Tristan showed the scar over his right eye and replied that it was fine. "In fact," he said, "I navigated the taxi driver here. I couldn't see the green lights but I could see the reds."

Delaney laughed at the response and interjected, "A seafaring man." Tristan answered with a smile, and his dark eyes locked on Delaney's, causing Delaney to laugh again, but with a note of embarrassment. Recovering, he confessed with another laugh, "You'll get me into trouble before this program is over." With a broad smile Tristan quipped, "I hope so."

After a discussion about the whys and wherefores of travel, Delaney asked Tristan if he ever got lonely. Tristan came back with one of his standard and, it must be said, most annoying responses: "Only in the mating season." Delaney, an excellent interviewer and intelligent host, had trouble keeping his composure at that point. Laughing silently into his sleeve, he scratched his head to gain time. With another artful smile, Tristan jumped in to save him with a risqué qualifier, "And that's not too bad when the penguins are around."

There followed a rapid interchange between the two, with Delaney asking Tristan whether he missed intelligent conversation. After a flippant answer—"I've never had one"—Tristan straightened his face and replied, "Yes, I know what you mean, of course. I know what you're getting at." Delaney, perhaps not realizing the trap he was setting for himself, interrupted with, "And *I* know what *you're* getting at." Tristan leered at him and shot back, "Not yet, you don't."

In answer to Delaney's question, "Why do you travel?" Sir Laurens van der Post and Patrick Fermour each gave an intelligent, though long-winded, assessment of his feelings on the subject. Tristan's reply was basic: "Because it gets me from A to B. Why does anybody travel? You go from this place to that place."

Contrary to Tristan's words in *Outward Leg*, where he vowed his comments sent the studio audience into an uproar, a few members of the audience chuckled politely for a second, maybe two.

Comfortable with his status as a minor celebrity, happy that his books were continuing to sell reasonably well, and, after almost a year, resigned to being an amputee, Tristan should have been content to live in New York and write. His editors (Euan Cameron from Bodley Head in particular) and his friends, wanting him to grow as an author, advised him to do just that—stay in New York and write. Tristan the sailor, however, was restless and bad-tempered. He'd been in New York six years, he'd seen eight of his books published, and he was finishing *Yarns*—a collection of short features, both fact and fiction. Once *Yarns* was out of the way he embarked on *Heart of Oak*, another "autobiographical" book—this time about his naval career. Still, it wasn't enough.

His letters to friends and acquaintances for the first half of 1983 constantly refer to his need for a boat, preferably a trimaran, initially to sail to Mexico, where he could live cheaply while writing, later to cross the Atlantic solo—with only a dog for company. He needed another adventure—another long voyage—another story to tell. Maybe he missed the taste of salt on the wind.

CHAPTER 15

Once More, Down to the Sea

While an unhappy Tristan languished ashore, writing a new book while dreaming of another boat and endless horizons, a young Australian boat designer was making an impact in San Diego. With a series of trimaran designs from twenty-eight feet to forty-eight feet behind him, Leonard Surtees was keen to show another facet of his talents. He had developed an innovative rerightable system for trimarans—three-hulled sailboats—and wanted to test it. As Len explained, "The rerightable feature was intrinsically designed into the trimaran right from the concept of making available a safe world class family cruising yacht."

With the help of his wife, Maryanne, he built *Osprey 36*. Much to the surprise of the media and assembled boaters, Surtees launched the brand-new boat upside down on San Diego Bay in November 1980. He then single-handedly flipped the trimaran upright, aided, he said, by the rerightable system—a concrete-filled keel and a couple of leverage poles attached under the wings. Len and Maryanne, with their young daughter Sarah, had planned to sail *Osprey 36* home to Australia until a serious illness in the family called for a change of plans. Len listed his boat for sale with West Coast Yacht Brokers in San Diego and flew home to Sydney.

Larry Haftl, president of California-based H & S Bluewater Multihulls Inc., was a Tristan Jones fan. In a press release he affirmed that, having read Tristan's first four books, "I had come to greatly admire the man behind those books, his beliefs, his abilities, his compassion and his sense of right." Haftl made himself a promise. If Tristan Jones ever needed his help, it would be forthcoming. Fate, in the form of Tristan's "fatalistic synchronism," stepped in.

Tristan was in a yacht broker's office in San Diego when Haftl and his then business partner, Bob Smith, walked through the door. Haftl described the incident as meeting "a piece of lunar landscape in the flesh." Over coffee on the patio, Tristan told the yacht manufacturers of his dreams for a new voyage, in a trimaran. H & S Bluewater Multihulls just happened to know where there was a thirty-six-foot Osprey class trimaran available. After a nod from his smiling partner, Haftl offered Tristan the use of the trimaran for free—if Haftl could get it—for a two-year charter. At no time was there any mention that H & S Bluewater Multihulls would financially support the voyage. Until that time, other than being paid to skipper *Barbara* on her far-reaching voyage, Tristan had avoided funding from others to achieve his goals, preferring to make his own way. The sailor who prided himself on never accepting any form of sponsorship was about to embark on a new approach, one he would not always enjoy. In the euphoria of the moment, such thoughts were no doubt far from Tristan's mind.

Speechless at the generosity of the offer, Tristan sat in silence for a few moments, probably wondering how fate had led him to San Diego. By the time the two entrepreneurs and the craggy mariner parted late at night after that initial meeting, Tristan was ecstatic. He had his boat, and he could pay his way by writing. Soon after, Len Surtees received a phone call from Larry Haftl. When Haftl told Surtees that he wanted to buy *Osprey 36* for Tristan Jones to sail around the world against the prevailing winds and ocean currents, Len's professional interest was aroused. As soon as Haftl asked him if he would be interested in preparing the boat for the voyage, Len's decision was made. "I was practically on the next plane out of Sydney, full of a sense of adventure and a mission to accomplish."

A press release from the offices of H & S Bluewater Multihulls of Winnetka, California, dated July 11, 1983, announced:

PROJECT STAR
Single-handed circumnavigation of the earth by Tristan Jones aboard a trimaran.
Primary purpose: to demonstrate to the world the capabilities and potentialities of "handicapped" people.

The news brief explained that special modifications would be made and fittings would be designed to maximize the safety and comfort of the amputee.

On his return to San Diego Len had just seven days to prepare *Osprey 36* for rigorous sea trials in the rough and unpredictable waters off Point Conception—known by ocean sailors as the Cape Horn of California. Seven days to get ready before Tristan's arrival on board. Surtees was excited, and in his handwritten notes about the big day there is a sign of nervousness. "Sitting in the cockpit I saw Larry Haftl's car pull up and both Larry and Tristan head towards us, about 100 yards. I couldn't help but notice two contrasting individuals, with Larry being about 6′4″ tall and 200 plus lbs with an amiable gait. Then there was Tristan. Smallish, frail-looking (how wrong first impressions can be!) hobbling along dressed in light brown safari trousers and jacket, topped off with a 'Mad Dogs and Englishmen' safari hat. More noticeable was the peg leg protruding from under his trouser cuff."

Len had planned a few pleasant words of welcome and introduction as they shook hands. Tristan beat him to it. In a gravelly voice he asked, "How's it going, Mate?" And that, said Surtees, was all it took. In an instant a mutual respect and friendship was born.

Osprey 36 as a name for the boat did not fit Tristan's personality. Expressing his topical and rather morbid sense of humor, he quickly changed it to *Outward Leg*. And so another legend was born to join *Sea Dart* in the annals of sailing.

Sea trials and outfitting the boat to Tristan's exacting specifications filled the rest of July, August, and September 1983. When *Outward Leg* sailed out of San Diego harbor and set course northward for the toughest test, Tristan was at the helm, on one good leg and one peg. He admiringly absorbed the sensations of a well-bred multihull as she rose and fell with the Pacific Ocean's never-ending swells. Beside him Len Surtees and Larry Haftl studied the boat's every movement with a mix of anxiety and pride.

Point Conception lived up to its reputation. *Outward Leg*'s sea trials took place in a howling gale and proved to be a roaring success. Haftl was pleased to have found a safe and seaworthy yacht, while Tristan's introduction to a modern trimaran, to quote Surtees, "blew him away. Never before had Tristan experienced the safe stable platform that this multihull offered along with outstanding bursts of speed. Tristan was like a little boy with a new toy. He especially enjoyed the incredible control he had while surfing down waves as *Osprey [Outward Leg]* obeyed his every demand on the helm."

Bob Smith filmed the trials from a helicopter, an extravagance that annoyed Tristan, who would rather have seen the money used for the voyage. Other than that, he was reasonably content. Before he pronounced himself satisfied with the trimaran's performance, however, the skipper required one more test. How did she handle when hove-to in a gale? The crew soon found out. Flying a small expanse of sail for stability and with the rudder on opposite lock and the bows at forty-five degrees to the oncoming sea, the boat sat stable enough for all on board to enjoy hot tea or coffee. Surtees watched Tristan's reaction with great interest. He said later, "Tristan's confidence and open affection for *Osprey* warmed us as this was Tristan's first sailing adventure since having his leg amputated."

In August Tristan sent the doctored logbooks of *Barbara* and *Sea Dart* to Wally Herbert as a donation to Herbert's planned "Explorer's Museum" in Devon, England. In a near repetition of a comment to Arthur Cohen a few years before, on the opening page of *Barbara*'s second logbook, Tristan wrote, "This is one of the most unique logs ever!" On the same page, perhaps to establish his ownership of the book, he childishly wrote, "Bought by T. Jones with his own money."

H & S Bluewater Multihulls paid $38,000 for the trimaran, then poured in more money to equip her for the circumnavigation. The investment is a measure of the high regard the two partners had for Tristan's reputation and sailing ability. With Tristan Jones as captain on a circumnavigation, it looked as though the company had an excellent marketing tool for at least two years. Somewhere between the concept and the execution, however, plans changed drastically.

The July 1983 press release from H & S Bluewater Multihulls included the basic route and timing proposed by Tristan. Departure from San Diego was set for October 10, 1983. After provisioning in Cabo San Lucas, Mexico, the trimaran would cross the Pacific to Australia—planning to arrive about New Year's Day 1984 for a six-week layover. She would then continue directly across the Indian Ocean to the Seychelles. By the end of May or the beginning of June, she would be through the Red Sea and Suez Canal and enter the Mediterranean, where she would cruise gradually west from June through September. In October she would tackle the Atlantic, intending a November landfall in Antigua. During December, January, and February she would cruise the Caribbean toward Panama. The plan called for a return to San Diego in March 1985, seventeen months after departure.

Larry Haftl expressed some concern at the tightness of the schedule, adding, "I want to emphasize that it is now and always will be his [Tristan's] choice of route and schedule and that he is under no obligation, as far as I am concerned, to stick to this or any other route plan and schedule. Nor for that matter is he required to complete the voyage. All is at his discretion, his safety and survival being the paramount concern."

This statement gave Tristan absolute freedom of movement with the boat: an unconditional authority he would soon exercise once at sea. Late in the preparations, Project Star's stated purpose changed. The idea of a solo voyage was dropped. When Tristan sailed out of San Diego harbor on October 17, 1983, as far as anyone was aware, he was en route for Australia after a brief stop at the foot of the Baja peninsula. With him went Mrs. Brimstone—a cat—and Wally Rediske as crew. Another crew member, Ivan Gonzalez, a Spaniard, joined them in Costa Rica.

Tristan took Haftl's words about his authority seriously. He aborted the Pacific crossing during the initial weeks, cruising, south along the Mexican and Central American coasts. Instead of sailing southwest on the long haul through the South Pacific islands to Australia as planned, he altered course for Panama—without telling anyone. News clips from San Diego papers at that time charted his anticipated course, even to estimating when he would cross the equator. Interested parties first learned of the change of route when *Outward Leg* arrived in Balboa to transit the Panama Canal.

Tristan's rationale for his radical change of direction was simply that he wanted to revisit Colombia, and he thought crossing the Caribbean west to east, the Atlantic against the Equatorial Current, and then the Mediterranean would be a more attractive challenge than tackling the Pacific Ocean.

Considering that he had already sailed the Caribbean in a much smaller boat, albeit in the opposite direction, and crossed the North Atlantic from west to east, as well as spending large amounts of time in the Mediterranean—including the west-to-east cruise in *Barbara*, Tristan's explanation is at best confusing and at worst weak. Crossing the Pacific, a voyage he had not so far undertaken and one *he* had planned for *Outward Leg*, would have been a new experience for him. He had never visited the South Sea islands or Australia. Why then would he go against his own maxim of preferring not to sail a course he had already navigated? The answer, perhaps, is that he felt a routine "milk run" circumnavigation would offer little scope for exotic adventures and therefore provide limited material for an exciting new book. By contrast, he knew Colombia and its potential for producing trouble. He knew the

Caribbean, Europe, and the Mediterranean. He knew where to find that excitement.

Tristan's earlier nautical adventures with *Cresswell, Barbara,* and *Sea Dart* were conducted in private, away from public scrutiny. As such he had enormous leeway to fictionalize his voyages. With *Outward Leg* that anonymity was lost. Under the glare of media interest, urged on by press releases, he was compelled to be somewhat more circumspect with his stories. Rather than fabricating hazardous situations to enliven his next books, the peripatetic sailor would have to seek out real adventures—ones he could handle with one living leg and one false one. He wrote of long weeks spent on the notorious Colombian coast, ostensibly studying piracy. Few sensible boaters deliberately dally where drug smugglers hold virtually unlimited sway. Tristan's Colombian sojourn made little sense considering Project Star's objectives, but Tristan apparently went looking for trouble to make a stronger story.

As early as Curaçao, only five months into the voyage, he began expressing concerns about H & S Bluewater Multihulls to Richard Curtis. In spite of there being no agreement to do so, he seems to have expected Haftl and Smith to finance the voyage as well as supplying the boat. Complaining that he had had no communications from H & S since he left San Diego, he wrote, "If I hear no word from H & S by NYC I may have to consider abandoning the voyage of *Outward Leg.*" He later suggested fleeing with the boat if the owners tried to take it away from him.

Outward Leg's voyage from San Diego to New York was well documented in the book of the same name, and the story was well written— if one ignores Tristan's new soapbox-orator attitude. The conversion of the early author into his new persona is reflected in his writing, the lighthearted tone of earlier books replaced by a cynical and pugnacious appraisal of the world and his place in it. In his next few books he railed at the gods and shouted his displeasure with the hand he had been dealt. Obvious embellishments became fewer, and anger was more often expressed. Perhaps he felt that the void created by eliminating fictional anecdotes must be filled with preaching and complaining.

On arriving in New York, seven months after leaving San Diego, Tristan said Mrs. Brimstone was the first of his crew to disappear. Next was Wally Rediske, who hoped to find work at a diving museum. Ivan left soon after. Tristan, however, was not alone.

Across the street from *Outward Leg*'s berth at the South Street Seaport stood the North Star Pub and a host of ears eager to listen to his tales. Manager Deven Black remembered Tristan well. "He used to sit on that stool there," he pointed across the bar. "He'd come in every day for a few weeks and have a meal and drinks. A lot of drinks." Black said he didn't much like Tristan, but he did appreciate that he attracted a lot of custom to the pub. His truculent nature, he said, caused many a verbal battle in the bar. "He'd deliberately pit one man against another," Deven said. "He'd provoke an argument between two guys and then sit back to watch the results."

Tristan always signed for his drinks and his meals rather than paying cash. The local representative of Watneys, a British brewery, eventually paid the bill, on the order of $1,000. In return, on arriving in London Tristan and a new crew were to be photographed wearing T-shirts advertising Watneys Red Barrel beer. Tristan further agreed to arrive at St. Katherine's Dock in London at a time and date of his choice. If he was successful, he would have a free berth alongside one of the brewery's pubs.

In New York Tristan began to talk about changing his plans again. Instead of cruising through the Mediterranean, he pondered crossing Europe via the Rhine and Danube. He deferred the decision until after the Atlantic crossing.

In June 1984 *Heart of Oak* was released. Tristan and his new crew, Pat Quinn and Terry Johannsen, sailed from New York to Newport on July 17, 1984. Tristan signed his books, including the new one, at the boat show for a couple of days. He got drunk with well-known boating author Don Street Jr. and with his pal Henry Wagner. And then it was time to return to the sea. Across an ocean a free berth waited.

Martha (later *Cresswell*) being launched from the beach at Cresswell, Northumberland, 1935.
Courtesy Royal National Lifeboat Institution.

Cresswell having her masts stepped, probably in the Mediterranean circa 1965.
Courtesy Henry Wagner Collection.

A young Pete Kelly on *Banjo* off
Espalmador, Balearic Islands, 1967.
Courtesy Henry Wagner Collection.

A party of daytrippers on *Banjo* off Espalmador, Balearic Islands, 1967. Tristan
claimed the seated woman on the right was
Sissie. Pete Kelly said she was actually
a Norwegian secretary.
Courtesy Henry Wagner Collection.

Tristan Jones at the helm of *Barbara* in
the Mediterranean, 1970.
Courtesy Henry Wagner Collection.

Arthur Cohen, *Barbara*'s owner, at her
helm in the Mediterranean, 1970.
Courtesy Henry Wagner Collection.

Tristan Jones on board *Barbara*...

...and at her helm at sea, circa 1970–71.
Courtesy Henry Wagner Collection.

Barbara about to be lowered into the Gulf of Aqaba at Eilat, Israel, December 1970.
Courtesy Henry Wagner Collection.

(left to right) Tristan Jones, Conrad Jelinek, and Alem Desta in Kenya, 1971.
Courtesy Henry Wagner Collection.

Jones and *Barbara* at sea, circa 1971.
Courtesy Henry Wagner Collection.

Sea Dart careened at Taboga Island, Panama, 1973.
Courtesy Henry Wagner Collection.

Tristan points to *Sea Dart*'s damaged propeller after hitting rocks off Ecuador, 1973.
Courtesy Henry Wagner Collection.

Tristan feeding water to an exhausted bird off the Pacific coast of South America, 1973.
Courtesy Henry Wagner Collection.

Tristan and *Sea Dart* outside the Peruvian Yacht Club, Callao, 1973.
Courtesy Henry Wagner Collection.

Sea Dart passing volcano Misty en route to
Lake Titicaca, December 1973.
Courtesy Henry Wagner Collection.

With *Sea Dart* at Puno, Peru,
after the long haul by truck up
to Lake Titicaca, December 1973. *Courtesy
Henry Wagner Collection.*

Sea Dart being lowered into Lake Titicaca
at Puno, Peru . . .

. . . and in Puno harbor, Lake Titicaca,
January 1974.
Courtesy Henry Wagner Collection.

Quechuas and their reed boats, and *Sea Dart* on Lake Titicaca, 1974.
Courtesy Henry Wagner Collection.

Crossing the Gran Chaco of Bolivia by train, September 1974.
Courtesy Henry Wagner Collection.

Edwin "Huanapaco" Mejia on the Paraguay
River after helping Tristan haul
Sea Dart from Lake Titicaca to
Asunción, Paraguay, 1974.
Courtesy Henry Wagner Collection.

Sea Dart moored on the Paraná River,
possibly at Asunción, 1974.
Courtesy Henry Wagner Collection.

In New York City,
circa 1980. © *Carl Paler.*

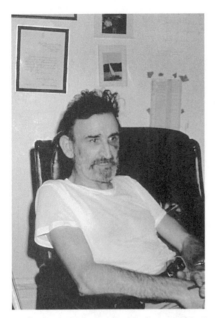

Tristan with a black eye, in his Greenwich Village apartment, June 1982.
Note the bookshelves lined with writing manuals. © *Mike Anderson.*

In Germany, on the Rhine–Danube crossing of Europe, winter 1984.
© *Manfred Peter, courtesy Willi Zeiss.*

With Martin Shaw (left) and Terry Johannsen (center) on *Outward Leg* on the Rhine, 1984.
© *Manfred Peter, courtesy Willi Zeiss.*

With thank-you sign on board *Outward Leg* on the Rhine,
winter 1984–85. © *Manfred Peter, courtesy Willi Zeiss.*

Outward Leg on the Donau Canal, 1985. © *Manfred Peter, courtesy Willi Zeiss.*

With Thomas Ettenhuber (left) on *Outward Leg* in Germany, 1985.
© *DONAUKURIER Ingolstadt, courtesy Willi Zeiss.*

Thomas Ettenhuber in Phuket, Thailand, 1987. *Courtesy Kriemhild Ettenhuber.*

Thomas Ettenhuber's grave in Bavaria. © *Kriemhild Ettenhuber.*

Tong Chai, the elephant, hauls *Henry Wagner* upstream during the Kra expedition, 1987. © *Thomas Ettenhuber.*

Tristan says a prayer before launching *Little Leg End* from his bungalow on the beach, Phuket, Thailand, 1992. © *Tristan Jones, courtesy Mike Warburton Collection.*

A legless Tristan Jones aboard
the catamaran *Gabriel* off Phuket,
Thailand, 1993. © *Matthew Burns,*
courtesy Jeff Ritchie Collection.

Circa 1994–95. © *Matthew Burns, courtesy*
Jeff Ritchie Collection.

Tristan aboard his dinghy
Little Leg End off Phuket,
Thailand, 1993. © *Tristan Jones,*
courtesy Mike Warburton Collection.

Henry Wagner, 2001. © *Anthony Dalton.*

Pete "the Manxman" Kelly, February 2001.
© *Anthony Dalton*

Mike Warburton, whose letter to King Hussein raised the funds to buy *Gabriel*.
© *Mike Warburton.*

CHAPTER 16

A Heart of Oak

In *Heart of Oak*, said to be the true story of Tristan's role in World War II, the author described that conflict from the point of view of a young man faithfully serving his country on the lower decks of a variety of His Majesty King George VI's Royal Navy fighting ships. The young Tristan of that book, we are told, fresh and tough from two years' coastal voyaging on a sailing barge, enlisted in the navy as a boy sailor in 1940 and was sent to HMS *Ganges* for his initial training.

Tristan's view of life at HMS *Ganges*, the Royal Navy's notorious shore establishment at Shotley on England's low-lying, windswept east coast, has been confirmed as accurate by former boy sailors who suffered the indignities heaped on them during their training. His research obviously paid off. He almost got it right, too. Almost, but not quite. He told his readers in *Heart of Oak* that he arrived at *Ganges* in early May 1940 as a sixteen-year-old. The weather, he added, was kind. Spring had shaken off winter. Southern England basked in warm sunshine.

He confided that he felt he'd been fortunate in getting accepted for one of the last boy sailors' classes to train at *Ganges* until the end of the war. What Tristan failed to learn from his reading, or his questioning of former *Ganges* recruits, was that the Lords of the Admiralty closed HMS *Ganges* as a Boys Training Establishment in the spring of

1940. In April of that year 264 men, known as "HOs" because they were drafted for "hostilities only"—in other words, for the duration of the war—arrived at Shotley to briefly join the 1,500 boys. On May 16, 1940, eight days after Tristan's birthday, 600 of those boys left *Ganges* for HMS *St. George*, on the Isle of Man. One day later the remaining boys left for training establishments at Devonport and Liverpool. And there, at three different stations, they continued their preparations for naval service. Meanwhile, the Shotley ground was used to initiate HOs into the dubious pleasures of military service.

A total of 60,968 HO ratings passed through HMS *Ganges* between May 1940 and the end of the war. Of those, 689 were Newfoundlanders, 545 were New Zealanders, and 13 were Falkland Islanders. In October 1945, with peace assured, the first batch of 152 new boys marched through the main gate at *Ganges*. By January 1946 HMS *Ganges*, the Boys Training Establishment, was back to full strength, with approximately 1,500 teenagers learning the nautical ropes.

Arthur Jones, the boy who would one day become Tristan Jones, obviously could not have joined HMS *Ganges* at Shotley in May 1940 as he recounted in *Heart of Oak*. Further, and far more important, in 1940 Britain may have been desperate for manpower to swell the ranks of her armed forces for her battle against the might of Hitler's Nazi war machine, but she was not so callous as to enlist eleven-year-olds.

As with stories of his earlier life in previous books, the tales in *Heart of Oak*—although loosely based on fact—are mostly fiction. The young Arthur Jones did not go to war. He was nowhere near old enough and so missed those frightening years of never knowing when an enemy torpedo might hit below the waterline and blow his ship to smithereens. Tales of his war wounds and of being sunk three times before he was eighteen are nothing more than fantasy.

Heart of Oak incorporates some of the best writing Tristan ever produced, with vivid and gory descriptions of major sea battles on the North Atlantic. Those tales are cleverly drawn from documented history. Tristan's powerful story of joining his first ship and the subsequent fire at sea is based on a real event. He said he and other recruits were detailed to join the armed merchant cruiser HMS *Cameroon* toward the end of February 1941. The ill-fated *Cameroon* caught fire at sea, and the author allowed his considerable imagination and writing skills free rein while maintaining the basic facts of a well-documented event.

His moving descriptions of *Cameroon*'s last hours, and the heroic rescue attempts, are intensely exciting and written with a passion strong enough to persuade any but the most skeptical to believe the story immediately. Tristan forces his readers to stand shoulder to shoulder with him as horrified witnesses in the midst of terror.

> *As I write I remember many things, all in a rush, with extreme vividness; I could try to set down in words the rush of the sea between the ships, the grinding rumble and screech as* Brooke *scrunched her hull alongside* Cameroon; *the shouts of the men, some jocular now, some crying in their despair and fright, as one sickening lurch and crash of both ships, one against the other, followed the previous one. It will not do. So that you will clearly understand what happened I must write down what followed in cold, precise phrases, just as, when I try to dissect my memories, they come to me like frames in a fast-moving film suddenly stopped for a few seconds. It is only thus that I can write what followed* Brooke's *sacrificial gesture. The facts are visible, tangible to me; part of my senses, part of me, keeping their place in space and time, in part of my life. They needed only a U-boat or two, a 1,000 ton destroyer and a converted liner of about 20,000 tons, an Atlantic gale, a raging fire, about one and a half thousand men and about three and a half hours before and after dusk. These facts made a whole that had facets galore, a complicated series of menacing events that could be seen in glimpses by the eye. But there was something else beside. Something invisible, a directing spirit of comradely essence, a willingness to lay lives down for the sake of friends. Here, now, my writing is slower . . . slower than it has ever been, with images surging up before me, as though to cut me off from all the modern shoreside world about me and everyone else in it.*

His epic tale continues with long, heartfelt descriptions of the dramatic scenes as HMS *Hayes*, a destroyer, braves mountainous seas to send Carley floats over to take off the endangered crew of *Cameroon*. HMS *Brooke* fights the storm to pick up survivors. Men scream in agony from burns, while others drown in the dreadful gray seas. And a few are crushed between two unyielding steel hulls.

Tristan continues his barrage of high drama and emotion as *Cameroon*, the former comfortable passenger liner, sinks into deep oceanic darkness before the gray of an Atlantic daybreak can bathe her in a soft light once more. With her, we are told, she took hundreds of dead and dying to an abysmally cold grave.

Naval records show that the heroic destroyers described in *Heart of Oak*, HMS *Brooke* and HMS *Hayes*, did not exist; neither did the armed merchant cruiser HMS *Cameroon*. However, records of British merchant shipping sunk during World War II describe the loss of the 15,241-ton former P&O liner SS *Comorin*. Formerly employed on the Britain-to-Australia run, she was requisitioned by the Admiralty in 1939 and converted to an armed merchant cruiser. Designated HMS *Comorin* for the duration of war, she was basically a troopship. There is little doubt that it was *Comorin*'s last voyage that Tristan described so ably in *Heart of Oak*.

HMS *Comorin* was on a passage from England to the West African port of Freetown, Sierra Leone, in April 1941. In addition to her crew she carried four hundred Royal Navy recruits bound for duty in more tropical waters than the unrelenting cold of the North Atlantic. On April 5, off the southwest coast of Ireland, *Comorin* caught fire. High winds and great Atlantic waves, thirty to forty feet high, slammed into the stricken ship, hampering efforts to put out the blaze. Fortunately, three other British ships were close enough to assist. They were the destroyers HMS *Broke* and HMS *Lincoln*, plus another armed merchant vessel, HMS *Glenartney*.

On Sunday, April 6, with no letup in the winter gale, HMS *Broke*'s captain, Lieutenant Peter Scott (later Sir Peter Scott—son of Robert Falcon Scott of Antarctic fame), made a valiant attempt to come alongside *Comorin* to take off as many men as possible. The punishing waves thwarted his maneuver, causing him to ram *Comorin*—a collision that opened a huge gash in the destroyer's bow. Undeterred, the captain made other, more successful attempts in spite of his ship's wounds.

With most of *Comorin*'s complement of crew and naval passengers safely aboard the three rescue ships, HMS *Broke* fired a torpedo into *Comorin* while *Lincoln*'s guns shelled her. She went down quickly, giant North Atlantic waves washing the flames from her decks and superstructure. The records show that twenty men died—not the hundreds reported by Tristan.

Although *Heart of Oak* is a fine example of wartime literature, it cannot possibly qualify as nonfiction. There are many excellent books available on the transatlantic convoys during World War II, which feature strongly in *Heart of Oak*. Tristan could have had his pick of half a dozen or more volumes—any one of which would have helped him keep his facts straight. Instead, Tristan struck out on a dangerous course. He chose to change history to suit his book and the role he wanted his readers to believe he had played in the Royal Navy's fight against Nazi Germany. Not content with coloring battles at sea with his own imprecise observations, he regularly added one extra destroyer to the fray—the one, of course, he claimed to have served on. The Royal Navy has no record of an HMS *Eclectic* or an HMS *Obstinate*, yet Tristan has them playing major roles in the Atlantic war, with him on board.

He knew that if he wasn't careful this book could raise embarrassing questions. In a letter to Richard Curtis he noted, "I have asked Bodley Head not to send the book for review by any ex-Naval officer or present one." Any competent naval officer, retired or serving, would certainly have picked up the many inaccuracies in the book.

As a preface to *Heart of Oak* he noted that, to avoid embarrassment to relatives, he had altered the names of some ships he served on, as well as the names of some characters. The comment about the change of characters' names makes sense; it's difficult, however, to understand what embarrassment might be caused by Tristan's revealing the ships he supposedly served on, or other ships involved in the actions he describes. Nonfiction books by the dozen have been written about wartime convoys across the North Atlantic and through Arctic waters. The ships that made up the convoys, and their proud naval escorts, are well documented. Tristan, not content with changing the names of the ships he says he was on, also inexplicably changed the names of other vessels—even when no crew member's name was mentioned.

Not one to shy away from personal glory, Tristan would have us believe he was there when HMS *Hood* went down, was involved in the sinking of the *Bismarck*, fought actions against *Hipper, Scharnhorst,* and *Gneisenau,* and experienced the horrors of Arctic convoys in winter.

His description of Convoy JW51B falls apart early, since he erred not only in the convoy's port of departure but also the country of departure. While his narrative of the ensuing battle, when the German raider *Hipper* attacked, bristles with courageous men and ships fighting off a determined assault, it is incorrect. He has his destroyer, HMS *Obstinate,* take over when the escort's command vessel is damaged and her captain severely wounded. When HMS *Achates* is hit hard by *Hipper* and eventually capsizes, he tells of a merchantman, *Northern Light,* rescuing her crew. With official reports readily available, it should have been a simple task to report the action with absolute precision.

Convoy JW51B's real story is a strong one. The convoy assembled in and sailed from Loch Ewe, Scotland (not Iceland as he described), on December 22, 1942. Its western escort, which covered the merchant ships from December 22 to December 25, consisted of three destroyers,

Blankney, Chiddingford, and *Ledbury.* The ocean escort, detailed to provide cover from Loch Ewe to Murmansk, consisted of two corvettes, one minesweeper, and two Royal Navy trawlers, *Vizalma* and *Northern Gem.* Christmas Day, when the western escort departed, saw the convoy joined by the destroyers *Achates, Obedient, Obdurate, Onslow* (vessel in charge), *Oribi,* and *Orwell.* The heavy cruisers *Sheffield* and *Jamaica,* already in Murmansk, were to meet the convoy northwest of Kola Inlet. In addition, distant cover was provided by a battleship, *Anson,* another cruiser, *Cumberland,* and the destroyers *Blankney, Chiddingford, Icarus, Forester,* and *Impulsive.*

At midday on December 30, as the convoy steamed south of Bear Island, the force was identified by a U-boat, *U-354,* which managed to transmit a sighting report. The weather was about normal for subarctic Atlantic waters: high winds, big seas, temperatures below zero, and occasional snow flurries.

Lützow, Hipper, and six destroyers attacked the convoy's escort of fighting ships on the morning of December 31. The Royal Navy's ships took a pounding, as did the Germans. *Hipper* put HMS *Onslow* and her skipper out of commission early. Command of the flotilla shifted to Lieutenant Commander Kinloch, captain of HMS *Obedient. Hipper* shelled the minesweeper, HMS *Bramble;* she was later sunk by one of the German destroyers. *Hipper* next turned on *Achates* and crippled her, then quickly damaged *Obedient.* Just before she turned over, the crew of *Achates* was taken off by the Royal Navy trawler *Northern Gem*—not *Northern Light* as Tristan reported. Surprisingly, only one merchant ship was damaged in the fray.

Stoker Arthur Jones did eventually serve in two of the destroyers from that battle. In 1952 he was posted to HMS *Orwell,* and in 1956 he was aboard HMS *Obdurate* for five months.

The juvenile Arthur Jones would probably have been thrilled to participate in the battle of the *Bismarck,* or to have been a stunned witness when the pride of Britain's naval armament, the mighty HMS

Hood, went down from pummeling delivered by a titanic fist, or to have been on board a destroyer during the running fights against *Hipper* and *Lützow*, *Scharnhorst*, and *Gneisenau*. Perhaps the adult Tristan would have been too, but he wasn't. As Royal Navy records have shown, Jones's naval career began several years later: eighteen months after World War II ended in Europe.

CHAPTER 17

Cold Rivers, Warm Seas

With sales of *Heart of Oak* climbing, Tristan and his crew made a relatively uneventful Atlantic crossing—Tristan's third under sail. Pat Quinn flew home from Horta, in the Azores, to be replaced by the much more experienced Englishman Martin Shaw. Quinn later talked with Henry Wagner about the Atlantic crossing aboard *Outward Leg*, in particular about the skipper's penchant for intimidating people. "Tristan was really a bully on the way over [to Europe]. We had to have two or three talks with him to get him to stop it."

Outward Leg arrived at St. Katherine's Dock in London on the afternoon of August 31, 1984. There was no welcoming committee from the brewery, Tristan said, and no free berth waiting. Help was at hand, though. Clare Francis stopped by for a visit and helped him obtain a new stove and an inflatable dinghy.

By this time Tristan had made up his mind to attempt a river crossing of Europe. With winter approaching it was, as events showed, not his most practical idea—and it wasn't well planned. Europe was to experience one of the worst winters for many years—and Tristan knew there was no direct water link between the Rhine and the Danube. He had been told of that gap in the inland waterway system on September 24. The typed memo states in part, "Have ascertained that 60K of the canal is still virgin forest. This apparently is a completely new canal connection and has not yet opened up. . . . Completion is not due until 1990."

On October 14 *Outward Leg* headed back down the Thames bound for a short North Sea crossing before tackling two of Europe's greatest rivers; crossing a continent from end to end—with a noticeable absence of water in the middle. Tristan was looking for trouble, and a salable story, again.

Tristan hadn't visited Amsterdam since just before losing his leg. The city again caused him pain when he slipped on wet decking and fell down the companionway, breaking three ribs and puncturing a lung. He spent over a week in the hospital, and the delay gave winter a chance to catch up and conspire with other obstacles to stall his efforts. At Nuremberg, Germany, the navigable waterway came to an end at a closed lock gate, beyond which the canal was dry. In late December, with no possibility of the trimaran's advancing to the Danube by water, the Rhine froze hard. *Outward Leg* became trapped in more ways than one.

If we ignore his unnecessary belligerence, Tristan proved once and for all his tenacity and determination to succeed—even though he had effectively created his own problem. He left out no angle in his quest to keep his boat moving eastward. He fought daily battles with local bu-reaucrats, arguing for permission to haul the unwieldy boat by road from the Rhine to the Danube.

With *Outward Leg* caught in ice on the upper Rhine and his progress blocked by the lack of access to the Danube, Tristan flew to London to appear on the Terry Wogan Show on BBC Television, an opportunity to promote his books and to publicize his current predica-ment. Notwithstanding the Irish host's supercilious smile and frivo-lous quips, the interview was a good one for Tristan—with both men coming across well.

Asked if he had a crew with him on *Outward Leg*, Tristan answered with a twinkle in his eye, "Yes, two—and they're both handicapped.

One's English, the other's American." It took Wogan, and the audience, a moment to appreciate Tristan's sly comment. Tristan was never an easy person to interview. Television and radio hosts needed to be constantly on guard for his unusual sense of humor and his impeccable timing. When Wogan asked him if, as a globetrotter, he still got itchy feet, Tristan immediately corrected him. "Foot. Itchy foot." While Wogan and the audience laughed, Tristan prepared his next broadside. "Do you know I still get athlete's foot in this one?" He joked, pointing to his artificial leg. Warming to his audience's laughter as only a professional entertainer can, Tristan continued, "For years my only sensual enjoyment at sea was scratching that athlete's foot. Now when I try it, what have I got? Fiberglass and steel."

In a serious moment, referring to his crisis on the iced-over Rhine, he reverted to a more militant attitude. "I'm not barmy. I've beaten down German bureaucracy. *[He hadn't. He was still negotiating with local officials.]* I've sailed the lowest in the world. I've sailed the highest, and now I've beaten the Krauts." Wogan promptly offered an apology to any Germans watching the program, with a half smile he could not completely suppress.

News clips from German television show *Outward Leg* trapped on the Rhine. Ice covers the river from bank to bank. Only a small pool of open water is visible around the trimaran. In the pool, warmly wrapped against the frigid conditions, Terry Johannsen and Martin Shaw keep the water circulating by cruising back and forth in the inflatable dinghy with the outboard motor running. As fresh crystals begin to form, they force the dinghy over them to shatter the ice before it can solidify. The operation had to proceed round the clock until the temperature rose enough to alleviate the conditions. If the ice ever got a grip on the hull and the two amas (the floats or pontoons of the trimaran), *Outward Leg* would have been severely damaged.

He may have been in a tight corner, but Tristan never forgot the people who mattered to him most—his reading public. A photograph from January 1985 published in a German newspaper showed him standing in *Outward Leg*'s cockpit. In one hand he held his walking stick, in the other a Nuremberg newspaper and a sheet of white paper with the handwritten words, "Thanks to all readers! Tristan Jones."

Manfred Peter, a photojournalist, and his wife Gabby, along with yachtsmen Michael von Tülff and Peter Steinhäuser, plus Alexander Pufahl, among others, stepped in to help. Michael remembered Tristan's telling him he kept a pistol under his pillow in case his crew attacked him. Two sources said this was because he believed they were smoking pot in town at night. His fears were unjustified. The current crew members were unlikely to attack Tristan for any reason. They simply quit. Manfred, Gabby, Michael, Peter, and a few others took over, helping Tristan in every possible way. Teenager Alexander Pufahl helped out whenever he could.

Peter Steinhäuser talked to noted single-hander Wolfgang Quix about the problem. In Nuremburg Quix sent Tristan unexpected assistance. Thomas Ettenhuber, a skinny twenty-one-year-old Bavarian with spiky red hair and glasses, arrived on March 21, 1985, to offer his services. It was to be the start of a special relationship, more like father and son than skipper and crew.

Thomas Ettenhuber, born in Munich on May 22, 1964, had a privileged education. He attended elementary school in Munich before being sent to a private boarding school in the Bavarian Alps. Kloster Schule Ettal, near Garmisch-Partenkirchen, was a Benedictine institution. During his seven years at Ettal, Thomas showed a facility for languages, excelling particularly in Latin, a strong requirement at the religious school. He also had a flair for painting watercolors and acting in amateur dramatics. He was highly intelligent, yet often critical of himself, constantly demanding more of his mind than he could possibly deliver. He returned to Munich a well-educated and disciplined teenager.

After the strictures of Kloster Schule Ettal, high school in Munich opened up a whole new world to him. Thomas's studies suffered as he relaxed and began to enjoy himself. School and education gradually lost their appeal. He dropped out before graduation. "Often he would disappear for days at a time," his mother, Kriemhild Ettenhuber, said. "He'd stay with friends, or somewhere else. We sometimes didn't know where he was."

His mother confirmed that Thomas was often introverted yet could turn outward when he felt the need. Before long he began to mix with what she termed "the wrong crowd": other dropouts, punk rockers, and the like. Unless someone stepped in and rescued him, he was heading for trouble. Wolfgang Quix—single-hander and astute family friend—knew exactly what he was doing for the Ettenhubers, including Thomas, when he sent the skinny boy to help Tristan Jones.

Waiting for permission to haul his boat out of the water and transport her a short distance overland to the Danube, Tristan complained to anyone who would listen about bureaucracy and the lack of understanding and assistance from German authorities. A televised newscast showed a stiff and formal Tristan, forcefully explaining his needs to the German public. Speaking slowly and clearly in English, he outlined his lack of success in dealing with German embassies in Panama, Caracas, and London, plus German consulates in New York and Amsterdam. "And in each case," he growled, "Nuremberg and Regensberg might just as well have been in the middle of the Brazilian jungle."

While an interpreter translated, Tristan fidgeted with his walking stick, impatient to say more. He wanted the German people to know he attached no blame to them for his delays. "But, understand, I'm not complaining," he growled. "Because they [the bureaucrats] have done me the favor of making it possible for me to meet many wonderful people in Germany." Those placatory words out of the way, the focus of his attack continued. "I have been to that autobahn. I have measured that autobahn, and I know that boat can be pulled along it." Looking tired and frustrated, Tristan, leaning on his stick, told the interviewer, "It's very, very difficult. This is the hardest journey I have ever made."

A few minutes later he talked emphatically about his expedition goals, particularly those of reaching out to handicapped people, "I shall reach them. It doesn't matter about any authorities. It doesn't matter about bureaucracy. I shall reach them!" At the end of the program the interviewer wished Tristan good luck. "It's not good luck I need, it's a helicopter," he shot back.

Tristan's prayers were eventually answered. In the middle of March 1985 *Outward Leg* was finally lifted out of the Rhine by a crane and carefully lowered onto a flatbed truck. Supported by stacks of wooden pallets borrowed from Nuremberg Docks, the trimaran was as steady and stable as a professional trucker could make her.

Asked a question by a German interviewer at the loading site in the dark of night, an obviously tired Tristan admitted he was very happy the boat was finally on the move. A follow-up query in German provoked Tristan's fiery temper when it was translated. "Well, you told me to keep it short," he snapped.

The spectacle of the huge trimaran being carried on the back of a truck was startling by day, especially as the truck was maneuvered around corners. At night, with an escort of police cars, the illuminated truck with its cargo of an oceangoing sailing vessel was a stirring sight as it progressed down the autobahn from one waterway to the next.

Once they were under way again, a heartwarming television news clip showed Tristan and Thomas welcoming youngsters on board *Outward Leg* on the Donau Canal. While Thomas made tea, Tristan took the boys on a tour of the boat and explained the workings of his sextant and compass. After the school party left, Tristan commented to the camera, "They don't understand that adventure isn't just on film or in books. It's alive. It's well, and it's kicking, and they should take part in it."

The story of that cold winter, the frustrations of dealing with bureaucracy, the unexpected departure of Martin Shaw and Terry Johannsen, and the warm hands of friendship offered by German people was effectively told in *The Improbable Voyage*. So too were tales, true and untrue, of Tristan's battles against intractable communist officials as *Outward Leg* worked her way down the Danube to the Black Sea. Thomas, no longer sporting spiky red hair and now wearing contact lenses, viewed the voyage quite differently from Tristan.

"Now the voyage has begun," Thomas wrote home from Budapest. "Until Vienna it was a test. From Vienna it really started, and now I feel really at home here. And it is not a bad home, past which all the pretty places drift as decoration to the living room. Or, it's like sitting inside a TV set which travels around the world."

In Thomas Tristan discovered far more than a crew member. He found a friend, as dedicated to the voyage as Conrad Jelinek had been over a decade before in *Barbara*, and a source of occasionally needed funds. After Thomas's mother sent him and Tristan the equivalent of $500, Thomas wrote home from Veliko Gradiste, in Yugoslavia, about the problems of getting foreign currency changed there.

> *We got the money the same day you sent it. But did you know that they only pay out in dinars? Well, there we sat with 13,000 dinars in cash, and no bank will change them into foreign currency. And they are worthless as soon as you leave Jugoslavia. For five hours I ran from bank to bank, to the post office and back to a bank, to a post office, to and fro, with 13,000 useless scraps of paper. Fully into the tourist trap. The German, American, and British embassies would not help at all. The Germans just searched me. Tristan was swearing and told me I was an idiot and a lousy secretary. That I had no idea: an innocent provincial. I simply replied that he should not send me to do these things. Am I right? Banks, money, and me?*

No doubt there was a noisy argument about the situation. Thomas's family had supplied the money, yet Tristan blamed the problems on Thomas. They soon put aside their differences and combined forces to see what could be done.

Tristan sailed into the post office as if he was likely to sink it if they would not pay out our money. Or as if he wanted to kill the grimy, unshaved postmaster every minute. They sent us off to the headquarters [presumably the main post office]. We used all our ammunition. Tristan a writer; articles about the miserable conditions in Jugoslavia, TV Belgrade, everything, until they gave us dinar travelers checks and sent us to a bank. There we were told we could only cash them for dinars. Back to the main post office again, arriving just as it was closing. There we met the director, who knew everything. The wires ran hot between the banks, post office, and the police. The director then called someone at a bank and, with a trick, a lie, we finally got our money. A day—a nightmare.

He ended the letter with an expression in English, straight out of Tristan's repertoire: "If in danger or in doubt, hoist the sails and fuck off out."

With money in their pockets, or in Tristan's pocket, they left Belgrade immediately. Thomas's letter spoke of his excitement at the voyage and his awe of Tristan. "From here we will go with maximum speed to the Black Sea, set up the mast and go sailing. That's what I'm waiting for. There's something else, that I can't really judge, because I only have a slight idea about it . . . what it means to me, for my life, to be on board *Outward Leg*. How great Tristan is, in what style he goes down the Danube. What a power it is to me and an unbelievably tremendous matter to hear, 'Thomas, you are my friend.' "

He closes the letter with evidence that he has done a fair amount of thinking about the voyage, and about his captain: "History is not made when someone makes something for the first time. This one [Tristan] makes history, creates legends. What he does may not be so important; it is nevertheless great."

In Romania an inebriated Tristan lost his temper and punched a policeman. He took that undisciplined act of aggression and turned it into a major story. He was right, he insisted. The police were wrong. He claimed that he was thrown out of Romania for his sins. He wasn't.

Somehow he and Thomas were allowed to leave without penalty. When they arrived at the Black Sea, under sail at last, Thomas still wasn't fully satisfied. He found sailing less interesting than anticipated, partly because he was homesick and partly, perhaps, because he was becoming claustrophobic on board. He wrote from Varna, Bulgaria:

> *Now the mast is standing and we can sail. I'm waiting until we really start. Some days I believe it will never really begin; sailing is boring and much work. Two hours work, two hours watch, and everywhere you come to is the same. I am a tourist no longer: I live in whichever country I happen to be in. Everywhere you have to make new contacts. Sometimes I am really homesick, Munich was easier.*
>
> *The Danube is finished. It's a kind of anticlimax. Next time it will be interesting, when we get out, out of the Mediterranean—next year. Anyway, it will be better when we are finally out of the Black Sea. Interesting is okay, but it can also become too much.*

A week later Thomas sat on *Outward Leg* happily watching the sun go down over Topkapi Palace and Istanbul from the eastern shore of the Bosporus. The Mediterranean proved more to his liking than the Danube.

During the crossing of Europe Tristan, with Thomas's help, had written a guide to the river system for boaters, called *The Danube Pilot*. He hoped to eventually sell copies for a high price.

For the next few months after leaving the Black Sea Tristan took his time voyaging from port to port, waiting for the right season to tackle the Indian Ocean. By the time he reached Greece he was again concerned about losing *Outward Leg*. Animosity had arisen again between him and the boat's owners, yet Tristan neglected to explain why. "I have to keep one step ahead of those buggers in California," he wrote to Henry Wagner, "in case they pull the boat from under me."

In Kastellorizon, Greece, Alexander Pufahl joined the crew and found the situation less than satisfactory. "When I was on board *Outward Leg* I felt like a third wheel. Thomas and Tristan had already bonded into a love/hate relationship. They often shouted at each other. Thomas regularly threatened to leave. Tristan told him to go, but he didn't. They both knew Tristan needed Thomas."

From Cyprus, Tristan informed Wally Herbert he was exploring a change of direction. He discussed the possibility of hauling *Outward Leg* across Israel, following *Barbara's* truck route of 1971. Plus, he looked directly east. "I have feelers out in Syria for a haul from their Med coast to the river Euphrates, but I don't have too many hopes for it. The passage through Iraq is the problem, once all the Syrian stuff is somehow got through. Then of course there's the war in the Persian Gulf just to liven up the show." As with an overland haul across Israel, this idea of another river journey failed to gain any momentum, but Tristan was not finished with exploring rivers.

Leaving Alexander in charge of the boat in Akko, Israel, in January 1986, Tristan and Thomas flew to the States to promote Tristan's books. When they returned, Tristan summarily fired Pufahl on the young man's birthday.

Outward Leg sailed from Israel for the Suez Canal and the Red Sea at the end of February. On board were the skipper, Thomas, and a young Swede—Svante Wagnerius. Their destination was Thailand, with stops in the Red Sea and the Indian Ocean en route. Other than a badly timed entry into Aden to have Tristan's teeth seen to (they arrived with appalling timing, flying the Stars and Stripes, about the time United States forces bombed Qaddafi's Libya) and almost running out of water and diesel fuel halfway across the ocean, the voyage to Cochin, India, was mostly uneventful. In Galle, Sri Lanka, Svante quit.

Tristan's thoughts returned to exploring rivers when he wrote to Henry Wagner from Galle about his "crazy scheme to haul the boat *[Outward Leg]* over the Kra peninsula." After the trials of crossing Europe, a new expedition on rivers and over a difficult watershed with a large trimaran appears at first glance to be an enormous mistake. It was for the moment a vague plan, yet one with potential for a new book.

Without Svante, Tristan and Thomas sailed the final leg to Phuket, Thailand, by themselves. Thomas dropped anchor in Ao Chalong Bay on July 1, 1986, and made *Outward Leg* secure, then the pair went ashore in the dinghy. The trimaran's circumnavigation was more than half completed. Tristan announced that he would be back in California in about a year. In fact the voyage was already over. *Outward Leg* would never return to San Diego.

CHAPTER 18

Exploring Thailand

Letters Thomas sent to his mother when he arrived in Thailand show it was time for him and Tristan to give each other some badly needed room. After well over a year together, living in the confined space of a trimaran had begun to grate on Thomas. Even so, despite his apparent depression, Thomas found the mental energy to compliment his mentor. "I was so tired," he wrote. "I'd had enough of Tristan. We made the trip from Sri Lanka to Thailand with only the two of us. [I'm] so tired of the continuous work for somebody else, of sitting on each other every minute of the day. No longer could I listen when an old experienced man talked."

With *Outward Leg* swinging comfortably at anchor on Ao Chalong Bay, rolling gently to the ceaseless rhythm of Indian Ocean swells, Tristan sat down in his rented house to write a book and articles about the recently completed voyage from Istanbul. Two or three Thai boys tended to cooking and cleaning chores, leaving Tristan to write while Thomas busied himself learning the local language. As far as Thomas knew, the plan was to stay in Thailand for about six months before sailing on to China. Often at loose ends, he roamed the bars and restaurants of Phuket, talking with tourists and locals. Each day his knowledge of the Thai language improved.

In the late 1980s Thailand had approximately 55 million people in a country the size of France. Roughly 8 million lived in Bangkok, the capital, with about 200,000 in Chiang Mai—the second largest city. Ably guided by the steady hand of King Bhumidol and his government, the hot and humid country had enjoyed a decade of continuing economic improvement. Although 90 percent of Thais practice Buddhism, there is a large Muslim community in the south, primarily around Phuket and down to the border with Malaysia. Unfortunately, Thailand had developed a reputation as an exotic destination for males, and sex—straight and gay—was readily available. Underage girls and boys were easy to obtain, anxious to please, eager to earn money. When Tristan and Thomas arrived, Phuket was adjusting to several busy years of beach hotel expansion occasioned by a tourism boom. Between November and March (outside the monsoon season), Europeans found the combination of sandy beaches, hot sun, and a colorful culture irresistible. Foreign yachties also discovered a haven virtually impossible to pass without stopping for a while. Most let go their anchors off Nai Han Beach, site of the Phuket Yacht Club Hotel.

Tristan was well pleased with his temporary abode in Phuket. He told Henry Wagner he had paid the $270 monthly rent for six months and that he was mobile on land. Thomas had either adapted a motorcycle and welded on a sidecar or had arranged for it to be done. Tristan said of his new home, "This is Avalon, Camelot and Shangri-La all rolled into one."

Later in the same letter he assured Henry that his planned extended stay in Thailand did not mean the circumnavigation was over. "I shall still head east in Jan/Feb (1987)," he said.

In mid-September 1986 Tristan and Thomas left *Outward Leg* at anchor, watched over by the house staff, and flew to New York, with tickets, as usual, supplied by Henry. Tristan signed books at boat shows in Stamford, Annapolis, and Houston and lectured in Boston. At one show Tristan made a grave error when he talked about rounding the

Horn while speaking to a real Cape Horner, delivery skipper and author John Kretschmer:

> *I first suspected TJ was a bit of a bullshitter when my book* Cape Horn to Starboard *was published. I remember standing in Henry's booth [Henry Wagner of Sailor's Bookshelf], rather meekly trying to promote it at the Annapolis show. Jones was also there and he took a look at my book and muttered something like, "Cape Horn, oh yes, I've been there." I knew most of his writing and was surprised to hear that he'd been around the Horn, especially when he told me that, like me, he'd doubled the Cape from east to west against the wind. When I pressed him for details he gave them to me. Unfortunately, I knew exactly what he was talking about. He described Edward C. Allcard's voyage of 1966, when he sailed his 36 foot ketch,* Sea Wanderer, *around the Horn. I had done a lot of Cape Horn research so I was well aware of Allcard's passage.*
>
> *I didn't push him or question him, it somehow just seemed disrespectful even though I knew full well he was lying. From that moment on . . . I was always suspicious of his stories. Of course, that didn't stop [me] buying and enjoying everything he wrote.*

It's interesting to note here, in view of the alleged South American circumnavigation, that Tristan never did write about rounding Cape Horn—the Holy Grail for the most adventurous of ocean sailors. Had he really doubled the Horn it would have guaranteed him a published article, probably a book, a literary opportunity he could hardly ignore. The only time Tristan came close to Cape Horn was in late 1977 and early 1978 while he was a guest lecturer on board the *Lindblad Explorer.*

Thomas, normally quiet, reserved, and dependable, disappeared while in Annapolis. Tristan told Henry not to worry, that Thomas was probably hiding somewhere. He liked to be alone at times. This time Tristan was wrong. Thomas wasn't hiding. Thomas was in trouble.

Thomas had gone to a bar by himself. He drank far too much and created a disturbance that culminated in a visit from the police. When an officer attempted to quiet the agitated young sailor, Thomas got mad. He ripped the badge from the policeman's shirt and began to throw punches. While Tristan and Henry searched for him in the hotel, a battered Thomas spent the night in the local jail. Thomas mentioned the incident in a letter to his mother: "When I came out of jail, beaten blue and green, with a hangover that would have knocked down an elephant, and I know elephants, Tristan said, 'It's good that you beat up this rozzer, but why didn't you do it in Romania?' That's where he beat one up after we'd been drinking rum on an English warship."

Henry and some of the boat show exhibitors found Thomas's plight highly amusing. As Henry told him, he was far from the first sailor to be thrown in jail in Annapolis for being drunk and disorderly. Fortunately for Thomas, he wasn't charged and escaped with, as he put it, "my honor."

After a stop in Austria to deliver a copy of their *Danube Pilot* to Vienna University, Tristan and Thomas returned to Phuket at the end of October 1986. *The Danube Pilot* was never published.

In 1981 Tristan had set up the Atlantis Society as a registered charity. No doubt thinking in terms of a new book, he planned an expedition to discover the lost city of Atlantis—sponsored by the Atlantis Society. Like many of his plans, the idea fizzled. The society had to wait a few years before becoming useful.

The long-dormant Atlantis Society was resurrected with a new direction soon after the duo arrived in Thailand in 1986. A "nonprofit" organization with bank accounts in New York and Thailand, its new function was to assist in the development and rehabilitation of handicapped young people. Regular newsletters reported Tristan's activities and solicited donations to the society. Perhaps not surprising in a largely Muslim community, of the handicapped people it is known that Tristan helped, only a couple were female.

Initially funds were used to buy a traditional longtail fishing boat, which Tristan promptly named *Henry Wagner*. Tristan's next newsletter wrote glowingly of his new boat. It's role, the letter announced, would be as a training vessel to teach handicapped youngsters to earn a living from the sea. The newsletter, like the previous one, asked for tax-deductible contributions to the Atlantis Society to help finance the training venture. Although part of the funds appear to have gone to support Tristan, he used most of the money honestly, in service of the needy. Atlantis paid for a series of operations to repair horrific damage to a teenage boy's face and supplied arm and leg prostheses to Thai amputees.

Meanwhile *Outward Leg* was supposedly being readied for an expedition across the Isthmus of Kra, followed by a long voyage to the Yangtze River in China. In *The Improbable Voyage*, his story of the European crossing, Tristan wrote of his fascination with rivers. The Kra, and later the Yangtze River, would feed that interest and—with luck— provide him with new stories to tell, new books to write. With the Kra and the Yangtze behind him, Tristan intended to leave *Outward Leg* in either Hong Kong or Japan for the winter of 1987–88, before sailing the Pacific to San Diego to complete the circumnavigation. He told Wagner he had been in contact with Larry Haftl and said he was confident H & S Bluewater Multihulls would let him keep the boat longer, although he worried about the company's finances.

"On our return from the Yangtze, by air," one issue of the newsletter reported, "we hope to purchase and refurbish two more fishing-training craft for handicapped youngsters here in Phuket." But like so many of his plans, the Yangtze trip had to be set aside indefinitely— eventually to be forgotten altogether.

Henry Wagner visited Phuket in January 1987 for a couple of weeks, shortly after Tristan and Thomas returned from a quick survey of the first part of the route over the Kra. A home video shot by Thomas shows Tristan, Henry, and a group of Thai boys cruising Ao Chalong Bay in *Henry Wagner*. It also has footage of the boat motoring slowly up a jungle river. Having seen Tristan and Thomas together only on two or three brief visits to the States, Henry was surprised at the way Tristan dominated his mate in Thailand.

"He was a Captain Bligh to Thomas," Wagner said. "He was so afraid Thomas would get distracted by a woman, or a pleasure boat, and leave Tristan to go off and do something better. He was very protective of Thomas and tried to keep him out of contact with other people, especially local yachties. I remember one time we were having dinner in Phuket, down by this big hotel. A lot of French people vacation there. I pointed out the topless women on the beach to Thomas and told him, 'You should go over there and take care of business, as any young man should. Go and look after the lonely tourist ladies.' You know, Tristan became so outraged that I brought that up. Totally outraged. That was the only time he really read me the riot act. He could see Thomas going over there and becoming the center of attention. You know, a handsome young man and these beautiful young women from France. If Thomas got among them, Tristan knew, he would no longer matter."

Although Tristan was hard on the young man, Thomas did get out by himself at times. "I know he went to the cat house one night because he told me about it," Henry said. "He got drunk there and lost his wallet and his passport, but he got them back later."

Defending Tristan's often hard-hearted determination, Henry said, "When Tristan had his course set, there was nothing could bother him. No one else's sacrifice was too large if it meant Tristan getting from A to B, from C to D. He made sacrifices and he expected everyone else to do the same. I mean, it wasn't like he was living in luxury hotels at every one of his stops. He definitely made sacrifices."

On one visit to the States to attend boat shows and deliver lectures, Thomas too had to make sacrifices. His mother arrived in New York for a ten-day visit while he was there. She was allowed to see her son for one afternoon and that same night—no more. Thomas, under orders from Tristan, left first thing in the morning to return to Brunswick, New Jersey, where he and Tristan were staying with the Wagners. Kriemhild Ettenhuber phoned Tristan to ask why she couldn't spend more time with her son. "Because we have work to do," came the curt answer. Tristan and Thomas, with Henry, were preparing for the Stamford Boat Show and Tristan—Henry said—did not want Thomas's mother to intrude on their work in any way.

"*Outward Leg* was not in good shape when I was in Phuket [in early 1987]," Henry said. "The head didn't work. Nothing else seemed to work either. The stanchions were all loose. You didn't dare grab them to hold on to, especially in rough weather. If you were in the water you just didn't reach up to pull yourself out. Whatever you held on to would probably fall off. I don't think a dime of upkeep went into that boat from the time it left the harbor in San Diego. I don't think it was seaworthy enough to continue the voyage back home [to San Diego]."

Henry talked about his departure from Phuket after that visit. He, Tristan, and Thomas were planning to sail *Outward Leg* to Penang, Malaysia. From there Henry would fly to Perth, in Western Australia, to watch the America's Cup races. Tristan and Thomas would renew their Thai visas and then sail back to Phuket.

"When we were getting ready to leave Phuket, Thomas went around [the coast] to get *Outward Leg* and bring it to the beach in front of Tristan's house. We waited and waited. No Thomas. No Thomas. It was getting late in the afternoon, and Tristan said, 'Maybe there's a problem.' Now, Tristan had a motorbike with a shopping cart welded to it for a sidecar. I got in the side and Tristan drove. Off we went tearing down the road. It was a hair-raising drive on three-quarter-inflated tires with Tristan weaving in and out of traffic. The metal of the cart was cutting right into my ass. It was really uncomfortable. The local Thais knew Tristan as the madman. He sure proved it on that trip."

Reaching the shore opposite *Outward Leg*'s mooring, Tristan and Henry took a dinghy out to the boat. "She won't move," Thomas explained. "Maybe it's the prop," suggested Tristan. Thomas and Henry went over the side to take a look. "The prop and shaft were so covered in barnacles you could hardly see them," Henry said. With Henry watching, Thomas hammered enough barnacles and other crustaceans off the propeller to give the blades some semblance of pitch. "Enough to get the boat moving, so we could get her out of the harbor," Henry explained.

Outward Leg was a mess, yet, as Henry said with a certain amount of awe, "That boat could fly. We were doing almost eleven knots one night going to Penang. Oh, she was just flying."

Henry had nothing but praise for Tristan's plucky mate, "Thomas was an iron man. On the voyage from Phuket to Penang he did everything. He'd shinny up the mast. He'd fight to get the anchor up by himself. He'd have a go at anything."

Perhaps as a precursor to terminating the circumnavigation voyage, Tristan wrote H & S Bluewater Multihulls from Penang offering to return *Outward Leg* to them. Alternatively, he suggested, he could perhaps continue with the voyage. H & S agreed to Tristan's staying in command, though they had no funds to assist the voyage. At that point, in February, Tristan still pondered the idea of taking the trimaran over the Isthmus of Kra by river. There's an element of confusion in his notes and letters at this time regarding his plans, possibly caused by concerns about his health. His few remaining teeth desperately needed attention, and the stump of his left leg continually broke out in painful sores. He was scheduled to return to North America for lectures in Vancouver and San Diego in March 1987 but cancelled for medical reasons. Early that month he confided to Henry that he felt his voyaging days were over. "I think you could tell that my general state just isn't up to the wear and tear of cruising much more—at least not for long sustained periods of effort. It's time to call it a day, and I've always said and written that unfit people (unfit for sea) shouldn't do it, as they will only be a burden to others."

Having said that, he admitted he thought he could manage the Kra crossing. At the end of March he sent out an appeal through his Atlantis Society newsletter for donations to help defray the cost of the expedition, which he judged to be about $4,000. Instead of using the impossibly cumbersome *Outward Leg*, he sensibly decided to employ two longtail fishing boats, one of them *Henry Wagner*. The avowed purpose of the expedition was to publicize the plight of handicapped young people in Southeast Asia and at the same time to promote their aspirations and abilities. The newsletter ended with a strongly worded appeal: "Thomas Ettenhuber and I have [put] and will put all we have into this endeavor, including, if need be, our lives. Please help us with anything you can spare. We could, probably, at this stage, get big business to support us, but the price we would have to pay in delays, first— the loss of freedom of intent and action, would be heavy and might even put the whole endeavor in hazard through the setting of deadlines, or the demand for extra people to accompany us. Your support will make that approach unnecessary and preserve our independence."

Using money earned from his lectures and book sales, and aided by donations totaling $734 to the Atlantis Society, Tristan scraped enough together to equip the Kra expedition—which would start in Phuket and end in Bangkok. By this time Thomas's photography was illustrating Tristan's magazine articles, and that income too went directly into the Atlantis bank account.

Instead of two boats Tristan settled on one, *Henry Wagner*. On June 16, 1987, Tristan and Thomas set off from Phuket with their handicapped crew: Som, age nineteen, with one arm; Anant, fifteen, with one leg; and Nok, fifteen, with his upper lip and palate severely damaged by a large fish hook when he was a little boy. Ahead of them lay a sea voyage of roughly 90 miles followed by another 170 miles on unknown rivers. Compared with his previous expeditions, the Kra crossing was a relatively short distance and should take only a few weeks— an important feature considering Tristan's physical condition. A successful crossing would, however, give him another first for his collection of records.

All the official notifications of the voyage from Tristan either neglected to mention Thomas Ettenhuber altogether or labeled him legally blind—a characterization Tristan had used since the beginning of their association in Germany. In *To Venture Further*, the book of the Kra expedition, Tristan said Thomas dropped his spectacles and trod on them early in the voyage, shattering the lenses. Of course, on an expedition there is nowhere to get them repaired. Thomas was short-sighted but far from "legally blind," and he usually wore contact lenses. He tells us in his log of racing upriver in the dinghy, noting the location of obstacles and projections that might endanger *Henry Wagner*. It doesn't take much imagination to realize the impossibility of such a task for someone with extreme myopia. At no time does Thomas complain of having broken his glasses.

In his foreword to *To Venture Further*, Thomas noted that at times he had "thought things had been a mite different" from Tristan's version. Tristan agreed that he was right to do so. And he was. The most significant differences between Tristan's official version of the voyage and Thomas's logbook once again represent Tristan's need to create drama where none existed.

In most respects Thomas's logbook parallels what Tristan wrote in *To Venture Further*. There are anomalies, and there are obvious embellishments from Tristan's side. Also, the Isthmus of Kra is actually far to the north of the route *Henry Wagner* took from Kantang to Surat Thani. Nevertheless, fifty-eight-year-old one-legged Tristan Jones, with Thomas Ettenhuber and a trio of handicapped Thai boys, did haul a heavy boat up jungle rivers and across the Malay Peninsula (on a much wider route than the isthmus) from the Andaman Sea to the Gulf of Thailand. Under any conditions, it was a phenomenal achievement. Both Tristan and Thomas, as well as the Thai crew, were justifiably proud of the accomplishment.

Some of Thomas's personal comments from his log are worth considering here. Three days after leaving Phuket, there is a note of concern, "Too much panic in the morning—got to improve." And then a hint of potential problems brewing. "Sometimes 5 captains no good. Tristan and I interfere with each other. Got to improve too."

Early on, Tristan developed a sore on one toe that resisted all efforts to heal it. The open wound became increasingly painful and perhaps offered a portent of what was to come. Tristan later wrote of his foot becoming so painful that, combined with the heat and humidity and his age, he had slowed down to the point where he could "no longer jot down lucid notes." Perhaps that was why Thomas took charge of the logbook entries.

On June 30 Thomas wrote in the log: "Leave early in the morning. Navigation still very difficult, river winding, steering *Henry Wagner* with Yanni *[the Yanmar engine]* not too difficult, need strength though lifting the propeller out of the water and dropping it in 90-degree angle, then the boat swings on the spot, in very sharp bends with 3–4 knots current. We reach our only recently fallen big tree that reaches right across the river. Some old men and girls come down. Old men help cutting. Our equipment undersized a bit. Cut through and went on with old men. They wouldn't leave until Tristan paid some money. They sat on the boat so she couldn't pass shallow parts. Everybody thinks we're tourists, don't realize the difficulties we've already overcome. Nobody knows more than 500 m ahead, or doesn't tell. Pass little bamboo bridge 100 m upstream river blocked by rocks and old fallen log on other side. Stop below for the night, organize chainsaw for next day."

Tristan's published version in *To Venture Further* incorporated subtle changes. Immediately after the line about sharp bends he added, as if Thomas had written it, "Wish my sight better." Tristan's version is a smoother read, and perhaps we should be grateful for that, although Thomas's words are easy enough to follow without an editor's pen. *To Venture Further* has wonderful scenes of Tong Chai, a working elephant, hauling *Henry Wagner* over the shallowest parts of the river. Without doubt one of the most amusing revolves around a basic animal function. It may be true, it may not. Either way it is a fine example of Tristan's sense of humor. He has Tong Chai, the elephant, relieving himself with a tremendous fart and covering Tristan with, "about a quarter of a ton of digested vegetation all over me and our bow."

The elephant towed *Henry Wagner* up the shallow river for eleven exhausting and worrying days for Tristan. In his book Tristan threatens to burn *Henry Wagner* as a ploy to keep the elephant's mercenary mahout working. Thomas's log says nothing of that incident. It does, however, tell of the chaotic scene when the river virtually disappeared at a road bridge. The media, foreign as well as Thai, appeared in force to record Tong Chai hauling *Henry Wagner* along an almost dry river bed.

That bridge could have spelled the end of the journey for Tristan's expedition. After a mammoth upstream battle and against incredible odds, the crew had reached the high point of the crossing. The next river they needed, the Mae Nam Ta Pi, was thirty-nine statute miles away. Thanks to the Thai army, a crane hauled *Henry Wagner* out and lowered her carefully onto the back of a truck. As Thomas wrote in his log, "Today 18/7/87 it looks like we cracked the Kra hard nut."

One day later they were traveling downhill at last, on a new river. Still, in spite of their efforts nothing, least of all success, came easy. The Mae Nam Ta Pi flows into the Mae Nam Chawong. The latter carries vast amounts of sand and silt along with its flow and deposits them wherever they will do the most harm. *Henry Wagner* ran aground regularly as she drew closer and closer to the South China Sea. And there were more troubles with the motor. Most important though, after the uphill battle on the other side of the isthmus, the boat was moving with the current and with enough water under her keel most of the time to keep her afloat. At Surat Thani, on July 20, 1987, Thomas noted with some satisfaction, "1st crossing completed."

The following day Tristan sent an exultant cable to Henry Wagner: "Your name now part of boating history. HW completed first Kra crossing 20th July. Arduous effort. Lifted boat 132 times to cover 520 km river.

Inform NQ *[Nautical Quarterly]*, *Cruising World*, Marty Luray, *Sail*, Ray Kennedy. Cheers, Tristan."

In Surat Thani Tristan had minor surgery on his remaining leg to clean deepening infections. He said the operation was a success. Surat Thani sits on the east coast of Thailand, the end of the land crossing for *Henry Wagner*, but the voyage was far from over. Tristan planned to take his boat on to Bangkok, hundreds of miles to the north. In getting to the capital Tristan told of great adventures in rough coastal seas, and of being stalked by pirate vessels, on the voyage along the coast to Hua Hin before crossing the Gulf of Thailand to Pattaya. Thomas's logbook is of little help in confirming the stories. It ceases abruptly on July 26 in the lovely Ko Wiang Bay and doesn't recommence until nearly five months later.

We know Tristan and crew returned to Phuket from Bangkok. Once again, before Tristan settled down to write, he and Thomas set off for the United States and Europe to publicize their recently completed expedition and promote the newly released *Improbable Voyage*. The Thai boys went back to looking after the other boats. In November Tristan and Thomas flew back to North America again to promote books in Canada. On the way home they stopped off in Tokyo to talk with Japanese publishers.

Buoyed by the success of the expedition and determined to carry his message of hope for the handicapped as far as possible, Tristan began planning a new river venture when he returned to Thailand. He intended to take *Henry Wagner* all the way up the Mae Nam Chao Phraya, north to Chiang Rai in northernmost, mountainous Thailand. From there he and his crew would sail the boat on the Mae Nam Kok northeast to the Mekong River at Chiang Saen. Once across the border in Laos, but still to the west of Luang Prabang, Tristan reasoned that he could recruit a small crew of handicapped Laotian children from villages and towns on the banks of the Mekong, then follow that great river back to the vast delta below Ho Chi Minh City and so, once again, to the South China Sea. As with the Kra crossing, the Mekong River expedition was designed to publicize the plight of handicapped children in Southeast Asia. What his current crew thought of the idea is not known. They and Thomas appear to have gone along with whatever plans Tristan put forward.

Ahead, before they could reach the Mekong, stretched over four hundred miles of winding rivers—and little information was available on river courses, depths, and currents. Then came the potential dangers of the Golden Triangle, center of an enormous illegal drug-producing operation, where the borders of Burma (now Myanmar), Laos, and Thailand meet. From the point of arrival at the Mekong's banks to the South China Sea, Tristan would have to navigate close to a thousand miles on a busy and unpredictable river. It was an ambitious undertaking with, in hindsight, little chance of success. But Tristan Jones had defied the odds before—in South America, in Europe, and in crossing the Malay Peninsula. If it could be done, he was the man to do it—he, Thomas, and a crew of handicapped boys.

During the hiatus *Henry Wagner* had been hauled out and left at Samut Phrakarn, downstream from Bangkok. In the second week of December 1987 Thomas, accompanied by Som, Nok, and Anant, arrived by bus from their respective homes in Phuket. Tristan apparently traveled separately at a later date. Thomas's log continues: "Fri 11th we launched the boat. She was taking a little water after five months being dry. We sailed to the Oriental [Hotel] for lunch and afterwards to the Krua Wangnar restaurant upstream of the King's Palace in BKK [Bangkok] where we stayed until Monday. The girls and Ladyboys were all over us. Nok and I got little love letters."

On Monday, December 14, they motored upstream for one hour to a ferry landing, where Tristan joined the boat that night. He was accompanied by a man named Lashion. "A big guy who looks like a Mafia hit man," noted Thomas, "and used to be the bouncer in a Patpong bar."

Early next morning they set course for Ayutthaya. Thomas the photographer was suitably impressed by the beauty of the scenery on this stretch of the Mae Nam Chao Phraya. "Houses on stilts, well kept, with little boats in sheds. Speedboats going up and down the river full with kids going to school. Rice barges going up empty and down loaded to the gunwales. It is very cool, the light from the sun gives everything a beautiful color, especially the temples with their golden ornaments. Everything is distinctively Thai, even the rice barges look like the temples ashore."

That night they moored under a tree in front of a group of wooden houses on a side stream. Opposite, on an island, stood a temple that the monks could reach only by cable car. For some reason Tristan thought they were in Ayutthaya and was disappointed to find they were a few miles short of their goal for the day. *Henry Wagner* reached Ayutthaya at midmorning the next day. Thomas, still waxing dreamy about the river, wrote, "The Chao Phraya is a most beautiful river. What scenery."

Tristan left immediately for Bangkok, with Nok and Lashion, to visit the Laotian embassy to discuss the forthcoming Mekong expedition. Lashion and Tristan must have fallen out over something or other, for Thomas scribbled in his journal on December 17, "Lashion returns early, he got the boot from Tristan. Later TJ returned. L was gone."

Tristan pronounced himself pleased with his reception at the embassy and confident of receiving approval for his next expedition. Three more days took *Henry Wagner* to Nakhon Sawan and the end of the Chao Phraya. From that junction, where the river splits into four, the two main streams are the Mae Nam Ping and the Mae Nam Nan. Told by locals that the Mae Nam Ping was the route to Chiang Mai, Tristan cruised slowly upriver on a short but wasted journey. Thomas described the Nan as muddy and the Ping as clear. Perhaps the difference in clarity between the two should have warned Tristan that the Ping was getting progressively shallower. *Henry Wagner* soon ran aground on a sandbar. Try as they might to find a safe channel through the obstructions, the exercise was doomed. The Mae Nam Ping could not carry the heavy expedition boat. Reluctantly Tristan turned back to Nakhon Sawan for help.

For three days, from December 22 to Christmas Day, the stymied crew waited for a contractor to meet Tristan to discuss hauling the boat to Chiang Rai. They waited in vain. At 10:00 A.M. on December 25 they set off again, this time to look for the railway station, in hopes of arranging a haul by train. Once again they were thwarted, though the excursion was successful in that they found a deep river, probably the Mae Nam Nan, flowing from the direction of Uttaradit, north of where they stood. Once under way on this river, Thomas noted, "Everybody is happy we're moving."

By the end of that afternoon they had reached Chum Saeng, where they enjoyed dinner at an outdoor noodle shop on the main square. Thomas commented in his log that the local boys and girls were very pleasant. And then a note of annoyance creeps in: "Nok and Anant take off for the whorehouse and don't return until next morning. Now something has to happen. [These] Kids are taking advantage too much."

That's the final entry in Thomas's logbook. We can only assume that from that day on he was too busy helping to move the boat over increasingly difficult terrain to write more. We are fortunate, however, that Tristan did find time to write an article about the journey for *Motor Boat and Yachting* magazine in England. "Into the Golden Triangle" was published in the December 1988 issue. And we have a later eyewitness account of the final stage of the river journey.

Henry Wagner pushed a further 120 miles north to Phitsanulok, where the river finally became too shallow for further travel. Sometime between Christmas and New Year's Eve Tristan took a train back to Bangkok to attempt to find ways to haul his boat to Chiang Rai, the final main town before Laos. His journey proved a waste of time. When he returned to Phitsanulok he installed himself in the Amarin Nakorn Hotel. Thomas and the boys continued to live on the boat. Thomas, ever restless, spent his days and nights over the Christmas season exploring Phitsanulok, searching for a way to continue the voyage. In that he was lucky. On January 1 he discovered Bibi's Pub.

Laid out along the lines of a real English pub, with a counter bar seating fifteen people, in addition to tables and chairs, Bibi's serves Western and Thai food in a cozy atmosphere. Since its opening in 1986 Bibi's Pub had collected a large number of regular customers. They included expatriate oilfield workers, Thai nationals, and local dignitaries. Jos Souer, Bibi's Dutch husband, an employee of Shell International temporarily assigned to Thai Shell, met Thomas on his first visit to the pub. Jos described the young man as he first saw him, seated quietly at the counter bar sipping a beer, looking rather rough but clean. He had dark hair and a dark complexion—dark enough from exposure to the sun to almost pass as a Thai.

Thomas told his story, and Bibi's regulars hustled into action. First, though, learning that the boys were sleeping on the boat under an awning, the American wife of a hotel owner offered accommodation for the crew in the Rajapruk Hotel. Thomas checked with Tristan, who promptly refused the offer, insisting that Thomas and the boys stay on the boat. Undeterred by Tristan's attitude, the regulars went out of their way to help, badgering local officials into giving permission to close a road bridge for a couple of hours and making all the arrangements to haul *Henry Wagner* out of the water. Jos Souer and other oil workers organized a truck and trailer. Thomas became the project's contact with Tristan, who stayed away. Apart from agreeing to pay the cost of diesel fuel for the truck's journey to Chiang Rai, he remained hidden in his hotel.

On January 4, 1988, Tristan surfaced to take charge of the operation as a crane hauled *Henry Wagner* from the river and deposited her on a large trailer. As he barked orders to everyone around, his presence was neither needed nor, it appears, appreciated. Thomas and the oilmen were perfectly capable of lifting the boat safely without his interference.

With *Henry Wagner* strapped and chocked in place, courtesy of the Americans, the truck hauled her north. Eight hours later she was afloat again on the Mae Nam Kok at Chiang Rai. Just before departure Thomas presented Bibi's Bar with an autographed photograph of the boat being towed by Tong Chai and a wood carving of the elephant. Tristan never did pay Jos Souer for the fuel. Jos did, however, see Thomas again a few weeks later when he passed through Phitsanulok by bus, en route to Bangkok to have an outboard motor repaired, and again on his return. Souer remembered that Thomas did not look happy but declined to say why.

With the rugged 1,600-mile journey from Phuket finally over, *Henry Wagner* floated close enough to the border to cross within hours once permission had been procured. It was not to be. A small local war broke out between Laos and Thailand, and the border was closed. *Henry Wagner* had reached her farthest north. Leaving her safely moored near Chiang Rai, Tristan and crew retreated 90 miles south to Chiang Mai, where Tristan rented a house to use as a northern base camp. Subsequent comments suggest they might have moved the boat to Chiang Mai as well.

A month later Tristan and Thomas returned to Bangkok, where they stayed for a few weeks in separate hotels in the red-light district. Tristan must have felt reasonably solvent at this juncture. He had rented houses in Phuket and Chiang Mai, in addition to a hotel room in Bangkok. From Bangkok Tristan, with enormous help from Henry Wagner in New Jersey, made plans for an extended book-selling trip to the United States. Two months was the duration Tristan discussed with Henry, expressing some concern at the projected cost. In late March 1988 Thomas went to Germany to visit his parents. Tristan, suffering from a pulled muscle in his lower back, stayed on in a Bangkok hotel to recuperate.

In early May the pair went to New York. Tristan appeared on Larry King's live radio show from Washington, D.C., on May 6, where he boasted of selling ten million books (the actual figure to date would have been closer to a quarter of a million), before they set off to raise funds by lecturing and selling books—with the emphasis on *Somewheres East of Suez*, Tristan's latest release. The third book in his *Outward Leg* trilogy, *Somewheres East of Suez* relates the story of the trimaran's voyage from the Black Sea to Phuket. Fully one third of the book takes place in the Red Sea. Compared with the almost nonstop adventures in *The Incredible Voyage*, which also featured the Red Sea, it is a lackluster tale—though an interesting read for armchair sailors.

From the United States they went to England, where, as Tristan told Henry, "The Bodley Head [publishers] in UK treated us very well, fixed us up with 2 national TV shows, 2 newspapers, 3 bookstores and 6 radio shows in London and Wales, all in 10 days."

In London Tristan once again appeared on the *Terry Wogan Show*, on July 1, 1988. Other guests included the English funnyman Frankie Howard and the American standup comedian Mort Sahl. Anyone in Britain who had not seen Tristan since his visit to the Clare Francis program on BBC-TV in January 1982, or to Frank Delaney's show at the end of that year, would have been shocked at how much he had aged. Even a liberal application of stage makeup could not disguise his pale complexion, drawn face, tired eyes, and drab gray hair. Obviously the harsh winter on the Rhine, the trials of the Danube, the subsequent long tropical voyage, and the arduous Kra expedition had taken far more out of Tristan than he or anyone else had anticipated. He looked like a walking corpse. Tired though he may have been, humorless he was not.

Denied the opportunity of displaying his latest book on the show, Tristan managed to get in a plug about *Somewheres East of Suez* while also taking a subtle shot at the program's producer. Then he pulled a Welsh flag out of his pocket and showed it to Terry. His pause for effect was perfectly timed. Folding it carefully, he pulled a homemade flag from another pocket. "This is my new flag for my country," he announced proudly. The new flag had a red elephant in place of the Welsh dragon. Tristan used it as a perfect prop to tell how he and his handicapped crew, assisted by an elephant, hauled the *Henry Wagner* over the watershed from one river to another on the Kra expedition.

Strangely, although Thomas was on the promotional tour with him and he routinely described Thomas as "legally blind," Tristan once again failed to mention his German mate when talking about his handicapped crew. He said, "Between the four of us we were missing two legs, one arm and half a head." Those references were for himself, Som, Nok, and Anant. He included no recognition of Thomas, who probably did more than anyone else to make the expedition successful.

Tristan and Thomas moved back into their rented house beside the river in Chiang Mai on July 25. There they learned that *Outward Leg* had set sail during their absence from Thailand. Tristan wrote to Henry, "[Larry] Haftl sent someone out to Phuket and they have sailed *Outward Leg* away—we think to Singapore, from where they will probably ship her back to the USA. I'm not at all affected by this, except perhaps relieved that it's all over."

Tristan's original agreement with Haftl and Smith was for a solo circumnavigation lasting up to two years, but he had never sailed her solo. He had kept her for almost four years yet failed to complete the circumnavigation. He did earn considerable publicity for *Outward Leg*, and himself, though it is unlikely much of this proved of advantage to Haftl and Smith's company. While it is not known where *Outward Leg* sailed to initially, she ended her days in sad condition on shore at a small marina in the Philippines.

The months passed, while Tristan continued to play diplomatic chess with the Laotian government. With each successive move he became more and more confident of winning the contest. He wrote an upbeat letter to Henry on September 17: "What a game! I mean with the Laotians. I set off in the first place asking for a tremendous great deal from them, in the hopes of getting something less—and I got it." Later in the same letter he noted, "I am marking time for a week or two. But that's only on the paper front. Back in the real world we are organizing now the haul of 500 kilometers back south of the boat 'HW' from Chiang Mai to a place called Nong Khai *[farther down the Mekong on the Thailand-Laos border, actually well east of Chiang Mai]*, where she'll be launched into the river Mekong next month."

Had he kept to that timetable, it's possible that the next few months would have proved far less traumatic. In the meantime Tristan kept busy, revising the manuscript of *Seagulls in My Soup*, a sequel to *Saga of a Wayward Sailor* that he had begun many years before, and in mid-September he started writing *To Venture Further*—the story of his Kra expedition. By October 27, he told Henry, he had completed the latter book and sent the manuscript to London. Later in the same letter he confusingly talked of going back to Europe with Thomas to continue work on *To Venture Further*.

The speed with which Tristan sometimes wrote his books created considerable problems for his publishers. Euan Cameron, his friend and editor at the Bodley Head, remarked, "I did find that he required more than the usual amount of editing, and this got worse as he got older and more slapdash. For the very last book [we published, *Somewheres East of Suez*,] we even had to employ an outside editor to work on the text." Whether they were written too hastily or not, publishers and readers still wanted Tristan's tales of adventure.

By the end of October Tristan had finished *Seagulls in My Soup* and turned his attention back to the Mekong River expedition. *Henry Wagner* was still in either Chiang Mai or Chiang Rai, waiting for her crew and for permission to proceed. Tristan wrote to Henry, "On the Laos front things are moving slow. A party of American MIA-family people from S. Carolina busted into Laos across the Mekong the other week, and got themselves, of course, arrested. They were (literally) casting money onto the River Mekong, offering rewards for information. I feel for their loss, but good God did they have to do that? Really! Do these people have any idea what it means to do a thing like that in SE Asia???? I wonder if they knew what utter fools EVERYBODY thinks they are??? They have really slowed things down and made everything awkward for us. The clumsy oafs have made the Laotians 1,000 times more paranoid than they were a month ago." A few lines later his frustration broke through, "The idiots! We can get more info on MIA's in a WEEK than they could have got for a million dollars a week for ten years!"

Tristan's outburst was justified to a certain extent. The well-meant intrusion by the South Carolina families almost certainly spelled the end of his chances at the Mekong. None of his subsequent letters in November or December mention the Mekong. Thomas, usually in the forefront, slid into the background as the expedition hopes faded. Some months earlier, in a letter to Henry, Tristan had said of his mate, "Thomas is disgustingly healthy and active." Years later Henry recalled, "Thomas was worried about the draft in Germany. *[He was of an age when he could expect to be inducted into the army at any time.]* He told my wife, 'I could pass the physical right now.'"

But the German military never did get a chance to see what kind of soldier Thomas Ettenhuber would make.

CHAPTER 19

The Strange Death
of Thomas Ettenhuber

"Thomas Ettenhuber died this morning. Tristan Jones." The stark ca-
bled announcement, delivered on December 28, 1988, could hardly have
been less sympathetic. For Kriemhild Ettenhuber it was a nightmare
come true. Tristan's terse sentence, devoid of feeling, shattered the
mother's world. Her Thomas, her only child, a healthy young man of
twenty-four, was dead. And that's all she knew. In desperation she
phoned Tristan in Chiang Mai. She learned nothing more. "Thomas is
dead," was all he would tell her.

Lacking confidence in her ability to comprehend the situation in
English, Ettenhuber asked for help. Tristan gave her the telephone number of Georg Brummer, a German brewmaster working in Chiang Mai.
Calls to Brummer elicited little new information. Ettenhuber decided to
fly to Thailand. In the Christmas season, a busy time for airlines flying
from Europe to Southeast Asia, getting a flight to Bangkok proved difficult. Fortunately, Rosemarie Vivell, Ettenhuber's sister-in-law, was a
travel agent. She used her contacts to arrange bookings on Lufthansa
for two people on January 3, 1989, six days after Thomas died.

Ettenhuber and her brother, Alfred (Fredi) Vivell, flew from Munich to Frankfurt. While waiting for the long-haul connection to
Bangkok, she telephoned her estranged husband. He told her he had received a call from the German embassy in Bangkok warning the family

that, owing to the holiday season, it was not a good time to travel to Thailand. Undeterred, Kriemhild and Fredi boarded Lufthansa flight 734 and departed at 7:35 P.M. Throughout the long flight they tried to come to grips with the reason for their hurried journey. Thomas was dead. Ettenhuber could not believe it—would not believe it—until she saw her son's lifeless body. Nine and a half hours after taking off from Frankfurt, the huge jet landed at Bangkok's Krung Thep Airport at 10:30 A.M. local time, January 4, 1989.

In Bangkok the bereaved pair went immediately to the German embassy to sign sheaves of official papers. They were not impressed by their reception. No one they spoke to mentioned Thomas by name. He was referred to, rather coldly, as "the body." With all papers in order, a tired and depressed Ettenhuber, with Fredi, boarded the evening flight for the one-hour hop north to Chiang Mai to identify and arrange to ship the remains home. Georg Brummer met them in the arrivals concourse with a friendly greeting yet offered a warning. "You shouldn't be here," he told them. "It is not safe for you."

Thomas had known Georg Brummer socially. Many years before, he and Brummer's son had attended Kloster Schule Ettal together. Soon after the Kra expedition Thomas and Georg met in Bangkok, where Brummer had built a brewery. In 1988 and early 1989 he was employed in setting up another brewery in Chiang Mai.

Strangely, when Kriemhild and Fredi landed, Brummer's car was parked not in the airport parking lot but close by, in a dark corner, which the recent arrivals considered odd enough to be of some significance. Other than offering the warning, Brummer said little on the tight-lipped drive to Tristan's riverfront house. Tristan greeted them at the door. Kriemhild said he was leaning on his stick, trembling with undisguised anger, his face lined with fear. "Tristan was really frightened," said Kriemhild. "He was already packed. He couldn't wait to get out of Chiang Mai."

Refusing to let the brewmaster in, Tristan offered a greeting that echoed the one heard at the airport. "You shouldn't have come. It's not safe." Kriemhild and Fredi were more confused than ever. Why was it not safe for them in Chiang Mai? What was happening? The concerns and questions flashed through their minds as they tried to make sense of the situation. Why was Tristan so frightened? Why didn't he trust Herr Brummer? Why did Brummer want them to leave as soon as possible? All they knew for certain was that Thomas was dead. The two checked into their hotel that night hopelessly confused.

Fear of the unknown is contagious. Paranoia was rampant. Tristan and Brummer, who had often spoken on the phone before the tragedy, were no longer on speaking terms. Kriemhild and Fredi turned down Brummer's invitation to dinner one night, nervous about his motives. They both felt the brewmaster was hiding something, yet many years later they could not adequately explain their concerns.

So, what instilled such palpable fear into Tristan Jones and Georg Brummer? There are no clues forthcoming from Tristan. He publicly referred to his mate's death at the end of *To Venture Further*, with a heartrending tribute to Thomas preceded by a few lines from Kipling's *Prelude to Barrack-Room Ballads*. The tribute began with a distorted version of events quite at odds with the truth.

Thomas Ettenhuber, he announced, died of a heart attack on the north bank of Chiang Mai's Nam Ping River on December 26, 1988. He explained that only Thomas's family knew of the heart problem. He said his friend's death at age twenty-four was completely unexpected and effectively wrecked the planned Mekong expedition. He continued his tribute with the statement that within two weeks he had returned to Phuket with *Henry Wagner*. The boat would have been hauled by truck and trailer. There, near his home, he said, he rebuilt a longtail fishing boat that he named *Thomas Ettenhuber*.

Tristan, as so often happened, got the date wrong. (In a letter to Henry Wagner dated December 28, 1988, he got it wrong again. He said, "Thomas died last night.") He also deliberately lied about an important event, intentionally misleading his readers for his own ends. Thomas's young heart had not failed. He was dead, but not from natural causes. A frightened Tristan had no wish to join his mate.

Only the previous summer, when Tristan and Thomas visited the United States to attend boat shows, Thomas had told Joan Wagner that, since he was so fit, if he was called to Germany he would have no problem passing the military medical examination and would be inducted into the army. Few who knew Thomas believed the story of a heart problem.

Two days after his letter to the Wagner family telling of Thomas's death, while waiting for Ettenhuber to arrive, Tristan wrote to the Wagners again. Much of that strange letter is worth including here because of its deliberate falsehoods. "Dear Henry and Joan, You see I knew something that others didn't. Maybe his mother did, I don't know yet, as she is not yet here. We are still waiting for the autopsy report. But his mother probably won't discuss it. TE had a built-in self-destruct mechanism. It was some form of cancer as I understand it. He told me about it in Germany in 1985. He looked strong, but inside he was very defective. All I could do, after I found out, was try to give him as good a life as his short time span allowed. I may have been wrong to do that, but I don't think so. He shone brilliantly and burned out suddenly."

And then Tristan refers to a couple of letters that, as far as Henry Wagner could recall, were sent for quite different reasons. "Henry you knew from my previous letter that I was worried about him and asked you to write to him. I had almost been on my knees to him to take it easy. Unfortunately your letter arrived after his death. But I read it to him anyway. I could not stop him going out. I could not send him away, for without me he would have gone sooner I am sure. I tell myself that I gave him a good two years of extra life. And he helped me to make his name immortal. He was liked by everyone. Perhaps that was the problem."

After a few lines about his immediate plans Tristan returned his attention to Thomas: "I am getting better. He had to go young, because the Gods loved him. I always knew that. But I am bereft, grieving, and see his face everywhere, and know he's up on a mountain, or on a sailboat somewhere, laughing. He depended on me much, much more than I did on him. Most people did not realize that I'm sure."

Actually, the reverse was true. Tristan relied on Thomas far more than the young man depended on him. Tristan then tossed in another interruption to talk about Som's passport before expressing his concern about Frau Ettenhuber's impending visit. "I dread Thomas' mother's arrival. A woman's grief is so much different to a man's. It is bottomless and there is no real consolation for a mother. Her child is part of her."

Once again Tristan went back to business matters before signing off. Henry's memory of the theme of the letters Tristan mentioned is somewhat different. He remembered, "Tristan was concerned about Thomas. He was worried Thomas might get sidetracked by his [Thai] girlfriend, and not want to continue [the expedition]. He asked me to write to Thomas and try to talk sense into him."

Thirteen years and one month after Thomas's untimely death, Kriemhild Ettenhuber sat in her Bavarian home discussing her son's life and death. In response to a question about Thomas's reported heart attack, she hesitated a moment, then said, softly, slowly, distinctly, "There was nothing wrong with Thomas's heart. He did not have a heart attack."

When asked if she was sure, she nodded, her eyes filling with tears.

"Was an autopsy performed on Thomas?"

"Yes," she replied. Almost a whisper.

"Where? Here, or in Thailand."

"In Thailand. In Chiang Mai."

"And what was the result of that autopsy?"

Kriemhild shook her head once, slowly. Then, raising her eyes, she replied in a surprisingly strong voice, "Thomas was found lying in a parking lot at six o'clock in the morning of December 28. The autopsy showed he had died as a result of a single puncture wound to one arm. He had been injected with an overdose of heroin."

For a few moments there was silence, then a searching question to her, "Are you saying you believe Thomas was murdered?"

"Yes. Yes. I think Thomas was murdered." It would take a further meeting, months later, with Ettenhuber and her brother and sister-in-law before the story began to make real sense.

Thomas spent Christmas Day 1988 with Tristan. On December 26, after receiving a phone call from his mother, he went to visit Georg Brummer. After dinner, as far as can be ascertained, Thomas left Brummer's residence for an undisclosed destination. He did not go home to Tristan. During the few days Kriemhild and Fredi spent in Chiang Mai they heard—from Brummer, they said—about Thomas's attraction to a Thai girl. It seems natural at this point to wonder if Thomas and the girl in question spent the night of December 26 together.

On December 27, according to Tristan, Thomas phoned to say he was going to the travel agency for some information; then he would be home. Tristan and a Thai helper cooked a special dinner to welcome Thomas back. The hours passed. The sun went down and darkness descended. Noisy cicadas, tiny creatures of the indigo tropical night, awoke and announced their presence with high-pitched vibrations. Thomas did not arrive. A worried Tristan went out on his motorcycle, searching without success the route he thought Thomas would take. As the night progressed and Thomas failed to appear, Tristan might have suspected something serious had happened. The unbelievable news, far more traumatic than his worst fears, greeted him at daybreak. Thomas Ettenhuber, his friend, his surrogate son, his mate for the past four years, was dead.

Kriemhild and Fredi talked to the authorities without getting much help. They found little sympathy at the German embassy in Bangkok, and the Thai police in Chiang Mai were no more helpful. Thomas's death was recorded as just one more European kid taking an accidental overdose. Someone, perhaps, knew better.

The obvious questions are these: Was Thomas Ettenhuber, the mild-mannered young German sailor, murdered? If so, why? He was an adventurer and a photographer. What could he possibly have done to provoke the ultimate violent reprisal? Was it something to do with a Thai girl? Or was he, with or without Tristan's knowledge, mixed up in drugs in some way?

Clearing up the last question is relatively easy. According to all reports, Tristan had a passionate hatred for anything to do with so-called recreational drugs. And Thomas, although he admitted he sometimes smoked marijuana in Thailand, had no trace in his system of any prior abuse of hard drugs. No other needle marks showed on his body. There is no evidence to support any theory that Thomas had strayed into the drug trade, knowingly or otherwise. On the other side of the coin, however, is the evidence offered by the examining physician.

The medical report, dated January 6, 1989, noted that the autopsy was performed on the morning of December 28, 1988, the day Thomas died, at Maharaj Nakern Chiang Mai Hospital. It says the examination revealed no evidence of violence. Samples of blood and urine were sent to the forensic toxicology laboratory for analysis. The results showed heroin metabolite in both blood and urine. Thomas's death, the report stated, was due to a heroin overdose.

With the cause of death established to the satisfaction of the authorities, the case was effectively closed to further investigation. Thomas's remains were embalmed on January 5, 1989, the day after Kriemhild and Fredi arrived in Chiang Mai.

At the time of Thomas's death, the supreme drug lord in the Golden Triangle of northern Thailand, Laos, and Myanmar was Khun Sa, a citizen of Myanmar. Only six months before, Tristan had publicly discussed the problems of travel between northern Thailand and Laos with British TV host Terry Wogan. In response to a question about the area Tristan replied, "It's very dangerous. The territory we're in now is controlled by a man called Khun Sa, the drug warlord of the northern triangle. And for the next 600 kilometers we've sort of got to duck down low and dodge the bullets. But when we get to a place called Luang Prabang we'll be safe." Wogan asked why Tristan thought he and his crew would be shot at. Tristan answered, "Because they [the drug lords] don't like any kind of outside interference."

Tristan and Thomas had been badgering officials in Thailand and Laos for months, asking for permission to sail *Henry Wagner* on the Mae Nam Kok from Chiang Rai to the Mekong River, which is in effect the border between the two countries at that point. The route they had chosen was through the middle of a notorious drug-smuggling region. Their previous expedition, across the Malay Peninsula, had garnered wide publicity in Thailand, on television and in newspapers. The drug lords would have known all about Tristan Jones and Thomas Ettenhuber and what their intentions were. They would not have wanted the expedition of disabled adventurers, with a potential media entourage, rampaging through their golden jungle. It is therefore strongly possible, though unlikely ever to be proved, that a drug lord, or one of his henchmen, had Thomas killed to dissuade Tristan from his plans. Certainly Tristan had been given a warning, perhaps verbal as well as graphic. As a deterrent, it worked. Tristan abandoned the idea of sailing the Mekong River. He fled northern Thailand, with his boat and crew on a truck, as soon as he was able.

During Ettenhuber's short, sad visit one of Tristan's Thai crew—she believes it was Som—approached her one day. "Missy," he called, holding a homemade wooden sailing ship, square-rigged with blue sails, in his one hand, "Missy, come with me." Ettenhuber went with Som to the river. There he tenderly placed a red candle on the ship's deck, lit the wick, and gently pushed the vessel out into the current. "Now Thomas's soul can go home," he said.

Tristan's version of the departure of Thomas's coffin from Chiang

Mai differs markedly from Ettenhuber's. She praised the thoughtfulness of the undertaker and said Thomas was taken in a hearse from the Chiang Mai morgue to Bangkok's Krung Thep Airport on January 6. There his casket was loaded on Lufthansa flight 737 for departure at ten minutes past midnight, January 7. Tristan wrote the story this way in a letter to Henry Wagner on January 7, 1989: "TE has gone back to Bavaria now. I comforted as well as I could his mother. I think she felt better when she left but what a job. All the able-bodied would-be Rambos, Sambos, Bambos and Bimbos were on holiday or drunk or 'indisposed' and one-arm Som and I wound up rolling his coffin out to the bus on rollers. There was a red and gold sign over the morgue exit, that Som told me said, 'Happy New Year!' "

Using the excuse that nothing was ready, Tristan promised to ship Thomas's possessions home to his mother as soon as he had collected them all together in Chiang Mai and Phuket. The only item of Thomas's that Tristan parted with at the time was a U.S. Navy pea jacket. Tristan gave it to Kriemhild, then asked Henry to get him another as that one was actually his, not Thomas's. Thomas's jacket, he explained, had been stolen during a burglary in December, along with Thomas's camera. Despite his promise, Tristan kept everything. Thomas's slide collection, and his mementos from four years of traveling with Tristan, remained with Tristan.

Kriemhild and Fredi flew from Chiang Mai to Bangkok during the evening of January 6. On checking in for their flight to Germany, with Thomas's casket already consigned as cargo, they were astounded to learn that someone—they were told the German embassy—had cancelled their tickets. Fredi immediately put in a call to Rosemarie. She went to work to get the reservations reinstated.

Thomas Ettenhuber, the lonely boy who became a confident ocean sailor, was buried far from the sea in his beloved Bavaria. His headstone is an oval granite boulder with a simple "Thomas" engraved in black. The shadowy outline of a sailing ship stands to the left of his name. A trio of orange candles brightens the sad scene. Kriemhild asked for donations to the Atlantis Society instead of flowers at Thomas's funeral. She sent every pfennig collected to Tristan, apparently unaware that it would be used primarily for his personal needs.

Months later Georg Brummer wrote a strange, disjointed letter to Fredi Vivell expressing his sadness at the tragic events. With the letter he enclosed a prayer he had written and read over the place where Thomas's body was found—a place to which, he complained, "neither you nor Frau Ettenhuber accompanied me." Tristan did not see the letter. By the time it reached Fredi Vivell, Tristan and Ettenhuber had all but ceased communicating with each other. Kriemhild mainly blamed their lack of a common language for the lapse.

One can't help wondering what effect the pressure of his constant lies had on Tristan during those dark months. He almost certainly knew, or suspected, that Thomas had been murdered. Tristan had carefully crafted an image for his public of an aggressive, hard-nosed adventurer, afraid of nothing that might stand in his way. He pictured himself as a heroic figure who had sailed mighty oceans and weathered terrible storms, who grappled with polar bears in the Arctic, fought his way through snake-infested jungles in South America, and backed down from no man. Considering this image, Tristan's cowardly retreat from Chiang Mai, and the weak explanation of a heart attack to cover up the facts of his friend's death, did him no service. It's true his life possibly was also at risk. Equally, it's reasonable to believe that without evidence, any formal accusations against the perpetrators would have come to nothing. Tristan was, however, in a unique position. He was a writer of books and magazine articles. He published a regular newsletter. Each of those could have been used to shout the truth about his mate's death, if only as a measure of his respect for a young man who had stood by him in a way few others would have done.

On January 1, 1989, the grieving Tristan officially canceled his round-the-world voyage in *Outward Leg* (deliberately ignoring the fact

that *Outward Leg* had already been taken from him), although the no-
tification did not get sent to Henry Wagner for distribution to fans
until February 5. The short statement read:

> *After 36,000 miles [sic], during which we visited 36 countries, I have de-*
> *cided not to resume my voyage in* Outward Leg. *My main reasons for*
> *this decision are:*
>
> *1) Voyage-long lack of support from the boat-owners.*
>
> *2) The realization that my own achievements on ocean passages do*
> *little to encourage young disadvantaged, disabled people [to] achieve*
> *themselves. To do this I must be among them, working with them, as I*
> *am at present.*
>
> *3) The death of my late Mate, Thomas Ettenhuber, of heart problems,*
> *at the age of 24. At this stage I have no wish to take on board another*
> *"apprentice."*
>
> *4) Personal disinclination to set another "record."*

Tristan never did reveal the true story behind Thomas's death, not
even to Henry Wagner and Wally Herbert, his best friends. However,
three weeks after Thomas's death Tristan's pain at his loss shows in a letter to Henry.

> *I keep myself busy all day every day. It doesn't help much to ease the void*
> *that Thomas' death caused, but it helps. Most of the time I am doing it*
> *all for him anyway, just as he would have done it. I don't think anyone*
> *who has not shared the hazards of small-craft voyaging with someone*
> *can understand what kind of relationship evolves. I know it was closer*
> *than any father-son or even brothers. The other person becomes an alter-*
> *ego, a shadow-self. When the other person is much younger he becomes a*
> *projection-vehicle of one's self into the future. On reflection, it's probably*
> *best for two people like TE and I to split up as soon as a voyage ends. But*
> *we were both Taurians, and would never know the ends or the edges of*
> *anything. Of course the Freudian-fed psychoanalysts would try to put*
> *some kind of sexual connotation to it, because that makes it easier to ex-*
> *plain, but they would be wrong about that, there's nothing of that in it,*
> *of course. It's strange, because it's never been really investigated or ex-*
> *plained. I know Polar explorers get like that about each other within the*

team. Big ship sailors, I know from my own experiences, know it in a much lighter way. It's the "ship-mate" thing. But I am positive that it is most deeply felt by small-craft voyagers. I cannot look at an anchor or a line, or a boat even, without TE being at my side. I doubt if two people could have been so alike and so dissimilar at the same time.

And then a telling sentence showing how low his spirits had sunk in the twenty-one days since December 28: "I have thought much about suicide since TE took off, but have decided it would be too much like surrender, and that I'll never do, of course."

Did Tristan contemplate suicide because he knew far more about Thomas's death than he was prepared to admit? We will never know.

CHAPTER 20

Another Devastating Blow

Tristan had two journeys planned for early 1989. The first was to attend boat shows in Japan and talk with Yanmar, his engine sponsors. Soon after, he was to fly to Hawaii for filming of the IMAX feature *To Race the Wind*. Without Thomas, who had been his traveling companion and aide for four years, Tristan took Som with him to Japan. He then went to Hawaii alone, the first long journey he had made without an assistant for many years.

On his return to Phuket he wrote his regular letter to Henry Wagner. The one-page letter, dated March 15, 1989, remarked on his solo journey. "I was pleased that I managed to go to Hawaii and back all by myself," Tristan wrote. "I took no luggage and returned with a small shoulder-bag only. But it shows I can do it."

Unusually for Tristan, in the same letter he admits to having a rough time in Honolulu, "as we were out in heavy seas every day, shooting over and over again. By the time I got returned to our hotel, usually late, I was so bone weary I could hardly move."

As a memorial to his deeply missed mate, Tristan had named one of his boats *Thomas Ettenhuber*. He later purchased another boat and named it *Joseph Gribbins* after his former editor at *Nautical Quarterly*. Both vessels were used, with *Henry Wagner*, to train young crews for fishing and taking tourists on day trips from Phuket.

At the end of April Tristan received a surprising invitation from Odessa to visit the Soviet Union by yacht, with up to six of his crew. His reply, sent through his agent Richard Curtis, said he was willing to fly there and discuss publication of his books in the USSR. Apparently anticipating substantial sales, he said he would then accept advances and royalties in the form of a Soviet-built forty-foot multihull. Nothing came of the suggestion, but Tristan did briefly look into having a boat built at a Black Sea port.

To Venture Further was accepted by Grafton Books in the United Kingdom. But getting it published in the United States, which he expected to be a formality given his track record, proved more difficult. Although he was worried, Tristan's biting wit comes through in the last paragraph of a July 1989 letter to Henry about his problems in getting the book accepted. "Connie Rooseveldt at Hearst says they [will] publish TVF if I 'add more story' (!!!!!) I've offered to include (in order of appearance) the following extra characters to liven it up for Ms Rooseveldt's imagined readers: Emperor Hirohito, Fidel Castro, the Two Jessie's (Helms and Jackson), Madonna, Michael Jackson, Rev. and Mrs. Bakker, Oprah Winfield [sic] (on her back in the outfield), Mrs. Thatcher's husband—Dennis, Donald and Daffie Duck, HRH Prince of Wales, (to act as a spinnaker), and 'Sting' and 'Boy George.' That should do it!"

It's probable that, as with *Somewheres East of Suez*, Tristan had relied on a more truthful approach to telling the expedition's story, and this time it appeared to have backfired. Hearst Marine, however, did eventually publish *To Venture Further* in 1991.

With plans well under way for Tristan to visit the States in September, and with nonrefundable tickets purchased (by Henry Wagner), Tristan suddenly decided he should visit Odessa after all on his way back to Thailand. Henry was not amused and reminded his errant friend that the tickets could not be changed or the cost refunded. In a few lines he admonished Tristan for constantly changing direction. "If you went to Odessa in Oct., you would miss 3 firm lectures and the Annapolis Boat Show, (800 books sold last time). Now, to be the devil's advocate. There is a great lack of continuity in your planned projects. You ask for contributions of money and equipment. Fans ask about the Yangtze River, *Outward Leg*, the catamaran trip across the Pacific and more. They are confused. Contributions are slow and small. I understand your problems: many do not."

Henry's letter worked. Tristan flew to the States and attended a series of boat shows. Seated at a table, with a stack of his books at hand, he proved yet again that he was the master at attracting custom, entertaining readers, and selling books. But he was not the Tristan Jones of previous visits. Few visitors to his display would have recognized the change; only those who knew him well could sense that his mind was not fully on his work. As soon as his commitments were over, Tristan returned directly to Phuket. He was well aware the trip had not been a complete success. Back home in Thailand, Tristan sent a note to Henry that included a half apology. "I hope I didn't alienate too many people on my trip. I had an awful lot on my mind—a hell of a lot at risk—that I couldn't talk about much. It's all settling down okay though."

His general health and money, or lack of it, were the problems. Book sales had slowed. Donations to the Atlantis Society were drying up. Living in Thailand, although inexpensive day to day, offered little opportunity for earning money from public appearances and lectures. Tristan needed a healthy shot in his financial arm.

His moneymaking campaigns strayed into the bizarre in May 1990 when he decided to attempt to extort a large sum of money from the Czechoslovakian government. A letter to Abner Stein, his British literary agent, explained:

> Now that the 5th anniversary of cracking the Iron-Curtain in US-flag vessel Outward Leg *has passed, I am publicly taking up a deep grievance, re: the attempt by the Czechoslovakian State Security Police, in Bratislava,*

on May 2nd, 1985, at approximately 08:00 hours, to cause the deaths of my crew, Thomas Ettenhuber (West German) and myself (British). Please arrange for Bodley Head to send to Czech author, now president, Vaclev Havel, a copy of my book The Improbable Voyage, *and include a note drawing his attention to Chapter 18—"The Set-Up." Please inform me when this has been done.*

The chapter referred to is my account, carefully written from records noted very shortly after the incident, and from my crew's statements, of how the Czechoslovakian State Police, with full knowledge of all ship movements about to be made in the area, ordered the US-flag yacht Outward Leg *out of Bratislava's No. 1 port and directly into the path of the Hungarian-flag river-ship* Mantra *and her tow, emerging from Bratislava's No. 2 port. In the ensuing unavoidable collision, only luck and skill saved the lives of myself and my crew. I ingested into my lungs large amounts of cold, polluted river-water which substantially contributed to the present poor state of my lungs. Apart from lung damage I suffered severe shock for several months after the incident which badly affected my general health. Even now I suffer from nightmares about the Bratislava incident.*

I am claiming ten million dollars US from the Czechoslovakian government for damages incurred when its servants issued wrongful orders with intent to murder me.

Stein sent the book and Tristan's letter to Havel. There was no reply, so the outrageous attempt at extortion failed. Money may have been tight, but Tristan's health was given a boost when he was advised to try a Chinese herb—he called it dong quoai—for his blood and lung problems, particularly the emphysema, probably the result of a lifelong addiction to cigarettes. With the help of his Haw-Chinese assistant, Ehd, he was able to try the cure and found it did indeed make his breathing a little easier.

He was invited to sail to Japan on a chartered catamaran but, expressing his utmost disappointment, had to refuse because of his emphysema. Even that debilitating lung condition could not slow him for long. In March 1990 he resurrected an old idea for a new book. The proposed story, *Sons of the Sea*, about his peacetime career in the navy, was intended to fit chronologically between *Heart of Oak* and *Ice!* Tristan talked about offering it to Richard Curtis to present to publishers. The project appears to have been little more than a good idea. Mentioned in the foreword to *Heart of Oak* as an eventual sequel, *Sons of the Sea* was—unfortunately—never written. Instead of his version of those years we have only the Royal Navy's spare, cold facts.

American sailor and author Reese Palley, who had known Tristan for some years, was in Romania in 1990 helping develop a marina at Constanta. He arranged a job for Tristan as commodore. Palley said, "He joined me in my mistaken belief that there would be hordes of yachts that would take this route [the Rhine-Danube] and, on entering the Black Sea via Bucharest, would need a harbor. By the time we asked Tris to join us we already knew that the Romanians were a recalcitrant and tricky breed. They would need a very firm hand and, knowing Tris as I did, I felt that if anyone could cow the Romanians it would be our terribly tempered Mr. Bang."

Tristan went to Constanta for three months over the summer of 1990, which he spent racing around the marina in his wheelchair terrifying everyone with his fiery temper. Through no fault of his own the exercise was not a success, and he retreated to Thailand and a quieter life. He later wrote to Reese Palley of the Romanian sojourn, "I'll tell you, boyo. The Gods were easy. They stood and fought. The Romanians melted away at the first hint of conflict. It's like jousting with shadows. The worst enemy I never bested."

Apart from learning that *Seagulls in My Soup*, the long-awaited follow-up to *Saga of a Wayward Sailor*, had been accepted for publication by Sheridan House, 1991 was an abysmal year for Tristan. First he scalded his hand badly. In March he was admitted to the Phuket Adventists Hospital suffering from a severe intestinal obstruction, necessitating surgery. Following that operation he developed a blood clot—in his right leg. A further operation was performed to correct the circulatory problem. Tristan later remarked that he had been in the Valley of Death for three painful weeks. Worse was to follow.

By the end of the first week in May he was recovering, yet he lacked feeling in his remaining foot. He was under no illusions about his situation. Desperate for any form of help, temporal or spiritual, he told his friends, "Please pray for the recovery of my right foot."

At home, and struggling mightily to regain the use of his right leg, he told Henry he was in a bad way but "thank God, I live to see *To Venture Further* in print *[British edition]*." On June 5 he admitted to feeling "pretty dismal" while praying he could stay alive until July 30, the anticipated release date for the Thai edition of *To Venture Further*.

A day later his doctor told him that if the circulation in his right leg did not improve quickly, part of his foot would have to be amputated. Clots had formed in the capillaries of his big toe and third toe. Somehow, despite intense pain and a strong feeling of impending death, Tristan fought on. A new diagnosis called for possibly amputating only the two toes. Tristan scrawled a fax to Henry that, apart from pleasantries and instructions, gave his friend heart. "If diagnosis by 28th [of June] indicates further chopping I'll go to London . . . and I swear and promise to hold on like a true bloody British Bulldog and with my American friends pulling for me, I will come through. I might be covered in Tauro-scat, but I'll come through. I may be howling, but I'll come through."

About this time Tristan began painting watercolors. He thought he was pretty good at it and said so. Henry thought different. "They were really childish," he said. Amateurish or not, the attempts at art helped take Tristan's mind off his condition.

For some time Tristan had signed occasional letters with references to Islam. "By the grace of Allah," is a typical example. In 1991 or thereabouts he was quoted in a newspaper interview as saying that if he had a second attempt at life he would like to come back as a Muslim. Rafiq Tschannen, a Swiss Muslim living in Bangkok, wrote thanking him for his positive remarks about Islam and sent him books on the subject. Tristan told Rafiq he had had a dream in which he saw an intense light. Rafiq interpreted the phenomenon for Tristan: "An intense light, signifying Allah, had a very good meaning in a dream and could mean he would enter paradise." As a result, Tristan adopted the Muslim faith.

The doctor gave some hope, telling his patient the decaying toes might renew their capillaries. Tristan, ordered to rest, complained of the physical pain of having "to lie facing left" all the time.

Another boost welcomed July. A happier Tristan faxed Henry, "Despairing of any progress with chemotherapy, I called in Chinese-medicine practitioner/monk. He sent an angel to inspect me last Sunday. He then provided herbs, etc., (some over 100 years old . . .) to make broth. After 3 days of nose-holding disgust my leg calf muscle is gaining strength and my foot, while yet painful, is less garish. I have more hopes of recovery now than a week ago."

Medically, Tristan was a mess. The wound from his stomach surgery had not completely healed. He suffered from emphysema and had recently had a cyst removed from his lung. The muscles in his leg below the knee were weak, and he had occasional sharp stabs of pain. An incision at the back of his knee and another down the outside of his calf muscle were both still healing. The muscles lower down in his leg were atrophying, and the nerves tingled. His foot looked dead yet had some color. The flesh on his heel had worn away as a result of his long stay in bed, but so far the open wound was clean. Not so his toes: the big toe and third toe were black. Gangrene had set in.

Delighted to discover he could move his calf muscles and toes, the invalid became convinced the Chinese medicine was working. His confidence was such that he said he hoped to be able to stand in three or four weeks. Despite his hopes of getting back on his feet, the boredom of remaining in one place was getting to him. He moaned to Henry, "I am yet a prisoner in bed, unless someone helps me get into a chair. A miserable existence if my surroundings were not beautiful, or if I did not keep myself busy."With a strength of will impressive in one whose body so desperately needed help, he did keep himself occupied. Although the days of locking himself in his room and writing for ten or twelve hours at a stretch were over, Tristan continued to sketch out articles and develop ideas for future books.

August dawned, with the stress continuing. Tristan's leg remained virtually paralyzed from the knee down. The only way he could maintain circulation and reduce the pain was to elevate his knee. His mood was getting desperate again. Although he had little money, he tried without success to arrange treatment with a specialist at Songkhla University Hospital. Again he spoke of returning to England, while doubting that the National Health Service there would be efficient enough to handle his case without delay.

On August 31 he sent Henry a morbid note: "Have gangrene in toes, starting to spread up. Doctor comes tomorrow. May go mission hospital . . . pray for me."

For Tristan there was to be no return to England, and no cure. Though the Chinese medicine may have helped for a while, nothing could stave off the inevitable. The tissues of his leg and toes were dying. Without drastic surgery his life would be forfeit. Accepting his fate with courageous resignation, he agreed to the operation.

With over six decades of hard years behind him, Tristan Jones was used to being in trouble. He'd lived with it since his earliest days. Often he'd gone looking for it, his aggressive nature urged on by adrenaline, stimulated by thoughts of an impending battle. In his youth and early manhood his mouth, backed up by his fists, regularly placed him in jeopardy. In those carefree days he was as happy fighting as he was drinking. Nothing stopped the tough little sailor: certainly not the threat of trouble. To Tristan trouble was simply another challenge, something to face up to, his hawk nose pointing aggressively at his opponent, his bearded chin thrust close to another's angry face. Trouble was an irresistible opportunity. Trouble equated to fun. In September

1991 all that changed. Real trouble, of a kind he knew only too well, trouble that had been threatening him for months, arrived with hurricane force.

Stretched out on a hospital bed in a tropical country, far from the land of his birth, Tristan's thoughts on that bleak day must have been somber in the extreme. The tiny blue star tattooed on his left earlobe, once a vibrant symbol of oceanic prowess, had faded along with his strength. A jagged scar over his right eyebrow merged with deep lines carved by hard living. Outside, the humidity of the monsoon season was lessening to a bearable level. West of where he lay in the Mission Hospital in Phuket, the Andaman Sea was calm; only a gentle swell rolled in to form tidy patterns of waves caressing golden beaches. Green-slatted palms waved slowly, fanning their trunks and their exotic fruit against the Asian heat. In the sterile room where he waited in contemplative silence, cooler air circulated from an overhead fan. Not far away his Thai crew—Anant, Nok, and Som—looking after the boats at Rawai Beach, kept a sad vigil for their suffering captain and mentor.

Tristan had unwittingly prophesied this moment in one of his books thirteen years earlier. In *Ice!* he wrote about his feelings while lying on a hospital bed with a back injury. At that time he eloquently expressed the fears of a young sailor forced to consider a life of inactivity ashore—a sailor who could no longer take comfort from the restless ocean swells.

Perhaps on that oppressive September day in 1991, his gray hair and beard showing the ravages of time against the stark white freshness of his pillow, Tristan reached down to feel his gangrene-defiled right leg one more time and asked himself whether the Thailand expedition had really been worth all the anguish and pain it had caused him and others. Maybe his long, slender fingers ruefully touched the scars on the stump of his left leg, which he'd lost nearly a decade ago.

While he waited for a Thai orderly to wheel him to the operating theater, where surgical staff prepared their instruments and readied their trained hands to sever his remaining leg, Tristan knew his chances of ever going to sea again were virtually nil.

Two days before, on September 2, Tristan had written a terse note to Henry Wagner: "Amputation above knee tomorrow Sep 3rd. Should mean loss of pain by end of Oct . . . will be under sedation about five days. My blood is clear, not diabetic. May god preserve you and yours." He signed it and, with a morbid flash of humor, added, "The Legless Wonder."

He was given a one-day reprieve. The operation was rescheduled for September 4. Another day to think about the future. Another day to dwell on old age without legs. Another day to consider a life—such as it would be—away from the sea.

Tristan's fascination with the Royal Navy was well documented in *Heart of Oak*. Perhaps, while waiting for the surgeon's knife, he ruefully thought of those who long before—during Lord Nelson's time—had limbs amputated without any anesthetic other than a vaguely soporific tot of rum.

Unlike the harsh, primitive surgical practices commonly employed during historic naval battles like that fought off Cape Trafalgar, modern medical technology has advanced enough to spare a patient's mind while under deep anesthesia. Seconds after the hypodermic needle entered Tristan's vein and the anesthetic flowed with his life's blood to paralyze his nerves and his brain temporarily, Tristan would have slipped into a nether world—a world of blackness where thoughts of the past, pain of the present, or fear of the future could not intrude. The next few hours, until he gradually awakened in the recovery room, would be lost to him forever. The evidence of his deathlike sleep would unfortunately be there when he awoke and would never leave him.

While the surgeon and operating staff cut away decaying flesh and aging bone, Tristan mercifully was suspended in a far better place. The dying leg, with its blackened foot, no longer useful to a living body, was discarded. Quickly the medical team sealed the blood vessels, trimmed the end of the bone, and folded healthy flesh over it. With the delicacy of a skilled seamstress, one of them stitched the flaps of skin over the remains of a once strong leg.

Monitored carefully as each day passed, Tristan slowly returned to some semblance of life, though morphine clouded his mind as it subdued the pain created by the surgeon's tools. Tristan, always a scrapper, fought the invasion of the drug, knowing instinctively that if he was to survive, it would have to be by his strength of will.

On September 13, out of danger and becoming clear-headed, he wrote to his London publisher from his own bed: "Don't know what chapter this is I'm 'living' now. Had right leg amputated on 4th. Now back home 'being brave,' taking each hour as it comes. No friends except Thai employees here as off-season. Very, very depressed but determined [to] exercise and stick it out and, if I can, *write about it*. Am in less leg-pain but heart-stricken and sanity-sore. I need words of encouragement."

A few days later he was rallying and, although depressed, sounding more like himself—more like the gutsy Tristan Jones of his books. Another letter addressed to Henry Wagner told of his mental condition and his pain at the recent accidental death of an employee: "Henry— whilst worse off than last year, my physical state has prospect of improving. The sudden withdrawal from morphine, after 10 days, was a great shock. To return home to bereavement (Ehd, 15, used to help with 'office work,' faxes, etc.) was devastating—correction, *is* devastating. The double shock almost finished me. I am still weak but my main aim—apart from survival—is to try to remain here at least until the Thai version of *To Venture Further* is out. One delay after another, but I think the end of this month it should be out. Your fax cheered me greatly. I can only dream of things like an electric wheelchair."

Dream he may have done but, rarely one to miss an opportunity, he continued with a brief reminder of the electrical power in Phuket. Just in case.

Electricity in Thailand 240 volts. We've now organized a local male nurse to attend me until my new stump heals. Healing here in humidity is slow. *You must understand that normally Thais avoid conflict and misfortune, so if a couple of things seem slightly* odd *don't jump to Western-type conclusions and bear in mind I'm* surviving *hour by hour and so far am doing alright. Your response gave me* great *encouragement.* Thank you. *Mentally I am fighting intense depression. I don't know why yet—but I do know that there must be a reason and am searching diligently. The thought of my readers helps me. We are a team—all of us. The thought I may have helped others is a great consolation. I am greatly changed. Humble, but not* humbled. *Does this make sense? I look forward to news of your visit. It is a lifesaver. Henry you are . . . (What can I say?) . . . my friend, and thank God!*

Tristan Jones, a man who had always tackled life head on, who never backed down from a fight, who told enthusiastic tales of surviving the terrors of rafting ice in the Arctic and beating the green hell of Brazil's Mato Grosso, who mastered jungle rivers in Thailand and sailed the oceans of the world for much of his life, no longer had his own two feet to stand on. His strength of character, his natural stubbornness, his determination to survive and to succeed would, from that day forth, be taxed to the limit. For whatever life he had left, Tristan, never a quitter, would battle with all the resources at his command.

Thoughts of death preyed on his mind for weeks after the amputation. On September 19 he informed Henry he wanted his ashes to be placed somewhere on the town jetty at Kastellorizon, Greece. "This can best be handled through my good friend (fellow author) Liz Carr. Liz is a good all round woman deckhand/mate. She's been at it since before 'Lib' meant anything. She can make a mainsail or a splice with both hands tied. Socially she's fantastic," he said. "It looks like I'm going to survive at least for a while. But I want to get the ashes thing settled. I might get myself to Kastellorizon and kick off there. But in case not, when Snyder (local law-advisor) advises you, tell him (under terms of my will) to send the ashes to Liz. Sorry to be morbid, but the prospect of my remains resting in the birthplace of democratic thought is irresistible."

His spirits received a considerable boost on October 2, when he learned from the Welsh Union of Writers that he was the joint winner of the John Morgan Prize for Literature for *To Venture Further*. Awarded for investigative journalism and for travel writing, his share amounted to £1,000—a much needed payday. Even with that unexpected windfall he was still deeply in debt for his medical care. Tristan appealed to his fans for help. Such had been his impact on readers, editors, and publishers over the fourteen years he had been in the public eye that help soon arrived in a dynamic way.

Patience Wales, then managing editor of *Sail* magazine, heard about Tristan's second amputation and his dire need for financial support. She mentioned the seriousness of his situation in her next monthly editorial. Using Henry Wagner's Sailor's Bookshelf as a mail drop, the widespread plea raised over $35,000 for Tristan. One check for more than $500 came from a psychiatrist who used to read passages from *Ice!* to his young daughters.

Henry opened all the envelopes, read the letters, and deposited the checks. Donations ranged from a couple of dollars to hundreds. After banking the money, Henry sent the letters and deposit statements to Tristan in Thailand. "That was one of the few times he had excess money in the bank," Henry said.

Needless to say, Tristan was delighted with the letters of encouragement and enormously relieved to benefit from the largesse of his fans. For the time being his financial worries were over. With that burden removed, he could concentrate on staying alive and rebuilding his health. Somehow he also found time to wage war on imagined foes.

CHAPTER 21

Wounded Pride

A magazine article based on a 1991 interview in Phuket quotes Tristan as saying, "I was crossing the Atlantic alone, in 1969, and I heard on my small radio that men had landed on the moon." On July 21, 1969, when astronauts Neil Armstrong and Edwin "Buzz" Aldrin landed on the moon, Tristan was sailing across the Atlantic in *Barbara*. With him were Anton Elbers, Hank Kelly, and Dan Burt. Faced with such outright falsehoods, it's not surprising that other writers, and some readers, cast doubt on Tristan's honesty in reporting his adventures.

In 1978 Hal Roth, noted American blue-water sailor and author, wrote a critical letter about *The Incredible Voyage* to the editor of *Sail* magazine. Published in the March issue that year, it read, "I must agree with Anne Christensen's letter (*Sail*, November 1977) in which she pointed out the gross inaccuracies, the vulgarity, the exaggerated style and the holier-than-thou attitude of Tristan Jones in his book *The Incredible Voyage*. After spending the last 3½ years sailing around South America, I agree with most librarians who classify the book as fiction. Jones is an expert writer but he needs to learn the meaning of truth and responsibility to his readers, some of whom may actually try to follow Jones's route. For Jones to embroider a notable trip with exaggerations in order to sell books may be enterprising, but it is cheap sensationalism in my view. His book might better have been entitled *The Incredible Fantasy*."

As a worried Tristan prepared for his second amputation in 1991 he read Rod Heikell's *The Danube: A River Guide*, published earlier that year. In it Heikell wrote about Tristan and *The Improbable Voyage*. Heikell, a well-respected author of seven sailing guides, including four on the Mediterranean and two on the French waterways, wrote:

> *It is not until 20 years later that there is another account of a trip down the Danube, made by the irascible Tristan Jones in the same year I wandered down the river for the first time. Readers either adore or hate Tristan Jones's racy prose and pugnacious adventures. In* The Improbable Voyage *he recounts his voyage and his battles against German bureaucracy, a Czechoslovakian set-up (he believed) designed to wreck his boat, Bulgarian piracy and his single-handed attempts to reform Romania and free its people. You cannot deny the allure of the ripe tales, but there is a lot of fantasy mixed into the book and worse, a jingoism, a waving of the American flag though he is Welsh, that has little to do with an understanding of eastern Europe and its peoples and promotes the sort of stereotypes that need to be dismantled rather than reinforced.*

Toward the end of his book, under the heading "Useful Books," Heikell takes another dig at Tristan with this brief comment on *The Improbable Voyage*: "Racy prose and a thrilling read; but your own voyaging on the Danube is unlikely ever to encompass all that Tristan Jones manages to fit in."

Tristan read those two excerpts and went berserk. In a flurry of insulting letters to Rod Heikell and his publisher, Tristan's temper took him beyond reality to let them know that he was prepared for a duel. In a childish diatribe to the publisher of *The Danube*, Tristan described Heikell and his book: "Rod Heikell's book *The Danube* is plagiaristic, full of errors and will certainly place in jeopardy the vessel of any voyager using it for reference in navigation of the River Danube. In future, until I get satisfactory word back from either Heikell or his publisher, I shall refer to him as 'Butch.' Certain mannerisms in the way he writes about his women companions—plus his first name—lead me to suspect that, besides being a fascist, Heikell is also a lesbian. Reliable witnesses have told me that Ms Heikell emptied her toilet-bucket straight into the Danube all the way downstream, and that both her companions looked like KGB drivers in drag."

Rod Heikell replied, in part, "Dear Tristan Jones, For a paragraph in an inconsequential book on the Danube which will probably only sell a few thousand [copies] if I'm lucky you seem to have developed an intense hatred of me. Why? We've never met so you don't have any idea of me, apart from a few hints here and there in *The Danube*. I think you take me too seriously as a threat to your name and your books. I think you take me more seriously than I do."

Heikell stuck the knife in deep, reminding Tristan that not only was *Outward Leg* not the first oceangoing craft to sail across Europe, but he was not even the first handicapped person to do it. Although his letters have a conciliatory tone, Heikell provoked Tristan anew with this rejoinder: "And you are emphatically a bully. You are a bully in your faxes and letters." Heikell finished with a challenge: "Contact the yachting magazine of your choice in the UK and I'll forward the correspondence between us to them. I doubt you've got the balls for it."

Tristan was not in the least mollified by anything in Heikell's reply, though he failed to pick up the gauntlet. Instead he shot back three pages of type to emphasize his complaints and wounded pride. Tristan, now a Muslim at least in spirit, began by invoking the holy book of Islam. "On the Holy Koran—I swear: Heikell: your part-apology to me for my hurt on reading (on what seemed my death-bed) your words about me in your book *The Danube* has now arrived."

After lecturing Heikell for a few lines about the seriousness of a writer's craft, Tristan quoted the ten-line paragraph that he considered so highly offensive, underlining every word. He continued by dissecting the paragraph and ranting about each of his accuser's points. And he let himself be carried away on the tide of his own anger by announcing himself as both a prophet and a political soldier. "In 1978, in *Saga of a*

Wayward Sailor, I clearly forecast the collapse of the Soviet system. *[He didn't.]* By 1980 I was certain it would happen before the end of this terrible century; in October 1984 I set out from London to help it happen quicker. Unlike most Western pro-freedom 'intellectuals' I put myself where my mouth was."

Although it is congruent with what his former crews and his friends have said about his tactics afloat and on land, Tristan could not let the accusation of bullying pass. In a line in the letter's final paragraph he shouts, "I am not and have never been a bully."

The argument raged back and forth for months, with Tristan blustering and threatening legal action, before it finally faded. "I went to Thailand on holiday in 1995," Rod Heikell said. "I thought it would be a good idea, while I was there, to visit Tristan and try to become friends. I was too late. The old bastard died before I got to Phuket." A 1987 review of *The Improbable Voyage* in the *Geographical Journal* treated Tristan's work rather more kindly, referring to it as "a most enjoyable book."

In September 1994 Tristan discovered another slur against his name. Richard Henderson, author of *Singlehanded Sailing*, vaguely maligned Tristan in his book. Tristan complained to Richard Curtis, "I've only now discovered the reported slander about me, which Henderson repeated as libel in his second edition of *Single Handed Sailing.* He says of me, 'Two Bluewater Medallists of my acquaintance have called him a charlatan.' "

To Tristan, sick though he may have been, those were fighting words. Once again he took up the cudgel to defend his honor. And for the first time he admits his change of name. He continued, "[The book] seems to have been public for some time, but no-one has informed me before. When was it published please, and by whom? I never claimed to have made all my voyages under my present name *[he claimed exactly that]*; what Henderson published was improperly researched, irresponsible and utterly mischievous. If Henderson heard gossip, most probably from my arch-enemy, Don (Squeaky) Street (I was in Grenada when his first wife was brutally murdered, I hit a rock he hadn't charted, etc., etc.) he should have checked with me before publishing."

As an appendix to his latest manuscript, *The Sound of a Different Drum*, Tristan had planned a list of books for "an ideal yacht's library." Among them are volumes by such classic boating or adventure writers as Jack London, Erskine Childers, Joseph Conrad, Vito Dumas, and Ernest Shackleton. On hearing of Henderson's attack, he promptly added to the manuscript a vitriolic page or so on *Singlehanded Sailing*.

> *One book no yacht's library; no library at all, should contain is* Single Handed Sailing, *by a self-appointed guru called Henderson. Apart from egregious inaccuracies scattered throughout, Machiavellian stabs and sly nuances here and there, it is the most amateurishly dull book ever written on a subject which should sparkle with professionalism and life. Henderson's writing is so banal that it's less mean sentences would seem, to the impartial reader, to verge on mumbled dirges. Its so called "author" (perhaps "cobbler" might be a better term) seems to depend in part purely on drunken gossip for his sources. In small-craft passage making, in which sobriety, precision, compassion and certainty are so vital, knowing the true history of sailing, all sailing, is as necessary as knowing anything else about it. Don't look for it here with* maître *Henderson.*

With the metaphoric bit firmly between his false teeth, Tristan added insult to injury:

> *Giving valuable space onboard to* Single Handed Sailing *might be compared to giving space to* Mein Kampf; *it has the same manic ring, of ill-intent and ignorance, disguised as good-purpose.*
>
> *As an exemplar in some junior-Eng-Lit classroom, this shoddy shambles:* Single Handed Sailing, *might serve to show how random-clips from others' works, and gossipy, moronic, drunken or out-of-context "sound-bites," thrown together into cheap collages by careless dilettantes, who demonstrably know little of their subject's history and even less of it's literature, should neither be proffered by the publishers, nor accepted by the public, as authoritative references. It is one of the few ill-founded works*

*which, as electronics-communications burgeon, helps toll the knell of sea-
literature in print.*

Tristan raved on to wonder why, if Henderson was such an expert,
he hadn't mentioned the sexual abuse case against Joshua Slocum.
What that unfortunate episode in Slocum's life has to do with the skills
of single-handed sailing is not made clear.

Tristan wrote a couple of letters to Henderson's publishers, International Marine/McGraw-Hill, the first of which demanded both
McGraw-Hill and Henderson publish apologies in the February 1995 issue of *Sail* and the spring 1995 edition of *Explorer's Journal*. He further
requested he be allowed a 2,000-word rebuttal in the next edition of
Singlehanded Sailing. As sole redress, McGraw-Hill's lawyers countered
with an offer for the inclusion of a single paragraph. Tristan sent the
following: "The collator of this work in the 2nd edition never checked
with me for an explanation, which will be found in my book 'Rough
Trade' [aka The Taming of a Tough Guy, *this unpublished book bears
no such explanation*]. In a couple of my earlier yarns I may have em-
broidered a mite; but only to make specks of brighter color on my tap-
estry. In my books published prior to 1995 I left out a thousand times
as much of even-more-amazing facts and feats; they did not suit, then,
my telling of my tales. In greatly helping to resurrect sea-literature,
which had died well before 1977, I attacked a pompous yacht elitism and
certain forms of yacht-chartering which make whimpering pimps out
of honest people; of course I made enemies. But my tales will endure,
and that, for me, along with thousands of treasured expressions of enjoyment of them from all around our planet, and evidently the spiteful
envy of a couple of frustrated-would-be-sailing-authors, is reward
enough."

Richard Henderson's *Singlehanded Sailing* is an excellent work by a
lifelong sailor with nineteen books on sailing to his credit. If, or when,
a new edition of *Singlehanded Sailing* is published, it will carry an edited version of Tristan's rambling statement as agreed. In reality it is un-

likely that Tristan actually read any more of Henderson's book than the few lines that mentioned him.

So, what terrible words did Mr. Henderson write about Tristan Jones? *Singlehanded Sailing* has one long paragraph about him, in a chapter focusing on a variety of famous, and not so famous, single-handed sailors. We see immediately that Tristan had taken Henderson's comment out of context. The full paragraph reads:

> *Then there is the salt-encrusted Welshman, Tristan Jones. I don't quite know how to deal with the page-long list of record claims he sent me, as two Blue Water Medallists of my acquaintance have called him a charlatan. Jones is a colorful writer, and there seems little doubt that he sometimes mixes fiction with fact. But even if he "draws a long bow" on occasions, he has accomplished many astonishing feats. He claims to have sailed "the farthest north ever reached in a sailing vessel," although an Arctic explorer tells me Jones's geography is mixed up. Nevertheless, he drifted alone for many months, apparently less than 500 miles from the North Pole, after his 36-foot ketch* Cresswell *became trapped in the ice. Other claims include the most singlehanded passages under sail across the Atlantic in craft under 40 feet long—a total of 17 between 1952 and 1975, as well as the most miles of singlehanded sailing in boats under 40 feet— approximately 345,000 miles between 1952 and 1976. Presently Jones is sailing a multihull around the world with one crewmember, after having had his leg amputated. What a man!*

Henderson's book includes an annotated list of books about single-handed sailing. Of Tristan's *The Incredible Voyage*, Henderson writes: "Entertaining solo exploits by the colorful Welsh shellback who, one suspects, does not allow the telling of his amazing experiences to be overly hampered by facts. More practical how to information is to be found in Jones's *One Hand for Yourself, One for the Ship*."

Tristan, never one to forget a grudge, would have another go at Henderson in an Atlantis Society newsletter dated September 30, 1994. He also managed to include an insult aimed at the man he called his "arch-enemy." "That was while the Blue-Water Gang (if the Olympics ever hold Gossip Contests D. M. Street should be U.S. team-leader) and the world's least quoted 'author,' Richard Henderson, sat criticizing boat show visitors (and probably their unfortunate wives) and scratching (whatever)."

Tristan's stated archenemy, Don Street Jr., treated his supposed nemesis with considerably more kindness. Rather than the enmity Tristan suggests, Don Street remembered him with something approaching affection. In a privately taped series of informal memories Street opened with, "Whoever gave you the story that I did not get along with Tristan Jones strictly gave you bum dope. Tristan was a very amusing character. I didn't believe half of what he said, but I do respect him tremendously, for a man who really fought against physical disability. He never gave up."

Commenting on this book, Don laughed: "If you're writing a biography of Tristan you'll have a hell of a job, because trying to figure out what really happened in Tristan's life from what Tristan said happened in his life is one of the great projects of the world. But if you ever want anything in there for endorsements for people to buy Tristan's books . . . just say the well-known yachting author Don Street states that he feels that an awful lot of what Tristan wrote was a figment of Tristan's imagination, but he said it so wonderfully, and in such an amusing fashion, that I advise anyone at any time who sees a Tristan Jones book for sale to pick it up and read it. It will be well worth the investment."

Street recalled that he first met Tristan way back in the 1960s when he had about a forty-foot sloop. Based on additional comments, it became clear that he was referring to Tristan on *Barbara* in the early 1970s, probably in the Caribbean. When *The Incredible Voyage* was published (in 1977) Street obviously read and enjoyed it, no matter how cynical he may have been about some of the content. His fondest memories of Tristan hark back to days of relaxing in marina bars, telling each other tall stories and drinking heartily. "We crossed tracks up in Boston at *Sail* magazine a couple of times. Drank some beer and told each other lies," Street said. "But the most momentous incident was really funny. I was moored out on the end of the yacht haven dock *[at Newport]* on *Iolaire* and Tristan arrived, unbeknownst to me, in his trimaran *Outward Leg*. The crew came down and said 'Tristan would like you to come up to the bar to have a drink with him.' Well, I would rather have had a drink on *Iolaire*, but Tristan only having one leg I said, 'Sure, I'll come up there,' rather than him walk all the way down to *Iolaire*."

The two talked for a while about Tristan's voyage along the dangerous Caribbean coast of Colombia. It wasn't long before their conversation was interrupted. Don continues, "With the two of us sitting there talking, people came up and wanted to take photographs of us, and Tristan said, 'Sure, you can take photographs of us, but you've got to buy us some more beer.' So Tristan started telling stories and I started telling stories, and then people came up and one thing led to another."

Don Street didn't know how the one-legged Tristan got back to *Outward Leg*. He thought one of his crew might have carried him. "I know I had trouble getting back to my boat. We'd been there [drinking] for about three or four hours. The guys who ran the Bridge Bar made themselves a fortune, because everyone was coming up, buying us drinks and listening to the stories, and buying themselves drinks, and a good time was had by all."

Don Street repeated that he didn't believe much more than a third of what Tristan said or wrote. He did say he loved to listen to his tales and to read his stories—a fine compliment from one boating icon to another.

Don told a wonderful anecdote about a sailor named Phil (he did not offer the surname), someone he and Tristan both knew. Hearing that Phil had cancer and had been given no more than eighteen months to live, Don sent Tristan a note asking him to write to Phil with words of comfort. According to Street, Tristan wrote a passionate motivating letter, including: "Don't believe what the doctors tell you. Go fight it. Go fight." Those words galvanized the much younger Phil into battling the cancer with every ounce of his energy. Perhaps as a result of Tristan's encouragement, Phil made a couple of sailing expeditions to Arctic waters on a vessel named *War Baby*. Each time he was warned by doctors that the voyage would kill him. Each time he survived to return rejuvenated. Much to the surprise of his medical advisers, Phil came home in better condition than when he left.

"And that was strictly on account of Tristan," Don Street explained. "If Tristan hadn't lit the fire under him, there's no two ways that Phil would have lasted as long as he did." If the story is true, and there's no reason to disbelieve it, Tristan's urging got Phil through those eighteen months and extended his life by about ten years.

Compassionate though he could be to others, Tristan was without doubt his own worst enemy. If only he could have learned to temper his fictionalizing of known facts, he would have had a much easier time from journalists and from his fellow authors and sailors. A classic example of pointless fabrication is written in his own hand in a letter to his English pen pal Mike Warburton, dated May 8, 1992 (Tristan's sixty-third birthday). After listing his numerous overseas greetings, Tristan began a new paragraph: "Did you know that in 1965, in Ibiza, I taught Francis Chichester sailing & navigation in boats (he'd been a plane-pilot)? I didn't like him much but felt sorry for him. . . . If I'd had a Mrs. like his I'd have NEVER come ashore! He & she—real 'toffee-noses.'"

The facts, as most ocean sailors already know, are quite different. Francis Chichester was no ordinary "plane-pilot." In November 1929, only six months after Arthur Jones was born, Chichester made a flight around Europe in a Gipsy I Moth. From December 1929 to January 1930 he covered the enormous distance from London to Sydney, Australia, using the same aircraft, in 180½ hours flying time. He accomplished the first east–west solo crossing of the Tasman Sea in 1931, and later that year he flew from Australia to Japan, where he had a spectacular crash. In 1936 Chichester, with Frank Herrick, piloted a De Havilland Puss

Moth from Sydney to London. Before 1939 Francis Chichester wrote four short books on astronavigation and taught the subject to Royal Air Force personnel.

In September 1953 Chichester traded the lonely sky for equally empty seas when he purchased a sailboat, which he later renamed *Gipsy Moth II*. By 1960 Chichester had won the first solo transatlantic race under sail. He repeated the feat in 1962, creating a new record. Not content with his achievements, he broke his own record again in 1964. Chichester's final sailing triumph came on May 28, 1967, when he and *Gipsy Moth IV* arrived in Plymouth after a solo voyage around the world. Sixty-five-year-old Francis Chichester was subsequently knighted by Queen Elizabeth II in recognition of his accomplishments. That last well-publicized feat was almost certainly one of the sailing events that precipitated Tristan on his quest for a vertical record.

There was obviously nothing Tristan Jones could have taught the sprightly old aviator and ocean racer about either navigation or sailing. And Tristan would probably have enjoyed meeting Sheila Chichester, who was a competent sailor herself, having been a member of her husband's crew in the Cowes–Dinard Race (Isle of Wight, England, to France) in the mid-1950s and crossed the Atlantic twice with him in *Gipsy Moth II*, in 1960 and 1962.

CHAPTER 22

The Saga of Gabriel

Mike Warburton introduced himself to Tristan through a fan letter early in 1992. The two never met, yet they formed a strong and lasting friendship. Mike sent CDs of classical music to boost his friend's morale when his spirits were down. He wrote a few newspaper and magazine articles to help promote Tristan's books and his causes. Most of all he was there, at the end of a telephone line, to give his hero support whenever he needed it, as he often did. Mike would eventually pull off a stunning coup for Tristan.

Tristan discussed an idea for a new book with Richard Curtis in March 1992. With a working title of *You Cannot Say "I Cannot"!* it sparked thoughts about an autobiography. As Tristan described the premise, "This is the book about getting to glory from the utter depths of pain, misery and despair by helping others do the same. But I doubt I'll write it; I won't let one goddam thing delay or interfere with the tremendous efforts that I'm making—right now it is my immense privilege to be the only one that can make it in such a telling (and visual) way. To allow what strength I have remaining to be sapped by writing-effort and to fail in my exemplary task would be to spit at a zillion suffering fellow beings. Should we ask an aspiring young author to be my Boswell—what do you think?"

Instead of writing the book, Tristan talked of buying a catamaran and mounting a filming expedition to the Andaman Islands, although he neglected to state any clear objectives for the trip. Meanwhile he busied himself building a dinghy, *Little Leg End*, and preparing a system of tracks so he could launch the boat from his bungalow, with himself on board, down the beach and into Ao Chalong Bay. He wrote to Richard, "My hands are blistered and scabbed from handling concrete tiles and my back is killing me."

A few days later he summarily dismissed Richard Curtis as his agent—without explaining why. Within a few months he reinstated the Curtis agency.

He spent his birthday with Anna Borzello, a young British journalist, whom he described as "a very bright 'n' beautiful writer." Anna interviewed Tristan at his beach bungalow. Seated in his wheelchair surrounded by small boys, Tristan watched with Anna as one of the disabled boys tested the new dinghy launching ramps. Anna said, "I remember the boys whizzing down the plank into the water and lots of jubilation." She said Tristan was thrilled that his help would enable such boys to go to sea. Referring with a certain pride to the launching system, he said, "I suppose that to most people it doesn't look like very much—a bit of concrete, a few bricks, a bit of plastic. But actually it's three months' effort and the amazing thing is—as far as I know—it's the very first boat in the world that legless people can launch themselves and bring back themselves. [You] put a line from there down to the sea on an anchor, and the boatman can turn the boat around, as long as he has arms, then pull himself up and down the track."

Over the next few months Tristan and Anna corresponded regularly by fax, often discussing writers and their works. He told her of adopting Islam in 1991 and of his feelings about a fellow author: "For me Rushdie is despicable beyond argument." (On February 15, 1989, the Ayatollah Khomeini, political and religious leader of Iran, had ordered Salman Rushdie executed for what he condemned as blasphemy against Islam in his novel *The Satanic Verses*.)

Tristan asked Anna to issue a challenge to Salman Rushdie on his behalf, "to meet me, under firm guarantee of safe passage until the main event, any time, in any country where dueling is legal, and let's have it out with any lethal hand-weapon he chooses." Anna, of course, did no such thing.

August 1992 saw Tristan bedridden again. Dozens of small blisters had broken out on the right side of his chest, accompanied by severe chest pain. A doctor confirmed that he was suffering from shingles (herpes zoster), a condition Tristan described as "very painful." Tristan admitted he had always imagined herpes could only be contracted sexually and was relieved to learn he was incorrect—that his condition was a different form of herpes. Shingles is caused by reactivation of the chicken-pox virus. The painful condition persisted for some weeks, keeping him confined until late September, when he finally felt well enough to do more than write to friends and associates.

While Tristan recovered, Mike Warburton, the faithful pen pal, went to work on his behalf. Many of his letters seeking help went unanswered. One, directed to a noted philanthropist, was spectacularly successful. Mike wrote to King Hussein of Jordan on September 20, 1992, describing Tristan's sailing achievements and mentioning plans for the expedition to the Andaman Islands.

On October 7 Mike received a reply saying that His Majesty would contact Tristan directly. The speed with which the royal court operated was impressive. A stunned Tristan received a fax from Amman, the Jordanian capital, the next day. Once he'd recovered from the shock, his first call was to Mike, who related the conversation in a message to his brother, Ralph: "I've just had a phone call from Tristan re—my success with King Hussein! He was close to tears by the sound of him and could hardly get the words out. I can't believe it myself!! All the work has paid off. Yippee! It was great to hear his voice too. Thanks for your help. As T.J. says—Tally Ho!"

Mike's euphoria was matched by Tristan's when he learned that

King Hussein would donate $20,000, enough for him to purchase an oceangoing catamaran outright. He wrote back to Mike: "You really hit the main jackpot with HM King Hussein. I cannot thank you enough. This tale is becoming even more incredible: that several so-called 'biggies' in UK should ignore or turn deaf ears to us, and you have put in such time, expense and effort and persisted on what seemed to be becoming a forlorn cause . . . and I have not even met you. And now a king comes to our aid. No author would dare to write such a tale except as fantasy."

Recognizing the promotional value of King Hussein's donation and suddenly feeling he had financial security within his grasp, Tristan quickly developed a conviction that if one royal figure was prepared to help his cause, then other regal families could be persuaded to dig into their own gilt-edged pockets. He remarked to Warburton, "Whether this will work or not I don't know, we'll have to wait and see. But 'keeping up with the Jones's' must work among royalty, too; and some houses need all the goodwill they can muster."

To another associate he wrote, "Now (through third parties) I'm approaching other crowned heads of state for additional funding towards this endeavor, which will cost US$20,000 to complete the voyage, and another US$20,000 for maintenance and paid crew and some air-flights in 1993."

It was an ambitious plan—doomed to failure. The remaining crowned heads—of Europe and elsewhere on the planet—ignored Tristan's begging letters and wisely sent him no money.

At one time Tristan had decried those who relied on sponsorship or donations to fund their voyages and other adventures. Once he sampled the king's silver, however, he became as mercenary as any other sponsored adventurer. A few weeks later he reckoned that, with King Hussein's donation, he had $30,000 in the expedition kitty. His budget was a simple one: the boat, which he would call *Sinbad Legend*, would cost $22,000, plus outfitting at roughly $5,000 and the expenses of the voyage at $3,000, for a total financial outlay of $30,000—exactly the amount he had. With those figures in mind, there is good reason to wonder at his asking for considerably more.

Tristan apparently forgot about his recent windfall, about H & S Bluewater Multihulls, which lent him *Outward Leg*, and about Yanmar, which supplied engines for his longtail boats. His cynical views on sponsorship came to the fore in a press release written specifically for journals in the United States. Headed "Right Values," and written as an interview with himself, it is part comedy, part slap in the face at Britain, and a strident rant at Chay Blyth's British Steel Challenge Race around the world.

> *In Phuket, Thailand, Tristan Jones, while recuperating from his second leg amputation, has worked day and night for eight months this year trying to interest British organizations in his work on researching and developing disabled mobility, and in trying to raise the funds to provide a sailboat for training "leg-disabled."*
>
> *Tristan says he might as well have bayed at the moon. "In late September," he said, "ten expensive identical ocean yachts, each with eleven $25,000 fee-paying amateurs onboard set out from UK on the British Steel Challenge Race around the world, to fanfares of British Grit and making ordinary lives into real adventure.... "God only knows," growls Tristan, "what the whole BSCR will cost. But I do know that the fare alone of every single one of those crew persons was the same as the total delivered cost of the catamaran, Sinbad Legend, lock, stock, and barrel."*
>
> *Tristan went on: "If you have tears to shed, prepare to shed them now. In 1994 all those British amateurs will (hopefully) be back home, having seen an awful lot of water and a few marinas, and of course they will have helped provide the British Steel Company with 2 years of publicity. Let us pray it will all be joyful."*
>
> *Tristan continued: "But, for the self-same amount of money as the BSCR total crew-fees alone there could have been built one hundred and eleven Sinbad Legends ... with a working life of about twenty years each ... and each year each boat could have provided one hundred and twenty disabled kids a month's sailing course ... and that would have made a*

total of 260,400 youngsters charged with the self dependence that sailing can instill."

Tristan's voice rose: "If I had knees I'd be on 'em. Great God! Is my country, Great Britain, untouched by the sea-change in human values over the past twenty years? What's more worthwhile? A few better-off, able-bodied, white, middle-class Britons button-pushing their way round the world, or a wholesale effort to end, once and for all, disabled-sea-sport 'apartheid' all around the world?"

He reflected: "What I say will probably be considered in UK as dog in the manger." He grinned as he lumbered off under the waving palms on his 3-wheel bike towards the beach and his waiting self-launch dinghy. He waved his good arm out towards the magnificent tropical scenery; "Well . . . some bloody manger!" Then he was gone.

Note: I've no hope of this being published in UK.

Whether the delightfully sarcastic press release was ever submitted is not known. Considering its content, it was unlikely to be published, as Tristan guessed, particularly in Britain. Perhaps, to Tristan, publication in this instance was not so important. Venting his frustration at so much money being wasted (to his way of thinking) on undeserving people was the therapy he needed.

An Australian TV film production company arrived during the first week of November, intent on making a documentary featuring Tristan. Once again he stuck his hand out. He described the premise of the film: "It will show a one-legged lad launching *Little Legend* [sic] and also *Henry Wagner* etc. then I'll do an interview on our aims and what we've managed so far. As it's not [yet] for payment I will not perform myself with the dinghy. If the Aussies decide to support the voyage [with a contract] I will." Tristan did get his contract and a fee for appearing on camera.

While he waited for his catamaran to arrive, he continued to rail against the injustices of the media, especially when he could see a vague association to his own situation in the reports. A BBC World Service (radio) news brief raised his ire on November 7. He moaned that it mentioned "an American leg-less-below-the-knees who is motorcycling around the world on a Harley-Davidson."

Ever ready to take umbrage at any slight, real or imagined, against himself or any other amputee, Tristan the pompous leaped into action. "Compared to boating and sailing for above-knees amputees," he trumpeted, "motor-cycling with two knees is a luxurious push-over! Daily motor-cycling for me is routine, and only *starts* my day's endeavors!"

Tristan filled his November days with activities concerning his new love. *Sinbad Legend*, however, never did go to sea—as such. At the last moment Tristan changed his new vessel's name. On November 25 an issue of the Atlantis Society newsletter went out from the house on Rawai Beach.

> *TO ALL OUR FRIENDS WORLD-WIDE:*
> *Rejoice on the delivery of our 42´ sailing catamaran.*
>   *As twin-hulls anchored I reflected that old Sinbad never, so far as I know, sailed a multihull. So, as our purposes are to wake the half-dead and demolish the cynics, I name our cat:*
>   *Gabriel & Michael [for the archangels]*
>   GABRIEL *for short,*
>   *pronounced gah-breeal and mee-shell, as in most languages.*

He said he hoped that he and his crew would be ready for the Andaman voyage by December 26, 1992. But Tristan hadn't yet taken possession of the catamaran when he sent out the newsletter, and his plans for a December departure were too optimistic. By the end of November he was sending out letters to potential suppliers, and anyone else who might read them, soliciting complimentary equipment and additional funds. Tristan, relatively unused to sponsorship deals, had not yet learned that obtaining freebies was a time-consuming and soul-destroying process. Time ran out. The expedition date was put back to sometime in January 1993. In the meantime, the preparations continued.

Busy preparing *Gabriel* for her voyage, Tristan found reserves of mental and physical energy he'd long forgotten. Getting ready for sea put him right back in his element. The frenzy of last-minute work was exactly what his depressed spirits needed. On December 5, 1992, he was triumphant. For the first time since his second amputation, fifteen months before, he went aboard an oceangoing sailboat. A cryptic note faxed to Warburton tells of his excitement: "Mike! I did it! After trials and tribulations inexpressible I got on board and ashore safely and without pain. I am overjoyed. *This* Is the achievement. The coming voyage is like a molehill compared to this, but who will understand except leg-less? Bless you! Tristan."

On December 6 Tristan officially took over the yacht from Andre Dumestre, the previous owner. After appointing two Thais as crew, Montri Samawang as skipper and someone called Mek as deckhand, he had the boat careened at Vichid Beach. There, on the relative safety of the sand, his crew practiced hoisting Tristan's chair into the cockpit using the boom as a crane. That night a happy Tristan hosted Mr. Y. Kobayashi, of the Yanmar Company, on board for dinner.

The next evening *Gabriel* motored round to Rawai Beach and careened bows-on at Bahn Lek. Tristan slept on board for the first time but found it uncomfortable. He also complained that the dining table seat was too narrow and that he couldn't get down into the amas.

In the morning the crew landed all loose gear for temporary storage at Bahn Lek and installed a new sunshade over the deck and cockpit. Afraid of being dumped in the sea, Tristan again had his boys spend the day hoisting him from the beach into the cockpit and back again, using the boom as a crane. Once he was satisfied they wouldn't drop him, he allowed hired carpenters on board to make a new bridge deck over the cockpit well from marine plywood and hardwood. They also installed a wheelchair ramp into the main cabin. Sailmaker John Batt inspected all the sails and took a jib away for repair. And another deckhand, Lee, joined the crew.

Tristan made his final payment on the catamaran on December 11.

The crew cleaned and antifouled both ama hulls and painted the forward cabin white. Tristan occupied himself by designing a steel hoisting cage to replace the lifting chair. He obviously felt safer with protection all around him, though if the crew dropped him in the water, his chances of survival would have been severely limited.

For the next few days people must have been tripping over each other on and around the boat. Carpenters built cupboards and doors while the crew painted the interior aft and a small dinghy. They also installed bigger anchoring cleats on the foredeck. Tristan ordered new companionway boards and a dozen T-shirts, had the rudders unshipped, and appointed an agent. An electrician came aboard to check the wiring and radios. Khun Ith, Tristan's Thai lawyer, took the ship's papers to register her in the new owner's name. He also drafted a charter agreement. Paul Dark, another friend, arranged for new berth mattresses. In his spare time Tristan taught Lee, Mek, and another crew member, Sarayut "Looey" Chokku, to tie simple knots.

Khun Ith returned in the afternoon of December 15 to report that Montri would have to go to Chachasao, near Ayutthaya, about six hundred miles north, to transfer registration to Phuket. Once that was done Tristan would officially own the boat. With the interior now finished, attention turned to the dinghy, *Little Leg End*. Someone fitted a plastic fender around the gunwales while she was being adapted to accommodate Tristan's new lifting contraption.

On December 16 Tristan was hoisted aboard in his new cage without incident. He began to feel confident about getting to sea again as he surveyed the work completed. Montri and Looey left for Ayutthaya. Tristan noted in his log, "Everything to plan and so far on time."

By December 18 he still had not received permission from the Indian government to sail to the Andaman Islands. Eager to be back at sea and cruising again, he talked of Penang as an alternative destination. In truth it didn't matter to him where they went—being on the sea was all that counted to Tristan. And he knew that if he could just get away he would be able to write at least one magazine article about the voyage to help defray expenses. The sad reality, however, is that Tristan, despite his determination, was not fit enough to go on an ocean voyage, even a relatively short one, and he knew it.

On Christmas Eve he managed a few hours under sail and wrote an exultant fax to Mike Warburton immediately on coming ashore. "If I hadn't been there this morning I would not have believed it. 12m cat, steered by some old guy with no legs from a wheelchair, sheets handled by a one-armed guy and a one-legged bloke, MAKING 15 KNOTS PLUS IN A FORCE 3 BREEZE. SUCCESS! SUCCESS!! YOU HELPED A GREAT DEAL TO MAKE THIS WILD DREAM A REALITY. MERRY CHRISTMAS INDEED!"

Weeks passed, and *Gabriel* remained close to shore. On January 21, 1993, Warburton received a depressing note: "Dear Mike, Any longish voyage is off for at least a month. My stump is playing up. I banged it some days ago and it's open, all sore. It'll take some time & patience to heal." He later confessed he had jerked in his sleep just after the New Year and knocked the stump against his bedside table.

At the end of January plans for the Andaman voyage had to be cancelled. The injury to Tristan's stump had not healed, making it impossible for him to travel. Further, he heard news of another sailing expedition that had attempted a landfall in the Andamans, only to be turned back by the Indian navy when less than a day's sail from Port Blair. He changed *Gabriel*'s initial cruise destination to Langkawi Island, Malaysia.

Thai TV gave the frustrated skipper something new to think about by approaching Tristan to shoot a fifteen-minute segment on board *Gabriel* at the end of February. Although no money was offered up front, Tristan did receive assurances that he would share in profits from sales outside Thailand.

With all the excitement and activity surrounding *Gabriel*, Tristan somehow still found time to write. For months he had been secretly working on a trilogy of new novels, led by *The Sound of a Different Drum*. He also began work on the second draft of another book, *Dinner*

On Board—Come As You Are. Tristan completed *Dinner On Board* and sent it to Richard Curtis, then withdrew it almost immediately, explaining he felt it was an inferior work. Later he blamed lack of interest from his agent and publishers for the withdrawal. Whatever the reason, he ordered all copies of the original manuscript destroyed, except perhaps the one on his computer.

Once again Tristan changed the destination for *Gabriel*'s maiden voyage. With departure now set for mid-March 1993, he planned to sail down the coast to Kantang, though well offshore, out into the Strait of Malacca, then back to Krabi, on the mainland, before returning to Rawai Beach. The triangular course, Tristan estimated, would take *Gabriel* roughly 180 nautical miles on each leg. Once more fate intervened.

Montri Samawang, *Gabriel*'s skipper, resigned, then Looey was injured in a motorbike accident and Som got married. *Gabriel*'s first ocean voyage had to be delayed yet again, until April 15. This time they did put out to sea, albeit a day late. Tristan reported the short voyage in a two-page note to Mike Warburton on April 22.

> Gabriel *crept back in this afternoon. My concern at our lack of radios was much misplaced. There was no way we could have reached Malaysia in less than ten days. We headed south-east on the 16th, and waited for wind . . . and waited . . . and waited. Then we'd move on, and waited. . . . The strongest breeze was usually in the evenings, about ten knots for an hour or two. The rest was flat calm. We anchored twice off small islets and once off a small place on the mainland called Si-kao. The only other craft we sighted were fishermen.*
>
> *The crew, Looey, Som and Prasert, were first class, with good spirits even when it was obvious we'd never get far. The one bad thing was the breakdown of our Yanmar long-tail engine. As we'd run out of petrol for the Yamaha outboard it meant we had to beat back to Ao-Chalong under very light breezes, much of the time hardly moving, or being drifted back east by strong currents. The weather was very hot. The temperature on deck in the afternoon sun was up to 130 Fahrenheit. The total miles covered on this trip could have been no more than 250. But still: total since we started in* Gabriel: *about 2,000. I'm not too disconsolate, as it's all been*

under tremendous handicaps, and we got useful data and probably good
pictures. For me the only really risky times was boarding and landing,
but we learned a lot more about those two exercises too. In some perverse
way I'm almost content we didn't get to Malaysian waters: I suppose it
gives me another shot at the aim.

The estimate of 2,000 nautical miles covered in *Gabriel* since her
purchase has to be taken with more than a grain of salt. The catamaran had spent most of the five months under Tristan's command in
sight of his house. Her only voyage, apart from a few local coastal trips,
was the one just completed. That short voyage, however, probably did
more to bolster Tristan's self-esteem than anything else could do—except perhaps publication of a new book. Legless at sixty-four, he had
proved to others—and more important, to himself—that he was still a
competent sailor and capable of commanding respect as captain of a
small sailing vessel. Sadly, it was to be his last voyage. Lack of money
and failing health kept him ashore in Phuket for the remaining two
years of his life.

In May 1993 his health suffered another setback when he contracted
a viral infection in his chest. While recovering he listened to the sooth-
ing sounds of Sibelius on a CD Mike Warburton sent as a birthday present. Mike later sent him music by Debussy and Schubert. In thanking
him, Tristan acknowledged a sore point that had bothered him for a few
years—a perceived lack of interest in Britain in his books and his struggles. He wrote, "I reflect that about 50,000 of my books will be published in Sweden and Netherlands this winter, while in UK no-one except you seems to want to know."

The complaint is based mostly on his being unable to raise any form
of sponsorship from the United Kingdom. His most recent book, *To
Venture Further*, was published in Britain before it was released in the
United States, and he had been awarded a literary prize for it. But he
hadn't been offered anything new since. The trilogy he started, headed
by *The Sound of a Different Drum*, had been planned for submission in

the United States only. The dedication to *Different Drum* would explain why.

The year 1993 came to a close with Tristan planning to take *Gabriel*, plus an escort multihull suitable for a film crew, on a two-week expedition to the Mergui Islands of southern Myanmar in late January or early February 1994. As so often happened, the plans were vague and depended to a great extent on someone's raising a lot of money (£20,000 was the figure Tristan quoted) and obtaining a filming contract. The project came to nothing.

By mid-January 1994 *Gabriel* had been converted into a charter boat to earn much-needed income. With Looey, age twenty-one, as skipper, and Ali Chartri, also twenty-one, as mate, *Gabriel* successfully completed a five-day charter to the islands of Kho Raja Yi, Kho Phi Phi Don, and Ao Nang—plus, on the mainland, Krabi, Ao Pot, and Kho Lon—and returned to base at Ya Noi. It was a voyage of 160 nautical miles. Tristan remained ashore.

Confident of a successful new direction for *Gabriel*, Tristan set charter rates at £266 a day, including meals. Once again fate intervened to spoil his plans. With his work on *Dinner On Board* wasted, hence no publisher's advance, Tristan's income had sunk to a new low. He had no spare funds for advertising his charters. *Gabriel* had to be sold. Any thoughts of sailing to Myanmar vanished on the tropical wind. Fortunately Tristan quickly found a buyer, and the sale went through without delay. Included in the purchase price of $32,000 was the four-year lease on the beach bungalow at Bahn Lek. We can assume that King Hussein was not informed of the sale.

CHAPTER 23

The Sound of a Different Drum

In September 1994 Tristan sent Richard Curtis a set of computer diskettes. Each contained a manuscript: *The Sound of a Different Drum*, *A Sensitive Saga*, and *The Taming of a Tough Guy* (aka *Rough Trade*). The accompanying letter suggested which publisher they should be sent to; one who, in Tristan's words, "runs a lot of gay books."

The dedication for *The Sound of a Different Drum* reads, "To the moderating, in 1994, of laws which, for so many, for so long, made of Britain: a country of fear and violence." It is followed by an author's note: "In the mid-1960's, at the start of this narrative, the words 'gay' and 'pride' had been rarely, if ever, used in the same sentence; the acronym 'AIDS' had not been invented."

The Sound of a Different Drum, written mostly during 1992 yet harking back, perhaps, to Tristan's life in Greenwich Village in the late 1970s and early 1980s, is an unassuming gay novel with sailing as the theme. Set for half the book in the Azores, *The Sound of a Different Drum* tells of two gay men, Roger Ingham and Jack Botham, each building a boat for a long voyage. Despite its potentially controversial content, the book offers vivid descriptions of a traditional Azores whale hunt in open boats and careful descriptions of boatbuilding lore. It's a love story with a twist. The sailing episodes are magnificent as the narrative follows Roger across the Atlantic in his boat, *Different Drum*, from Horta to Barbados, to catch up with his lover, Jack—who left months before.

Tristan introduced the book with an enigmatic foreword: "Sailing skippers used to say, 'There are four kinds of sailors: novices, dead, retired and pessimists'; but we know—we've always known: there's— not another kind, but another tag to be added on to the rest: *gay*. That at least doubles the number of varieties of sailors to: *eight*.

"I started to write this romance in 1981, in New York City, but it was interrupted, partly by a leg-amputation and a sail voyage half-way round the world. For the rest; it would have been false; I'd wanted to display a whole plant, and yet had shown only some roots, and to me those were of an alien variety. In 1991 my other leg was amputated in Thailand, and I thought—What the hell? What can they do? Give me a hard time?

"Here, my friends, are roots, stem and blossom, in full bloom. It's fragile, yet it can go anywhere; it's impervious to sea-water; storm, sand, torrential rain, hail, ice, snow, high winds, fast rivers; all these hazards, to it, are—joys—."

As one would expect from Tristan Jones, *The Sound of a Different Drum* is an entertaining and well-written tale. Many of Tristan's die-hard fans, however, may have problems with the subject matter should the book ever be published. A trio of short unedited excerpts offer hints about the flavor of the story. "Jim, the young barman in the 'Lion's Head,' (whom I suspected realized my own inclinations, but he was far too young for me), while he made a pretence of being coyly shocked by some of Griffith's tales, was clearly attracted to him. It seemed to me that in an unassuming way Griffith knew it; he coolly took it for granted, and with Jim, Griffith was like an expert fly fisherman landing a trout."

It's possible there is as much fact as fiction in *Different Drum*. Certainly Tristan brings in a character, Owen Griffith, who could only be himself, and he refers to incidents so explicit that they sound like life experiences.

"I recalled my past infrequent dives into the gentlemen's underground toilet in Victoria Station. There I would stand for a few minutes, sometimes really peeing, as the usual 'cottagers' and a few strangers sidled in and rushed out. To this resort had the British laws on homosexual activity driven grown, otherwise respectable, well-educated men. I tried to recall what Rex Clements had written about the call of the sea . . . about what was exciting me inside every time I thought about it or about 'cottaging;' how had Rex put it? ' . . . wherein lies the lure (he meant of the sea)? The irrefutable fascination to the spirit of man of the unknown, of what might lie between that tumbling expanse of water and the empty blue vault above.' " ("Cottaging" is a gay euphemism for fornicating in public washrooms.)

And later we read, "Jack kissed him passionately and long and after the first bittersweet taste of his kiss, as Jack tightened his hold, Roger knew again the stir at his loins. Jack sensed it and pressed to him. He thought of the time long ago when he had been a jaunty young sailor and had imagined that by the time he reached 50 all this would be but a memory. Now, he thought, as Jack eased himself away, it was even worse—better?—worse? It certainly was deeper."

The Sound of a Different Drum is an original work of fiction. Had it been written as a "straight" novel it would certainly have been published, and the ensuing income would have made Tristan's last months far more comfortable.

A Sensitive Saga, subtitled *A Masculist Allegory*, on the other hand, is nothing more than the beautiful *Aka*—Tristan's excellent 1981 novel about dolphins and a solo sailor—rewritten with a cast of gay characters. *A Sensitive Saga* has the same story line as *Aka*. It is, in fact, almost word for word, scene for scene, the same. The only difference is that in *Aka* we meet Conan—a middle-aged single-hander in an around-the-world yacht race—and his longtime love, Ruth. In *A Sensitive Saga* we once again meet the stars of *The Sound of a Different Drum*, Roger Ingham, the solo sailor, and his lover, Jack Botham. Tristan describes

Roger as he might, perhaps, have liked to describe himself: "The type of man that most heterosexuals are hardly aware of: he was *an all-male homosexual.* When he relaxed there was a passivity about him, but there was nothing of *woman* in him."

Similarly, *The Taming of a Tough Guy*, which Tristan claimed was a candid autobiography, is a version of *Seagulls in My Soup*, combined with a few of the anecdotes found in the final pages of *Saga of a Wayward Sailor* with a gay twist at the end. While *Seagulls* and *Saga* may have flimsy autobiographical bases, they are in the main delightful and amusing fiction. Originally, according to Tristan's notes, it appears that *The Taming of a Tough Guy* was a much longer manuscript and may have included important facets of his early life: details different from those used to fill the pages of *A Steady Trade* and *Heart of Oak.* For reasons he did not reveal, Tristan acknowledged having cut over twenty thousand words from the book, including his birth, childhood, and Royal Navy years.

For those who would see them as such, there are many clues to Tristan's homosexuality in his books and in his life, particularly in his attraction to handsome young men—of which he employed many as crew. There is a suggestion of it in *The Incredible Voyage.* His World War II novel *Dutch Treat* features a couple of gay characters. *Heart of Oak* brings up the subject again. A behavioral psychologist who previously knew nothing of Tristan or his books read *Ice!* and immediately identified its author as gay.

Tristan's homosexuality, while hidden from all but the most perceptive of his readers, was well known to his closest friends although most of them preferred to ignore it and he never discussed it with them. Conrad Jelinek saw evidence of it, though he firmly believed Tristan was probably bisexual—and that more emotional than physical. Chip Croft, who produced the video *The Incredible Tristan Jones*, remembered Tristan as acting and sounding gay only when he was with his gay friends. Others agreed that Tristan's public persona was that of a hard-drinking, hard-sailing adventure writer. Rarely did he allow any hint of the more personal aspects of his life to surface.

Tristan's resolution to allow the public access to his carefully protected secret was a courageous one. Perhaps, too, there was an element of the indefatigable self-promoter in the decision. A public announcement of his homosexuality, in the form of a new novel, while it might shock some of his more staid readers, would inevitably open up his books to a new and exceptionally loyal audience. With nothing to lose, Tristan sent the three manuscripts to New York. Unfortunately, because Tristan had so obviously plagiarized two of his own books, Richard Curtis saw little potential in offering the works to a publisher. And so the manuscripts remain in the sad, claustrophic darkness of a hall closet in New York.

Although much of the work is unpublishable, *The Sound of a Different Drum*, while not a dynamic book, does have the unmistakable stamp of Tristan's experience and imagination. Above all, it is a fine novel about boatbuilding and sailing, written by an expert seaman. As such, perhaps it will be published one day and stand proudly beside its author's sixteen other volumes.

CHAPTER 24

The End of a Long Voyage

Undeterred by the latest setback with *Gabriel*, Tristan continued trying to interest film companies in his plans. As always, the asking price was £20,000. As usual, there was no response. Having destroyed all possibility of making money from *Dinner On Board*, Tristan prayed his three gay novels would be accepted and began work on a collection of stories to be called *Encounters of a Wayward Sailor*. He also proposed a new biography of Joshua Slocum. Locking himself in his room for long hours, he wrote—as he had in the past—with fierce concentration. "I have been so busy writing to catch up on wasted effort that I've not been out very much, and exercise mainly by mounting on and off my immobile motorbike on the balcony," he noted. "Thais think I've finally gone mad."

Encounters of a Wayward Sailor once again raises the subject of Tristan's years as a yacht delivery skipper. Like previous stories, the tales are fiction. Without actually mentioning his passport in the book, Tristan casually attempts to explain his early ability to move about freely without identification papers either for himself or for his boat: "Characteristically, in those days, before I made my departures, I did not bother to obtain clearance papers, registration, bill of health, or even evidence of ownership. Most officials at my destinations, especially in Latin America, were always too astonished, not to say impressed, to bother with such mundane matters."

The Barbadians and other West Indian officials, Latin American authorities, and the immigration and customs officers in Monaco would
certainly have demanded papers, including passport details of the captain and crew. Nowhere is there any hard evidence that Tristan delivered
even one yacht to the Caribbean or Latin America. Not content with
such obvious untruths, Tristan writes as if he were the first sailor to
deliver a yacht across an ocean. He continued the explanation of his
laissez-faire life with a belligerently condescending attitude toward of-
ficialdom: "As for the official who was not impressed, or who stuck to
the book, there was always a powerful local yacht-club member who
could threaten to stop his pension, or have him transferred to a jun-
gle-border hut, if he carried on at me for lack of bits of paper."

Having technically entered a country illegally, Tristan never did
tell us how he managed to bypass other government officials to board
an aircraft and leave that same backward country, or how he was able to
talk his way back into Britain without a passport.

Professional captain and author Jan de Groot considers Tristan's
claims of regularly delivering yachts to foreign ports without paperwork to be virtually impossible, regardless of the year. He said, "I delivered a yacht from Rotterdam, Holland, to Durban, South Africa, in
1952. We were inundated with paperwork to satisfy customs and immigration. Also in South America and the United States, if you didn't
have a passport and/or a visa, deportation was immediate. If all papers
were in order, crew could remain in the country as long as the ship or
yacht was in port. Admission was as 'seaman only.' This permit expired
the minute the vessel departed." Jan did concede that in some develop-
ing countries rules were a little more relaxed, or "less organized" as he
put it; consequently one might be able to confuse the authorities with
fake paperwork. But paperwork there had to be.

The late Peter Tangvald, a renowned Norwegian sailor with vast
experience at sea on small boats, echoed de Groot's words. In 1976 he
and his wife, Lydia, arrived in Singapore on his gaff-rigged yawl

L'Artemis de Pytheas. Before the boat and crew could be cleared, Tangvald had to produce a sheaf of papers and endure the attentions of customs and immigration officers, a quarantine doctor, police, harbormaster, and health inspector. His final words on the subject emphatically destroy Tristan's earlier haughty comments: "Papers are what count!"

Tristan told Mike Warburton that his efforts in raising money from King Hussein would be acknowledged in *Encounters of a Wayward Sailor,* as would His Majesty's benevolence. But as so often happened with Tristan, he just couldn't bring himself to recognize publicly that someone had helped him. Instead, insulting the intelligence of his faithful readers, Tristan wrote that the way he obtained the boat was too complex to be readily understood. Instead of thanking King Hussein and Mike Warburton, he restricted his accolades to God.

Besides ignoring King Hussein's gift, which would not have materialized without Mike Warburton's efforts, Tristan takes credit in the book for adapting the motorcycle to his needs. The late Thomas Ettenhuber, who either did the conversion or organized it, would probably have shrugged and forgiven him, as Mike Warburton did when the deliberate omission was pointed out to him over a drink in a London bar.

With little income from his writing and no opportunity for lecturing to his many admirers in America, Tristan was fast becoming a mendicant. The rattle of coins in his figurative tin cup began to be heard wherever in the world he had fans. His newsletters cried out for donations to the Atlantis Society, which by then was little more than an excuse to maintain Tristan and his staff of Thai boys in Phuket. The thousands of dollars he earned from the sale of *Gabriel* were never mentioned again.

As the year progressed, Tristan's output of faxes and letters rapidly declined. "I had to cut down on all correspondence to economize," he wrote in November 1994. "I won't be faxing often."

Broke and increasingly worried about his situation, Tristan talked seriously about returning to Britain. "My aim is to go to UK in the spring, to stay for long enough to qualify for a disability pension, then we'll see. I will need an address to claim. Maybe I can rent a small ground floor place, for me and one attendant, not far from shops. It is pointless to go before March, as my blood is too thin for cold weather. There are a couple of possibilities for when the time comes around."

Jeff Ritchie, a former U.S. Navy computer technician, contacted Henry Wagner in November 1994 and asked if he thought it would be appropriate to visit Tristan during a forthcoming business trip to the Orient. Henry said, "Why not write and ask him?" Tristan, never slow to take advantage of a situation, replied to the request with a shopping list of necessary items, mostly computer parts and accessories, none of which he could pay for. To help out, Henry purchased two cheap suitcases and filled them with Tristan's books for sale in Thailand. At the time, Tristan was living off the proceeds of occasional articles published in Thailand and the few donations still trickling in. Even that latter erratic and undependable source of funds was steadily drying up.

When Ritchie arrived at Tristan's home in Phuket he was dumbstruck when Tristan rolled his wheelchair out onto the veranda. "He looked so small." Tristan, rarely at a loss for words and continuing to perpetuate the myth of his wartime naval service, lit a cigarette, sized up his visitor, and greeted him with a hefty slice of fiction: "Hello. It's not every day one meets someone who was there at the sinking of the *Bismarck*, is it?"

Later, in a poignant moment during an extended conversation, Tristan told Ritchie he thought he was dying. He had expressed the same premonition a few times over the previous years. This time he was closer than he knew.

Downcast Tristan may have been, but there was still room for pleasure in his life. He sold many of the chapters from *Encounters of a Wayward Sailor* to *Phuket Magazine* as individual articles. He also had been playing with a computer for a couple of years, and by January 1995 he was thoroughly enjoying his first forays into the cyberworld and eagerly anticipating his imminent access to e-mail. More than that, he had already astutely ascertained that electronic publishing was the future for writers. Had he lived longer he would almost certainly have taken advantage of its many opportunities. "I haven't been able yet to analyze it enough to comment deeply on it," he said of the Internet, "but I will."

Once online Tristan embarked on a project to have all public places in Thailand with wheelchair access placed on a list. "By later this year," he wrote, "I expect to have enough data to compile a disk or book: 'Access in Thailand.' So far, any kind of movement or travel within Thailand, and especially in the cities, has been unthinkable for wheelchair cases, except in cars, or ambulances, where such exist."

American Steve Rosse, employed in public relations at the Boathouse hotel and restaurant in Phuket, invited Tristan to lunch half a dozen times. Most of their discussions, Rosse recalled, consisted of Tristan talking about Tristan and his host talking about himself. He also arranged for Tristan to deliver occasional talks to a local literary society at the Boathouse. The most notable one was an excellent dissertation on Boswell's biography of Samuel Johnson. A drawback to Tristan's involvement at the meetings, or at lunch, Steve remembered, was that his ears and beard were usually dirty and he smelled so bad that the waiters winced when they approached the table. Steve was not the first person to make such a comment. Tristan's standards of personal hygiene were never high.

In his last few months Tristan wrote almost daily letters to the *Bangkok Post*. Frightened for his safety, he told Rosse they were signal flares in case he was robbed and left immobilized. If the letters ceased, he hoped someone would come looking for him.

By this time Rosse had accepted that Tristan was a bitter, defeated, and angry man. The wealthy yachties despised him—as he despised them—and his original Thai crew had long gone. The lower order of transient expatriate boat crews detested him and on at least one occasion threw empty beer bottles at him as he passed on his motorcycle. Tristan had a sign made, in English and in Thai, warning aggressors that he knew every policeman on the island. Fortunately, his friends, among them Paul Dark and Julie Hirunchai, owner of a bookshop, always had time for him. So did Henry, Richard, Wally, and Mike, thousands of miles away.

June found Tristan ailing again. He suffered a stroke, and Paul Dark took him to the hospital. Complications set in, and at 11:00 A.M. on June 21, 1995, Tristan Jones put down his pen and slipped peacefully from this life to embark on his last great adventure—an eternal voyage into the unknown.

On being told of Tristan's death, Paul Dark went straight to Tristan's house, as did Steve Rosse when he heard soon after. Both were worried that the local Thais might break in and remove everything of value. When Rosse walked in he found Dark examining the contents of a drawer in Tristan's bedside table. Among other personal effects Dark found three passports. One correctly gave Tristan's year of birth as 1929. On another, with the identical number, the birth date had been altered to read 1924. The third passport too was a forgery; perhaps it was the one giving a birth year of 1927 that Tristan had used years before when arranging landing permits for himself and his crew on *Barbara* to enter the Seychelles.

Three books lay on the table, among an assortment of medicine bottles: a Rand McNally world atlas; a biography of Samuel Johnson by Boswell, from which Tristan had been quoting for many years; and a volume sympathetic toward Adolf Hitler.

Mike Warburton remembers events surrounding Tristan's death well. A day or two after Tristan passed away, but before Mike heard the news, he was on a flight over the Bay of Biscay, working as a steward for British Airways. Five years later he wrote of a strange aura that had engulfed him: "It's difficult to describe, but felt as though I had been transported from where I was and into a boat, at the tiller on a calm sea, with the water just rippling, the air warm and feeling like lotion on my bare skin, the sun shining intensely on the water. I felt the most incredible feeling of calm and well being. I remember thinking, ah, so this is what Tristan loved so much. . . . The following day I received the devastating news. Make what you will, my friend. Me, I got the feeling that somehow he had told me he was now at peace."

When he died Tristan had been a prisoner of the persona he created for himself for twenty-two years, a full third of his life, and the most successful part of it. Having built the man and promoted him in a collection of books, he had little choice but to live with his creation for the rest of his days: it was either that or admit to making fraudulent claims. Living as he did, for so many years, never knowing when he might make a slip and expose the truth or whether someone else might stumble on his secrets, must have been a considerable burden. Given that in his last few years Tristan Jones was physically an extremely sick man, he bore the encumbrance with stoic intelligence and considerable craft.

Did anyone know the truth? It is doubtful. Certainly Henry Wagner and Wally Herbert, his closest friends, did not. Thomas Ettenhuber was with Tristan almost daily for four years. He may have seen Tristan's legal passport at some time, yet there is nothing in his letters or notes to suggest that he knew his skipper was five years younger than he claimed. Tristan Jones intended to take his closely guarded secret with him to eternity.

His earlier intention to have his ashes interred in the harbor wall at Kastellorizon in Greece had been replaced in his will with a new burial site. Five days after his death, at his own request, Tristan's cremated remains were scattered on the Andaman Sea at sunset. *Gabriel*, borrowed for the occasion, carried his ashes and a host of onlookers a few miles from shore for the ceremony. In an early will Tristan had requested, "And pour a bottle of dark rum after me." Unable to get to Thailand for the funeral, Richard Curtis sent a message to Paul Dark asking him to do just that.

Brice Keller, a fan, contributed to an Internet guest book about Tristan. His words make a fitting epitaph: "Tris was a great sailor and storyteller, I don't care if he never left his flat and dreamt up every one of his books. They have provided countless hours of enjoyment for myself and many others."

CHAPTER 25

Afterword

Tristan Jones was an enigma. No one really knew him. He lived to be sixty-six years old and managed to keep the first forty a mystery. He had friends during the last twenty-five years or so, good friends, yet none were ever allowed so much as a peek at his real past. To fill that enormous gap in the four decades between his birth and his arrival on the scene as skipper of *Barbara*, he fabricated a series of stories for friends and acquaintances, interviewers, and his readers. He told people what he wanted them to believe, and he told the tales so well that he was in fact believed. Henry Wagner accepted his friend's history without question, as did Wally and Marie Herbert and Richard Curtis.

No one could accuse Tristan of being self-effacing. He promoted his sixteen books on radio, on television, and in person with impressive arrogance—usually with charm, occasionally directing thinly veiled sarcasm at his interviewer. He exuded the confidence that comes with a certain success, secure in the knowledge that he had hoodwinked the world.

Tristan Jones's record claims were mighty. They encompassed over 345,000 miles under sail in small boats, 180,000 of those sailed solo. He boasted of crossing the Atlantic nineteen times under sail (a world record, he said), with nine of the trips single-handed. (In a biographical sketch he wrote in April 1992, he claimed twenty-two Atlantic crossings under sail.) He honored himself with the titles of farthest north, first to circumnavigate Iceland, farthest up the Amazon, first to transit the Panama Canal under sail alone, first to sail on both the highest and the lowest bodies of navigable water in the world, first to cross the width of South America with a boat, first to sail on the Mato Grosso, first across Europe with an oceangoing sailboat, first across Thailand's Isthmus of Kra.

The records he was really entitled to put his name on are considerably fewer. It's possible he was the first to sail a foreign boat on Lake Titicaca—highest navigable lake in the world. He was almost certainly the first person to take a boat across the width of South America. He was probably the first to sail in the Mato Grosso. He was the first to take an oceangoing trimaran across Europe, from the North Sea to the Black Sea. And he did lead the first expedition to cross the Malay Peninsula by river—although not at the Isthmus of Kra.

The deception of so many fraudulent claims is disturbing. It's one thing to fictionalize a book and pass it off as true adventure. Claiming unearned records is far more serious. It is significant that in spite of his many declared long-distance oceanic voyages in small boats, he was never awarded the Blue Water Medal. That trophy, presented by the Cruising Club of America for "meritorious examples of seamanship," would surely have decorated his cabin at some time had he really sailed all the voyages he wrote about. (In 1987, however, Tristan was awarded a lifetime membership to the Bluewater Cruising Association, based in Vancouver, Canada.) The fact is, few experienced cruising sailors believed his preposterous tales. Among them, Tristan Jones's reputation as a sailor will be forever tarnished by his obvious mendacity. And that is unfortunate, because had he exercised more honesty in promoting himself, his legacy could have been much greater. Perhaps the fact that he misled his readers so enthusiastically is more a measure of his lifelong insecurity than of his duplicity.

Tristan Jones made only three long voyages under sail in his life.

The actual distance he sailed, however, is impressive. In *Cresswell* he possibly sailed up to 1,000 miles: we can discount the Arctic voyage. *Banjo*'s short trips among the Balearic Islands collected a few more miles, let's say another 1,000. And short deliveries of other people's boats between Mediterranean ports perhaps accumulated another 4,000 miles at most. *Barbara*'s four-year cruise, the first properly documented voyage, added 31,242 miles, including two Atlantic crossings. *Sea Dart*'s impressive South American odyssey racked up a further 3,600 miles at sea, an estimated 500 on Lake Titicaca, 1,800 statute miles overland by truck and train, and another 1,500 nautical miles on the Paraguay and Paraná Rivers.

Sundowner's charters in the Caribbean can be estimated at a maximum of 4,000 miles, including the delivery voyage from New York. *Outward Leg*, Tristan's first multihull, sailed 25,000 miles from San Diego to Phuket, Thailand, including a third Atlantic crossing. *Henry Wagner* navigated close to 1,000 miles of coastal seas and rivers in Thailand. Finally, Tristan skippered *Gabriel* a maximum of 500 miles in the Andaman Sea.

Those figures, the true rather than the false, while nowhere near as awe-inspiring as the claimed distances, are impressive by any sailor's standards. They total close to 47,000 miles on seas and rivers in monohulls. With one leg, he traveled another 25,000 miles in a trimaran, also on seas and rivers. The longtail fishing boat added 1,000 miles more, and finally, a catamaran—skippered by a man with no legs—brings the grand total to almost 75,000 miles, equal to three times the circumference of the Earth. Unfortunately, of that amount the total he sailed solo is unlikely to tally more than a very few nautical miles—certainly nowhere near the 180,000 he claimed.

It was inevitable that one day someone studying Tristan Jones in the fishbowl he had created would uncover proof of his fabrications. The covering letter to Wally Herbert that accompanied the logbooks of *Barbara* and *Sea Dart* requests that they be made freely available for researchers after his death. He later wrote his will in such a way as to all but nullify that possibility. Any researcher worthy of the name would need no more than a cursory glance to see that extensive tampering had dramatically changed the nature of the information in the logbooks.

In a more positive light, on Tristan's voyage through the latter half of his life he roamed the world in search of adventure stories. As a result of his travels, his books gave great pleasure to thousands of readers. He endured immense personal suffering—two amputations and chronic emphysema would have slowed or stopped a lesser man—yet he continued his explorations. Late in life he became a father figure and mentor to handicapped youngsters.

Tristan Jones's true record as an adventurer, a writer, and a seaman is one he had every reason to be proud of. His actual voyages are evidence that he was an accomplished sailor, and his books are written by a skilled author who was awarded two literary prizes in Wales.

In the foreword to *Encounters of a Wayward Sailor*, published soon after Tristan's death, his literary agent, Richard Curtis, noted with sadness that the world at large had failed to recognize Tristan in his lifetime, a fact that upset both Curtis and Jones. Richard Curtis, a gifted author himself, knew Tristan was an exceptionally talented wordsmith. Perhaps we should let that stand as his memorial and ignore his extravagant claims as the blustering obfuscation of a man, initially lacking in self-confidence, who became trapped by his own falsehoods.

Maybe, however, those pretensions had much to do with his heritage. If we accept that he was Welsh, as he claimed (and it's possible that he was), he was far from alone in his ability to weave fabulous tales. British author Melvyn Bragg, in his excellent biography of Welsh actor Richard Burton, said of Burton: "In his cups he was a story-teller and embellished whenever necessary, and expected the brighter listeners to understand the art." Bragg's statements about his subject sound tailor-made to describe the narrative style of the late Tristan Jones. Bragg commented further on Burton and the Welsh art of tall tales: "The

Welsh way was to talk it up: Celtic stories were tall stories and if your audience was daft enough to swallow it whole—so much the worse for them. He truly didn't give a damn."

Tristan often didn't give a damn what people thought about his stories either. Arthur Jones was a nobody for forty years before his metamorphosis into Tristan Jones—a literary meteor rocketing through unsuspecting skies above unpredictable seas. He had a dark side, subject to fits of uncontrollable anger, aggression, and depression, and a lighter, playful side. He used both to great effect in his books and his public appearances. By the time nature extinguished his fire in a hot and humid land, his name was known around the world. "Tris," as his friends called him, the illegitimate son of a working-class Lancashire girl, had made his indelible mark on nautical literature.

Notes

"TJ" refers to "Tristan Jones." Publication details for books are given in the bibliography and the annotated bibliography for Tristan Jones.

CHAPTER 1. THE EARLY YEARS

10 On TJ's early years and family tree, as he represented them, see *A Steady Trade* and *Ice!* Details of Margaret Jones's residences and pregnancy are conjecture based on birth certificate number BXBZ533173 from the West Derby Registration District entering the birth of Arthur Jones.

11 "In an unpublished book": *The Taming of a Tough Guy* (aka *Rough Trade*).

11 Historical details of the era are from the CD-ROM, *Chronicle of the 20th Century*.

CHAPTER 2. TRISTAN'S NAVY

16 Although the Royal Navy would not supply full details of Arthur Jones's service, the Armed Forces Personnel Administration Agency did provide a list of shore establishments and ships in which he served, with the corresponding dates, and reported his conduct and the reason for his discharge. His legal passport details were supplied by the U.K. Passport Agency in a letter dated 7 March 2001.

CHAPTER 3. WITH *CRESSWELL* AND *BANJO*

19 Royal Navy and merchant navy service numbers are from Tristan's pension payment receipts from HM Paymaster General. *Cresswell*'s history is documented in *The Story of the Cresswell Lifeboats*, written by Jill Mitchell for the RNLI, and in the yacht registers at Lloyd's Register in London.

21 "We did one whisky [smuggling] trip": Ian Spooner, e-mail to the author, 25 November 2002.

22 The derivation of the name Tristan comes from *The Oxford Dictionary of English Christian Names* and *A Dictionary of British Surnames*.

24 My accounts of Tristan's escapades with Pete Kelly are based on fourteen hours of conversation with Kelly in the bar of the Green Man Hotel, Old Harlow, Essex, England, in February 2000, and in subsequent e-mails. I met with Rob Cohen at his home on 20 April 2001.

26 "I begin to understand": Ibid.

26 "Tristan said he carried 150 crates": See *Ice!* "More than 90,000 bottles": BBC-TV *Clare Francis Show*, 29 January 1982, and BBC-TV *Frank Delaney Show*, 26 November 1982.

27 Forged passport in Guernsey: The first factual evidence that Tristan had a forged passport comes in 1971 in a letter to Arthur Cohen when he was applying for landing permits for the Seychelles (see page 75). I conjecture he obtained the forgery in 1965, since as a convicted felon he would not otherwise have been able to reenter France.

28 "Once I had to sail his boat": David Morgan, e-mail to the author, 3 May 2002.

29 Tristan's tattoo story is from *Saga of a Wayward Sailor*, as is his tale of the Barbary apes.

35 "During the two years I spent": Guus Schohaus, e-mail to the author, 12 September 2002.

35 "David Murray, owner of La Taberna": David Murray, e-mail to the author, 10 September 2002.

36 Naviza letterhead held in Rob Cohen's archives.

37 S. Morse Brown letter and other papers held in Rob Cohen's archives.

38 "fatalistic synchronism": TJ used this term, in various guises, in his books and articles.

CHAPTER 4. *BARBARA'S LONG CRUISE*

Sources include conversations with Rob Cohen at his home, his archives, *Barbara*'s logbook, letters and reports from TJ to Arthur Cohen, the unpublished *Track of the "Barbara,"* and Conrad Jelinek. All distances from *Barbara*'s logbook are in nautical miles. Elsewhere, distances on sea and rivers are also in nautical miles unless otherwise stated; land distances are measured in statute miles unless otherwise indicated. *Barbara*'s logbook is in Sir Wally Herbert's archives.

40   "The passage between": from *Track of the "Barbara."*

41   "His flight home to Ibiza": Ibid.

41   "A quick glance over her": Ibid.

41   Tristan's arrest: E-mail from Rob Cohen dated 6 March 2001.

42   "I am sad to leave": From *Track of the "Barbara."*

43   Anton Elbers: Letter from Elbers to the author, 12 June 2000.

44   "The first two days and nights were rough": From *Track of the "Barbara."*

46   Donald Crowhurst: From *Barbara*'s logbook.

47   "We were racing along": From *Track of the "Barbara."*

48   "They had no idea at all": Ibid.

50   Cohen read the manuscript: Letter from Arthur Cohen to TJ, 13 March 1970.

CHAPTER 5. ISRAEL AND HOSTILE SHORES

Sources include letters to Arthur Cohen, conversations with Rob Cohen, Conrad Jelinek, *Barbara*'s logbook, *The Incredible Voyage*, and *Rudder* magazine, January 1977.

54   "I thought there was": Letter to Arthur Cohen, 25 November 1970.

54   "Conrad is very loyal": Letter to Arthur Cohen, 13 December 1970.

57   "I usually backed Tristan": Conrad Jelinek, e-mail to the author, 23 May 2001.

58   "We got her up to": Letter to Arthur Cohen, 16 December 1970.

59   "Some shots passed": Letter to Arthur Cohen, 14 January 1971.

60   "There were not the amount": Conrad Jelinek, e-mail to the author, 28 May 2001.

61   "So I sailed a safe triangle": Letter to Arthur Cohen, 14 January 1971.

61   "January 9th": Ibid.

62   "Well, as I write": Ibid.

63   "About as useful": Ibid.

63 Captain Bob Jones: Letter to Arthur Cohen, 11 February 1971.

64 "The difficulty is": Ibid.

64 "It is vital": Ibid.

65 "Assab is the last": Ibid.

65 "Well Arthur, this is": Ibid.

65 "The easy period": Letter to Arthur Cohen, 12 February 1971.

66 "The yacht club escorted us": Conrad Jelinek, e-mail to the author, 28 May 2001.

CHAPTER 6. INDIAN OCEAN SAGA

Sources include TJ's letters to Arthur Cohen, Rob Cohen, Conrad Jelinek, *Barbara*'s logbook, and *The Incredible Voyage*.

68 "Whilst messing about around": Letter to Arthur Cohen, 23 March 1971.

68 "He knows absolutely nothing": Ibid.

69 "On the Indian Ocean leg": Ibid.

69 "If you don't catch it": Ibid.

70 "I wish I knew": Ibid.

71 "It's as well something": Conrad Jelinek, e-mail to the author, 14 February 2002.

72 "For ventilation": Ibid.

74 The U.S. magazine in which parts of "Islands of the Moon" were published, under the title "Hot Passage," was probably *Rudder* (January 1977).

74 "What a struggle": Letter to Arthur Cohen, 14 May 1971.

74 "The Seychelles sound so good": Letter from Arthur Cohen, 7 May 1971.

75 "The change of voyage plan": Letter to Arthur Cohen, 26 May 1971.

75 "There is a continual swell": Ibid.

77 "Going like a train all day": from *Barbara*'s logbook.

79 The Inhambane Port Authority stamp is in *Barbara*'s logbook.

79 "*Barbara* found herself": Conrad Jelinek, e-mail to the author, 24 November 2001.

80 " 'Tristan,' Conrad said": Conrad Jelinek, e-mail to the author, 23 May 2001.

81 "In the Indian Ocean": Conrad Jelinek, e-mail to the author, 25 May 2001.

CHAPTER 7. THE AMAZON AND A NEW *BANJO*

Sources include letters to Arthur Cohen, Rob Cohen, Conrad Jelinek, *Barbara*'s logbook, and *The Incredible Voyage.*

85 "Now whizzing along": *Barbara*'s logbook, 15 February 1972.

89 Building catamarans in Macapá: Letter to Arthur Cohen, 8 May 1972.

90 "Studying the tides": See *The Incredible Voyage.*

91 Peter "Champy" Evans: Evans, telephone conversation with the author, 21 March 2001.

93 "My own position": Letter to Arthur Cohen, 29 June 1972.

93 "I fell into a stroke of luck": Letter to Arthur Cohen, 14 July 1972.

93 "In August he sent the manuscript": Letter to Arthur Cohen, 20 August 1972.

93 "I don't think I can keep": Letter to Arthur Cohen, 12 September 1972.

95 *A Sailor's Odyssey*: Letter to Arthur Cohen, undated.

95 "I found a buyer for *Banjo*": Letter to Arthur Cohen, 17 October 1972.

96 "He confirmed his agreement": Letter to Arthur Cohen, 5 December 1972.

96 *Singora*: Ibid.

96 "Good news!": Ibid.

96 "The deal with *Singora*": Letter to Arthur Cohen, 9 December 1972.

97 *Ring Anderson*: Jan de Groot, e-mail to the author, 23 April 2001.

CHAPTER 8. TRISTAN MEETS *SEA DART*

Sources include e-mails from Ron Reil, Ron Reil's website, TJ's *The Incredible Voyage*, Laurel Wagers's *Sailing Among the Stars*, and *Sea Dart*'s logbook (held in Sir Wally Herbert's archives).

CHAPTER 9. CRUISING TO PERU

Sources include *Sea Dart*'s logbook, *The Incredible Voyage*, a letter to Arthur Cohen (courtesy of Rob Cohen), and newspaper clippings.

104 "A Bogotá newspaper": *El Tiempo*, 10 May 1973.

108 "I'm a bit worried": Letter to Arthur Cohen, 22 September 1973.

CHAPTER 10. REACHING FOR THE STARS

Sources include *Sea Dart*'s logbook, *The Incredible Voyage*, and newspaper clippings.

122 "And all the time": *The Incredible Voyage*.

123 "Temporary importation certificate": Translated from the Spanish by Erwin Jurgensen.

125 Robert J. Austin: E-mails and telephone conversations, 23 and 25 February 2001.

127 "[It's] hot, dusty, dirty": *Sea Dart*'s logbook, 5 September 1973.

134 Hal Roth: E-mails to the author, 22 November 2002.

137 Roberto Zaldivia: *El Día*, Montevideo, Uruguay, 29 June 1975.

137 "With her he sent all standard sailing equipment": Copy of the shipping manifest placed in *Sea Dart*'s logbook.

CHAPTER 11. A NEW LIFE

Sources include *Adrift*, e-mails and conversations with Robert Grosby between January and March 2001, letters between TJ and Wally Herbert, and telephone conversations with David and Margaret Shields, October 2002.

138 Harrods: Tristan's version is in *Adrift*. Harrods could not confirm his employment, stating that they no longer have the personnel records from that period.

140 Call to Joe Gribbins: From "A Tribute: The Little Guy from Distant Wales," *Sailing Magazine*, September 1995.

140 *Sundowner*: See "The Infernal Triangle," *Motor Boat and Yachting*, January 1977.

142 "He set himself a new goal": From a letter to Wally and Marie Herbert, 25 November 1978.

144 Grey Owl: See Dickson, *Wilderness Man*.

144 Sir Laurens van der Post: See Jones, *Storyteller*.

144 Patrick O'Brian: See King, *Patrick O'Brian*.

145 Jeffrey Archer: See Crick, *Jeffrey Archer*.

146 "His speech patterns": Based on study of extant tapes of television shows, and other audio media.

147 For information on lying I relied on Ford, *Lies! Lies! Lies!*

149 John Hemming: Letter from Hemming to the author, 7 March 2002.

149 Ruth Cohen wrote to *Motor Boating and Sailing* in a letter dated 11 March 1977. Jeff Hammond replied on 16 March 1977.

151 Bob Shnayerson: E-mail to the author, September 2002.

152 "The young truck driver": See Wagers, *Sailing Among the Stars.*

152 "Through the Bering Strait": From a letter to Wally and Marie Herbert, 25 November 1978.

CHAPTER 12. COLD FACTS, ARCTIC FICTION

Sources include *Ice!* and *Saga of a Wayward Sailor*, H. W. Tilman's books, Dod Orsborne's books, and Nansen's *Farthest North*. Historical details of St. Kilda are from Steel, *The Life and Death of St. Kilda.* Ice conditions in the Denmark Strait are from *The Ice Conditions in the Greenland Waters, 1959* (Danish Meteorological Institute).

153 Dod Orsborne: See Orsborne's books in the bibliography.

159 Edward Allcard: See *Temptress Returns* by Allcard.

160 *Arctic Pilot*: Volume 2, 8th ed., Her Majesty's Stationery Office, 1996.

161 "Bill Tilman and his crew": See Tilman, *In* Mischief*'s Wake.*

165 "East Greenland has": As reported by Tilman, *In* Mischief*'s Wake*, and attributed to *The American Pilot Chart*, U.S. Hydrographic Office, n.d.

165 Quotations from the *Admiralty Pilot* and *Arctic Pilot* are from Tilman, *In* Mischief*'s Wake.*

166 *Gustav Holm*: Details supplied by Helge Schultz-Lorentzen, adviser to the Danish National Museum.

CHAPTER 13. BLENDING FICTION WITH FACT

Sources include *Ice!*, *Saga of a Wayward Sailor*, and *Encounters of a Wayward Sailor.*

170 "In a magazine article": See *Rudder*, January 1977.

170 "In a much later book": See *Encounters of a Wayward Sailor.*

173 Welsh Arts Council prize: Press release from Welsh Arts Council, 9 March 1979.

173 "What a grand sight": Jan Morris, e-mail to the author, 18 June 2001.

174 "You make me remember": Quoted by Jan Morris, ibid.

174 "Busy though he was": Letters between TJ and Wally Herbert, 1978–79.

175 "Captain Tom Drake": See Klein and King, *Great Adventures in Small Boats*.

175 Joshua Slocum: Ibid.

177 "John Kretschmer quoted Tristan": E-mail to the author, 2 November 2001.

178 "Photographer Carl Paler": Telephone conversations and e-mails with the author, September 2002.

179 New York literary agent Richard Curtis: Conversations with the author, February 2000; Richard Curtis's files; and Wally Herbert's archives.

181 "In Earls Court": Card to Wally Herbert, dated "Xmas 1981."

181 "He once told Conrad Jelinek": E-mail to the author, 23 May 2001.

181 "Carl Paler recalled": Telephone conversation with the author, September 2002.

182 Patience Wales: Telephone conversation with the author, October 2002.

182 Lin Pardey: Telephone conversation with the author, October 2002.

182 Chip Croft: Conversation with the author, March 2001.

CHAPTER 14. DOWN BUT NOT OUT

Sources include conversations with Chip Croft in New York, March 2001. Telephone conversations with David and Margaret Shields, October 2002. Telephone conversations with Dave and Jaynie Horner, 28 June 2000. Telephone conversation with Lin Pardey, October 2002. Telephone conversations with Carl Paler, September 2002. Conversations with Henry Wagner in New York, March 2001, and subsequent telephone conversations through January 2003. Telephone conversation with and e-mails from Robert Grosby between January and March 2001. In addition, Tor Pinney's website, TJ's *A Steady Trade*, and TJ's *Outward Leg*.

184 "Some tiny bits": From Tristan Jones, "And Not to Yield," *Nautical Quarterly*, autumn 1984.

184 "In 1982 he was": From Ken Ringle, "The Unsinkable Tristan Jones," *Washington Post*, 31 July 1988.

184 "He lost his leg to cancer": Richard North, "Tristan Jones Salt and Pepper," obituary, *Guardian* (U.K.), 30 June 1995.

184 "Complications from Old": Ellen Lochaya, "Such a Glorious Man," obituary, *Phuket Magazine* (Thailand), 1995.

184 "An obituary noted": Rosse, "The Rock: The Life and Death of Tristan Jones."

187 "Larry Pardey offered": From a telephone conversation with Lin Pardey.

188 "Joan Wagner, from Sailor's Bookshelf": From conversation with Henry Wagner, New York, March 2001.

189 "Among the patrons": From Tor Pinney's website.

195 "rudimentary education": See Tony Allison, "Tristan Waives the Rules," *Asia Magazine*, 1991.

195 "nineteen elementary schools": See "Obituary of Tristan Jones," *Daily Telegraph*, 29 June 1995.

198 "His letters to friends": From letters in Sir Wally Herbert's archives.

CHAPTER 15. ONCE MORE, DOWN TO THE SEA

Sources include *Outward Leg* and Leonard Surtees, who sent e-mails and wrote a long letter from Australia, 4 July 2001, discussing the events concerning *Outward Leg*.

199 "I had come to greatly admire": Press release from H & S Bluewater Multihulls, 8 July 1983.

200 "a piece of lunar landscape": From the Project Star press release by H & S Bluewater Multihulls, 11 July 1983.

203 "H & S Bluewater Multihulls paid": Letter from Leonard Surtees to the author, 7 July 2001.

203 "I want to emphasize": Press release from H & S Bluewater Multihulls, 8 July 1983.

204 "Tristan's rationale": From a letter to D. Sleightholme at *Motor Boat and Yachting*, 23 January 1984.

205 "As early as Curaçao": Tristan's letters expressing his concerns to Richard Curtis from Curaçao and Venezuela, March 1984.

206 "In New York": Undated letter to Wally Herbert.

CHAPTER 16. A HEART OF OAK

207 Details of HMS *Ganges*: From the HMS *Ganges* Association.

209 "As I write": From *Heart of Oak*.

210 Loss of the *Comorin*: From the Royal Naval Association.

211 "I have asked Bodley Head": Letter to Richard Curtis, 19 July 1983.

212 "Convoy JW51B": See Kemp, Convoy.

CHAPTER 17. COLD RIVERS, WARM SEAS

Sources include Henry Wagner, conversations in Germany with Manfred and Gabby Peter, Michael von Tülff, and Willi Zeiss, plus *The Improbable Voyage*, letters from Thomas Ettenhuber to his parents (translated by Willi Zeiss), and conversations with Kriemhild Ettenhuber and Alexander Pufahl.

215 "Tristan was really a bully": Conversation with Henry Wagner, March 2001.

215 "The typed memo states": Memo to TJ from Sydney J. Moore, on Taylor Woodrow Group letterhead, 24 September 1984.

218 "Thanks to all readers": From *Nürnberger Nachrichten*, 22 January 1985.

219 Television newscasts: See under Television in the bibliography.

220 Television newscast: Ibid.

224 "I have feelers out": Letter to Wally and Marie Herbert, 7 November 1985, and letter to Dr. Ibrahim Nahal, University of Aleppo, Syria, 6 November 1985.

224 "crazy scheme to haul the boat": Letter to Henry Wagner, 1 June 1986.

CHAPTER 18. EXPLORING THAILAND

Sources include letters from Thomas Ettenhuber to his mother, Atlantis Society newsletters, conversations with Henry Wagner, *To Venture Further*, Thomas Ettenhuber's logbook, and Jos Souer.

227 "Tristan was well pleased": Letter to Henry Wagner, 20 August 1986.

228 "I first suspected TJ": John Kretschmer, e-mail to the author, 2 November 2001.

229 *Danube Pilot*: Although Tristan said he deposited a copy with the University of Vienna in 1986, a search of the university's catalogs failed to locate the manuscript.

230 Atlantis Society newsletters, held in Henry Wagner's archives.

230 "He told Wagner he had been": Letter to Henry Wagner, 15 July 1986.

230 "On our return from the Yangtze": Atlantis Society newsletter, November–December 1986.

233 "Tristan wrote H & S": Letter from TJ to Henry Wagner, 20 February 1987.

233 "H & S agreed": Ibid.

234 "Thomas Ettenhuber and I": Atlantis Society newsletter, 23 March 1987.

238 "Tristan began planning": From Atlantis Society newsletter, 25 July 1987.

242 "On January 1 he discovered": Details of the events in Phitsanulok provided by Jos Souer in a series of e-mails.

246 "I did find that he required": Euan Cameron, e-mail to the author, 8 September 2001.

246 "On the Laos front": Letter to Henry Wagner, 27 October 1988.

CHAPTER 19. THE STRANGE DEATH OF
THOMAS ETTENHUBER

Sources: conversations with Kriemhild Ettenhuber, Werner Umwherle, Fredi and Rosemarie Vivell, and Willi Zeiss in Germany, February 2001 and August 2001, plus letters from TJ to Henry Wagner.

CHAPTER 20. ANOTHER DEVASTATING BLOW

Sources: conversations with Henry Wagner and Beverly Baroff, plus letters held in Henry Wagner's archives.

260 Beverly Baroff: Conversations in Los Angeles, March 2001.

261 "At the end of April": Letter from Larissa Vasiliev, deputy chairman, Odessa Regional Peace Committee, 22 April 1989.

262 "If you went to Odessa": Letter from Henry Wagner, 7 August 1989.

262 "I hope I didn't": Letter to Henry Wagner, 13 November 1989.

262 "Now that the 5th anniversary": Letter to Abner Stein, 8 May 1990, photocopy held by Henry Wagner.

263 "He was invited": From Atlantis Society newsletter, 30 March 1990.

264 *Sons of the Sea*: Letter to Henry Wagner, 22 March 1990.

264 "He joined me in my mistaken belief": Reese Palley, e-mail to the author, 17 September 2002.

264 "He later wrote to Reese": Reese Palley, e-mail to the author, 21 February 2002.

264 "Apart from learning": Note to Henry Wagner, 8 February 1991.

264 "First he scalded": Ibid.

265 "A day later his doctor": Letter to Henry Wagner, 7 June 1991.

265 "A new diagnosis called": Letter/fax to Henry Wagner, 15 June 1991.

265 Rafiq Tschannen: Rafiq Tschannen, e-mails to the author, September 2002.

266 "The doctor gave some hope": Note to Phil Saracin, via Henry Wagner, 21 June 1991.

266 "Medically, Tristan was a mess": Diagrams and descriptions faxed to Henry Wagner, 10 July 1991.

266 "I am yet a prisoner": Letter to Henry Wagner, 28 July 1991.

267 "Again he spoke of": Letter to Henry Wagner, 7 August 1991.

270 "Don't know what chapter": Letter to Ian Paten, Grafton Books, with copy to Henry Wagner.

270 "Henry—whilst worse off": Letter to Henry Wagner, 16 September 1991.

272 John Morgan Prize for Literature: Fax from Jo Menell (award employee).

272 Patience Wales: *Sail* magazine, November 1991.

CHAPTER 21. WOUNDED PRIDE

Sources include *The Danube: A River Guide* by Rod Heikell, *Singlehanded Sailing* by Richard Henderson, and an audio tape supplied by Don Street Jr.

273 "A magazine article": From Tony Allison, "Tristan Waives the Rules," *Asia Magazine*, 1991.

273 "In 1978 Hal Roth": *Sail* magazine, March 1978.

274 "Rod Heikell's book": Letter to W. G. Wilson, Imray, Laurie, Norie & Wilson Ltd., 8 March 1992.

275 "Dear Tristan Jones": Letter from Rod Heikell, 12 March 1992.

275 "On the Holy Koran": Letter to Rod Heikell, 12 May 1992.

276 "A 1987 review": *Geographical Journal*, July 1987.

276 "I've only now discovered": Letter to Richard Curtis, 26 September 1994.

276 "[The book] seems to have been": Ibid.

277 "As an appendix": Ibid.

277 "One book no yacht's library": From the manuscript of *Sound of a Different Drum*.

278 "The collator of this work": Correspondence with Jonathan Eaton, editorial director, International Marine/Ragged Mountain Press, 2 and 22 December 1994.

282 "Did you know that in 1965": Letter to Mike Warburton, 8 May 1992.

CHAPTER 22. THE SAGA OF *GABRIEL*

Sources include conversations with and e-mails from Mike Warburton and Anna Borzello, plus *Encounters of a Wayward Sailor*.

284 "Tristan discussed an idea": Letter to Richard Curtis, 8 March 1992.

284 "Instead of writing the book": Letters to Richard Curtis, 3, 8, 12, and 17 March 1992.

285 "A few days later": Fax to Richard Curtis, 19 March 1992.

286 "A doctor confirmed": Letter to Mike Warburton, 15 August 1992.

287 "King Hussein would donate": Letter to Mike Warburton, 17 October 1992.

287 "You really hit the main jackpot": Letter to Mike Warburton, 18 October 1992.

287 "Whether this will work": Letter to Mike Warburton, 22 October 1992.

287 "Now (through third parties)": Letter to James Jermain, *Yachting Monthly*, 22 October 1992.

287 "A few weeks later": Letter to Mike Warburton, 13 November 1992.

288 Press release "Right Values": Press release, October 1992.

289 "An Australian TV film": Letters to Mike Warburton, 3 and 11 November 1992.

289 "A BBC World Service": From a letter to Mike Warburton, 8 November 1992.

291 "Mike! I did it!": Fax to Mike Warburton, 5 December 1992.

291 "On December 6": From *Gabriel*'s log, as faxed to Mike Warburton.

291 "Tristan made his final payment": Ibid.

292 "On December 16": Ibid.

292 "By December 18": Note to Mike Warburton, 18 December 1992.

293 "Dear Mike, Any longish": Note to Mike Warburton, 21 January 1993.

293 "At the end of January": Letters to Mike Warburton, 21 January and 1 February 1993.

293 "Thai TV gave": Letter to Mike Warburton, 24 February 1993.

293 *Dinner On Board*: Fax to Richard Curtis and to Sheridan House, 10 February 1993.

295 "I reflect that": Letter to Mike Warburton, 2 September 1993.

296 Expedition to the Mergui Islands: Announced in a letter to Mike Warburton, 10 December 1993.

296 "By mid-January 1994": Letter to Mike Warburton, 10 January 1994.

296 "Fortunately Tristan quickly found a buyer": Letter to Mike Warburton, 11 February 1994.

CHAPTER 23. THE SOUND OF A DIFFERENT DRUM

Sources include the unpublished manuscripts and 1 September 1994 cover letter to Richard Curtis.

CHAPTER 24. THE END OF A LONG VOYAGE

302 TJ's proposed biography of Joshua Slocum was to be titled *The Mystery of Joshua Slocum*. TJ proposed it to Richard Curtis in a 22 August 1994 letter. The book was never written.

303 "I delivered a yacht from Rotterdam": Jan de Groot, e-mail to the author, 23 April 2001.

303 "The late Peter Tangvald": From *At Any Cost* by Peter Tangvald.

304 "Tristan told Mike Warburton": Letter to Mike Warburton, 20 July 1993.

304 "I had to cut down": Letter to Mike Warburton, 6 November 1994.

305 "My aim is to go": Ibid.

305 Jeff Ritchie: Telephone conversation with Jeff Ritchie, 18 October 2001.

306 "I haven't been able": Letter to Mike Warburton, 15 January 1995.

306 "Once online": Letter to Mike Warburton, 8 March 1995.

306 Steve Rosse: Telephone conversations and e-mails with the author throughout 2001.

307 "at 11:00 A.M. on June 21": Fax from Paul Dark to Richard Curtis.

307 "Mike Warburton remembers": Mike Warburton, e-mail to the author, 11 May 2000.

309 "Brice Keller": From the original Tristan Jones Guest Book, www.net nickels.com/tristan, January 2001.

CHAPTER 25. AFTERWORD

310 "In a biographical sketch": Sent to Henry Wagner, 27 April 1992.

Selected Bibliography

BOOKS

Allcard, Edward C. *Temptress Returns.* New York: Norton, 1953.

Bragg, Melvyn. *Richard Burton: A Life.* Boston: Little, Brown, 1988.

Crick, Michael. *Jeffrey Archer: Stranger Than Fiction.* London: Fourth Estate, 2000.

Dickson, Lovat. *Wilderness Man: The Strange Story of Grey Owl.* Toronto: Macmillan of Canada, 1973.

Ford, Charles V. *Lies! Lies! Lies! The Psychology of Deceit.* Washington DC: American Psychiatric Press, 1999.

Gardner, John. *The Art of Fiction: Notes on Craft for Young Writers.* New York: Knopf, 1984.

Groot, Jan J. de. *No Shoes Allowed,* 3rd. ed. Langley BC: Emerald Point Publications, 1996.

Heikell, Rod. *The Danube: A River Guide.* St. Ives UK: Imray, Laurie, Norie & Wilson, 1991.

Henderson, Richard. *Singlehanded Sailing: The Experiences and Techniques of the Lone Voyagers,* 2nd ed. Camden ME: International Marine/McGraw-Hill, 1988.

Herbert, Wally. *The Noose of Laurels: The Discovery of the North Pole.* London: Hodder & Stoughton, 1989.

Jones, J. D. F. *Storyteller: The Many Lives of Laurens van der Post.* London: John Murray, 2001.

Kemp, Paul. *Convoy: Drama in Arctic Waters.* London: Cassell, 2000.

King, Dean. *Patrick O'Brian: A Life Revealed.* New York: Henry Holt, 2000.

Klein, David, and Mary Louise King. *Great Adventures in Small Boats.* New York: Collier, 1963.

Kurbiel, J., and J. M. Barrault. *Vagabond et les aventures polaires d'aujourd'hui.* Paris: Éditions Maritimes et d'Outre Mer, 1981.

Mitchell, Jill. *The Story of the Cresswell Lifeboats.* Poole UK: Royal National Lifeboat Institution, 1986.

Nansen, Fridtjof. *Fridtjof Nansen's Farthest North.* London: A. Constable, 1897.

Orsborne, Dod. *Master of the "Girl Pat."* Edited by Joe McCarthy. Garden City NY: Doubleday, 1949.

Orsborne, Dod, with Merle Severy. *Danger Is My Destiny.* New York: Prentice-Hall, 1955.

Orsborne, Captain Dod. *Voyage of the "Victory."* London: Muller, 1956.

Palley, Reese. *Unlikely People.* Dobbs Ferry NY: Sheridan House, 1998.

Reaney, Percy Hide. *A Dictionary of British Surnames.* London: Routledge & Paul, 1958.

Roberts, David. *Great Exploration Hoaxes.* New York: Modern Library, 2001.

Steel, Tom. *The Life and Death of St. Kilda,* rev. ed. London: Fontana, 1988.

Tangvald, Peter. *At Any Cost: Love, Life and Death at Sea: An Autobiography.* Dunedin FL: Cruising Guide Publications, 1991.

Tilman, H. W. *The Eight Sailing/Mountain-Exploration Books.* Seattle: Mountaineers, 1987.

———. *In* Mischief's *Wake.* London: Hollis & Carter, 1971.

Tomalin, Nicholas, and Ron Hall. *The Strange Last Voyage of Donald Crowhurst.* London: Hodder & Stoughton, 1970. Reprint, Camden ME: International Marine/McGraw-Hill, 2001, 2003.

Wagers, Laurel. *Sailing Among the Stars: The Story of "Sea Dart."* Dobbs Ferry NY: Sheridan House, 1999.

Withycombe, Elizabeth Gidley. *The Oxford Dictionary of English Christian Names,* 2nd ed. Oxford: Clarendon, 1950.

MAGAZINES

Allison, Tony. "Tristan Waives the Rules," *Asia Magazine,* 1991.

Cusick, Patrick. "Tales of Truth of a Modern Day Seafaring Adventurer." *Phuket Magazine* (Phuket, Thailand) 1, no. 6 (May 1990): 10–15.

E.A.R.T. (reviewer's initials) Reviews. *Geographical Journal* (Royal Geographical Society) 153, part 2 (July 1987): 285.

Gribbins, Joseph. "A Tribute: The Little Guy from Distant Wales; An Obituary." *Sailing Magazine*, 1995.

Kennedy, Ray. "A New Voyage for an Old Salt." *Sports Illustrated*, May 1984: 82–96.

Lochaya, Ellen. "Such a Glorious Man." *Phuket Magazine* (Phuket, Thailand) 6, no. 6 (1995).

Neilsen, Sheila. "Factors Used to Assess Whether Law Is for You: The 'Tristan Jones' Factor." *Illinois Legal Times*, February 1996.

Rosse, Steve. "The Rock: The Life and Death of Tristan Jones." *Nation* (Bangkok), 2 July 1995.

———. "The Rock: Publishing, Yachting and a Bit of Dumb Luck." *Nation* (Bangkok), 28 July 1996.

———. "Sailing with Mr. Jones." *Living in Thailand* (Bangkok), March 1997.

Suzuki, T. "Tristan Jones in Japan." *Yanmar Scope* (Tokyo), April 1989: 1–9.

Warburton, Mike. "Courage Ahoy: Tristan Jones, Intrepid Voyager." *Phab Magazine* (Peterborough UK), April 1993.

Wright, John. Reviews. *Geographical Journal* (Royal Geographical Society) 146, part 2 (July 1980): 313–14.

NEWSPAPERS

Batty, Jennifer. "Adventurer Tristan Jones Takes on the High Seas with Physically Challenged Crew." *PT Bulletin* (Alexandria VA), 29 November 1989.

Cameron, Euan. "Tristan Jones." *Independent* (London), 27 June 1995, Obituaries.

Cusick, Patrick. "Tristan Readies for His Last Voyage." *Sunday Post* (Bangkok), 18 October 1992, Leisure.

Goldman, Stu, and Joe McCann. "The Incredible Tristan Jones Visits Seattle." Unidentified Seattle newspaper, 21 September 1977. In the papers of Henry Wagner.

Jackson, Paul. "Record-Breaking on Just Ten Dollars a Day." *Western Mail* (Cardiff, Wales), 7 November 1986.

Lee, Mimi. "Tristan's 'Outward Leg' Sailing Here." *Bangkok Post*, 1 June 1987, Outlook.

Mauro, Luis Alberto. "Navegante solitario complio travesia por Rios Bolivianos." *Hoy* (La Paz, Bolivia), 24 October 1974.

North, Richard. "Tristan Jones Salt and Pepper," obituary. *Manchester Guardian* (U.K.), 30 June 1995.

"Record-Breaking Adventurer and Author Dies in Far East after Illness." *Western Mail* (Cardiff), 24 June 1995.

Ringle, Ken. "The Unsinkable Tristan Jones." *Washington Post*, 31 July 1988.

Ritchie, J. M. " 'Where the Best Is Worst'—with Captain Tristan Jones in Thailand." *Circleville (Ohio) Herald*, 6 December 1996.

Thevenin, Michel. "Il y a encore des albatros." *Le Reveil de Djibouti*, 25 February 1971.

"Tristan Jones, hombre que hace 'lo que debe hacer.' " *El Día* (Montevideo, Uruguay), 29 June 1975.

"Tristan Jones." *Times* (London), 24 June 1995, Obituaries.

TELEVISION

Delaney, Frank. *Frank Delaney Show.* BBC-TV (London), 26 November 1982.

Evening Magazine. ORF-TV (Austria), 21 March 0985, news.

Evening Magazine. ORF-TV (Austria), 27 March 0985, news.

Francis, Clare. "Clare Francis Interviews Tristan Jones." BBC-TV (London), 29 January 1982.

Tele Illustrierte. ZDF-TV (Germany), 16 January 1985, news.

Tele Illustrierte. ZDF-TV (Germany), 21 March 1985, news.

Terry Wogan Show. BBC-TV (London), 22 February 1985; 1 July 1988.

RADIO

King, Larry. *The Larry King Show.* Mutual Broadcasting System, 6 May 1988.

MULTIMEDIA

Chronicle of the 20th Century (CD-ROM). New York: DK Multimedia, 1996. Also available in the U.K. in print (Dorling Kindersley, 1995).

Race the Wind (film). Produced by Macgillivray Freeman Films for NTT and IMAX Corporation, 1989.

INTERNET SITES FEATURING TRISTAN JONES

Idaho, State of. Idaho Parks. www.idahoparks.org/about/support.html and www.seadart.org.

Murray, Scott. www.scottmurray.com.

Pinney, Tor. *The Old Salt at the Boat Show.* 1996. www.tor.cc/tales.htm and www.anchoryachts.com/tales.htm.

Reil, Ron. www.reilo.net/dart.shtml.

Sarjeant, Stuart. http://webmaster.daytonatrophy.com/jones.

Swartz, Don. www.netnickels.com/tristan.

Annotated Tristan Jones Bibliography

PUBLISHED BOOKS

The Incredible Voyage. Kansas City: Sheed, Andrews & McMeel, 1977. Tristan's
most successful book spanned six years of voyaging in *Barbara* and *Sea Dart.*
It was published in the U.K. by Bodley Head in 1978. A German language
edition, translated by Willi Zeiss, was published by Pietsch Verlag, Stuttgart,
in 2000. It is currently in print in the U.S. in a 1996 Sheridan House paperback edition, and in the U.K. in a 1996 Adlard Coles Nautical paperback
edition.

Ice! Kansas City: Sheed, Andrews & McMeel, 1978. Tristan and Nelson, a one-eyed
three-legged black Labrador, exploring Arctic waters aboard *Cresswell.* Published in the U.K. by Bodley Head in 1979. A German language edition, translated by Irina and Willi Zeiss, was published by Pietsch Verlag, Stuttgart, in
2000. It is currently in print in the U.S. in a 1995 Sheridan House paperback
edition, and in the U.K. in a 1996 Adlard Coles Nautical paperback edition.

Saga of a Wayward Sailor. Kansas City: Andrews & McMeel, 1979. Tristan and Nelson go to the Mediterranean where they meet an eclectic cast of characters.
Published in the U.K. by Bodley Head in 1980. A German language edition,
translated by Irina and Willi Zeiss, was published by Pietsch Verlag, Stuttgart,
in 2001. It is currently in print in the U.S. in a 1995 Sheridan House paperback
edition, and in the U.K. in a 1995 Adlard Coles Nautical paperback edition.

Dutch Treat. Kansas City: Andrews & McMeel, 1979. A novel of World War II at
the time of Dunkirk and the German blitzkrieg. Published in the U.K. by
Bodley Head in 1980. It is currently in print in the U.S. in a 2000 Sheridan

House paperback edition, and in the U.K. in a 2001 Adlard Coles Nautical paperback edition.

Adrift. New York: Macmillan, 1980. Tristan ashore in Montevideo, London, and New York. Published in the U.K. by Bodley Head in 1980. A German language edition, translated by Irina and Willi Zeiss, was published by Pietsch Verlag, Stuttgart, in 2001. It is currently in print in the U.S. in a 1992 Sheridan House paperback edition, and in the U.K. in a 1995 Adlard Coles Nautical paperback edition.

Aka. New York: Macmillan, 1981. A novel of a solo sailor and a tribe of dolphins. It is currently in print in the U.S. in a 1998 Sheridan House paperback edition, and in the U.K. in a 1998 Adlard Coles Nautical paperback edition.

One Hand for Yourself, One for the Ship: The Essentials of Single-Handed Sailing. New York: Macmillan, 1982. Useful information for the single-hander. Published in the U.K. by Granada in 1983. It is currently in print in the U.S. in a 1990 Sheridan House paperback edition, and in the U.K. in a 1995 Adlard Coles Nautical paperback edition.

A Steady Trade. New York: St. Martin's Press, 1982. A young boy's early life in Wales and his two years at sea on a coastal sailing barge. Published in the U.K. by Bodley Head in 1982, two years after it was written. It is currently in print in the U.S. in a 1996 Sheridan House paperback edition.

Yarns. Boston: Sail Books, 1983. Published in the U.K. by Adlard Coles in 1984. A collection of fictional and factual tales. It is currently in print in the U.S. in a 1990 Sheridan House paperback edition, and in the U.K. in a 2000 Adlard Coles Nautical paperback edition.

Heart of Oak. New York: St. Martin's Press, 1984. The horrors of World War II as viewed from the lower decks of Royal Navy fighting ships. Published in the U.K. by Bodley Head in 1984. It is currently in print in the U.S. in a 1997 Sheridan House paperback edition.

Outward Leg. New York: Hearst Marine, 1985. Tristan's trimaran voyage from San Diego to London, on one leg. Published in the U.K. by Bodley Head as *A Star to Steer Her By* in 1985. Currently in print in the U.S. in a 1998 Sheridan House paperback edition, and in the U.K. as a 1999 Adlard Coles Nautical paperback edition.

The Improbable Voyage. New York: Hearst Marine, 1986. Tristan and crew force a trimaran across a wintry Europe on the Rhine and Danube rivers to the Black Sea. Published in the U.K. by Bodley Head in 1986. A German language edition, translated by Irina and Willi Zeiss, was published by Pietsch Verlag, Stuttgart, in 2002. Currently in print in the U.S. in a 1998 Sheridan House paperback edition, and in the U.K. in a 1999 Adlard Coles Nautical paperback edition.

Somewheres East of Suez. New York: Hearst Marine, 1988. The continuation of the trimaran voyage from the Black Sea to Phuket, Thailand. Published in the U.K. by Bodley Head in 1988. Currently in print in the U.S. in a 1999 Sheridan House paperback edition, and in the U.K. in a 1999 Adlard Coles Nautical paperback edition.

To Venture Further. New York: Hearst Marine, 1991. Tristan and a crew of handicapped boys navigate a traditional long-tail fishing boat on Thailand's jungle rivers. Published in paperback in the U.K. by Grafton Books in 1991, with color photographs (the only edition of this book with photographs). Currently in print in the U.S. in a 1999 Sheridan House paperback edition, and in the U.K. in a 1999 Adlard Coles Nautical paperback edition. A Thai edition was published in 1991, for which details are not available.

Seagulls in My Soup. Dobbs Ferry, New York: Sheridan House, 1991. More humorous fictional Mediterranean adventures loosely based on fact. A German language edition, translated by Irina and Willi Zeiss, was published by Pietsch Verlag, Stuttgart, in 2001. Currently in print in the U.S. in a 1996 Sheridan House paperback edition, and in the U.K. in a 2000 Adlard Coles Nautical paperback edition.

Encounters of a Wayward Sailor. Dobbs Ferry, NY: Sheridan House, 1995 (posthumous), paperback. A final collection of fictional and factual tales. Currently in print in the U.K. in a 1996 Adlard Coles Nautical paperback edition.

UNPUBLISHED BOOK MANUSCRIPTS

Track of the "Barbara," 1969–70. TJ's first book-length work, written during the early part of *Barbara*'s voyage.

Indian Ocean Saga, 1971. Portions of this planned but only partially written book manuscript were eventually incorporated into *The Incredible Voyage.*

Purity, with J. Doyle, ca. 1979. One-act stage play, theme unknown. It is mentioned in an undated list of TJ's writing accomplishments.

Echoes of Distant Thunder, 1981. TJ claimed this manuscript was his translation from the Welsh of the romantic tales from *The Mabinogion.*

The Danube Pilot, with Thomas Ettenhuber, 1985–86. A boater's guide to the Danube River. No known copies exist.

A Sensitive Saga: A Masculist Allegory, 1992–94. A gay version of TJ's *Aka*. The original manuscript is held by Richard Curtis Associates, New York.

The Sound of a Different Drum, 1992. A love story of two gay boatbuilders. Original manuscript is held by Richard Curtis Associates, New York.

The Taming of a Tough Guy (aka *Rough Trade*), 1992–94. *Seagulls in My Soup* with a renamed cast and a gay twist to the ending. Original manuscript is held by Richard Curtis Associates, New York.

Dinner On Board—Come As You Are, 1993. No known copies remain of this manuscript, which TJ ordered destroyed.

Index

Notes are not indexed.